LEADING COPS IN TURBULENT TIMES

THE PRACTICAL ROADMAP TO HIGHLY-EFFECTIVE POLICE LEADERSHIP

GEORGE SAADEH

CONTENTS

Disclaimers

Although the author has made every effort to ensure that the information in this book was correct at press time, the author and publisher do not assume and hereby disclaim any liability to any party for any loss, damage, or disruption caused by errors or omissions, whether such errors or omissions result from negligence, accident, or any other cause. Unless a name is provided, any similarities to anyone, living or dead, is purely coincidental. In describing certain examples and situations, and to protect the identities of real people, the author has created composites to illustrate relevant points. None of the content in this book is meant to be relied upon as legal advice or to substitute for advice from public safety lawyers, legal advisors or any agency's policies and procedures. The information provided within this Book is for general informational purposes only. While we try to keep the information up-to-date and correct, there are no representations or warranties, express or implied, about the completeness, accuracy, reliability, suitability or availability with respect to the information, products, services, or related graphics and data contained in this eBook for any purpose. Any use of this information is at your own risk. The methods describe within this eBook are the author's personal thoughts and opinions based on experience and observations. They are not intended to be a definitive set of instructions for this topic. You may discover there are other methods and theories to accomplish the same end result.

❀ Created with Vellum

To my wife Laura, and my daughters Jillian and Kayla, without whom my life would have little meaning.

To all the great law enforcement officers in this nation who risk their lives to keep our communities safe. It is for them that I wrote this book.

In memory of my good friend Retired Police Sergeant Irma Vasquez-Mandel, one of the most effective, conscientious and hard-working police professionals I have known. May she rest in peace (see chapter 21).

"Leadership is solving problems. The day soldiers stop bringing you their problems is the day you have stopped leading them. They have either lost confidence that you can help or concluded you do not care. Either case is a failure of leadership."

Colin Powell

PREFACE

Today's policing environment is fraught with complex, seemingly intractable problems which require police leaders who use their intellect as well as their emotional intelligence to achieve long-lasting results. These leaders recognize that they have external and internal stakeholders—community members and police employees—who will demand from them not only an ability to innovate, but more importantly, an abiding competence and integrity necessary to build and retain trust from the community and the cops in the field. Police professionals who are in positions of authority, or who aspire to fill such roles, will find Leading Cops in Turbulent Times a clear roadmap to building high-performing organizations. This book will help you build or improve the hard and soft skills that are essential to great leadership. These police agencies will build capacity in good times and prove resilient in bad times. Regardless of rank or position, cops at all levels will find this book a significant resource in building personal and professional competence.

This book is exceedingly practical and utilitarian. While meant to be read from the beginning, it can also serve as reference so one can easily click on a hyperlink to read specific sections. The book is also, at times, brutally honest to challenge assumptions and the status quo. I focus on day-to-day application of fundamental but simple principles. It is available as a paperback and as an eBook with in-text hyperlinks to resources, citations and other information. The price of the eBook is little more than a fancy cup of latte at your local coffee shop. I don't want cost to be a barrier to anyone interested in making a difference by studying leadership and applying helpful concepts in real life, so it's readily available online to anyone who cares about self-improvement.

Although the principles and ideas I will discuss apply to most any industry, its primary audience is anyone who cares about public safety and wants to be a respected leader—or those who should know what great leadership looks like so they can hold their management teams accountable. Whether in a police department, a sheriff's office or a state agency like parole or probation, application of the ideas we discuss will take a little work and focus. In particular, this book is aimed at new leaders who want to learn from the mistakes and successes of others, but it will certainly benefit seasoned professionals as well. With the benefit of hindsight, I hope you learn from the mistakes we made, as well as the things we did right.

Much of the content involves personal experience, observations, anecdotes or practical real-life scenarios that will be instinctively familiar to you if you've worked in law enforcement or public safety for any length of time. Even if you're a firefighter or any other type of public servant, the principles apply. In addition to contemporary examples—such as the sad case of Los Angeles County Sheriff Lee Baca—to illustrate the pitfalls and challenges in police leadership, I incorporate stories of historical figures from whom we can learn valuable lessons, such as Abraham Lincoln, Winston Churchill, and John F. Kennedy. I chose them as models because they led their nations during war or in difficult times, and they persevered.

In my opinion, Lincoln is perhaps the greatest president this nation has had, so we'll talk about what made him such a formidable leader and how he was able to put together an implausible team to help him end slavery and heal the nation's wounds. Churchill was the driving force behind Britain's grit and resolve to resist and defeat the Nazis, and there are key lessons for the rest of us in his story. Kennedy was a charismatic and talented president who performed beyond his years and learned, the hard way, to buck the military establishment, trust his instincts, and take on the Soviet Union—his way. Primarily because of those instincts, our nation avoided a disastrous nuclear war. These folks illustrate what it is like to lead men and women in tough times. They show us the depth of character, initiative and intestinal fortitude we should all aspire to develop. They were human in so many ways, even flawed, but extraordinarily endowed with the skills and abilities it takes to lead.

There were other leaders in history that were talented but used those talents in the wrong ways or for the wrong purpose. Look no further than Adolph Hitler, who was charismatic and viscerally connected with the German people at the right time. In the early years, he was idolized and loved by many, if not most, of Germany's population. He was able to crystalize a vision of a Greater Germany, a People that he considered superior to all others. Hitler didn't start out to be a charismatic individual. He learned how to transform a middling existence born out of humble beginnings, into the man who would lead the German people to overwhelming military prowess and, ultimately, to ruin and destruction. According to The Dark Charisma of Adolph Hitler (BBC, 2012), Hitler was a tailor's apprentice and an amateur painter in southern Munich who grew angry that his work wasn't recognized. He became a soldier and fought the British in World War I, becoming a rabid nationalist. During his service he learned about leadership and how to influence others.

After Germany had lost the war and more than two million German lives, Hitler was able to capitalize on the despair and discontent sweeping through the country, seizing the opportunity to mobilize the population so they'd view Jews as the cause of their defeat and the ensuing economic problems. In essence, Hitler and others took advantage of the dispossessed and disenfranchised who were looking for someone who had a positive, uplifting message. He told them what they wanted to hear, what they longed for, to overcome the disastrous results of the war. Germany was humiliated, and its people—fragile and longing for Germany's redemption—were ripe to embrace anyone who could paint them a picture of a better future. Hitler delivered. He saw a chance to build his image as a savior who could rescue the German people from nefarious forces. We know the rest of the story.

* * *

For better or for worse, leadership and charisma have inevitably allowed historical figures to influence the course of history through an art that can be learned and applied successfully and for good purpose. Hence, the power of leadership, when used for the good, is seemingly infinite. Imagine what would have happened had Hitler used his considerable intelligence and charisma for the betterment of his nation. On a recent trip to Germany I stood on the banks of the Danube in the port of Passau, not far from Munich, where I over-heard a local guide telling a story about how when Hitler was a boy he fell into the very waters near which we were standing. Hitler could not swim, so according to the legend a Catholic priest jumped in and saved him from drowning. I heard a man nearby exclaim: "Wow, that priest changed the course of history!"

If the story were true, and I can't dispute it, the course of history would have indeed changed if the priest had not saved Hitler. Many examples show how a charismatic individual can affect the lives of many. In the absence of good, decent people in positions of authority who are willing to resist evil, a charismatic person with less than good intentions can divert the course of history with calamitous results. The same can be said for organizations of all types. Modern police leaders must use whatever tools they have to improve the lives of people in their communities and make their organizations great places in which to work.

So, what makes great leaders so good at shaping policy, changing behavior or leveraging resources? What skills or personality traits do they possess that allows them to convey a sense of purpose where others have failed? To what extent are these characteristics innate or learned? What or whom gives them the moral and organizational authority and credibility that is required to influence behavior? Is rank power or position a prerequisite for anyone who wants to alter the course of any public safety agency? To what extent does charisma play a role in a leader's ability to build great teams and get things done? Are hard skills more important than soft skills?

Hundreds of leadership books have dealt with these questions, with answers as varied as the authors. The tendency is to provide clinical, scholarly or textbook answers that focus on supervision or management principles that we've heard about for decades. But over the years I've found a dearth of material that focuses on common sense, practical, contemporary advice and experience-based information to help supervisors and managers, especially new or aspiring ones, become excellent leaders. Hence this book. I synthesize leadership principles into practical actions and methods that will achieve results. In other words, I crystalize theory for you by using experience, observations, and examples—historical and contemporary. Having witnessed leadership successes and failures in my thirty years in the business, I have the advantage of hindsight. So, for those of you who think: "It's easy for you to say now," you are right. And that's precisely the point! We must learn from our successes and failures, and in that process, hindsight is our best friend.

In my attempt at retrospection, I freely admit my mistakes and share with you what worked and what didn't for me. I will bring to life the composite characters of supervisors and managers with whom we've all worked and either hated, respected or admired, drilling down to determine in practical terms what made them a success or a failure—or just plain mediocre. I will criticize myself freely but will also share what I did that was right or worked well. In particular, the book's practical advice will help you minimize early career mistakes and help you recognize opportunities to do the right thing and build your career legitimately. I'll also show you how to come up on top in your quest for promotion. This book has the potential to make a difference in your personal and professional life and the way you view and perform your job. Even if you consider yourself a good leader, I will prompt you to think a second time and reflect on any changes you can make.

If you only get a few nuggets of useful information and put them to good use, I will have fulfilled my goal. Let's face it, law enforcement is a demanding profession that now requires ever greater sophistication, education, and training. Leaders must focus on solving organizational and community problems by being introspective and inclusive of diversity in every way. Not easy you say? It may not be, but you can do it with a little hard work and determination. I hope that in these difficult times when law enforcement is on its heels against an onslaught from the media and other groups—and some communities have lost faith in their cops—the suggestions and examples I cite will inspire you to tackle problems head-on to become the leader your organization needs.

* * *

I undertook this effort for the good cops—the ones that care about their mission, work hard and treat members of their communities with dignity and respect. I wrote it for the supervisors, managers and executives that carry the political and administrative weight of police organizations everywhere and, despite overwhelming odds stacked against them, make things better every day. I also wrote this book for the civilian members of your department that are often undervalued, and without whom police work would quickly grind to a halt. They deserve recognition, appreciation and outstanding leadership. I also took on this project because of the mediocre supervisors and managers who take the path of least resistance and coast through their careers, leaving behind failed initiatives, weak results and unfulfilled potential in organizations all over this nation.

We will learn from their mistakes and take steps to avoid repeating them. Although they may be relatively few in numbers, these are incompetent individuals that damage police departments everywhere. These are the supervisors and managers that should have never been promoted—the ones that destroy morale, cause employees to leave or retire early, and cost the organization dearly in treasure and productivity. They aren't merely weak leaders, they are toxic ones, meriting the full attention of management because even a few of these individuals can bring an organization to its knees.

Lastly, I hope city and county administrators will read this book to increase their understanding of public safety leadership, and what they can do to maximize their relationship with police managers and executives. I have a chapter just for them. These relationships are of particular importance because public safety agencies consume between fifty and seventy-five percent of a jurisdiction's general fund budget. That is a substantial investment that needs meaningful oversight, yet some local government administrators fail to engage with public safety leaders to solve problems and keep financial expenditures under reasonable control.

Some of these folks are intimidated by police chiefs and sheriffs or fail to engage beyond the selection of a chief executive whom they think will look at things the way they do, or who will do their bidding—right or wrong. That won't cut it. As a city manager or county administrator, you'll have to learn the business of policing and the dynamics at play between the rank and file, management, the community and the unions. You'll have to get in the weeds occasionally, but the more you understand the business the better you'll deal with the thorny issues that inevitably arise. Most importantly, you will have a decent chance to influence policing in your community for the good of its residents and businesses.

We will also look at some important topics and functions that tend to get police organizations in trouble or hinder good results if not handled or performed correctly. These are functions to which a sworn supervisor or manager is often assigned oversight, regardless of expertise, and which can have a significant impact on the agency and the overarching organization. These are areas of responsibility that go directly to why competence is an essential trait in all police managers and leaders. Among others, you'll find segments on:

- The importance of organizational audits
- Managing the budget effectively
- Managing the property and evidence room
- Dealing effectively with police unions
- The media and public relations function
- Dealing with misconduct and discipline
- Hiring and background Investigations
- The workers' compensation system

I don't mean for these discussions to be exhaustive, but after having dealt with these issues for over thirty years, I hope you'll find my insights helpful and thought-provoking. I believe this modest book will help you understand these issues better, especially if you're a new supervisor or manager, or aspire to become one. Again, I'll try to avoid theory because I'm not an academic. What you'll get is practical, honest and reality-based information to help stimulate your thinking on what it takes to build great teams and departments. Lastly, I'll give you my formula for getting ready for promotion and navigating the promotional process, so you come up on top.

THE NAYSAYERS

I know there'll be some who will say that this book contains basic information that every leader should already know and practice. If that's the case, why is it that an unacceptable number of supervisors and managers in all industries fail to practice such simple principles? Why is it that despite all available guidance on how to treat people, we continue to see some overbearing and incompetent individuals in positions of authority? If these principles are so obvious, why is it that some (too many in my view) in positions of power in police organizations continue to sap the spirit and dedication of good employees, while allowing the mediocre ones to keep lowering the bar? Why is it that we hear about public safety managers who bungle critical projects because they lack competence or the work ethic to get things done right? Why is it that sometimes the only punishment is a transfer to another division or assignment where they can continue their pattern of behavior? Why do researchers continue to find that inept or abusive supervisors and managers, in all manner of industry, sap resources, depress productivity and cost organizations millions in sick leave and workers' compensation costs? And, finally, why does empirical research suggest cops have lost faith in their management teams' ability to deal with bad cops?

An article in the Washington Post (Shannonhouse, October 20, 2014) described how bad bosses can affect subordinates in real, physical ways, leading to poor health, reduced productivity and increased workers' compensation claims and costs. According to the article: "The evidence is clear that the leadership qualities of 'bad' bosses over time exert a heavy toll on employees' health," says Jonathan D. Quick, an instructor in medicine at Harvard Medical School and a co-author of the book Preventive Stress Management in Organizations. "The evidence is also clear that despite the rationalizations some leaders may use to defend their stress-inducing, unsupportive style, such behavior by leaders does not contribute to improved individual performance or organizational productivity." This article—and the attendant studies and research—is one of the best I've ever read. It makes an irrefutable case that bad bosses of all types harm organizations in so many ways, that ensuring supervisors and managers are competent and enlightened leaders must be a priority for all public safety agencies. I recommend that chief executives and managers read the material and consider making it mandatory reading for all in positions of authority in their departments.

http://www.washingtonpost.com/national/health-science/is-your-boss-making-you-sick/2014/10/20/60cd5d44-2953-11e4-8593-da634b334390_story.html?hpid=z8

Knowing what you're supposed to do and doing it well are two different things. Look at the money your agency spends on sending supervisors and managers to seminars and other educational opportunities. If being a competent leader were that easy, then the return on investment in training would be apparent. I'm here to tell you it isn't always so. I am convinced, and you will be as well, that leadership by example, competence and integrity are the three essential qualities in any public safety manager or supervisor. We'll explore each in some detail, and I'll provide a roadmap for assessing your competencies and honing your skills in these areas. I'll also describe what makes some supervisors and managers so good at what they do, and how you can learn from them to improve not only the organization but your stake in it as well. To paraphrase Plato, the measure of a man or a woman is what he or she does with power. That power comes with tremendous responsibilities, so I urge you to entertain differing points of view and look at your performance to see if there is anything that can be improved.

There are thousands of good leaders out there who work hard and treat people with decency and respect. In fact, most police leaders are worthy of the noblest of law enforcement traditions. What I do in the book is share my experience, observations and examples to help you understand the essence of these principles and follow them in practical form. It is this essence that you'll have to put into practice to achieve both personal and organizational results. Trust me when I tell you that you can do it with a little effort and a desire to do well, for you and the agency in which you work.

One last housekeeping item: In the ebook I have provided in-text hyperlinks to the resources I mention in this book, but not all may be current. I've tried to give you as many resources in line with the text, rather than endnotes alone, but if you find a broken link or one that doesn't lead you to the source cited, try Googling the keywords to find it. Of course, I've also included them in the end notes. I will update the book periodically, and if you've purchased it as an eBook, you'll likely get those updates automatically. Now let's get started.

THE STATE OF POLICING IN AMERICA

"A true leader has the confidence to stand alone, the courage to make tough decisions, and the compassion to listen to the needs of others. He does not set out to be a leader, but becomes one by the equality of his actions and the integrity of his intent." — Douglas MacArthur

We indeed live in turbulent times. Rarely have police-community relations been more strained than they are today, with some communities rapidly losing trust in their cops, and cops losing confidence in their management teams. Law enforcement agencies across the country struggle to change the narrative. The headlines blare in the media with a din that is pitch-perfect for those who have for years asserted that law enforcement officers lie and kill minorities with impunity. The talking heads on television rev at full speed, with some headlines portraying cops as blood-thirsty killers who awake each morning wondering whom they can "kill today." The tone of the discussion that seeks to paint all cops with the same broad brush is disturbing, and as a result, many cops feel discouraged and under siege.

Recently, the PEW Research Center, a well-respected non-partisan organization, surveyed over eight thousand police officers from across the country seeking to find out how they felt about their jobs. The results are sobering and ought to be a wake-up call for government and communities. In light of the current state of police-community relations and the media headlines, fully 93% of officers are concerned about their safety, and 72% have become less willing to stop and question suspicious persons—an astonishing statistic that ought to worry us all. According to the report, more than eight-in-ten (86%) say police work is harder today as a result of the high-profile incidents we've witnessed in the last few years. While most police officers give their workplaces a positive rating, only three-in-ten (roughly 30%) say they are supportive in the direction that top management is taking their organization. Ninety-six percent say they are firmly committed to making their agency successful, but 86% percent say their organizations don't have enough officers to police the community adequately.

According to the report, when they are asked more specifically about the extent to which underperforming officers are held accountable, police officers give a more negative assessment of their departments: "Only 27% agree that officers who consistently do a poor job are held accountable, while 72% don't agree with this." That suggests that as many as three-quarters of our cops have lost confidence that their management teams can control errant or bad cops. Think about that: the vast majority of cops think police management is doing a poor job of controlling and weeding out toxic cops! Further, officers in general feel that a few individuals in every department taint the others with their actions.

These revelations should surprise no one who deals or talks with street cops in our nation. This sobering report must concern management and labor alike, and unions should be particularly alarmed about bad cops and how they hurt the general membership. While you may not hear open complaints in union meetings, union leaders will tell you that in private they get an earful about the bad apples in their midst. The current crisis is a defining moment for police unions insofar as their responsibility to members must include a willingness to work with police leadership to improve hiring, training, and retention of the most qualified applicants, as well as remove from the organization those who commit serious misconduct. As the PEW report illustrates, this isn't simply a management problem; It is a shared system problem, which includes labor groups as key stake-holders.

http://www.pewsocialtrends.org/2017/01/11/behind-the-badge/

To complicate matters and buttress the results of the PEW survey, arrests by officers in many jurisdictions, especially larger ones, have declined precipitously. According to the Los Angeles Times (Queally, April 1, 2017), police arrests across California are plummeting, fueling alarm and questions. While statewide propositions that reduced some felonies to misdemeanors have impacted arrests, many believe officers and deputies are now much more reluctant to initiate stops and make arrests given the scrutiny from the media and activist organizations. LAPD Chief Charlie Beck, while acknowledging the issue, was a bit more guarded: "I'd be denying human nature if I didn't say police are very cautious about what they do now because of the scrutiny. But do I see it? I don't really see things that make me think that the workforce as a body is retreating. I don't see that at all." Sheriff Sandra Hutchens told me the same thing, asserting that while cops may be more cautious, they'll continue to do their job if they feel supported by their departments. That support is critical, as is the will to remove from agencies the bad cops largely responsible for most incidents.

Others are more direct in their assessment, such as ex-FBI Director James Comey, who has publicly proclaimed that the so-called "Ferguson Effect" appears real and has caused police to be less proactive in stops, field interviews, and arrests. According to Comey (Newsmax-Swanson, May 12, 2016), "There's a perception that police are less likely to do the marginal additional policing that suppresses crime—the getting out of your car at 2 in the morning and saying to a group of guys, Hey, what are you doing here?" I find it hard to deny the apparent inverse relationship between crime rates and arrests, or reduced police activity in general. In my experience, proactive cops in the field do make a difference, so it ought to concern us all when a significant number of good cops make the following calculus: Do I get involved and risk tragedy for me, my family or the community, or do I sit back and let the crooks go?

A retired police captain I know put it a bit more colorfully during a discussion on Inside OC with Rick Reiff, a show broadcast on a local PBS affiliate: "Some cops are becoming firefighters...If you call,

I'll come, but to expect me to get out of my car and do proactive work and expose myself to be the latest YouTube video that will be broadcast across the country with a false narrative, is just taxing to some people." I hadn't heard it described quite that way before, but I'm sure there are some officers who may think of their jobs in those terms.

To illustrate why we must collectively deal with these issues sooner rather than later, take a look at the Chicago Police Department (CPD). In 2016 more than 700 people were murdered and over 4,000 were shot. Just as violent crime was on the rise, investigative field contacts by police—the bread and butter of street cops—fell by eighty percent, while arrests dropped by at least a third! The inverse relationship between active police work and violent crime in Chicago is almost incontrovertible when you consider all the evidence. Enlightened police chiefs will tell you there is a clear relationship between dogged police work and crime reduction.

The history of the Chicago P.D. is a troubled one, but the recent wave of violence can be proximately tracked back to the shooting death of Laquan McDonald in 2014. McDonald was a 17-year-old African-American who was reported to have been breaking into vehicles and ignored police commands to stop. According to police reports, he lunged at one of them with a knife. But according to news reports, dashboard video appears to show McDonald was moving away when he was shot 16 times by a white officer. When I look at the available video footage, which shows McDonald walking away from officers, I am at a loss to explain why the officer shot him, especially given that all others present, including officers who were at the scene earlier and had a better vantage point, did not.

On June 27, 2017, the New York Times reported that three CPD officers were charged with conspiracy, official misconduct and obstruction of justice in connection with the investigation that followed Laquan's death. According to the Times, "The three officers are accused of conspiring in the hours and days after the shooting to 'conceal the true facts' to protect Jason Van Dyke, a fellow officer, who fired 16 times at Mr. McDonald, who was 17." The indicted officers have over 50 years of experience. I'll be the first to tell you that all of these officers deserve their day in court to answer these allegations. However, once again, the actions of one officer created a public backlash and media coverage that was overwhelmingly negative, affecting every officer on the department. In that environment, many believe that many Chicago cops, fearing termination or worse, have retreated from doing aggressive police work or field contacts, instead focusing on answering calls for service. When you look at the evidence, the lack of police activity appears to be a contributing factor to the historical and devastating increase in violent crime in Chicago.

The key question about police management in general—which I attempt to answer in this book—is how the leadership of the Chicago Police Department could have intervened sooner to address the cultural issues that allowed some bad apples to influence the performance of thousands of cops to the detriment not only of the department, but the community as well. To what extent does a competent and dedicated management team affect the trajectory of a police department and, more importantly, how do agencies create leaders who lead by example and become a factor in the solution.

https://www.nytimes.com/2017/06/27/us/chicago-officers-indicted-laquan-mcdonald-shooting.html

An FBI report published in 2017 titled The FBI Assailant Study – Mindsets and Behaviors, provides additional insight into the effects of the current political and media atmosphere on those who assault police officers. The FBI carefully examined 50 of 53 incidents in which officers were killed in 2016, including the assailants' mindsets and behaviors, to determine what may have influenced the assailants and contributed to the attacks. Over the course of this study, the FBI interviewed law enforcement command staff and officers from 13 departments where an officer was killed in the line of duty. According to the report, the FBI analyzed an additional 37 incidents in 2016 through open-source information and law enforcement databases. In total, the FBI examined 50 incidents that occurred in 2016. The report concluded the following:

Since 2014 multiple high-profile police incidents across the country have occurred that law enforcement officials believe influenced the mindset and behaviors of the assailants. Specifically, the Michael Brown shooting in Ferguson, MO, in 2014, and the social disturbances that followed, initiated a movement that some perceived made it socially acceptable to challenge and discredit the actions of law enforcement. This attitude was fueled by the narrative of police misconduct and excessive force perpetuated through politicians and the media. Nearly every police official interviewed agreed that for the first time, law enforcement not only felt that their national political leaders publicly stood against them, but also that the politicians' words and actions signified that disrespect to law enforcement was acceptable in the aftermath of the Brown shooting. Police officials across the country agreed that while the majority of Americans still support law enforcement, this change in social mores allows assailants to become more emboldened to question, resist, and fight law enforcement.

http://lawofficer.com/wp-content/uploads/2017/05/MindsetReport.pdf

Undoubtedly, there are errant and even criminal cops in almost every agency. Some police officers across the nation have done things for which they should be fired—in some cases even prosecuted. To be sure, more than a few police leaders have failed to hold these officers accountable for their actions and, more importantly, allowed a culture of mediocrity and lack of accountability to permeate their agencies. But those in the media and government, along with some activist organizations, purposely leave out of the discussion the fact that this is a systemic problem, one for which society has largely abdicated its responsibility. Instead of developing comprehensive legislative, social and economic reforms to address the issues, society has placed cops in charge of fixing the problems without giving them the funding and the tools to do the job.

The strain in the criminal justice system is not only depleting precious police resources, but is also creating a permanent class of offender whose mental illness and drug addiction is overwhelming our jails, with little relief in sight. In the middle of it all are police officers, deputy sheriffs and probation/parole officers who, in the vast majority of the time, do their best to keep communities safe. The frustration and concern for the safety of cops and their families, along with the community's vulnerability to bad cops, must be the immediate focus of police executives and local governing bodies everywhere.

There is no question that cops have always been an easy target for criticism, primarily because the job they do is like no other. It is more visible, complicated and impactful than most public service jobs and arguably much more challenging than any other regulatory function. Police contacts are largely not pleasant events for most people because something has happened in their lives that is negative. Most of those who come in contact with law enforcement are victims or suspects, and neither has a pleasant story to tell. We task the police with helping those in need despite the lack of adequate tools and resources to do so. The mentally ill, the infirm and the homeless rely on cops to get them through difficult circumstances. Often, frustrated family members have relinquished control of troubled individuals to the police since cops are the only ones who come when called twenty-four hours a day. And when cops show up, the family expects a magic resolution to the problem that doesn't rely on force or arrest.

Thus, we find ourselves in a crisis the likes of which we have not seen since the civil rights era. Because there hasn't been a strategic, comprehensive, informed, and data-driven approach to the problems, they've simmered for decades. Compounding the situation is the fact that few critics are courageous or interested enough to look beyond the tactical and transactional problems with police agencies across the country, neglecting to point out the underlying strategic issues that must be tackled to find lasting solutions.

In other words, we've always known these problems needed attention and would someday boil over, but we collectively decided to ignore them and let the cops deal with the results. When I say we, I mean the people of this nation, the legislature, our government, and yes, police leaders. Given the enormity of the task, law enforcement has done an admirable job considering that staffing and budget issues have hammered police agencies hard in the last decade. As a result of cutbacks from the Great Recession, patrol officers in most major cities are going from call to call, with little time to do proactive police work or engage in meaningful community policing strategies. For the most part, cops take seriously their duty to safeguard the public, and despite the media's portrayal, they place their lives at risk to do so every day. I've been there. Despite the lack of a backup officer, I often rolled on calls and handled dangerous situations alone because I felt responsible for the safety of those I was sworn to protect. I am not alone. Most cops feel the same way, but when they work in a system that doesn't value that type of sacrifice, a good number of officers become callous and hardened by the job.

The political courage to fix the problem is conspicuously absent. Look no further than Baltimore or Tulsa for instances where cops were criminally charged only days after incidents occurred, only to have most acquitted at trial. And, by the way, there have been several high-profile acquittals or hung juries in other police-related cases in 2017, which may point to overcharging by prosecutors, charging based on politics, or the reluctance by juries to convict cops when they make mistakes in the heat of rapidly changing field situations. In some cases, this rush to judgment is perhaps evidence that the officers were overcharged, but I and other law enforcement professionals believe that some of these cases were worthy of prosecution. Cops should not be immune from the law, but charges must follow comprehensive, thorough, apolitical and unbiased investigations. Furthermore, we need to look deeply into the psychology that undoubtedly plays a role in how cops act and react to field situations, including the effects of the job on their ability to handle the work.

If you'd like to read an excellent article that highlights the physical as well as psychological dangers of police work, go here:

http://www.wsj.com/articles/the-hidden-hurt-of-life-on-the-police-beat-1482090105

To read an article on police shooting acquittals go here:

https://nyti.ms/2sZlFOX

According to bipartisan research, including the Pew Research Center, trust in government is at an all-time low. Only nineteen percent of Americans trust the federal government to do the right thing most of the time. Depending on where you live and work, confidence in local authorities and police agencies is not much better. Within organizations, the trust of employees in their management teams is also declining, pointing to an acute crisis in management competence. Elaine Kamarck, in her book: Why Presidents Fail (Brookings Institution Press, 2016), makes a persuasive argument that Bush and Obama (and now Trump) failed to grasp the importance of managing the federal bureaucracy. The results were impactful and negative: think the ill-planned invasion of Iraq; the bungled response to hurricane Katrina; the incompetent rollout of the refugee ban and the mishandled firing of FBI Director Comey by the Trump administration; and the botched implementation of the online marketplace for the Affordable Care Act, known as Obamacare, among many others.

Kamarck argues that what we need now is a "managerial" president who should focus on "old-fashioned management," such as paying attention to implementation of initiatives, conducting performance audits and setting up early warning systems, so one isn't blindsided by problems that are mostly predictable and thus eminently preventable. In other words, she's talking about competence, and she could just as easily be describing what public safety agencies throughout the country need. Communities are looking for visionary leaders for sure, but they desperately need those who can provide competent management of resources and initiatives. The community wants a seat at the table to help shape that vision, a leader that goes beyond rhetoric, and managers and supervisors who set the example and lead with unassailable integrity.

These are lofty principles to be sure, but they are qualities communities should expect and demand nonetheless. These ideals are aspirational, but they won't become the standard until police agencies require superior leadership from those in positions of authority. In this book, I make the case that in these turbulent times, police leadership would do well to focus on the basics, including leading by example, developing supremely skilled teams, and demanding straight-up honesty from themselves and those around them.

Make no mistake, the quality of leadership in any law enforcement agency is the key factor that influences officer behavior, how the officers treat the community, and the extent to which a department can help control or reduce crime and fear in cities across the nation. Given the complexities and realities of today's policing environment, we need leaders that not only offer a vision of hope and progress but have the skills to restore trust. Despite the winds buffeting law enforcement, there is much more leaders can do to transform their agencies into more effective and accountable organizations. Our communities need unrelenting and enlightened police leadership that seeks to forge strong community ties and build accountable agencies. These are the leadership qualities that create superb organizations, serve communities well, and ensure employees are treated with dignity and respect.

While the majority of police leaders work hard and do the right thing, hardly a week goes by that I don't read or hear about serious police misconduct or abysmally poor performance by some police supervisor or manager. In some instances, we, as police leaders, have abdicated our responsibility to act as thoughtful stewards of the public trust. Likewise, we too often have failed to do the right thing, choosing instead to take the path of least resistance. In my opinion, law enforcement has reached an inflection point: either we markedly change the system and return to our true guiding principles to turn the ship around, or we risk further loss of community and organizational trust, leading to ever-present turmoil, litigation and increased scrutiny at all levels. Either we lead effectively, or our organizations will become mediocre or worse. We must deal with these issues now, as kicking the proverbial can down the road is no longer an option.

To help us learn from the mistakes of others, I explore cases such as that of former Los Angeles County Sheriff Lee Baca, who was recently convicted in federal court of obstruction of justice and lying to federal investigators. Ten other sheriff's officials were also convicted or pled guilty in the case. I sought to find out what it takes to lead cops not only as a general principle but specifically during difficult times. I spoke with police officers and deputy sheriffs of all ranks to get a sense of how they viewed the issues and their jurisdictions. When I asked officers and supervisors what police management can do to improve ties with the community and help the rank and file weather the storm, one typical response was to give officers due process and not condemn their actions without a thorough, fair and dispassionate investigation. They recognize that there are bad cops out there that are tarnishing the reputations of the good police officers who care deeply about their jobs. For the community's sake, they want the bad cops dealt with swiftly and steadily, but not by politicians in the media—and not in a carnival atmosphere on the streets of America.

Street cops want to see their chiefs and sheriffs do the right thing by weeding out the officers who willfully commit misconduct or purposely use excessive force, but they want enlightened leaders that can discern mistakes of the mind from those of the heart. Most of all, cops want their bosses to lead by example and have their backs when they make well-intentioned mistakes. This fairness is the minimum our communities, and our cops, have a right to expect. Leadership by example, competence and integrity are the cornerstones of success for anyone wishing to lead men and women in policing, especially in these turbulent times. This concept is akin to a three-legged stool in that if one of the legs fails, the stool crashes. That equilibrium is fragile, so it requires an abiding commitment to improving wellness in the community and creating a respectful and effective workplace.

I will show you, in practical terms, how to build these leadership skills and use them to make a difference—regardless of your rank or position in the organization. I give you concrete examples of dysfunction at all levels and ways to move forward. I focus on practical, common-sense advice for aspiring or current public safety leaders who want to become great leaders by practicing the cornerstone concepts mentioned above. I prompt you to lead not only with your intellect, but with your heart as well, focusing keenly on developing your emotional intelligence. Finally, I synthesize police leadership theory into a practical, effective formula that will help you become a better leader for the cops and the people in your cities.

2

THE SANTA ANA POLICE DEPARTMENT

"High sentiments always win in the end. The leaders who offer blood, toil, tears and sweat always get more out of their followers than those who offer safety and a good time. When it comes to the pinch, human beings are heroic."
George Orwell

I remember the day well. It was circa 1978 on a Friday afternoon, and we had just started the early swing-shift roll call at 1500 hours. We worked the 5/8 schedule back then, and only the most senior officers had a piece of the weekend off. I started with Monday and Tuesday as my days off, so having Wednesday and Thursday off was like Manna from Heaven! I was assigned to Team One in the West End of town. As the sergeant finished calling out our names from the duty roster, the station supervisor walked in and told us our officers had just called a 997 (officer needs help) at Fifth and Euclid, the home turf of the Fifth Street gang. He added that it was a major incident with our cops fighting gang members and few units in the field during shift change. Keep in mind that Fifth Street was then a major violent gang involved in turf wars with several other gangs. The sergeant quickly ended the roll call and told us to "get out there code three!" (Lights and siren).

The room emptied quicker than you could blink and soon you

had twenty-five patrol units headed code three westbound toward the riverbed, which divided the West End from the rest of the city, all in a majestic row. The rush of adrenalin and the feeling I had as I drove westbound on Fifth Street and saw the overhead lights of our units, rising with the contours and changing elevations of the road, was indescribable! I guess exhilaration is one way to put it, but pride may be a more appropriate description. You see, back in those days, Santa Ana was the premier police agency in Orange County. We were the Gold Standard of law enforcement in California. I venture to say it remains one of the best police agencies anywhere.

As I got to Euclid, I could see an investigator from the gang unit jumping over a fence into a mobile home park just southeast of the intersection. A gang-banger was breaking a wooden chair over an officer's back as he took another suspect into custody in the driveway of a house whose inhabitants were well known to us—and not for being upstanding citizens! That officer was John Diehl, aka The Hulk! His muscular physique was intimidating, but he was a gentle, friendly police officer and a hard worker. It didn't surprise me to see him in the middle of the action.

As several of us pulled up to the house, I could see gang-bangers scurrying like rats throughout the neighborhood and our cops giving chase in every direction. It was almost surreal. I could see that John was hardly affected by the chair, which broke into pieces, and we quickly took the banger down and placed him in a marked unit. If I remember correctly, we took over ten suspects into custody that afternoon, and none of our cops were seriously injured—which is more than I can say for the gang bangers. Among them were bad folks who'd committed murders and assaults and had been plaguing their neighborhoods for decades. We quickly took control of the situation and got to work handling the scene. It was all second nature to us. We were an unrivaled professional police force, of which I will be perpetually proud.

I can go on with many anecdotes like that one, but I'll get down to business and the reason for including the story in this book. I am now retired after having spent over three decades with the Santa Ana Police Department (SAPD). When I retired, I was the Captain in charge of Field Operations, a time in my life that I will fondly remember because I got to work with blue-suiters who in my humble opinion carry the weight of the organization on their shoulders. I bleed Santa Ana Blue, a characteristic I'll have for the rest of my life. Growing up in the department I saw how every other agency wanted to be like SAPD, and cops from other agencies wanted to work at SAPD. We were respected and envied. When Santa Ana showed up at the scene to assist another department, everyone knew we'd take care of business, period. Even to this day, a Santa Ana cop gets more experience in one month than some in other departments get in a year. We were the agency to emulate, to admire and to have at your side in time of trouble. I still think of our department in those terms, and I'm sure the agency remains one of the best in the minds of most who know its history and traditions.

Maintaining such a reputation wasn't always easy. There were rough periods, such as the 1960s and 1970s when there was political unrest throughout the country, and outstanding Santa Ana police officers were killed in the line of duty—like Officer Nelson Sasscer, who was murdered by Black Panthers on a street corner in 1969, and Officer Dan Hale, who was murdered by parolees in a gun battle at the scene of a burglary in 1977. Or the mid-1980s when we had union problems that resulted in discord between the rank and file and city management. There were times when we were perilously understaffed, like in the late 1980s's when crime was rampant, and our homicide count reached 89 one year—which for a city of 350,000 was unheard of. We had so many vacancies that we developed a Marshall Plan-like effort to hire 45 cops in less than a year—without sacrificing the quality of our officers!

Turmoil, challenges, and difficulties have never been new to this great police department and the City of Santa Ana. What is clear is that we've always risen to the occasion by summoning up one galvanizing thought: We're in this together as a cohesive team with one mission. That level of professionalism and reputation has always been sowed on the backs of great cops and excellent leaders at all levels of the department. The traditions and history of any law enforcement organization endure because of the people in it, whose hard work, dedication and perseverance remain the purpose of those in leadership positions. It is for them that we must strive to do better.

3

A LITTLE HISTORY

"But if I was loved by everyone, I wouldn't be doing my job, would I?" Chief Raymond C. Davis

I t was about 3:30 P.M. on a sunny Sunday afternoon in the 1970s and I wanted to get out of the station after roll call as quickly as possible. I had been out of the police academy for about two years. Santa Ana, a relatively large metropolitan municipal agency and the seat of Orange County, California, was then the largest city in the county—and the busiest regarding crime and police activity. I worked in the West End of town, and I needed to traverse half the city to get there. I knew the city well because I had been assigned there as a Community Service Officer (CSO) for two years before being hired as a sworn officer. During those years, I had the privilege of being part of a large effort to educate the community to help reduce crime and, more importantly, the fear of crime.

As I'll explain later, those were formative years for me in police work. They helped me understand the concern and anxiety community members felt concerning crime and allowed me to get to know the good people that formed the bulk of the population. I now realize that it also helped me avoid cynicism throughout my career by reminding me that it was these folks in the community that made it all worth it. I got to know many of them personally, and it wasn't uncommon for them to invite us to dinner or a neighborhood picnic. We developed those relationships by building trust and a sense of being in it together, with a single purpose, and with the same goals in mind.

In the 1970s Santa Ana saw a major increase in property crimes and gang activity, which prompted the establishment of a utility users' tax to hire over 100 bilingual lateral transfers (experienced officers from other agencies) to supplement the 250 existing cops in the department. (more about the impact of that move—good and bad —later.) The Chief of Police at the time, Raymond C. Davis, was a no-nonsense, progressive leader and pioneer of community policing principles. A towering hulk of a man (we affectionately called him "Big Foot"), he believed in crime prevention through community education and the CPTED principles (Crime Prevention Through Environmental Design). In brief, we educated the community through nightly seminars at the homes of block captains and hard-ened the target by conducting home and business security inspec-tions, providing recommendations as to how a house or business could be secured. We placed CPTED into practice through a model crime prevention ordinance, which mandated that police employees formally review building plans for new construction, as well as modi-fications to existing buildings, to ensure that adequate security measures were designed in from the start, thus hardening the target in perpetuity.

The program worked, and soon agencies throughout the country were using it. We didn't invent it, but we used it so well it was widely cited as an example of progressive policing. CPTED was one prong of our crime reduction strategy. The others were aggressive community education and field deployment of officers according to team policing principles. Officers were assigned to the same area for a minimum of two years, thus getting to know not only the community and geography but the crooks as well. It all worked like a charm, but it took lots of hard work by sworn and civilian personnel.

I gained invaluable experience while working as a CSO. I cut my teeth by working with the community and making presentations to groups of all types. I learned home security principles that I used later as an officer every time I took a burglary report when I'd counsel the victims on how to secure their property. In those days, Santa Ana went all-in to knock back crime by using every resource available to the City, one of which was the twenty-member crime prevention unit. The supervisors in the unit were young and innovative and demanded that we work hard. One of them, Joseph Brann, later went on to head the Office of Community Policing Services for President Bill Clinton. Another was Robert Helton, who was an experienced cop and had little patience for fools. In fact, I remember him yelling at me as CSO when I chased hot calls in the field. Even though he scared the hell out of me, I knew he was right!

These folks treated us with respect and gave us their support as long as we did the right thing, so needless to say, I learned from them even at that early stage in my career. My heart, though, was always in sworn police work, and I got in some trouble for chasing police calls and assisting officers at crime scenes. I remember one day another CSO and I were conducting a vacation patrol check when we caught a burglar in the act. We held him at the "point of our flashlights" until the cops got there. We didn't stop to think what the suspect would have done had he figured out we were unarmed! Those were fun days.

Chief Davis also believed in aggressive—but lawful—policing. The Department was respected throughout the nation and known for its innovative policing philosophy and tactics. The cops in our town were, for the most part, hardworking and committed to proactive police work. Many were military veterans who had spent time in Vietnam. It was common back then for Vietnam vets to gravitate toward law enforcement agencies because of the paramilitary environment and a similar culture of order and respect for the chain of command. Given the level of activity and challenging police work, lots of cops in other cities and counties wanted to work in Santa Ana. We were proud of that reputation and zealously guarded it.

When I became a Police Officer I was in heaven. I got to work two hours early and didn't want to go home at the end of my shift! I wasn't the only one. Many of us simply loved our jobs and felt as though we couldn't find a better place in which to work. In fact, like many officers at the time, I couldn't believe they were paying me to do the job. For a young officer who wanted to make arrests and stay busy, Santa Ana was the place to be. If you were motivated, it didn't take long to find hypes (heroin addicts), gang members and many a variety of criminals. All you had to do was stay alert—actually just stay awake!—and you'd end up with a few arrests, a good number of field interviews and a couple of traffic citations each day to keep the sergeant off your back.

That's how it worked back then; you had to produce, or you'd have your sergeant's proverbial boot up your ass. At least the good sergeants operated that way and, like in all organizations, there were good and bad supervisors. We knew who the good ones were and tried to sign up for their teams as often as possible. If you worked hard, you didn't have any problems finding a good sergeant for whom to work. The weak supervisors also had fans: those who wanted to coast and be left alone. They, too, had some cops signing up to work for them, but for the wrong reasons. The sad truth is that everyone knew who the slackers were, but the civil service system allowed them to do the minimum to keep their jobs, and the bad supervisors became complicit in that mission. Most departments are like any other business: there are good workers, mediocre ones and some who are toxic. The difference is, in the civil service it is much harder to dismiss the bad ones. In Santa Ana, we were blessed to have the best cops in Orange County, bar none. Sure, there were the slugs, but the hard workers outnumbered them. I distinctly remember the lazy officers and how we all used to commiserate about them.

The Santa Ana Police Department became my home for over thirty years, and I loved it. The hard work and camaraderie that existed in our agency back then became legendary in law enforcement circles, even among federal and state agencies. With over four hundred officers at the peak, Santa Ana was relatively large—most police departments in the nation have twenty-five officers or less—but small enough so that you knew most of the organization. You could work hard and take advantage of different assignments, and our size allowed for a wide variety of positions for which you could apply. I worked in Homicide and the Gang Unit for years and learned to treat suspects with dignity and respect to get confessions from them. I had great partners who taught me persistence and the meaning of work ethic. We had such a good reputation that when we went to seminars or external training, other cops always approached us about joining the department. The time I spent in Santa Ana is what I consider the golden age of the agency. It was a great place to work. Don't get me wrong, we had problems, but all in all, it was a great organization.

So, on that Sunday afternoon at the start of my shift, I heard the radio crackle and my sergeant's voice asking me to switch to a tactical channel for a chat. He told me to meet him in a nearby parking lot. He was new to our policing team and would only be there a couple of months due to the rotation period being almost over. Although I'd met him, I wasn't sure what to expect. Each sergeant had his or her (we only had one female field sergeant at the time) own expectations and leadership style, and for a grunt like me, it was my responsibility to adapt, like it or not. That attitude emanated from the paramilitary culture prevalent in law enforcement agencies at the time. I learned from these veterans how to exhibit command presence to control calls and incidents. I also learned about discipline and the concept of teamwork, lessons that would serve me well throughout my career. As was often customary for quick field meetings, I pulled up close and parallel to the sergeant's police unit, hood-to-trunk, so we could talk without getting out of the car. Our respective fields of vision were covered, giving us the tactical advantage so we could stay alert and make a quick departure if we got a hot call.

As I arrived, I could see he was reading the newspaper. After some pleasantries, he got down to business. He would only be in the team a short while, he told me, but he had a few rules I'd need to follow, and we'd get along just fine. First, he said, "Don't cause me any paper." In other words, don't get too many complaints or use too much force, requiring him to write administrative reports. Second, "You won't see much of me in the field, and I'll only show up when you need me. Got any questions?" That was it. He went back to reading the paper, and I drove off after agreeing to his terms. I figured two months would go by quickly. At first, I thought he must have had a bad day, and I'd have to wait to see how he operated. I also thought he might have been trying to tell me he would let me do my job and he'd stay out of the way. Unfortunately, he was true to his word in a more literal sense. Unless I needed arrest approvals or had a major incident—and I mean major!—I seldom saw my sergeant in the field. Not even to tell me I'd done a good job or to chew me out for having done a bad one; there was little other than the occasional hello or goodbye. I also seem to remember he left my performance evaluation in my work mailbox with a note to sign and return it.

Some cops would have liked it that way, but I was disappointed. I hadn't been an officer for long, but I had worked for some good supervisors and instinctively knew that was not a good way to do the job. I was lucky that later I worked with some darn good sergeants from whom I learned a great deal about supervision principles and human nature in general, but more about that later. This brief encounter early in my career had an effect on how I viewed my job, and the impact leaders have on the organization and the community. Admittedly, that was a relatively minor incident—and I can't tell you precisely why it had such an effect on me—but I witnessed many others during my career. Some were downright egregious, affecting employees in ways that harmed them and the organization. I soon discovered that even though the majority of supervisors were good folks, there were too many poor or mediocre ones, and it didn't take me long to see the damage they caused.

Unfortunately, there were, and still are, some supervisors and managers that believe leadership means just slapping on the stripes, bars or stars and sitting in their offices dictating policy and criticizing the troops for every mistake, intentional or not. In their minds, there is no need for situational guidance or the periodic inspection of work to make sure it is done right and complies with departmental standards. No "praise in public and criticize in private;" no professional guidance or counseling to aid development; most of all, no leadership by example. I worked for some good sergeants and lieutenants in my first few years as a cop, and I quickly learned to tell whether a supervisor was competent or just one of the laissez-faire types who would only show up when they had to. We had a good number of the former and some of the latter. It was then that I set my sights on becoming a sergeant and developing leadership skills that would allow me to help achieve the organization's goals and look out for the welfare of the front-line cops and support personnel—the ones who made up the backbone of the department. I promised myself that I would never act like the poor supervisors, and I would strive to emulate the good ones.

And there were great ones. One of them was William "Wim" Sirks, a young and energetic narcotics investigator who was wise beyond his years. He understood human nature, led by example and made you feel as though you were special. I remember when he first came out to the field from the narcotics division, he would frequently follow us on calls to make sure we were OK and to see how we did the job. It didn't take him long to figure things out and start taking educated risks to battle crime. He quickly recognized that two of us in the team had some of the highest statistics in the city regarding reports, arrests and field interviews. He gave us an unmarked police car, put us in plain clothes and told us to go after every crook and dope dealer we could identify in our area. He gave us a framework and let us do it for ninety days unfettered by calls for service. He did this a few months after he took over the team as a brand-new sergeant. We made hundreds of arrests and put several street narcotics dealers out of business. Keep in mind that he made that decision after making sure we understood our responsibility for reports and calls for service, making it crystal clear it was a team effort. I didn't ask him if the assignment was a reward or a calculated decision to suppress crime because it was obviously both.

He took a chance, and it paid off. Crime declined in our area for the subsequent months and property crimes especially plummeted for a time. He knew this was only a stop-gap measure, but the point was to take some action that was calculated to keep the residents and businesses in the area from being victimized, even for a few months. Back then anyone arrested and convicted for using heroin (California Health & Safety Code section 11550) got a mandatory 90-day sentence. Any subsequent convictions called for a year in jail. For us, arresting heroin users was one of the premier tools to reduce burglaries. We became narcotic experts through training, experience and testifying in court about the signs and symptoms of opiate use. It became an extremely useful tool to reduce crime because back then most property crimes were committed by heroin addicts. During that time, I was also introduced to the magical properties of Narcan™, the drug given to those who have overdosed on heroin and which is again popular given the heroin epidemic in our country. I remember the first time I saw it used. The addict had passed out in a bathtub and was on the verge of death when paramedics administered a dose of Narcan. It worked in seconds, and he was up and alert. It seemed almost like magic to me.

I write about Sergeant William Sirks because he made us feel as though we were special. We worked hard for him. He'd roll up his sleeves and worked cases with us. Once, he showed me how to properly kick down a door during a search warrant service after I nearly dislocated my shoulder doing it as I had seen on television! Don't tell me you never tried it? He took the time to provide guidance and leadership to a young crew of officers who needed it. Don't misunderstand; it wasn't all laughs and camaraderie. I remember him taking me aside and chastising me for taking a longer lunch than I should have when it was busy in the field (forty rather than thirty minutes!), but he took the time to explain why, and it made sense. He turned criticism into a learning moment, and I understood. I thought he was one of the best supervisors for whom I worked—ever. I learned from him critical lessons that would prove valuable. Unfortunately, he passed away prematurely of natural causes in the 1980s after he'd made lieutenant. I still think about him and miss him. I guess I admired him for many reasons, but primarily because he was there. He was present, rolling up his sleeves and, in contrast with the sergeant I mentioned earlier, becoming a role model for his team.

He was not the only one. I can name others who impacted the careers of many young officers like me and who exhibited the leadership qualities I aim to highlight in this book. One particular sergeant showed me how humility is a preferred trait in leaders. What struck me about Bob Sayne right away was how unassuming he was, and how he'd go out of his way to talk to you and help you in any way he could even though I was a young patrol officer and he was a seasoned detective sergeant in the Narcotics Division. He was one of the down to earth supervisors who worked hard alongside his troops, earning their respect and admiration. I worked for another in the Major Enforcement Team (MET), a special unit that worked on all manner of crime—in uniform or plain clothes. Don Blankenship took a chance on a young rookie and brought me to MET to work with seasoned veterans. What stood out about him was his ability to encourage you to do great work as he led by example. He'd get a piece of your ass if you screwed up, but he'd invite you for a beer after work if he thought you had potential. I learned a lot from these individuals, and their example stayed with me throughout my career.

These were folks who influenced me early on and whose leadership traits stuck with me.

The point is that the vast majority of individuals in positions of authority in public safety agencies ought to be of the highest caliber, helping to propel organizations to successful outcomes and subordinates to becoming better than they are. After all, the stakes are high, and the well-being of our communities hangs in the balance. An early, positive influence in a young officer's career becomes vital to his or her success. If you agree with my proposition that crime is a public health issue, then you'll agree that police departments play a significant role in the wellness of a community. After all, we're the first ones at the scene where those most in need present us with entrenched societal problems that are difficult to solve, but which nonetheless require us to make decisions and offer some resolution. We're also the ones that pick up the pieces when services for the poor are lacking, or when mental health programs fail to serve the marginal populations. So why shouldn't we expect police agencies to hire and promote the best, always demanding great leadership? I make a case for a focused effort on the part of chief executives and their command staff to take a critical look at their departments and carry out the necessary changes to help ensure enlightened and competent leadership at all levels. Nothing less will work.

4

PRACTICAL CONCEPTS IN LEADERSHIP

"Overnight, I learned that a leader is not simply someone who experiences the personal exhilaration of being in charge. A leader is someone whose actions have the most profound consequences on other people's lives, for better or for worse, sometimes for ever and ever." Warren Bennis, 1925-2014

I believe in the power of One: The power of one person to make a difference in the lives of many. History is replete with evidence that one person, a man or a woman, or even a child— think Malala Yousafzai—can have a profound effect on others through sheer will, energy and a relentless commitment to a vision. Whether you're talking about Mahatma Gandhi, Abraham Lincoln, Lech Walesa, Nelson Mandela or Winston Churchill on one spectrum, or Adolph Hitler, Benito Mussolini and Idi Amin on the other, history shows us that for better or worse, one committed person can influence people and change the course of history. The same applies to an individual in business, a city council or a police department. The only difference is scale.

While the historical figures I mentioned may have changed the world, individuals such as cops, firefighters and others who develop strong leadership skills can alter the course of entire organizations and communities. Given the current crisis in policing, effective leaders are needed now more than ever. Focusing on leadership basics, with unrelenting community outreach and empowerment, is the only way to build trust within and outside your organization. I am an ordinary person with the same faults and foibles as anyone, but I learned early on how one person who cares and works hard, and who strives to act on his or her convictions, can achieve extraordinary results.

I looked at folks with whom I worked who by all standards were ordinary human beings but were visibly and remarkably able to make a difference. I also looked at historical figures and inevitably came to the same conclusion: it's all about having a vision, backed by the leadership and management skills to carry it out, that fuels the power of a single person to make a difference in a meaningful way. These leaders —despite humble beginnings or lack of formal education—were able to impact others in ways that set them apart.

We've all read books and articles that provide many definitions of the term "leadership." Most of these definitions seek to connect the leader to his/her ability to accomplish organizational tasks and goals through others, ideally willingly and using little formal authority. Subordinates (I hate that term, but use it for the sake of clarity), the authors say, ought to follow a leader because they want to, not because they have to. There are many leadership styles, with some of the most prominent briefly summarized as charismatic leadership (influencing others through personality traits), transformational leadership (focusing on subordinates needs and wants), and transactional leadership (day-to-day communication and exchanges between leader and subordinate).

The fourth—and one which is in my view one of the most relevant—is servant leadership, which focuses first on serving, especially the needs of subordinates, even above one's own, to accomplish organizational goals and help others grow and become better people. Larry Spears, from the Spears Center, defines servant leadership as that which "seeks to involve others in decision making, is strongly based in ethical and caring behavior, and enhances the growth of workers while improving the caring and quality of organizational life." Spears believes that some of the essential qualities that define servant leaders include receptive listening, empathy and understanding, stewardship, and commitment to the growth of people.

Among the qualities Spears mentions, two are particularly relevant to police leaders. One, Conceptualization: "The ability to look at a problem or an organization from a conceptualizing perspective means that one must think beyond day-to-day realities." According to Psychology Wiki, "Conceptual thinking is the ability to understand a situation or problem by identifying patterns or connections and addressing key underlying issues. Conceptual thinking includes the integration of issues and factors into a conceptual framework. It involves using past professional or technical training and experience, creativity, inductive reasoning, and intuitive processes that lead to potential solutions or viable alternatives that may not be obviously related or easily identified."

Two, Foresight—"the ability to foresee the likely outcome of a situation is hard to define, but easier to identify. One knows foresight when one experiences it. Foresight is a characteristic that enables the servant leader to understand the lessons from the past, the realities of the present, and the likely consequence of a decision for the future." These skills are particularly relevant in times of distress and uncertainty, such as the law enforcement community finds itself in recent years, and they are certainly worth nurturing in young leaders.

To read Spears' Character and Servant Leadership: Ten Characteristics of Effective, Caring Leaders, go here:

https://www.regent.edu/acad/global/publications/jvl/vol1_iss1/Spears_Final.pdf

According to Robert Greenleaf, who first developed the servant leadership theory in 1970, "A new moral principle is emerging which holds that the only authority deserving one's allegiance is that which is freely and knowingly granted by the led to the leader in response to, and in proportion to, the clearly evident servant stature of the leader." This concept influenced my thinking about leadership early in my career and partly serves as an impetus for this project. I've always felt that a leader must work for the benefit of others even beyond his or her own interest, and that legitimate authority is willingly granted to the leader not because of position or rank, but because one is recognized as a servant leader through his or her actions. It isn't difficult to see this concept in practical terms when leaders in police organizations make their own interests subservient to those of the employees, striving to achieve common goals through the willing work of their subordinates.

To read Greenleaf's seminal essay on servant leadership—which should be mandatory reading in police organizations—go here:

https://www.essr.net/~jafundo/mestrado_material_it-gjkhnld/IV/Lideranças/The%20Servant%20as%20Leader.pdf

I'll add a concept that I consider just as influential in my life, and which is entirely congruent with and supportive of servant leadership: Leadership by example—the ability to influence others by consistently setting the example and modeling desired behavior, even when it's difficult. We'll look at this key concept in the following chapter. Most of these theories are important in understanding how leadership works and its value to any private or public enterprise. But in practical terms, what are the characteristics, skills, abilities and actions that make leaders successful, and can they be learned or are they hardwired in one's DNA? In this chapter, I'll make my case that leadership is an art that you can master, and that leadership by example is that process. By that I mean, in part, modeling the organization's desired behavior (assuming it wants ethical and exemplary conduct); not asking anyone to do anything you haven't done or aren't willing to do yourself, and always acting in the best interest of the organization and its members, all of which is manifested by one's actions, not merely words.

Bill Belichick, one of the most successful coaches in NFL history, says: "Leadership means building a team that's exhaustively prepared, but able to adjust in an instant." In the same interview with Suzy Welch (CNBC April 13, 2017), Belichick describes four additional leadership traits: One, deploying one's dependable employees, rather than the stars all the time; two, having the gumption to be the boss and not being afraid to confront problems; three, caring about what goes on in the lives of your employees; and four, never resting on your laurels.

You can read the article and view the entire interview through the link below.

http://www.cnbc.com/2017/04/13/bill-belichick-leadership-rules.html

In my opinion, leading by example is one the cornerstones of all leadership principles and, without a doubt, can be learned and practiced. Albert Schweitzer, the great German philosopher and medical missionary said: "Example is not the main thing in influencing others, it is the only thing." I couldn't agree more. Think about the leaders you respect and invariably you'll see that they lead by example, demanding the same from you. So, if you look at leadership through the prism of serving others and setting the example, you'll readily agree that those in positions of authority who adhere to these philosophies tend to achieve good things for the organization more frequently and are respected and trusted by those who do the work. Look at your experiences. Remember when you used to work for a supervisor or manager that talked a good game, was charismatic, and whom you liked, but you didn't respect because he took the path of least resistance and shirked his responsibility because he wanted to be "one of the guys?" What about the one who mounted the bully pulpit and preached like a southern minister, but didn't have the same expectations of himself that he did of you? Remember what that did to your zeal for the job? How about your desire to work hard and feel proud of your Department?

I don't need to spell it out for you, but individuals like those I've just described, if left unchecked, can run an organization to the ground. Or, at the very least, lower the bar to the point that mediocrity and complacency become the norm. Conversely, how about the leader who worked alongside you and set the tone and pace of work, who when things got difficult rolled up his sleeves to help do the job without being dictatorial? These are the types of leaders I respected and preferred in my career, especially when I was a street cop or investigator. They rolled up their sleeves and worked alongside you without getting in your way, and in the end made you want to be part of the team. The inspiration indeed came from the perspiration! These were leaders who embodied the leadership principles I mentioned above. More about leading by example in the next chapter.

Incompetent supervisors and managers can make your life miserable. At the very least, they can decrease your productivity, the quality of your work and your effectiveness, as well as make you want to go home and kick the cat! I've read credible studies that show that bad bosses account for a significant portion of sick leave and workers' compensation costs. Given the risk posed by unfit individuals in positions of authority, who can't or won't lead by example, why do we continue to give them a pass? The answer will probably not surprise you, but it boils down to this: doing the right thing isn't easy! Complicating matters are civil service rules, union contracts and legal precedent—some of which was established because police management overstepped its authority or willfully violated doctrines of fair practice that govern how a peace officer is treated in a disciplinary matter or performance improvement effort.

As a result, some law enforcement executives, managers, and supervisors take the path of least resistance. Too many want to be popular (Harry Truman once said that if you want to have a friend in Washington, you should get a dog!) and ignoring problem children usually gets them there with a small but significant and vocal portion of the agency's employees. Meanwhile, the problem festers until a major incident or lawsuit turns up and bites the organization in the proverbial ass. Most tragic events that ultimately result in termination or incarceration of an officer don't happen suddenly. They are usually a series of small performance or misconduct incidents that are ignored by supervision or management, ultimately adding up to bigger issues.

Take, for example, the case of Lt. Charles Joseph Gliniewicz from the Fox Lake Police Department in Illinois. He was initially reported to have died in September 2015 from gunshot wounds inflicted by an assailant he was chasing. He was hailed as a hero and held up as an example of good cops who do a tough job well. In early November of that year, his police agency reported that the lieutenant had committed suicide by self-inflicted gunshots. According to the AP, "The huge outpouring of grief [about his death] has now been replaced by a sense of betrayal after investigators revealed on Wednesday that he had elaborately planned his own killing after stealing and laundering money from a Police Explorers program he oversaw for seven years. In his last weeks, he feared he was about to be exposed by a new village administrator."

What's even more remarkable is that his personnel file, recently released under a Freedom of Information request, revealed that he had been a troubled employee for many years. The file showed Gliniewicz was involved in alleged misconduct throughout most of his career with Fox Lake but had been promoted even after serious allegations—including lying—were sustained and substantial suspensions imposed. According to the Chicago Tribune (Zumback, Hinkel, August 12, 2017) "A copy of Gliniewicz's personnel file released by the village documented trouble reaching back decades before the 52-year-old died Sept. 1. The file shows an officer whose career was marked by drunken indiscretions, sexual misconduct and threatening behavior." An anonymous letter from employees to the Mayor also detailed many acts of misconduct and inappropriate behavior on the part of Gliniewicz. Further, "Three north suburban men who said they were targeted as suspects in the 2015 shooting of Fox Lake police Lt. Charles Joseph Gliniewicz before authorities declared his death a staged suicide, filed a federal class-action lawsuit Thursday against several north suburban police departments, the FBI, Illinois State Police and the Lake County sheriff's office."

To read the AP and Chicago Tribune articles go here:

http://news.yahoo.com/personnel-records-show-years-complaints-against-officer-072632494.html

http://www.chicagotribune.com/news/local/breaking/ct-fox-lake-gliniewicz-investigation-lawsuit-met-20170413-story.html

So why, in the face of overwhelming evidence that an individual in a management position is unfit, would a police chief keep that employee and promote him? Why would the organization not intervene early on to help the lieutenant when the first indications of trouble surfaced, or at least impose disciplinary action to check the alleged misconduct? In this case, there were red flags and sustained allegations of misconduct, and indications the lieutenant was potentially a problematic manager. Why would an organization fail to do the right thing in light of all this evidence, exposing employees to dysfunctional working conditions and an unsafe environment? As you'll read in this book, doing the right thing can be difficult, and some in leadership positions are reluctant to exercise their authority to protect the rest of the organization.

Sometimes the accused employee is well liked, or is charismatic, or has managed to intimidate the boss with references to a lawsuit or union action. In some cases, the decision maker can't muster the wherewithal to impose harsh but appropriate discipline on a long-time employee. Whatever the reason, inaction can damage an organization and expose it to lawsuits, loss of public trust and issues of low morale. I've seen it happen too often in agencies across the country. In my opinion, this was one of those cases. My guess is that it will haunt the organization for years with lawsuits and, more importantly, loss of trust by the rank and file and the community.

This type of failure of leadership was a frequent theme when I spoke with law enforcement executives in preparation for this book. They lamented the inability of some supervisors and managers to make the transition from officer to supervisor, allowing them to understand their role better. A few freely admitted they didn't do a good job at mentoring, training and conditioning new supervisors for them to have a smooth transition and better performance down the road. Others told me that given the union's power over politicians, they simply couldn't do the job the way it was meant to be done. I'm not convinced unions always preclude police executives or others in positions of authority from doing the right thing, but more about that later. I suspect it isn't much different in other professions, but it can be most damaging in police work given the scope of responsibilities. When a business manager misses a profit or production goal, the consequences are detrimental to the bottom line. When a police manager can't or won't do his job, the effects can be devastating or dangerous to the organization and the community. You need only look at the newspaper to find the disastrous consequences suffered by law enforcement agencies and communities when leaders fail to hold bad employees accountable.

Given the stakes, what does successful leadership look like? As I said earlier, think of a great supervisor or manager for whom you've worked and the qualities he or she exhibited. Some of those qualities are easy to describe, while others are more amorphous but equally as powerful. I remember working for individuals who by their mere presence and strength of personality made you want to do the best job you could. You wanted to please them, make them proud and felt as though you could follow them to the gates of hell if necessary. Don't get me wrong, these individuals were not perfect; they had the same human frailties as most, but they were able to project their strengths in ways you understood and welcomed. They made you feel special as if you mattered! They didn't get in your way unnecessarily but didn't shirk from their responsibilities to guide and supervise you. They treated you with dignity and respect. While those two words may appear to be clichés, they are two of the most important in the leadership lexicon. Understand them and learn to apply them, and you'll be a great leader in many ways.

Effective leadership is quietly present but clearly visible. You know it, you feel it, and you welcome it. That's right: employees crave a disciplined workplace with leadership that walks the talk and treats employees like they matter. They want predictability in the way their supervisors and managers will act and react to various situations, rather than be kept guessing as to what will please or upset them on a given day. Members of a police organization expect that they will be disciplined when they engage in misconduct. Yes, even the errant employee expects to be punished! But they want discipline to be consistent and fair, and that a distinction will be made between mistakes of the mind and those of the heart: was it a good-faith mistake or a wanton action devoid of redeeming qualities? These are not lofty expectations. They constitute the minimum standard of practice to which all agencies should and must aspire. To achieve any less would relegate the department to mediocrity and failure. Unfortunately, some agencies throughout the country ignore these principles. I saw it in my own department more often than I should have. Again, Santa Ana was a great police department that served the community well, winning national accolades, but, it had its share of poor supervisors and managers.

I served as a police lieutenant for thirteen years—six of those years assigned as the commander of the Human Resources division. Despite "Dirty" Harry Callahan's comment: "personnel, that's for assholes," I consider that period as perhaps the most formative in my understanding of how a police organization, or any public safety organization, works. It exposed me to practically every system in city government and gave me a great perspective on how government can be useful, or how it can fail miserably. It also gave me the opportunity to be of help to many in the department. For those of you who seek promotion, there is no better way to broaden your experience and gain an understanding of city or county government. During that time, I saw how competent supervisors and managers helped employees do their best, and how poor ones caused them harm, sapped their energy and cost the organization in terms of lost productivity, workers' compensation costs or lawsuits.

I had some employees sitting in my office in tears after being treated unfairly or caustically by someone in a position of authority who lacked communication skills or was autocratic to the point of ruling with an iron fist. To be fair, a small percentage of these employees had an agenda, and it soon became obvious, but most were legitimately wronged in some way. I always made mental notes as I and others tried to deal with the problems created by people that should have never been selected for their positions. Again, these misfits represented a small minority, but even a few bad apples can cause tremendous harm. If you want to understand how a police department works, spend some time in your human resources department and your internal affairs unit. We'll talk about work experience later and how it is inextricably linked to your leadership potential. For now, just remember that bad leaders can damage an organization—sometimes even beyond repair—and it is incumbent upon you, the conscientious leader, to root out the bad ones and protect the remaining employees.

All those years in the business also exposed me to successful leaders who were able to accomplish great things for the organization. I got to watch them in action and learn from them, seeing how they quickly put you at ease and allowed you to do things of which you didn't think yourself capable. I saw how they influenced new recruits and supervisors in ways I considered artful more than intellectual, always trying to align the best interests of the agency with those of the employees. People wanted to work for them even though they knew they'd be working harder than if they worked for others. They sought them out precisely because these leaders had high expectations of themselves and those around them. These folks became my role models, and I set out to learn as much as I could from them.

I hope that by reading this small contribution to the body of knowledge on police leadership, you'll also want to emulate them and achieve exceptional results for your employees, the organization and yourself. I propose that great leadership skills can indeed be learned by anyone who is relatively intelligent, is a hard worker and wants to do the right thing. The process of becoming an exceptional police leader has to begin by understanding one's skills, abilities and limitations, and formulating a plan early on in one's career to improve on assets and reduce liabilities. I'll talk about gap analysis later on, but that is what you need to do. Where am I, and where do I want to be? Those are the relevant questions. The path in between should be your roadmap to success. That applies to your employees as well, and your job is to periodically do that gap analysis with them to help shape their futures.

On that road, a fair amount of introspection is required. Understanding yourself is critical as the first step to visualizing where you want to go and how you'll get there. Making a commitment to become a great supervisor or manager is the second one. Look at the outstanding leaders in your agency and figure out how and why they are as good as they are. What traits do they possess that sets them apart, and how do they treat the people with whom they work? How do they interact with their peers and superiors? How do they treat members of the community? How do they overcome temporary setbacks and failures? To what extent do they open up to others and give up positional power to get legitimate power and respect? In other words, do they exhibit vulnerabilities because they are humble leaders? Do they listen to ideas, concerns and the needs of others? Answering these questions will give you a clearer perspective on where you fit in and what you need to do to reach your destination. It isn't easy to introspectively look at yourself and define what skills and qualities you have, what weaknesses prevent you from being the best, and what you need to do to improve. But it is essential analysis, and it can be done if you have the desire to help yourself and others.

Recently I spoke with a friend who is now a supervisor and who had worked at several agencies throughout his twenty-year career. We reminisced about his days in the gang unit and the level of activity that management expected of everyone in the team. It was a busy period with homicides and assaults at their peak. Everyone worked hard—sometimes to the point of exhaustion—yet they did it willingly and gladly. He told me personally worked hard not only for the department but also for his supervisor. I asked him why, and he paused for a second. He then told me it was because he knew his sergeant cared about him and could be trusted to take care of his troops. He said, "I worked hard for him because I didn't want to disappoint him." He went on, "Don't get me wrong, he'd quickly let you know if you did something wrong and expected us to learn from mistakes, but he cared about us, and I cared about him." I asked him what other characteristics he admired about that sergeant, and he told me that he was competent, "knew what he was doing" and could easily be counted on to lead by example. He said: "He'd kick your ass if you strayed, but he was right there next to you serving that search warrant or making that arrest." Essentially, it was all about trust; trust that someone cares about you and is competent to lead you in a profession that could cost you your life.

Leading cops effectively is more of a marathon than a sprint: it takes solid, consistent work to gain the trust and respect of those who by design have to be skeptical. You can't fool them for long as they have the best instincts for ferreting out those who merely talk a good game, but lack substance. It isn't about the occasional flash of brilliance, either. The street cop or the seasoned investigator will tell you that time is the only way to tell if a leader is truly worth his or her salt. Developing the skills and abilities to withstand these tests is crucial for anyone wishing to lead, to set the example, to galvanize teams to achieve the organizational mission. And trust is that one bargain that one can never risk losing, as it is nearly impossible to gain back. Once you've lost the respect and trust of those around you, regaining it will require a gargantuan and sustained effort. You'll need to make amends and then prove yourself all over again. It can be done, but it takes a confident yet humble individual that recognizes her own mistakes and can admit them to subordinates. Learning to be introspective, to tear down walls and willingly become vulnerable are the hallmarks of great leaders.

THE WEST WING MODEL

I do my cardio workouts on a treadmill at home in front of the television for about an hour nearly every day, so I watch Netflix and try to pick out good shows that last about that long. Although I never watched the West Wing when it played on network television, I recently started with the first episode. (Look, I know that Aaron Sorkin's staccato dialogue and liberal political views aren't for everybody, but some of his shows are intelligent and offer views with which we may differ but yet captivate our intellect and force us to look at differing opinions in entertaining ways.)

Somewhere near the end of the first season, about 15 months into their first term, there is an episode where President Bartlett's Chief of Staff confronts the President about his timidity to voice his opinions and pursue the policies and legislation he saw as critical to the nation. At that point, the President's approval rating was 42%. Leo, his chief of staff, points out how everyone in Congress knows he won't have the intestinal fortitude to engage in fights about meaningful issues because he fears the political consequences. He aptly points out that doing the right thing is hard, but that it is more important than winning a second term. After a brief period of denial, the President seemingly sees the light and decides to take the gloves off to do the things he truly wanted to accomplish. He recognizes it won't be easy, and he'll lose some of the battles, but he becomes invigorated with the thought he no longer has to play the middle-of-the-road game all the time, feeling free to chase after the agenda he once cherished. His staff is also enthused and motivated to advance the agenda they all signed up to accomplish. It was, in my view, a turning point for the series, which I'm sure was part of Sorkin's game plan to slowly develop Martin Sheen's character.

After watching the episode, I thought about how timidity or lack of confidence can marginalize anyone in a position of authority. There are times when the prospect of defeat on an issue has to be considered, but it shouldn't paralyze you to the extent that little or nothing gets done and a future of mediocrity looms large. City and county governing bodies hire police chiefs and sheriffs based on their leadership skills and competence, as well as their views on a host of issues. Supervisors and managers generally get promoted based on similar criteria. But everyone expects that a leader will articulate and pursue an agenda that makes sense for the organization and will make the lives of people better. That means forcefully but constructively pursuing a vision and strategy without having to always pull back because the fight may be difficult, or the politics will make it uncomfortable. President Bartlett reached that conclusion only after his closest advisor and his staff had the gumption and confidence to confront him and point out why he ran for president. In other words, speaking truth to power! Everyone at some time or another has to suck it up and tell the boss he's wrong or he's not doing the right thing. If he's a good leader, he'll welcome the constructive feedback as long as it's well-intentioned.

Leading isn't always easy, as you'll repeatedly read in this book, but it is the only way to make your hard work and sacrifice worth it. It is the only way to give people in the community and the organization a sense that there is hope, and that together you can achieve a better future. Those that oppose you on the merits of an initiative or issue will respect you because you had the guts to try and fought a good, clean fight. They'll see that you are sincere and are willing to put yourself up front to get things done. If you've done your homework and thought strategically, they will also respect you for being someone with whom they can work. I'll grant you that Sorkin's TV show is simply that, a made–up set of circumstances easily achieved in film. But it's also instructional and motivating, urging you to aim high and achieve what you feel is the future of the organization. Look at other episodes, and you'll get leadership and political lessons that resonate with everyone's desire to have a competent, articulate and caring leader at the helm of any enterprise. Sure, we are all flawed in some way, but great leaders feed our aspirations and desires for the best way forward and for our need to belong to something greater than ourselves. That desire is in all of us to some extent, and it takes effective leadership to bring it out.

BUILD A TEAM LIKE LINCOLN'S

"Good leadership requires you to surround yourself with people of diverse perspectives who can disagree with you without fear of retaliation." Doris Kearns Goodwin

Winter was nearly over in March of 1861, and after a grueling election, Abraham Lincoln was inaugurated as President and officially thrust into a national crisis of epic proportions. Slavery and the threat to the union were foremost in his mind, but he lacked experience in dealing with national affairs. Lincoln knew that if he was to effectively address the nation's problems he needed a cabinet filled with individuals of different strengths, backgrounds, political persuasions and, strikingly, those who were perhaps more intelligent or accomplished than he was. Lincoln was a confident man, and he knew that selecting a team of political rivals to help lead the nation through what was, arguably, its most difficult period was a risky but necessary strategic decision.

Lincoln also knew he could handle the rivalries and disparate perspectives of the team to focus their collective skills and expertise on the nation's problems. He recognized that it would have been folly to surround himself with those with whom he agreed and felt most comfortable, risking the loss of critical insight, experience and political assets that would help him accomplish his vision for the nation. To crush his opponents after they lost would have been petty, vindictive and short sighted; not characteristics of visionary and magnanimous leaders. While Lincoln didn't have experience in national affairs, he had keen political instincts and readily recognized his limitations.

Lincoln, following his instincts, set out to form a cabinet that included those who had opposed him during the election and several others who were better educated—and more experienced—than he was. He deliberately avoided surrounding himself with "yes" men. He chose cabinet members who largely agreed with him on slavery, but whose personalities and animosities toward Lincoln and each other presented a challenge most men would have avoided. The civil war broke out six weeks later. While Lincoln didn't know many in his new cabinet well and had a frosty relationship with some of them from the start, he slowly gained their trust and confidence and managed to accomplish what many thought was impossible. Keep in mind that Lincoln's newly installed cabinet members often disagreed with each other, but Lincoln maintained a productive relationship with each of them. He sought their opinions and valued the expertise or knowledge they provided. For example, Lincoln appointed and trusted Edwin Stanton as War Secretary, but he often consulted with and sought the military advice of Montgomery Blair, his Postmaster General, who had a military education and had served as a military officer and had a better understanding of how soldiers thought and behaved. In Recollections of the Civil War, (157-58), Charles A. Dana wrote:

"The relations between Mr. Lincoln and the members of his Cabinet were always friendly and sincere on his part. He treated every one of them with unvarying candor, respect, and kindness; but though several of them were men of extraordinary force and self-assertion— this was true especially of Mr. Seward, Mr. Chase, and Mr. Stanton —and though there was nothing of selfhood or domination in his manner toward them, it was always plain that he was the master and they the subordinates. They constantly had to yield to his will in questions where responsibility fell upon him. If he ever yielded to

theirs, it was because they convinced him that the course they advised was judicious and appropriate. I fancied during the whole time of my intimate intercourse with him and with them that he was always prepared to receive the resignation of any one of them. At the same time I do not recollect a single occasion when any member of the Cabinet had got his mind ready to quit his post from any feeling of dissatisfaction with the policy or conduct of the President. Not that they were always satisfied with his actions; the members of the Cabinet, like human beings in general, were not pleased with everything. In their judgment much was imperfect in the administration; much, they felt, would have been done better if their views had been adopted and they individually had had charge of it. Not so with the President. He was calm, equable, uncomplaining. In the discussion of important questions, whatever he said showed the profoundest thought, even when he was joking. He seemed to see every side of every question. He never was impatient, he never was in a hurry, and he never tried to hurry anybody else. To every one he was pleasant and cordial. Yet they all felt it was his word that went at last; that every case was open until he gave his decision."

https://archive.org/details/recollectionsofc00danach

The lessons in leadership and management competence provided by Lincoln's example contain gold nuggets for us all. Learning, and practicing them, is essential. Building a team isn't an exclusive realm of chief executives. Managers and supervisors must also put together effective teams, so Lincoln's example is one with broad application in public safety environments. Without a variety of views, perspectives, and backgrounds, any leader will have a limited understanding of issues, problems, and opportunities. According to historian Doris Kearns Goodwin (Team of Rivals: The Political Genius of Abraham Lincoln, Simon and Schuster), Lincoln's selection of political rivals for his cabinet was a stroke of genius. He selected them for their intellect and their abilities, not their political persuasion. For the good of the country he ignored their dislike of him personally and professionally, taking calculated risks that he could overcome those obstacles. He was right. You know the rest of the story.

Some managers tend to surround themselves with people like themselves, and with whom they share opinions and beliefs. It's natural to want to feel comfortable with those around you in leadership positions, wanting to avoid conflict and take the path of least resistance. Who wants to consciously surround themselves with those who will disagree, sometimes vehemently, with the direction of the organization and the decisions you make? But that is what leaders must do.

To put it another way, constructive conflict is the key to understanding the complexity and intricacies of most organizational and community problems (see the section on Constructive Dissension). As a manager or supervisor, you must surround yourself with good people with different backgrounds and experience who are willing to present differing views and who won't tell you what you want to hear unless it's the truth. You want people to constructively and forcefully disagree with you when they believe you're making the wrong decision without fearing for their jobs or positions. The key, as Lincoln realized, is to manage that conflict and debate effectively, and to make it clear that once the debate is over, the boss has the right to make the decisions and have them followed as long as they are moral, legal and ethical.

Donald T. Phillips, in Lincoln on Leadership (Warner Books, 1992), describes how the two men who initially thought the worst of Lincoln became the two closest to him and became the most competent in the cabinet. William Seward, Lincoln's Secretary of State, thought Lincoln was totally unqualified and had been a political rival. Seward accepted the job and, perhaps thinking Lincoln would be a pushover, was soon attempting to influence Lincoln's selections for the rest of the cabinet. Lincoln resisted, and Seward submitted his resignation. According to Phillips, Lincoln met with Seward and appealed to his sense of patriotic duty and sense of self-worth and talked him out of the resignation. Despite other disagreements, Lincoln and Seward became close and faithful allies, and "shared a deep commitment to the nation, a strong penchant for common sense, and high ethics and values...in a very short period of time Seward had turned from an attitude of skepticism and mistrust toward Lincoln to one of loyalty and admiration."

Great leaders encourage spirited debate for the right reasons and work with their teams to develop rules for engagement. That means that everyone understands that they may speak freely as long as it's done respectfully and constructively, addressing issues rather than engaging in personal attacks. The team must feel as though the decision maker wants to hear opposing options, perspectives and direction, and that his/her mind has not been made up until the analysis is reasonably complete. Orange County Sheriff Sandra Hutchens told me she will often wait to weigh in on an issue to see how those around her feel, thus letting them express their honest opinions. She'll then ask what she calls the "right questions," without which you'll never get relevant answers.

In other words, the leader must genuinely want to hear these differing views before making up one's mind. Nothing destroys morale more quickly than a charade played out in some conference room where you're asked for your opinion when a plan is already in place or substantially decided. Great leaders frequently seek opposing thoughts and views and relish a good debate before deciding on critical paths for them or the organization. Lincoln was the type of leader who understood the dynamics of dissent and sought to understand conflicting opinions, eventually making a decision that he would ensure was carried out without unnecessary delay. His opponents quickly found out how tenacious he could be when he made up his mind.

In a recently-found interview, Steve Jobs, Apple's co-founder and prior Chief Executive Officer, said: "It's that through the team, through that group of incredibly talented people bumping up against each other, having arguments, having fights sometimes, making some noise, and working together they polish each other and they polish the ideas, and what comes out is really beautiful." Police executives needn't fear healthy debate and different perspectives. It is essential to their success. Having talented people around you that espouse different views and perspectives is the key to coming up with innovative and effective solutions to entrenched community and organizational problems. After all, regardless of how bright or experienced you think you are, differing view and ideas often lead to that beautiful result Jobs talked about. When you look at the results or work product of successful organizations, you inevitably discover talented teams that work together, free to disagree, but ultimately united in a common and lofty purpose.

Good leaders are not afraid to defer to those whose background and experience makes them uniquely qualified to understand an issue or problem. They purposely select team members whose skills and abilities will complement and even surpass their own. They seek to find lasting solutions to problems through the talent and work of others and are not afraid to give people an opportunity to prove themselves despite the potential for failure. In fact, they see failure as an opportunity to learn and assess, creating the conditions for success in the future. It doesn't mean that a leader abandons his intuition and problem-solving skills; he merely allows for thoughtful and constructive dialogue to help build consensus on matters of importance. He surrenders power to gain insight and coherence for a plan of action.

Whenever possible, I always tried to encourage honest debate of proposals and ideas, sometimes assigning a different point of view to managers or supervisors whom I knew disagreed with each other about a course of action. I wanted to hear an honest, spirited debate on the merits. What I had to guard against was a tendency on my part to take sides based on my preferences and background or give more weight to a particular lieutenant's point of view because I liked or respected him or her more. While in most cases I had an opinion and leaned a certain way, I consciously focused on the merits of the arguments on both sides. I tried to test any assumptions and proposals as best I could, but in the end, I knew I had to trust those around me and listen to their concerns. In many instances, I was swayed and changed my mind. In others, I went with my gut instinct. Regardless of my decision, I believe I gave all proposals a fair and thoughtful hearing. In every situation, without fail, I made the decisions and insisted on a unified front when the time for debate was over. When people feel as though they've been heard, and their opinions considered, even if their views are not adopted, they will likely support the final decision.

Lincoln's cabinet selections were likely thought crazy at the time: why would he surround himself with personal and political rivals, many must have wondered. At the end that strategic approach allowed him to form a legitimate and effective government, which helped end the civil war and slavery. Lincoln thought strategically and continually looked for ways to accomplish his political initiatives. It appears as though foremost in his mind was surrounding himself with competent, dedicated people who rounded out his team. Keep that in mind when building your team. Don't be afraid to take calculated risks and surround yourself with a diverse, talented and committed team, even if they are your rivals.

WHAT REALLY MOTIVATES PEOPLE TO PERFORM

The eternal question facing managers and supervisors is what motivates people to do great work and add value to any organization. Is it money? Or perquisites? Or another material benefit such as bonuses? Or is motivation a byproduct of the belief that what one's work is intrinsically satisfying and makes us feel good about what we do? I subscribe assiduously to the theory that people will almost perform miracles if you treat them with dignity and respect and if you recognize and encourage their work, giving them the context of how it fits with the overall effort of the agency. When I asked the question about motivation to people I trust and admire, they nearly always placed the qualitative benefit of recognition and support at the top of the list, with trust as the key ingredient in the formula. Not that money and advancement weren't necessary and appealing, but they almost always followed the non-material benefits.

Think of your career: When did you do your best work? Was it when you found out you were getting a raise or was it when your work mattered to the enterprise and made you feel as though you were doing something good that was appreciated? I'd venture to say it was the latter. When assigning a critical project to one of my team members, I always tried to give them enough information so they'd know how the project fit into the strategic goals of the organization, and how critical they were to the effort. I would ensure that they had a clear view of how the project would translate into a benefit not only for the department but also to the community. I would put it in context so that those performing the work could see the value of their labor.

Dan Ariely is a Duke University academic who has done significant research into behavioral economics. He recently published a book called Payoff: The Hidden Logic That Shapes Our Motivations (Ted Books 2016), in which he explores the complex nature of motivation. His findings are condensed in the book, and they include: making work rewarding so employees feel as though their work is important and they are contributing to the organization's goals and ultimate success; trusting and challenging employees so they don't feel as though they are a clog in the bureaucracy which has to be watched and supervised constantly; and rethinking cash bonuses, which he believes may be an initial enticement to do the job but which rarely produce the truly committed, innovative and loyal team member. Ariely's experiments and research point to the intrinsic nature of motivation, and how managers and supervisors can synthesize the research into practical application to make workplaces more productive and meaningful. Increasing the value of work for people can be as simple as giving employees challenging assignments or giving someone feedback and showing them you care about what they do and how they do it.

I recently saw a copy of an email from a friend, who is a police executive, to all of his troops in the field, in which he extolled the virtues of stopping gang bangers based on probable cause to seize illegal weapons. He specifically told them why such activities are important to the community and included photos of two automatic guns that officers had seized with a cache of ammunition the previous night. What I liked most about it is that the executive communicated directly with his officers, appropriately bypassing the layers of supervision and management to personally deliver an important message to those that do the work. Powerful! He told them the activity he wanted them to pursue was important to him and the department and put it all in context by citing the link between these weapons and gang homicides in his city. He reinforced it all by including the photos of the weapons. He then congratulated the officers that made the stop the previous night. Lastly, he told them how much he appreciated their work and that the management team looked forward to continually supporting them to do such good work. This type communication from the boss is what helps motivate those who do dangerous work: the belief and feeling that those in positions of authority appreciate and value your work, and that they care about you.

Look, this isn't rocket science, but you'd be surprised how many organizations fail to unequivocally link the work of their employees to the bottom line and the wellness of the community. I know, you're probably thinking that understanding how one's work fits in with organizational and community goals ought to be intrinsically understood by everyone in the department. I'm here to tell you that isn't always the case, especially in departments where the management team is inexperienced, not working together well or plain incompetent. So those in leadership roles have a duty to continually reinforce the cause and effect link between good, strategic leadership and police work, and a satisfied workforce that contributes to the community's well-being. That connection needs to be explained in specific terms—like the executive's actions I described above— frequently enough to engrain the idea in everyone's minds, not unlike the advertising industry's frequent airing of one commercial until folks remember the message subconsciously, without prompting.

After decades of research into what motivates people to work hard and do the right thing, it should be obvious to all of us that an enlightened chief executive and management team who lead by example and are trusted by the workforce because of their actions, not their words alone, is the best way to motivate employees. You'll always have the outliers and those who must be disciplined to adhere to organizational standards, but most of your employees will respond to the methods described in this book.

.

SPEAKING TRUTH TO POWER

I remember the day I was promoted to lieutenant when I met with the police chief for the final interview. Since this was a civil service process, he had the option of promoting any of the top three candidates through what we call the "rule of three." That meant that even though I was number one on the list he could pass me and select someone else out of the top three who was ostensibly more qualified or was a better fit for the management team. The rule of three was never meant to get back at your opponents, and chiefs during my tenure used it sparingly and generally as intended. While I was pretty sure he would appoint me, I knew it was not a done deal. We had talked for a good hour before he asked for any parting comments. I told him that if he promoted me, he could count on two things: One, I would always be honest with him and would give him the unvarnished truth regardless of the consequences; and two, I would work hard and lead by example. I also told him I would never be blindly loyal to him personally but would be loyal to his position as the chief executive, with the best interest of the organization at heart. In essence, these are my guiding principles when it comes to the issue of loyalty, and they served the organization and me well.

Over the years I witnessed some folks who pledged and delivered blind loyalty to their superiors regardless of the consequences, setting the stage for organizational dysfunction and loss of credibility with the troops. This practice will sooner or later catch up with you, diminishing your potential and that of others in your team. Some of you will accuse me of restating the obvious, but I once again point out how many so called "leaders" fail to tell their superiors the truth, instead telling them what they think they want to hear, getting them into trouble or making them ineffective because they'll operate under the wrong assumptions. Don't kid yourself, if you think this kind of practice doesn't happen, you're burying your head in the proverbial sand.

Always tell your boss the truth. Don't equivocate, hedge your bets or color it because you want to please him or her, or because you're afraid it may not be what they want to hear. If you are constructively honest, the boss will come to respect you and will understand you have the best interest of the organization at heart. If your honesty results in retribution or dismissal of your input, it's time to reevaluate whether this is the place for you. Look, there are individuals in positions of authority who always seek approval and accolades from their subordinates. These folks seek adulation, and they may get upset if you're honest. If your boss is one of them, your options are limited. But read on to see what you can do about it.

Those around me knew I wanted them to be loyal to the organization, period. I also told them I expected them to tell me the truth and feel free to disagree with me, even vehemently, as long as they did it constructively and respectfully. I insisted that they follow any criticism with thoughtful suggestions regarding the issues at hand. In other words, I wanted the unvarnished truth presented with the best interest of the organization at heart. If it was bad news, I wanted to hear it promptly and plainly. I then ensured everyone understood the consequences of doing otherwise and followed through by rewarding those that were upfront and honest about critical organizational issues. Conversely, those who failed to meet my loyalty test and tried to give me filtered or inaccurate information knew how I felt right away. Depending on the circumstances, they might have gotten a second chance, but if they did it again, they lost my trust and support. There were times when I didn't live up to my own expectations when I wasn't as forthcoming with my boss, and I beat myself up for it. But by and large I did the right thing, and I'm proud of it.

If you find yourself working for someone who feels entirely differently than I do, and he demands blind loyalty or prefers the soft-shoe rather than the truth, my advice is to engage in a meaningful discussion regarding the merits of operating under the right assumptions when making decisions. Point out how you will always seek to protect the interests of the organization and the executive himself by broaching difficult subjects promptly and thoroughly. More importantly, emphasize how you'll work hard not only to identify problems but to find solutions.

You'll be surprised how many people respect someone who stands up for what's right and manages to convey ideas in a non-threatening, constructive manner. If that doesn't work, consider seeking a transfer. If that's not an option—perhaps because the person is the head of the organization or high up in the hierarchy—make it clear you can't work that way and negotiate a mutual understanding whereby you will be constructively honest, and he can elect to ignore your input. Think of it this way: if you give in and fail to do what's right, eventually you and your boss will likely be in serious trouble, perhaps even lose your jobs or positions in the agency. The one thing I can guarantee will happen is that you will both lose the trust of the rank and file and ultimately the community you serve.

Don't confuse what I'm saying with the absence of personal loyalty to an individual whom you like and respect and who happens to be your boss. Personal loyalty—not blind loyalty—is fine as long as you don't sacrifice the organization's best interest. If you seek to do the right thing, those around you will feel as though you deserve their loyalty. And don't forget the boss' right to call the shots and your responsibility to carry out her directives as long as they are legal, moral and ethical. That should always be the line in the sand. You have to work with the boss you have, not the one you wish you had, and the quicker you accept that premise and move on the better you'll feel. I'll understand if you think these are platitudes that conflict with the real world. Standing up for what you believe isn't easy, and risking your job is perhaps the hardest thing to do.

I was confronted with these decisions a few times in my career and, thank God, I was able to do the right thing. It paid off for me, and I gained the respect of the superiors with whom I dealt. Think of the alternative: how do you live with yourself if you simply give in, fold your hand and retreat to the safety of your office? I suggest you wouldn't be very happy in any organization. One warning: just because you think your way is the right way doesn't mean everyone will agree. In other words, don't get so wrapped up in your machinations that you ignore everyone else's perspective. They may be more right than you think.

As a police sergeant, I once worked for a lieutenant whom I respected immensely. His name was Dan McCoy. He was the type of leader that worked hard and gave you opportunities to break outside your comfort zone. He taught me a lot, most of all persistence. He and I had worked together in the gang and homicide units as investigators, where I was able to see him doggedly clear difficult cases and obtain confessions. He was relentless, but he did it in such an honest way that once a gang banger whom he'd put in the joint for many years asked him to be the godfather to his son. I would kid him that he talked so much during interviews that suspects confessed just to shut him up! There was some truth to that, but I learned a great deal about how you must treat people, especially suspects, if you want them to open up and give you information. I was fortunate to work with him, and he showed me how treating suspects with respect and allowing them to keep their dignity paid off in the end. I also saw how he provided the chief of police with honest, constructive information and advice, even though at times that was a difficult thing to do.

Later in our careers I witnessed first-hand how he defined loyalty. When he was a captain and I a lieutenant, we would often have to walk into the chief's office with bad news, or to argue in favor or against a particular course of action the chief was considering. Early on we had talked about the approach to loyalty, and we agreed that blind loyalty was foolish. There were lively discussions when we disagreed with the "Old Man" (affectionate term for the chief) about policy, direction or discipline. We presented our point of view forcefully, but always constructively. At times the relationship with the chief strained a bit, and Dan and I commiserated in private about whether a decision was judicious and how it would affect the agency. There were times when the chief was right, and times when our approach was clearly the better way to go.

The bottom line is that we worked within the system to advocate for our positions, both individually and collectively, but when a decision was made we carried it out as long as it was, again, moral, legal and ethical. We never undermined him by going behind his back and, more importantly, he knew we had his best interest and that of the department at heart. He knew we cared and didn't have a political or nefarious motive when pushing for our point of view. Although he and I disagreed on some issues, I've always given Chief Paul Walters credit for having an open mind and a willingness to listen. I won some arguments and lost others, but my campaigns were always constructive and within the system. That was the key.

The foundation for loyalty is trust. After I had retired, I worked in private industry for a few years, which put me in frequent contact with agencies throughout the country. The CEO of a company where I worked decided on a pricing strategy for their product solely on the advice of a financial guru who felt the company was leaving lots of money on the table. The CEO had not asked those around him—who were experienced industry veterans—how the price increase would affect customers and, by extension, the company's client retention and bottom line. When I learned of the planned action after the CEO decided it, I immediately saw the significant downside, as did a high-level manager in the organization. I felt the decision-making process had been fatally flawed, and he had not considered all the relevant factors. At the risk of losing my contract, I wrote the CEO a lengthy email as to why I felt he was making a mistake. I was constructively honest and direct. The next day he called me and told me I was right and canceled the planned price increases.

To his credit, he admitted to having trusted an outsider's advice without consulting those in the business who could point out obvious problems. I worked with some bosses who were scrupulous about getting feedback on critical decisions before they were made, and I remember the feeling of actually being able to give input that truly mattered and made a difference. Conversely, there were a few times when decisions were made without a meaningful opportunity for stakeholders to point out important drawbacks or pitfalls simply because the decision maker felt he knew better. That is precisely how one can doom a project or initiative before it is even implemented. Leave your ego at the door and get enough input from different perspectives is the moral of the story. (See the section on Red Teams for a way to vet decisions before they are made.)

There are those in all organizations that believe loyalty means protecting your boss at all costs and soft-pedaling the truth. The opposite is true. Tell your boss what she least wants to hear, and back it up with facts and options. That's what your department needs the most: honest employees who, regardless of rank, will constructively tell you if you're about to make a mistake or decide on a course of action for which the decision-making process was flawed. As a leader you must nurture these types of employees; they are undoubtedly the most talented, loyal and the ones that help your agency thrive. Reward them and hold them up as examples for others to see. If you ignore them or discourage them in any way, you will cement the agency's deficient culture, miss opportunities, and keep your organization in a defensive, perpetual recovery mode. Not a good way to do business in any industry.

Most people know intuitively that integrity is the essential element of any personal or professional relationship. Whether one acts following that knowledge is the variable that sets folks apart. I write about integrity in the context of loyalty and ambition because they are often linked, and it is in that environment that some struggle with decisions. One's interest is a powerful motivator—for good or bad. It takes confidence and intestinal fortitude to act in a way that places your job, career or position in jeopardy. But think about integrity as the only way to ensure you are respected so you can help the organization and employees accomplish goals and objectives. It's truly the foundation for all you do at work and home. It is the ingredient without which the brew is bitter, the meal is poisonous, and the flavor is utterly atrocious. There are tons of courses, books, and websites that tout lessons on integrity. It isn't that complicated: Be constructively honest, strive to do the right thing regardless of the consequences, and commit to the purpose of your department wholeheartedly. Everything else follows.

MANAGEMENT IS NOT A DIRTY WORD

"Effective leadership is putting first things first. Effective management is discipline, carrying it out." Stephen Covey

How many times have you heard "managers do things right, but leaders do the right thing?" While it's true that competent managers do things right, they must also do the right thing. I can't tell you how often I've read books or articles and heard speakers denigrate "management" as less necessary than "true" leadership. Leaders, not managers, are placed on a pedestal and revered as truly special. There is often a subtle inclination to pit managers against leaders as if they were enemies on the battlefield. They aren't. Leadership and management are parts of the whole, complementing each other and building on the skills and competencies all managers and supervisors need. Leadership and management are skills that a person possesses. While it's true that there are good leaders that may not have the greatest management skills, most of them understand that good management is essential to competency. More importantly, they surround themselves with people that possess competencies they may lack. Lincoln's cabinet is a perfect example of a leader who knew what he didn't know or couldn't do and sought a team that could compensate for his weaknesses or lack of political clout.

Again, from Apple's Steve Jobs: "Many companies get the disease of thinking that a really great idea is 90 percent of the work. And if you just tell all these other people here's this great idea then of course they can go off and make it happen. And the problem with that is that there's just a tremendous amount of craftsmanship in between a great idea and a great product. Designing a product is keeping five thousand things in your brain and fitting them all together in new and different ways to get what you want. And every day you discover something new that is a new problem or a new opportunity to fit these things together a little differently." That's the essence of creative and enlightened management, and Steve Jobs relied on folks he could trust to carry out Apple's mission. But he was always interested and involved in the details, hence Apple's amazing execution to bring beautiful and useful products to market. Some would say Jobs obsessed over too many details, but that was, in my opinion, the key to Apple's tremendous product line. While private industry CEOs have more leeway in hiring talent, public safety leaders must rise to the occasion and build teams that can deliver. It may be a little more difficult, but it can be done.

For an excellent resource look here: https://rework.withgoogle.com/guides/

A Los Angeles Times headline once read: "Where's Obama the Manager?" The article referred to the group of challenges that had seemingly befuddled the administration, including health care, the NSA leaks, Libya, and others. It goes on to describe how even a popular leader with tremendous oratory skills can be damaged and thwarted by a lack of management skills and precise attention to details. Or, to be clearer, the lack of a management team that is competent enough to implement the President's vision. What good is it for the boss to have great ideas, break through barriers and develop alliances for critical projects, if the projects are not implemented in an effective and efficient manner? Worse yet, what happens to an organization that has many charismatic leaders but few good managers to achieve the boss' vision? Ideally, great leaders are also competent administrators, but if they lack certain skills or abilities, they surround themselves with those who have them.

Don't ever underestimate the importance of competence to your employees, peers and the community. I grant you that truly good leaders often have qualities that can set them apart from purely competent managers, such as vision, creativity and the ability to forge successful strategies for long-term success. But having those qualities is also consistent with being a great manager. Police agencies should seek to develop good managers who can also become great leaders through mentoring, education, training and exposure to different jobs. If you start out by setting a firewall between the two, you'll end up with bean counters and prima-donnas who never reach their potential and, at times, can even harm an agency. I may be splitting hairs here, but it's always bothered me that managers are seemingly denigrated because of their competence and their perceived lack of that amorphous "passion or vision." Bottom line: Strive to be a competent manager and a great leader because they aren't mutually exclusive.

The road to competence begins with your experience base, so that's where I'll start. Before we move on, however, I'd like to ask you to review the headlines in the media about local, state and federal projects that were botched, had huge cost overruns or took much longer to finish than was previously promised. These debacles cost government agencies much more than money; they erode or destroy what little confidence the public has in governmental organizations as it is. Look at the healthcare.gov debacle, or the bungled travel ban by the Trump administration, to see how botched government projects can affect public policy that may be worthwhile but isn't implemented well. These initiatives would have benefited from an organizational red team (see the chapter on risk management). The moral of the story is to manage these projects with prudent and competent stewardship, test extensively before implementation, and manage expectations so that that the result exceeds them. Setting high expectations requires the muscle and the intellect to deliver, but unless you're sure that you can do that, set realistic expectations and work hard to surpass them. Most of all, as the leader, don't relinquish responsibility by delegating and forgetting; follow Steve Jobs' example and stay involved to ensure the right path is taken.

The other crucial element of good management is to admit mistakes and fix them as quickly as possible. I was surprised when members of the Obama administration sought to downplay the problems with the healthcare website, ignoring reality and pretending that the outcry would pass if they just held firm. I know what you're thinking, but I'm not only piling on the previous administration. I am an independent voter, previously a Republican that got fed up with partisan politics—I voted for Obama, twice—who votes his conscience regardless of the politics. I believe that healthcare reform is of critical importance, but the implementation mistakes of the program were hard to ignore. Unfortunately, we don't learn from past mistakes, as the Trump administration is intent on surpassing Obama's in mistakes by displaying a breathtaking lack of competence. You need to look no further than the series of flops the Trump administration had in 2017 and the first part of 2018. Sadly, rather than admit mistakes, they doubled-down with illogical explanations and excuses. The way to blunt criticism and move forward is to quickly admit mistakes, develop a realistic plan of action to fix them, and then put a good team on the project and bring it to fruition on a realistic timeline. Denying the weaknesses and fatal flaws only makes you look like you're living in a parallel universe devoid of reality, none of which bodes well for the future of your organization. Remember that leadership, competence and integrity are inextricably linked and equal parts of the whole. Don't dismiss one at the expense of the others. Finally, you'll find that public safety organizations that focus on mentoring and training punch above their weight frequently —and achieve superior results for the community and their employees.

The bottom line is that incompetent managers can destroy any organization. I recently read a review by Andrew Hill, from the Financial Times of London, of a book written by Morgen Witzel, an author and management historian. The book is "Managing for Success: Spotting Danger Signals—And Fixing Problems Before They Happen" (Bloomsbury Press). His book is a stark reminder that as Witzel says: "Managerial incompetence is not consequence-free. It kills companies. And, sometimes, too, it kills people." That is a sobering truth, especially in law enforcement, where bad management actors degrade not only the effectiveness of the agency but destroy morale and sap the energy of valuable employees. Witzel argues that many business failures are not caused by one bad leader making a few bad decisions, but instead are the long-term effect of a broken organizational culture. Perhaps the most useful reminder in his book is that managers have an "important and humane mission to make things better" for staff and members of the public. As Hill states, the lessons in the book aren't new, but they bear repeating since managers make the same mistakes as their predecessors. Keeping your eye on the ball is not only good for your agency but is good for you as well.

So good managers, at times belittled, are no less critical to the well-being of any workplace than a visionary leader. Think of the projects or budgets that wouldn't survive if all you had was a charismatic leader who didn't have the expertise, knowledge and managerial competence required to bring it to fruition. The obvious ideal is to have a great leader who is also a great manager, but that combination may not exist in your organization for certain positions at the top at any given moment in time. The alternative is to have leaders who surround themselves with competent managers who can help carry out the department's mission, and who pursue a policy of mentoring and growth for those who seek these positions.

These leaders ensure that there is always a path to becoming a better supervisor or manager and that those who strive to be leaders get the opportunities to measure up for the job. Great leaders aim for redundancy in talent, giving people the chance to experience and develop different areas of work so they can assume more responsibility at the drop of a hat. Like the military's leadership program that rotates individuals through commands after a certain period, rather than selfishly keep someone in a particular job because they are so good at it, rotate them and have them develop a broad set of competencies. You'll help ensure a solid succession of command plan, as well as the ability to handle any crisis with reasonable success.

Many great leaders were competent supervisors and managers, proving themselves by delivering important initiatives and projects on time, or perhaps by looking deeply at community problems and helping design solutions that get to their root cause. There is often a fine line between a great manager and a great leader. A leadership newsletter to which I subscribe recently published a list of what its publishers consider the differences between leaders and managers. While I agree in principle that there are some differences, I differ on how these differences manifest themselves. The article described them in stark terms, while I see them as much more subtle.

One such difference, according to the article, is that leadership is about propelling the organization forward, while management is about maintaining what is already there. I happen to think that raising artificial walls between leaders and managers is foolhardy. Sure, chief executives are always concerned about strategic issues and looking around corners to best position the agency for success. But so do managers who care about their employer and feel invested strategically as well as tactically in the outcomes of their efforts.

Good leaders have broad knowledge about the business in their field, but they also have relatively strong competencies in the many facets of their profession. I don't mean that a good executive can't go from one industry to the other unless they are experienced in both. Take a look at Alan Mullally, the ex-CEO of Ford, who was an Executive Vice-President at Boeing before going to Ford as the CEO in 2006. Mullally, who didn't know much about the car business and went from planes to automobiles, is widely credited with turning Ford around and making it profitable again, and without government assistance. Mullaly is an example of a talented outsider coming into a company outside his field and doing well by using leadership and management skills that are universal in nature. Mullally undoubtedly relied on insiders who knew the business and the culture but applied his own principles and values to lead them to profitability and a bigger share of the market.

While possible, this may not be as easy to accomplish in para-military organizations such as police departments, where managers and chief executives typically rise through the ranks in their agencies after gaining experience that serves them well in making decisions, looking at critical issues and implementing difficult projects. I'm sure some could make the transition from private industry to a police agency as the top cop, but it requires superb individuals who are masters at sizing up workplace environments, cultures and politics to accomplish it. In police work, it is almost unheard of to bring in a top leader from another industry to lead an agency. It would be an interesting experiment though!

Google conducted a major experiment in 2002 when they got rid of all managers. It didn't go so well. (https://rework.withgoogle.com/subjects/managers/.) According to Google, in 2008 a team of researchers set out to prove that managers don't matter, which is what they suspected. The team soon discovered the opposite, that managers mattered, a lot. With Project Oxygen, they set out to find out what makes a great manager at Google. They analyzed performance reviews, responses to surveys and the qualities that led to management awards. They looked at all the data that was relevant and available and developed a set of skills, abilities and qualities that make a great manager at Google. It was based on their own data and, according to the New York Times (http://www.nytimes.com/2011/03/13/business/13hire.html? smid=pl-share), "In Project Oxygen, the statisticians gathered more than 10,000 observations about managers—across more than 100 variables, from various performance reviews, feedback surveys and other reports. Then they spent time coding the comments in order to look for patterns." In short, Google put its money where its mouth is and committed the resources needed to develop a list of eight key factors that make a great manager. The beauty of the project is that the recommendations were based on data from their own organization that they validated through exhaustive analysis and interviews. Once the list was released, Google provided their managers with one-on-one coaching and extensive training on the findings and the relevant principles. The result was significant short and long-term improvement in the quality of management. Their findings as to what makes a good manager:

A good manager:

- Is a good coach
- Empowers the team and does not micromanage
- Expresses interest in and concern for team members' success and personal well-being
- Is productive and results-oriented
- Is a good communicator—listens and shares information
- Helps with career development
- Has a clear vision and strategy for the team
- Has key technical skills that help him or her advise the team

While you may think these qualities have been known for years, ask yourself how well your agency has integrated them into the selection, training and mentoring of managers. How do your managers stack up to each of these elements, and what has your agency done to remediate those that lack one or more of these skills? The list wasn't released and left to improve conditions on its own. Google developed a massive training and coaching program and established critical processes for recruitment, hiring and remediation. That's what makes the program successful. I urge you to read a Harvard Business Review article that takes a deep dive into Project Oxygen and its aftermath. You'll find it useful and revealing, as well as informative at the granular level, which should help you develop your own programs. (It can be found here: https://hbr.org/2013/12/how-google-sold-its-engineers-on-management.)

The question, then, isn't whether managers are needed. The key issue is what makes a good manager and how do organizations ensure that all teams have good managers. Project Oxygen is one of a few initiatives that have sought to answer that question. Google spent tremendous resources and time to find out and follow up to make sure they used the findings in practical, measurable ways. Your department must make that commitment as well.

5

HARNESSING THE POWER OF
EXAMPLE

"Example is not the main thing in influencing others. It is the only thing."
Albert Schweitzer.

I t was near freezing in Washington DC at around 8:00 pm on March 10, 2004. Deputy Attorney General James Comey was leaving his office in the Justice Department when he got a call from Attorney General John Ashcroft's chief of staff. Sounding alarmed, the caller told him that two high-level officials from the George W. Bush administration (Andrew Card, his Chief of Staff, and Alberto Gonzales, General Counsel) were en route to George Washington hospital, where Ashcroft had undergone emergency gallbladder surgery. Ashcroft was suffering from a severe and potentially life-threatening case of pancreatitis.

Those who saw him described him as in pain and disoriented, thus not able to make critical decisions. He had transferred his powers to Comey. Despite his wife's request that he not be bothered, Card and Gonzales wanted to get the AG to sign off on the continuation of the then-secret National Security Agency's wiretapping program (Stellar Wind), which would expire the next day. Before falling ill, Ashcroft had already decided to reject the program, and days earlier Comey had attended a meeting at the White House and told Vice-President Cheney—who was furious with Comey—and his staff that the DOJ did not believe the program was legal and would not certify it as such. Comey, who later testified about the incident before the Senate Judiciary Committee, said he remembered where he was at the time (Constitution Avenue) and quickly decided he had to stop them (Card and Gonzales).

According to a media account of the incident and transcripts from the Committee, the following occurred:

"So I hung up the phone," Comey told the committee, and I "immediately called my chief of staff, told him to get as many of my people as possible to the hospital immediately. I hung up, called [FBI] Director [Robert] Mueller—with whom I'd been discussing this particular matter and had been a great help to me over that week—and told him what was happening. He said, 'I'll meet you at the hospital right now.' [I] told my security detail that I needed to get to George Washington Hospital immediately. They turned on the emergency equipment and drove very quickly to the hospital. I got out of the car and ran up—literally ran up the stairs with my security detail." The account gets better at this point as Comey's testimony reads like a detective story. Minutes later, there is a showdown in the hospital room. Ashcroft, buffered by his wife and three of his senior deputies, faces down Gonzales and Card and refuses to sign off on the spy program. Gonzales and Card storm out of the room. Card calls Comey and demands that he come to the White House, but Comey refuses to go until he can get Ted Olson, the solicitor general, to accompany him. "After what I just witnessed, I will not meet with you without a witness," Comey tells Card.

http://www.salon.com/2007/05/15/comey_testifies/

The White House meeting eventually takes place but does not resolve the issue. The Bush administration then decides to reauthorize the program without the DOJs approval, triggering intense activity and soul-searching at the highest levels of the DOJ and the FBI. Comey—undeterred by presidential power—drafts a letter of resignation that would be effective the next day. Ashcroft, Mueller and other executives at both agencies are apparently prepared to do the same, and they communicate their intentions to President Bush. Before his top law enforcement officials resign in protest—creating a constitutional, judicial and public relations nightmare for the president—Bush, to his credit, steps in and agrees to modify the NSA's program so it complies with the law, and the wiretapping act is reauthorized.

Comey told the Judiciary Committee that: "I was concerned that this was an effort to do an end-run around the acting attorney general and to get a very sick man to approve something that the Department of Justice had already concluded was unable to be certified as to its legality. And that was my concern." Comey went on to become the FBI director under President Obama and, as you probably know, was unceremoniously fired by President Trump in 2017. In another twist of fate, Mueller was appointed as Special Counsel to investigate alleged ties between the Russians and the Trump campaign. I guess the truth is stranger than fiction!

I remember following this entire debacle closely at the time it played out on the national stage. I was aghast that someone at the highest levels of government—no doubt with what they thought were good intentions—would attempt to take advantage of the AG as he lay on his hospital bed, dazed and confused from pain medication. The drama was better than a James Patterson thriller, complete with protagonists, antagonists and the ultimate "good guy wins" ending. In his book, A Higher Calling, Truth, Lies and Leadership (Flatiron Books, 2018), Comey recounts the incident in depth, and recalls how when Card and Gonzalez were leaving the room, Janet Ashcroft (the AG's wife) "scrunched her face and stuck her tongue out at them." You gotta love it—two of the most powerful men in the nation, who were representing the President of the United States, got stymied by good men displaying leadership and integrity. Doesn't get better than that!

For Comey and Mueller to be ready to resign their posts in protest of what they saw as an attempt to authorize an illegal program, took guts! They projected the ability to do the right thing despite the consequences, which would have undoubtedly affected their lives and careers. But that's precisely what we should expect from our leaders, especially those that guard our most cherished institutions such as the justice department and the FBI. It reminded me of the intent of the framers of the Constitution who, wisely, felt that executive power had to be checked by the legislature and the judiciary, lest those in power feel they can do anything with impunity. In this case, institutions within the executive branch checked the power of the President of the United States.

To be sure, I believe President Bush and those around him had good intentions. It was a scant few years after 9/11, and our nation was reeling from the effects of the attacks on the Twin Towers. There was a reasonable fear that more was to come and those in positions of authority felt powerless to divine the mode and time of the next attack. Nonetheless, principled people who understood the implications of resorting to unlawful programs prevailed. Our system worked, as it did during the Watergate era. During an interview with CBS' 60 Minutes years later as the FBI director, Comey said that the American people ought to be deeply distrustful of government power, which is the primary reason our founding fathers set up the three branches of government. Comey and Mueller gave life to the premise underlying our form of government and showed, in excruciating practicality, how committed and dedicated leaders can influence events and outcomes.

This incident crystallized for me the power of example as a critical component of leadership. I saw how individuals placed their jobs on the line and risked losing their livelihoods to do the right thing, regardless of the consequences. I also saw how the example they set for the thousands who worked for them was just as valuable a lesson. Comey and Mueller led by example and inspired others to do the right thing. They sent a message that defined their expectations of those around them—and, I argue, around the nation. I remember smiling in awe after reading about the incident, as I thought their actions defined courage.

For me, it was a life lesson that validated my efforts to strive to do the right thing and set the tone for those with whom I worked. When I was confronted with a decision that was complicated or placed me at professional risk, or which impacted others in significant ways, I asked myself if indeed it was the right thing to do. It was a way for me to come to terms with the human propensity to take the path of least resistance. I asked myself how my actions would look the next day, in a month and the years ahead. Ultimately, I asked myself if I'd be able to live with my decision and be proud of what I'd done. The answer always helped me take the best path, regardless of the consequences.

LEADING BY EXAMPLE WORKS AND
INSPIRES

One rainy day during the American Revolutionary War, George Washington rode up to a group of soldiers attempting to raise a wooded beam to a high position. The corporal in charge was shouting encouragement, but the soldiers couldn't get the beam in position. After watching their lack of success, Washington asked the corporal why he didn't join in and help, to which the corporal replied, "Don't you realize that I am the corporal?" Very politely, General Washington replied, "I beg your pardon, Mr. Corporal, I did." Washington dismounted his horse and went to work with the soldiers to get the oak beam in position. As they finished, General Washington wiped perspiration from his face, and said, "If you should need help again, call on Washington, your commander-in-chief, and I will come" (Maxwell, 2011).

As George Washington aptly illustrates, there is no better way to influence people than to lead by example. I know, I know, it sounds like a cliché, but believe me, truly walking the talk is essential and it pays handsome dividends. Heckman and Owens, in their seminal research into how a leader's humility impacts team performance (see endnote), wrote: "Our findings collectively support our theoretical model, demonstrating that leader behavior can spread via social contagion to followers, producing an emergent state that ultimately affects team performance. We contribute to the leadership literature by suggesting the need for leaders to lead by example and showing how a specific set of leader behaviors influence team performance, providing a template for future leadership research on a wide variety of leader behaviors." If you get nothing else from this book, I hope you will see how the ability to lead by example is a non-negotiable attribute of effective leaders.

What does "leading by example" really mean? It means modeling the behavior you and the organization expect, acting clearly in support of what you preach and not asking others to do what you have not done or are unwilling to do yourself. It means developing a firm commitment to do the right thing regardless of the consequences, even though your decisions may go against your own interests. It also means sticking to the right path even though you'll falter at times. But most importantly, it means plumbing the depths of your character to do the things that are right and matter most to those who trust you. Leading by example includes admitting when you're wrong and learning to respect the opinions of others. When you do, you'll learn from your mistakes and move forward understanding that you're not perfect but have the capacity to persevere for the right cause. This way of being requires you to follow the rules just as you expect others to do. But it also means not being afraid of—in fact relishing—the opportunity to immerse yourself in the work of your subordinates, without getting in their way.

As you read earlier, those that influenced me most were almost invariably the supervisors and managers that rolled up their sleeves and worked alongside me, especially when times were tough. Having a commitment to lead by example is not pie-in-the-sky or naive ideology. It is a fundamental requirement of all who seek to lead and influence others to accomplish organizational goals, as well as take care of the organization's most valuable resource: its people. If you aren't willing to make that commitment, I counsel you to reconsider your desire to assume a leadership position.

When I promoted to Police Captain and took charge of the Field Operations Bureau, which included Patrol, Traffic, and SWAT, I'd wear the uniform frequently and worked in the field as often as possible. I felt that working alongside patrol officers and supervisors was important, but I didn't want the troops to misunderstand my motivation: I wasn't out there to spy on them or to micromanage field personnel. I felt that to lead by example I needed to do what they did—to stay in touch with field issues and understand the problems my officers faced. It was also a lot of fun. I wanted to keep my skills current and get to know the officers and supervisors better.

I would go out and handle calls, assist officers and generally do what needed to be done, including making arrests. But as they say: "if I caught them I cleaned them," meaning I wrote the reports. I also learned about community problems and the needs of the officers, giving me insight into the state of our city and the agency. There were lieutenants that did the same thing, and these folks were respected by the troops. Many times, I returned to the station determined to fix a problem I'd noticed but which no one had brought to my attention, or obtained additional resources based on my observations and input from the troops. There is nothing more enlightening than to see for yourself the working conditions and morale of the troops you lead.

The reaction to my field days was overwhelmingly positive. It was the right thing to do, and I enjoyed doing it. I remember one day a seasoned officer with whom I'd worked for many years approached me. He told me that one of his co-workers had confided in him that he was starting to get burned out but got a second wind when he saw a police captain and other police managers in the field working with field grunts—his words, not mine. He said it gave him a new perspective and hoped he'd emerge from his slump. On one of my field days, I remember the station supervisor sending out a general broadcast on the mobile data terminal to all officers that the captain was in the field, and he didn't want me making more arrests than they did. It was energizing for me, and I often came back to the station armed with new insights into critical issues and concerns for our management team. I can unequivocally say that I enjoyed those moments immensely.

There are talented and motivated lieutenants and captains in my old agency that work alongside the troops as they recognize it should be the norm rather than the exception. Invariably, these are the most respected leaders in the organization. There is an emotional glue that binds cops working side-by-side regardless of rank or position. It bonds law enforcement officers in a way that is unique to those who put their lives in jeopardy by wearing a uniform. It is also something most civilians don't understand but goes a long way to explain why those who depend on each other for their safety—or their very lives—tend to socialize in the same groups. It goes beyond reason; it's a visceral feeling that is hard to verbalize. Cops have it even decades beyond retirement. It simply never leaves you. It also helps put in context the reality that it is often difficult for police officers to inform on or testify against their fellow cops when they commit misconduct. When you depend on someone for your very existence, it isn't easy to cause them harm, even if it's the right thing to do. Luckily, most come to realize that by allowing bad cops to skate they hurt the good ones.

Leading by example relies on making emotional as well as intellectual connections with others. By that I mean the visceral reaction, that gut feeling one has when a person in a leadership role actually walks the talk and behaves in a way that inspires and reinforces the shared vision and mission of an organization. Leading by example isn't merely a slogan. It is truly the foundation from which all managerial and supervisory work emanates. I make the case that it is, by necessity, demonstrative and responsive. I don't mean that a leader has to act emotionally or lose decorum to connect with subordinates and co-workers. Neither do I mean that as a sergeant or lieutenant you have to constantly wear your emotions on your sleeve or go out and party with your subordinates. (I hate that term but use it for the sake of brevity and clarity.) Nor do you have to be gregarious or outgoing all the time. I mean a leader has to model behavior that makes that connection with others not just cerebral but rooted in feelings as well. People have to believe you care about them and the organization; that you are genuine and truly want what's best for them in the workplace and their personal lives. When you roll up your sleeves to work with the troops, you make that connection.

To a certain extent, your personality will determine how you interact with others. But if you want to make a difference you must learn to build the connections with others that engender respect, trust, and loyalty. Think about those in leadership positions with whom you've worked that couldn't, or wouldn't, lead by example. Would you have gone the extra mile for them to accomplish an organizational goal or come up with a solution to a vexing community problem? Would you have worked hard to help that person build a team or enhance the department's effectiveness? You might have to a certain extent, but you probably did it because you had intrinsic qualities that motivated your actions. You cared and wanted to do the right thing. The problem is leaders have to influence everyone with whom they work, not just those that are predisposed to do the right thing. When leaders can impact only a portion of an organization, they become personally and professionally ineffective. What I'm trying to say is, if you want to lead men and women in policing successfully, you must exemplify the behavior you wish to see in others. And, most importantly, they have to believe you truly care; about them as well as the community.

I worked with some excellent supervisors early on and looking back I can see the common traits and characteristics that made them good at their job. For starters, they had an enthusiasm that was contagious. They made you glad to be at work and easily reconciled your experience with the need for supervision. These supervisors exhibited the sort of attitude they expected of you, demanding of themselves even more than they did of you. I had no trouble seeing and feeling what they stood for. That is, there were no half-measures; no vacillation as to what constituted good work. It was clear. They led by example, and we could all trust that they would be there for you if you ever needed them. They rolled up when you had a pedestrian stopped or cruised by to make sure you were code-four (no assistance needed) during a traffic stop. They weren't afraid to call you aside and chew you a new one if you did a boneheaded thing. Even though you couldn't put your finger on the reasons, their actions made you trust and support these leaders. They connected with you emotionally as well as intellectually. You understood they had a job to do and they seemingly turned unpleasant criticism into a life lesson they delivered with empathy.

Never forget about the little things—they mean a lot to those with whom you work. I always believed in being the first in and last out. I know, you'll accuse me of being a workaholic, incapable of balancing work and family, but you couldn't be more wrong. I used my time productively but being the first one to work and the last to leave set a tremendous example for others to follow. A good work ethic is paramount, so don't let anyone tell you to only put in your eight hours and go home as a way of doing business. If you do that consistently, then don't expect that others will work hard or go the extra mile.

They'll see you scooting out the door, and they'll know you've doubled down in favor of mediocrity.

If you expect your employees to adhere to company standards, you've got to do the same. In other words, what's good for them has to be good for you. Don't ever underestimate the effect of perceptions, whether accurate or not. I realize many managers work extra hours that aren't reflected in an eight-hour day, so don't take this literally. What I'm trying to say is you've got to put in at least as much time as your hardest workers. That's the best way to set the example, period.

Over the years I witnessed many examples of "do as I say but not as I do." I saw how the troops were disciplined, faulted on their performance or criticized for doing things their bosses freely practiced. Don't get me wrong, these instances were in the minority, but there were enough of them—including visible, egregious ones—to impact the morale and perceptions in the agency. As I've said in this book several times, ignore perceptions at your own risk. They are a powerful force that can shift momentum against your management team and damage the department.

On one recent morning, as I made mental notes for this chapter, I read about a fire chief in one of the largest fire agencies in the nation who had submitted his resignation under pressure from the firefighters' union and the governing board of the organization. By all accounts he had an impressive resume, having served in national organizations that set policy for fire departments across the country. According to articles in the media, the agency had problems with leadership, management, and competence, with abundant signs of dysfunction. Accusations ranged from inattention to details and failures in accountability, to an insidious morale problem. According to the article, the union distributed a photograph recently taken of the chief's car parked in a handicapped space at one of the stations. The incident allegedly occurred after the chief had sent out a memo reminding staff not to park in no-parking areas in the stations. Incidents such as these unambiguously point out how important perceptions are to any agency and why dealing with them is critical. To the chief's credit, he admitted his mistake and apologized in writing.

There are instances of failing to lead by example or ignoring negative perceptions as "only in the minds of the employees" at all levels in public safety agencies I actually heard managers utter that phrase in response to concerns from the troops and others about matters big and small. There is often a tendency to take the path of least resistance and hope problems or issues will only go away. They won't! In some situations, the chief executive and the management team are inexperienced or under-experienced, or perhaps have made a conscious decision to ignore problems they consider insignificant. In others, the team lacks the institutional knowledge to gauge how important some of the issues have been in the past, or how the experiences of the employees affect how they perceive management decisions. In virtually all of these cases, ignoring the problem only makes it worst and ends up damaging your department, often prompting drastic actions that could have been avoided.

My advice for dealing with perceptions, accurate or not, is simple: Deal with the issues in question head on, quickly and without equivocation. Find out what's feeding the perceptions and determine if they are accurate, or if there are circumstances that contribute to the confusion which you may be able to explain or improve relatively quickly. Meet with stakeholders, including the union, as soon as possible and get an understanding of the concerns. Explain the facts, as you know them, but only after you're confident you know them. If you reveal facts or adopt a position, make darn sure it's accurate or proper, or your credibility will be damaged—perhaps beyond repair.

Consider department-wide communications to deal with perceptions but be careful with personnel issues and confidential information. By showing concern and providing additional information, the members of your department will see that you are working to fix whatever may be wrong. There will be times when the perceptions aren't accurate, and setting the record straight, without sounding too defensive, will work. If you promise a fix, keep your promises. Don't overreach or offer a panacea, as it generally doesn't help. If you were wrong, admit it.

Avoiding the perception of wrong doing is a fundamental element of any leader's approach to his job. Astute managers know that if employees widely perceive them as behaving less than ethically, even though the behavior may be perfectly legal and in compliance with the organization's policies, they will question their integrity and fairness. If the allegations or perceptions are significant enough, it may even cripple a leader's ability to do his job. Thinking carefully about actions that lead to these perceptions requires a regular and introspective look at one's daily activities. I was once told to think of everything I did through the prism of the local newspaper. How would my actions look when printed on the front page of the local paper should be a test all leaders take when confronted with a moral or ethical dilemma. It isn't enough to avoid actual misbehavior or ethical lapses but aim to avoid those that could also be perceived as such. Not easy to do I grant you, but a key to maintaining the trust of the organization and its members.

If you're the chief executive and someone in your management team has been accused through the grapevine of misconduct or unethical behavior, it is critically important that you take swift action to determine the veracity of the allegations. If they appear true, ensure that a competent investigation is conducted promptly. If the rumors aren't true, you have a duty to forcefully set the record straight so the manager isn't maligned or rendered ineffective. The same applies to any other individual in the organization. The trick is to refute false allegations appropriately and without furthering unsubstantiated rumors. Not an easy thing to do, but one that must be done with sensitivity and determination.

GET YOUR HANDS DIRTY

Whether you believe Napoleon Bonaparte's accomplishments were worthy or self-serving, Napoleon was keenly aware of how the folks around him thought and felt because he understood that to influence their behavior he needed to understand their fears, concerns, and aspirations. He needed to shape his leadership approach to the dynamics of the moment and build a devout team that not only fought for their country but was intensely loyal to him as well. As Ralph Jean-Paul writes in Napoleon Bonaparte's Guide to Leadership: "When the people you are leading are not only devoted to the cause, but also loyal to you, there is a heightened enthusiasm and effort that is put into the work."

http://potential2success.com/napoleonbonaparteleadership.html

Over the years I worked with people in leadership positions that viewed their roles as overseers, standing back and letting subordinates and others get in the weeds—avoiding getting their hands dirty and remaining above the fray. Folks like that got little respect from the troops and never reached the hearts and minds of those who did the work. They underperformed and lost opportunities to build trust with those that mattered the most, and thus diminished their agency's accomplishments.

Too often the culture in organizations encourages leaders to see themselves as better and more important than others, relegating them to use organizational power rather than the legitimate power granted only by those leaders seek to influence. While organizations may survive using that approach, they tend to be mediocre and embroiled in controversy. Napoleon's example, while not always laudable for its objectives, illustrates how we, as legitimate leaders, must sometimes immerse ourselves in the work of our subordinates —not to micromanage, but to understand the nature of the job and set the example. Working hand-in-hand with your team members, showing that you aren't afraid to get your hands dirty, builds trust and overtly informs them that you care, are willing to work hard and will lead by example. It is self-evident and hard to ignore. They will come to the inescapable conclusion that you value them and their work.

Don't be afraid to roll up your sleeves and be hands-on. Jean-Paul vividly describes how Napoleon's hands-on approach to leadership allowed him to excel as a leader and in battle: "Usually when the battles were over and the opposing army's guns fell silent, Napoleon would rise up sweaty, dirty and covered in gun powder. This won the respect of the men around him. They felt that he was one of them, that he really cared about what he was fighting for. He knew everyone else's job and would take on task that he could have easily delegated to someone else." Jean-Paul describes how Napoleon, who was teased as a child for not being able to speak proper French, "was a great motivator of people. From the lowest soldier to the high-ranking generals and aristocrats, Bonaparte knew that in order for him to succeed he had to have the people around him enthusiastic about their mission. He understood that a leader must win the trust of the people he is leading."

Throughout my career I strived to get in the thick of things as often as was possible and prudent. I wanted to understand how we did our work and what the obstacles were so I could help remove them. I also had selfish reasons: I enjoyed doing police work when I could. While it concerned me that officers and others would think I was meddling in their work, I knew they appreciated the lieutenant or the captain's interest in their jobs and careers. Over time folks got used to the idea that I wanted to be meaningfully present even when their task was mundane. I'd make it a practice to spend time at someone's desk talking about their case load or following up an officer in the field during a call. They appreciated it and I know I did.

AN EARLY INFLUENCE

There are over 100 verses in the bible that extoll the importance of leading by or setting the example. Nearly every book I've read on leadership ranks it as an essential quality in every leader who has achieved great things or turned around an organization in trouble. There are hundreds of examples in history that are instructional on the importance of walking the talk. Early in my career, I had some supervisors who exemplified a great work ethic, which to me is a foundational quality for any leader. The one that sticks in my mind the most was a field corporal whose example influenced me greatly. I'll call him by the fictitious name of "Mike." He was in his mid-thirties, and we worked together for six months. He was a quiet, matter-of-fact individual who got right down to business. Although he had a tough exterior, his sense of humor and personality came through once you got to know him.

Mike was a fifteen-year veteran who was assigned to a patrol team in the days when the Santa Ana Police Department had sworn officers performing basic crime scene investigation duties in addition to their regular tasks. He never stopped working! I remember him taking me aside and telling me what he considered the secret to success in a police career: "Stay busy, do more than they ask you to do, and treat people the way you want to be treated." I'm paraphrasing him of course, but that was the gist of it. He explained that in police work you had to love the work to stay sane, and you had to stay as busy as possible to counteract the negative effects of sitting in a police car and driving around waiting for the dispatcher to send you somewhere. He cautioned me not to be a slave to the police radio. There are many crooks out there, he told me, so get out of the unit and look for them. That wasn't simply an exhortation for me to stay busy, but he was describing a philosophy, the way he saw himself in the organization. It was a work ethic that stuck with me. He was at least ten years older than I was, but he worked just as hard or harder. I decided then that's how I wanted to be.

Over the years Mike continued to work hard and set the example. Even though he was a senior officer and could have easily sat back and let the junior cops take the calls and do the reports, he'd volunteer for just about anything. I rarely saw him use force. He had a way of talking to people that conveyed confidence and a calm demeanor, often deescalating tense situations with ease. He never complained about anything and took more calls and reports that the rookies just out of the academy. He was never promoted beyond corporal because he hated taking tests and doing interviews, but everyone respected him; even the crooks. I admired him, and when I supervised my own units as a sergeant or lieutenant, I tried to bring him with me. I learned early on that to do well surround yourself with capable, independent people who know the job and enjoy learning.

Contrast that to some senior cops who want to drive around and only respond to calls when they are assigned by the dispatcher, feeling entitled because of their time on the job or their rank. The ones that roll up to a scene or a call for help and treat people with contempt, at times spending more time kissing off a call than they would have spent handling it. The ones that have a loud mouth and can't help but attract attention to themselves in an attempt to impress younger cops. Finally, the ones whose field investigations are so deficient no one who knows them would want them investigating a crime at their home. While these folks may be popular with a small, discontented segment of a police department, they are not respected. I would take one Mike versus ten of the former any day. If you want to enjoy your job and grow to be respected and effective, take Mike's example and run with it. You'll feel better about yourself and the organization for which you work. More importantly, you'll bring added value to the people in your department and the community it serves.

WINSTON CHURCHILL'S CALL
TO ARMS

"Success is not final, failure is not fatal, it is the courage to continue that counts." - *Winston Churchill*

September 7, 1940 will forever be remembered by the British people as Black Saturday—one of the darkest days in the nation's history. Hitler's campaign to bomb Britain into submission became widely known as the "Blitz," and lasted until May 1941, when Hitler turned his attention to the Russian front. According to some historical records, in August of 1940, Germany's Luftwaffe made a series of mistakes while targeting British oil fields, and some bombs fell on London, prompting Winston Churchill to order a retaliatory strike on Berlin. What followed was an escalation of the war and the relentless bombing of London that lasted two months before being expanded to other British cities.

According to the U.K. History Learning Site: "Black Saturday was a huge shock for Londoners. The Luftwaffe arrived in the late afternoon during a day of very good weather when many Londoners were on the streets enjoying the sunny weather. The sirens first started at 16.43 at the start of a twelve-hour attack. The 'all clear' was sounded at 05.00 on September 8th. Few could have believed the damage done to London in just one raid. 430 people were killed and over 1600 were seriously wounded. Hospitals simply could not cope. During September 8th Winston Churchill visited the East End—where the raids had been concentrated to destroy the docks."

http://www.historylearningsite.co.uk/impact_blitz_london.htm

Despite what is arguably the most brutal bombing campaign in history, the British people, who suffered unspeakably, held firm and resisted Hitler's tactics to break their national spirit. Winston Churchill rallied his people to defy Hitler by becoming the most visible politician of his time, refusing to leave London for safer ground despite pleas by those around him. He believed, like all great leaders do, that he had to lead by example to galvanize his nation into a coherent force that would withstand untold hardship. Churchill used his forceful persona and considerable oratory and literary skills to make his case not only at home, but also abroad to persuade President Franklin D. Roosevelt to assist Britain in the war effort.

This was an existential battle for Britain, which required shared sacrifice and a leader who rose to the occasion by summoning internal strength and skills he'd honed throughout his life. The power of Churchill's speeches (listen to his speeches at The Churchill Centre, http://www.winstonchurchill.org) and writings at the time were an essential component of Britain's intellectual and emotional arsenal against the Nazis. As in any battle worth fighting, the power of leadership—coupled with management talent and a keen sense of right and wrong—helped unite the world against Hitler and brought about his eventual defeat.

Churchill's speeches played a significant role in Britain's resolve to resist and ultimately help defeat Hitler's Germany. The following excerpt from the end of his "Finest Hour" speech (Library of Congress at https://www.loc.gov/exhibits/churchill/wc-hour.html or http://www.winstonchurchill.org) demonstrates how Churchill's passionate oratory helped change the course of the war:

"What General Weygand called the Battle of France is over. I expect that the Battle of Britain is about to begin. Upon this battle depends the survival of Christian civilization. Upon it depends our own British life, and the long continuity of our institutions and our Empire. The whole fury and might of the enemy must very soon be turned on us. Hitler knows that he will have to break us in this Island or lose the war. If we can stand up to him, all Europe may be free and the life of the world may move forward into broad, sunlit uplands. But if we fail, then the whole world, including the United States, including all that we have known and cared for, will sink into the abyss of a new Dark Age made more sinister, and perhaps more protracted, by the lights of perverted science. Let us therefore brace ourselves to our duties, and so bear ourselves that, if the British Empire and its Commonwealth last for a thousand years, men will still say, This was their finest hour." If that didn't move you, nothing will!

To read the entire speech go here:
http://www.winstonchurchill.org/learn/speeches/speeches-of-winston-churchill/122-their-finest-hour.)

These weren't empty words; Churchill backed them with action and determination. I believe without doubt that had Churchill not been elected Prime Minister in 1940, the world would be a markedly different place today. He was the glue that held Britain together during the war. Like the U.K. did then, modern police organizations require visible, articulate and emotionally connected leadership. While the battles police leaders wage in their organizations and communities pale in comparison to Churchill's, accomplishing great things requires the same skills and abilities to lead, persuade and inspire those around them. Changing or focusing the direction of an organization—or a smaller unit such as a patrol team or a sub-unit of the department—requires the strength of character and example that are evident in history's great leaders. Leaders must be visible and must shun privileges that separate and isolate them from those who do the agency's work. Management perks have a tendency to separate you from the effort in unintended ways. If your office is isolated, reducing access from the troops, how do you maintain that connection to the rest of the agency? You can spout platitudes all you want, but unless you back your words with actions you'll never gain the respect you need to be an effective leader.

Take, for example, a recent conversation I had with a conscientious police officer in a large agency. The officer lamented how senior cops in the field were being shielded from calls for service simply because they had more time on the job than the junior officers, who had to handle the bulk of the calls. She was actually disheartened and troubled by what she was telling me, and I could tell it was a critical issue for her. That sort of "I'm senior and you're not" attitude gets woven slowly into the fabric of the organization. In agencies of all sizes senior officers and deputies may feel entitled to sit back and let the younger folks carry the load. Unless checked by the leadership of the organization, that feeling of entitlement will lead to mediocrity and a disgruntled workforce. While such a system may be an unfortunate part of an agency's culture, it is counterproductive and helps destroy morale. Once quasi-caste systems take hold in a police force, the talented and hard-working employees begin to feel as though merit and good work aren't recognized or rewarded. The same applies when managers and supervisors, due to personal or organizational choice, become far removed from the daily rigors of police work. Committed leaders seek to weave their routines into the work of their agencies, remaining connected to the rank and file in ways that are noticeable and palpable.

Churchill's example is particularly relevant when an organization is in decline or trouble, and the leadership team has to muster the wherewithal to turn the ship around or accomplish an important objective. In times of trouble, the rank and file will look squarely at the chief or the sheriff, demanding a sense of confidence, a strategy that will work and behavior that is unassailable. It is in these challenging and turbulent times that great leaders can extoll the virtues of shared sacrifice, hard work, and unanimity in fighting for an organization's survival and eventual prosperity. These leaders are so visible and approachable that they are virtually everywhere. They are passionate and caring, with oratory that summons all hands on deck for a common purpose. They understand that without the support and energy of those in the trenches day in and day out, the battle can easily be lost. I believe that this battle, which leaders must fight, is the micro-equivalent of Churchill's rallying of his nation during the Blitz. After the war, he once said: "I was not the lion, but it fell to me to give the lion's roar." Churchill was conflicted about the course of the war, and he was mindful of the mistakes he had made at Gallipoli during World War I—which cost the lives of thousands of British soldiers. However, when faced with the defeat of his nation, he embraced the challenge and rose to the occasion with singular determination.

6

THE ORGANIZATIONAL CULTURE AND MEDIOCRITY

"Excellence is a better teacher than mediocrity. The lessons of the ordinary are everywhere. Truly profound and original insights are to be found only in studying the exemplary." Warren Bennis

For police organizations entrusted to guard public safety, avoiding mediocrity is essential to maintain that trust. When an agency becomes a poor performer—or engages in practices that marginalize the community—the fault nearly always lies with its leadership. I mean the entire leadership team, from the chief on down to the field-training officers. Mediocrity feeds on itself, relegating agencies to a downward spiral from which it is exceedingly hard to fully recover. Other than the obvious failures, there is little to learn from mediocre organizations. One of my favorite authors, Warren Bennis, co-wrote a book with Burt Nanus called "Leaders, Strategies for Taking Charge," which is, in my opinion, the best leadership book ever written. Bennis once said: "Excellence is a better teacher than mediocrity. The lessons of the ordinary are everywhere. Truly profound and original insights are to be found only in studying the exemplary."

When agencies allow their standards to fall, these low standards become the norm, and soon everyone begins to fulfill those requirements. This degradation becomes especially true in law enforcement organizations where some become conditioned to take the path of least resistance. The true believers, the bright, and hardworking begin to feel as though their efforts don't matter. You lose them, and you're done. Rising above the ordinary becomes an imperative for police management teams.

How do you avoid mediocrity? Look at the culture of your agency from the perspective of an officer in the first five years of her career. She works hard and takes pride in her job. She cares about the community and looks for innovative and effective ways to make the lives of its residents and business community better. She has intrinsic qualities that guide her behavior. Her work ethic is superb, and she often does more than she's asked to do, resulting in outstanding performance evaluations, pay incentives and recognition by superiors. Supervisors in investigative and administrative assignments of the department, always on the lookout for good cops, quickly recognize her abilities and trip over each other to snag her up for their units. Sound familiar? Whether you're a field cop, supervisor or manager, you'll recognize this story. Great cops aren't hard to spot. Unfortunately, in some organizations there aren't as many of them as there should be. Leaders ought to ask: why not? Is it the lack of qualified applicants, the selection process, the training? Or is it somehow the lack of expectations or motivation? It's all of the above.

But the most important factor is an organization's culture, which begins to affect new members of an agency slowly but inexorably, eventually sapping their desire to excel. What do I mean by "culture?" It's the norms, practices, standards and behavior that formally and informally govern the members of an agency and is established over years or decades. In other words, it's what people believe and how things are done. Wikipedia defines it as:

"Organizational culture is the collective behavior of people that are part of an organization, it is also formed by the organization['s] values, visions, norms, working language, systems, and symbols, it includes beliefs and habits. It is also the pattern of such collective behaviors and assumptions that are taught to new organizational members as a way of perceiving, and even thinking and feeling. Organizational culture affects the way people and groups interact with each other, with clients, and with stakeholders."

The key here is that for the most part, an agency's culture shapes the habits of new employees and reinforces the behavior of seasoned members of the team. Thus, it has significant influence on the organization's success or failure. If the culture is sound, then the agency will likely be exponentially more effective with each succeeding year. If the culture is deficient or substandard, the agency is—or will likely become—mediocre or worse. And it all starts and ends with leadership, especially at the top. Without exception, every current or retired chief of police whom I spoke to while researching this book told me the culture of any department is one key to success. One retired chief from a mid-size urban agency who had a successful career told me it took him seven years to change the culture of his last department.

Medium and large agencies don't turn on a dime, but it can happen much quicker if the CEO is talented and determined and he/she has a competent management team. The standards established by the leadership team of an agency will help determine the individual and collective performance of its members. If your actions show you willingly or tacitly tolerate inappropriate behavior, low productivity or poor performance, expect that mediocrity will take hold in your organization relatively quickly. Take, for example, how discipline and internal investigations are handled. If your management team sets the example and your department handles misconduct investigations promptly, equitably and professionally, then the culture will be such that employees know what to expect and what the consequences will be for inappropriate conduct. The same goes for productivity. Setting these expectations, adhering to them and having clear consequences for those who don't, goes a long way toward avoiding becoming a mediocre organization. Of course, if the management team doesn't adhere to those same standards, it all becomes an exercise in futility.

The leadership team must be closely attuned to emerging trends and risks to the norms that make up the organizational culture, as even subtle changes can have disastrous consequences over time. I don't mean just the management team, but supervisors and field training officers (FTOs) as well, as they often have greater influence on new employees than anyone else. A recent Time Magazine article that delved into the deep–seated problems in the Chicago Police Department (Weichselbaum, 2016) points out the role of culture, and

FTOs in particular, in the success or failures of a police department. Some of the key findings in investigations by sociologists and researchers regarding the CPD focus on a failed culture of neglect, ignoring officers who lie or commit misconduct, allowing politics to affect behavior and the lack of a robust, credible FTO program to protect the City's investment in new officers. According to the article, Officer Rialmo's (who was involved in a high-profile accidental shooting), "policing career illustrates many of the problems. After completing the police academy—which he dismisses as 'a complete joke,' long on theory and short on useful information—he began a three-month street training cycle by following a field training officer on rounds of the West Side. That, he says, was his real education." That feeling isn't unique to Chicago, as many academy recruits credit the FTO program with teaching them the "real" ropes in policing, pointing out the critical nature of any FTO program.

Most agencies consider the FTO position one of the most important roles in the organization and provide additional pay for the duties. The selection process for FTO must be a rigorous one and those selected the best models of behavior, intellect, and work ethic. The FTOs of any organization will shape the future of the agency for years to come, so take great care to ensure they are the cream of the crop. I like to think about the impact of an FTO on a recruit or new lateral officer as formative in nature. Much like a child's formative early years are shaped by their parents and surroundings, a new officer's view of the agency and his place in it will most likely be shaped by those early encounters—so the selection and training of FTOs is essential. That includes instilling the values of the agency into all the recruits and trainees and modeling those values and expectations at all times. If an FTO fails to set the example or acts contrary to the values of the agency, he or she should be promptly removed from the position. There is no room for inadequate performance in this job, period.

If your agency pays field training officers more for performing those duties, make it crystal clear from the start that the FTO serves at the pleasure of the chief of police, and that removal from the position is at his or her discretion. Some legal cases have held that pay for one of these assignments is considered a property right, so removal entitles the individual to an administrative hearing or due process, so be careful. Work with your legal advisor to establish a fair model for removing an FTO from these duties if the law requires it. Make sure all applicants to the FTO position understand not only the qualifications and duties but the importance of the function and their impact on the department. Trust me when I tell you that any haphazard attempt to remove an FTO will cost you dearly, and the entire effort will be seen as capricious. But don't be afraid to take action to preserve your management rights when it means so much to your agency. Just do it right.

The culture of a police agency will inevitably influence how those on the front lines act, react and perform their duties. If officers feel free to kiss-off calls or avoid taking reports when they should be taken, they will undoubtedly repeat that behavior. If laziness and inattention aren't challenged by supervisors, you'll end up with a lousy department that serves no one well. If managers and supervisors are reluctant to step up and set the example, the rest of the department will likely feel free to do the same. I've seen police officers spend a good half-hour or more trying to avoid doing an investigation or taking a report when the actual time to do the job right was probably about the same or less. In my experience, situations like that often end up biting agencies—and officers—in the behind at some point, making the clean-up process much more costly. When an FTO or a supervisor let that kind of behavior go unchallenged, the message is clear: it's OK to do a mediocre job in this organization.

Make no mistake, one of the most influential figures in a cop's life is another cop, especially in a cop's first year or two on the job. It is a fact of police life that cops learn to rely on each other for their safety, thus building an emotional connection and interdependence that makes it difficult for some supervisors to criticize or take action when an officer makes mistakes or acts inappropriately. But you need to think about the consequences of supervisory inaction on the officer and his career. I have seen a good number of officers who started out well enough, but who took the wrong path because no one called them on mistakes or wrongful behavior, setting them up for disciplinary action, termination or jail time. We don't do anyone a favor by ignoring their misconduct or by letting mistakes go unchallenged.

I understand how easy it is for some to turn a blind eye to obvious, or even latent signs of dysfunction. After all, taking the path of least resistance is a time-old tradition in bureaucracies. I urge you to stay vigilant and work hard to maintain a culture of respect, high expectations, and achievement at all levels. When you assume a position of leadership, you must view your duties as nearly sacrosanct. You will help build, and have in your hands, the future of the organization. I understand how difficult this can be, especially in agencies that have paid scant attention to these issues over time, but you must do your part, regardless of what others do or fail to do. Don't underestimate the power of one great leader on the morale and productivity of members of your team. Besides, it is the right thing to do!

I worked for some folks in my time that made me want to work hard. In retrospect, one of the key characteristics they shared was their ability to confront misconduct and mediocrity regardless of the circumstances. They faced problems and sought to improve how things were done, didn't give up and insisted you didn't either. If you look at mediocre places to work, you'll probably see an organization that had a leadership vacuum at some point. When the legitimate leaders fail to fill that vacuum, other do so quickly. These may be good folks that have an intrinsic desire to do well and keep the agency headed in the right direction, or they may be those that have an ax to grind and see an opportunity to elevate their stature in the department. Either way, you've left the direction and well-being of your agency to chance and an uncertain future.

Tackling mediocrity means setting up the support systems to rise beyond it, even if you don't always achieve everything you intend. Let me give you an example. In the early 1990s, I spearheaded an effort to completely revamp the Department's performance evaluation system. For too long we'd gotten away with using a generic form used throughout the City, which had neither police performance indicators nor police-specific performance standards. With little guidance on performance indicators, values and objectives—other than departmental orders aimed at governing procedural behavior—the system was flawed beyond redemption. It had simply become the thing to do because the municipal code called for it. In other words, the performance evaluation process was procedural, rather than reflective; wrought not explorative; ambiguous not specific, and it lacked the critical factors that would help individuals become better at their job.

There was little urgency to "fix what wasn't broken" at the time, and this wasn't a high priority. I felt otherwise, and so did a task force formed by Chief Paul Walters to look at critical issues in the department. I knew the damage this inferior system was inflicting, so for the next year, we convened a group of employees, sworn and nonsworn and at all rank levels, that researched and drafted performance standards for every category of employee. These standards incorporated community policing principles, thus providing a reward mechanism for those who practiced it. We also developed a new evaluation instrument that was specific to our agency and dovetailed with the standards. After prolonged negotiations with the employee unions and some revisions, we kicked off the new system.

The Department's intent was to have a system that was fair, performance-based and which provided honest and timely feedback to the employees. The entire exercise depended on supervisors and managers being honest and using concrete examples of behavior to justify ratings. We provided training and a grace period of a year to give the new performance standards a chance to sink in, and an opportunity for employees to model those standards. While we accomplished some of our goals, and the system was infinitely better than the previous one, we found that too many of the raters felt constrained by merit pay being tied to performance. By that I mean that if an employee was rated average or needing improvement, he or she was supposed to lose merit pay after being allowed an opportunity to improve and failing to do so. So many raters, not wanting an employee to lose pay, would artificially inflate an employee's performance rating, defeating a fundamental principle of the system. Also, some supervisors who tried to be honest felt management did not support them when the time came to take away merit pay. Other flaws have been corrected over the years, and the system remains in use today. But by and large, the effort failed to accomplish what we set out as the key objective: A system that resulted in timely, honest and specific evaluation of performance, along with a sound performance improvement program.

The issue of merit pay and how it was structured played a significant role in torpedoing the new performance evaluation system. In a recent article in Fortune Magazine (Fisher, 2016), the author spelled out why bonuses, and merit pay in particular, don't work. The article cited a study by Willis Towers Watson where 150 senior managers at large and mid-size companies were interviewed and admitted their incentive policies don't work. The research revealed that the least effective of incentive measures employed were: "Merit raises, which managers are supposed to give (or not) to employees based on, well, merit. Just one in five (20%) of the executives surveyed thinks merit pay 'drives higher levels of individual performance' in their companies." I wasn't surprised to find out that according to the research, the reason merit raises don't work is that individual managers "don't stick with the program." It's difficult for managers to hold performance-related conversations with employees, especially when financial incentives are involved.

Most managers and supervisors don't want conflict with their team members if they can help it, and they'll take the path of least resistance, handing out merit raises even when the employee's performance is deficient. By linking merit pay to a numerical rating in the evaluation when we devised the original system, we set the stage for the conflict avoidance that inevitably results when raters have to make subjective judgments on an employee's performance.

I can't give you an easy answer to this problem, but I can tell you that developing objective, job-related standards that become the basis for a complete performance evaluation system that is woven into the organizational culture is one part of the framework that helps you avoid mediocrity. The change must be incremental but sure and steady, with input from employees, supervisors, managers and the union. Anyone who evaluates performance must be thoroughly trained in the proper approach to give and obtain feedback, with fairness and impartiality serving as the cornerstone of any such system. Any agency interested in actually improving performance has to build in periodic feedback as to performance linked to specific organizational values, goals, and objectives. Without that linkage the entire exercise becomes subjective and meaningless. Furthermore, employees need to know there is a credible, positive performance improvement process that precedes any thought of negative action, such as loss of merit pay. As the Willis study points out, merit pay should be tied not only to individual performance but team and organizational results. Increasingly, agencies throughout the country are embracing community policing and problem-solving philosophies which are frequently team efforts. The collective approach to policing must be part of the culture and thus an accepted part of any evaluation system.

While the system at my former agency worked to a certain extent, it had too many holes to be called a success; at least back then. I blame our management team and myself for not being able to substantially overcome the problems we encountered, such as push-back from the unions and a deeply entrenched organizational culture. But we made the system better than it was. To be fair, this is a complex issue that demands supportive supervisors and managers, as well as union cooperation. Unfortunately, due to fair representation and fiduciary duties unions owe their members, they are often reluctant to support reforms that will cost their members money, even if it is the right thing to do. That's just the way it is, and good leaders learn to work within the system to accomplish as much as possible. Remember, human nature is such that many often take the path of least resistance. That's how organizations become mediocre. It's the job of an agency's leadership to find ways to overcome obstacles and do it in a way that maintains reasonable labor relations and allows employees to be treated fairly. A tall task, but one that can be accomplished by patiently and incrementally changing the organizational culture.

Don't get me wrong, changing the culture of an organization, especially a large one, can be a daunting task even for the best and most committed leaders. Using the discipline and reward system works to a certain extent, and effective leadership can make a significant difference in reducing and even eliminating impediments by using the principles outlined in this book. There will be some departments, however, where change proves difficult. In the end, if the agency's culture is so toxic and entrenched, the only way to remove cultural barriers to meaningful change may be, over time, to hire those who share your vision and values. That takes patience, but it can be done. Chief executives must relentlessly seek a hiring process that supports their mission, so background investigations and the interview process become the tools of the trade.

I admit that creating an outstanding, cohesive team is much easier in private industry, where a CEO has tremendous flexibility on who gets hired, fired and promoted, and where you can easily create financial incentives. In the public sector, one must inevitably deal with the civil service system, which imposes bureaucratic hurdles and processes for nearly all personnel decisions. But smart managers get to know the system and learn to work within it to overcome any perceived impediments. It can be done, but it takes a chief executive and management team that are enlightened, focused and determined to build a great organization.

I often hear about the lone individual who through tenure and protection by civil service rules can wreak havoc by being obstinate, blocking reform or making his subordinates miserable. Just one or two of these folks in positions of authority can thwart even the worthiest initiatives or plans from becoming a reality. So, what's a chief executive to do? If every conceivable method has been tried to get this person in line with organizational priorities and objectives to no avail, then it is time to do one of two things: Build a legitimate case to fire or demote him. Even with onerous civil service rules, you can always make a case that an individual, because of his or her actions, not only deserves to be terminated but also poses a systemic risk to the organization. If that doesn't work, then marginalize them, so they have the least amount of power and influence in the agency. Make them a "minister without portfolio," so to speak. Working with your legal advisor and within the civil service limitations, create an environment where this person has little opportunity to degrade others or harm the public service. The union may challenge you or take you to court, but as the CEO you must do all you can to remove such a harmful member of the team from the critical flow of power in your department. A critical caveat applies, however: Make sure your actions are legal, fair, in compliance with applicable laws, and calculated to accomplish a critical organizational need. In other words, don't act capriciously or vindictively, as it will make your job harder and more painful.

These are drastic steps, but they can be justified if you diligently document performance and the impact of such damaging individuals on your employees and your mission. In an interview in 2015 with appleinsider.com, a technology trade online magazine, Apple CEO Tim Cook said, referring to the importance of employees fitting into the organization's culture: Browett's failure (Apple's previous head of retailing) was "a reminder to me of the critical importance of cultural fit, and that it takes some time to learn that," Cook said. "Because you want to push the people who are doing great. And you want to either develop the people who are not or, in a worst case, they need to be somewhere else," he added. The chief of police or sheriff of any department must not shy away from heeding Cook's advice, especially when it comes to critical positions. The alternative is mediocrity or worse. Ask yourself these questions: What is the incentive for the good cops to go the extra mile and work hard if those who don't are allowed to muddle through with impunity? What is the incentive for supervisors and managers to do the right thing if the culture of the department doesn't support them when they take on low performers or those who commit misconduct? If you're an honest leader, the answers to these questions will shape your path to excellence.

Many public safety organizations are turning to at-will employment contracts for middle and top agency executives, even in promotions. At-will doctrines won't relieve you from acting reasonably and ensuring all rights—particularly those afforded through legislation, such as California's Peace Officers Bill of Rights Act—are observed when dealing with peace officers. These arrangements will allow you to mentor, select and terminate managers more easily than if they had civil service protection. Crafting a credible, legal employment scheme for management isn't simple, and you may have to amend your city or county governing code, or it might be a meet-and-confer topic with the union, but it can be done in conjunction with your legal advisor and elected officials. Furthermore, the system must be devoid of inappropriate, preferential or illegal treatment of employees for it to work well and provide you with the tools to build a great team. Most police chiefs and other unelected top law enforcement officials nowadays are at-will employees, so why not offer them the same advantage to build a team they can work with and trust to fulfill the agency's mission? It makes sense, and it's a strategy pursued with increasing frequency in law enforcement. It isn't without pitfalls, however. There is always the danger that politics will influence the behavior and performance of police managers, so creating a fair and well-designed at-will system is particularly important.

An agency's hiring and promotional practices form the cornerstone of any effort to build a good team. The people in your shop—

whether at the line level, supervisors or managers—will make or break your department. Gordon Graham, the nation's preeminent public safety risk management guru—with whom I had the pleasure of working for several years—believes that the financial and cultural health of police departments depends on how supervisors and managers discharge their duties vis-a-vis the employees, the agency's policies and their recognition of risk and opportunities. Thus, the hiring and promotional processes are the ground level prerequisites to all that follows. Rather than looking for those applicants that are physically fit and devoid of a criminal background, look for those who have—or can be taught—critical thinking skills. Rather than conformity, look for a willingness to challenge the system and the status quo in a practical, productive way. Look for the emotional intelligence that allows one to develop sympathy and empathy. I realize this isn't easy, but there is no other choice. Law enforcement is under a withering attack on many fronts, forcing police management to retool, rework and find innovative recruitment and training techniques to help organizations survive and thrive. This moment in time, with the attendant turbulence, is an inflection point for police departments nationwide. How we react will determine if we form better and healthier alliances with the communities we serve.

A final note on this topic. For a new police chief or sheriff who's been brought in from the outside, the task is formidable. However, the job becomes a bit easier if the chief looks for the folks within the department that are respected and have been in the organization for some time, and who may be amenable to playing a role in changing the culture. The key will be to include them early in the process and to listen carefully to what they have to say, coupled with a heartfelt plea for their help in making the organization better and its employees more committed. If they believe you are sincere and have the agency's best interest at heart they are much more likely to support you. In short, you need those who have credibility with the troops and management to drive the effort.

DEVELOPING A CULTURE OF
CONSTRUCTIVE DISSENSION

For nearly all of my career I witnessed how at times politics and internecine wars prevented our organization from developing a management team that was honed like a laser beam on the problems of the community and the development of the employees. Don't get me wrong, by and large, the managers at Santa Ana PD were smart, hard-working and talented, and we were effective. And, the Department was always a national leader in policing, achieving results and making the city safer with each succeeding year. But from the early years to the day I retired, I saw how we could have been even better had we been able to create a more open management environment that highly valued criticism and honest input. Perhaps a more unified, collegial team that wasn't divided by camps or allegiances to one captain or another, or those for or against a particular chief would have yielded even better results. It was wasted energy that could have been devoted to reducing fear in the community, or to improved systems and strategies internally.

This political game-playing is not unique to my agency or yours. It is a universal malady that affects private and public entities alike to one degree or another. The result is unfulfilled personal and organizational potential. There were a few times when I also played the game unwittingly or because at times I lacked the conviction to fight it. I'm not proud of that, but with time and experience I came to loath it and demanded that those who worked for me do the same.

I recently read a book about the Bush and Cheney years (Days of Fire: Bush and Cheney in the White House—Peter Baker, Knopf Doubleday), that paints a fascinating portrait of the personalities in the White House and how decisions were made on issues such as Iraq, Afghanistan and many others. The most illuminating parts related to internal power struggles and machinations by all the players, which made me wonder how we, as a nation, function as well as we do, given the power struggles within the government. I was particularly blown away by admissions from several of the key players that they harbored serious doubts about the decisions on Iraq, yet they failed to alert their boss—the President—of their misgivings. I got the distinct impression that those who held their tongues were unwilling to buck the political trend at best, or were perhaps afraid to be seen as weak in the face of strong support for the war by Cheney and Rumsfeld, at worse. In either case, their inaction helped us embark on what I consider the greatest strategic blunder our country ever committed. All you have to do is look at the rise of ISIS and the quagmires in Syria, Libya, Yemen and other places in the Middle East, which I and many others believe have their origin with the ill-fated invasion of Iraq.

How many times have you or others remained silent in the face of policy decisions with which you didn't agree, but were afraid to confront? To what extent did you rationalize decisions, activities or actions by others by trying to justify them in ways that caused you internal strife and stress? The culture in an organization largely dictates how its members and managers interact with each other when debating policy decisions. Some agencies frown upon the vigorous debate of ideas, instead of submitting to the wisdom of organizational elders. Others freely encourage what Mary Barra, the General Motors CEO, calls "constructive dissension," during which passionate, yet respectful, arguments are made for one position or the other regardless of politics or rank structure. That, I believe, is the structure that most supervisors and managers yearn for but don't often find. There are well established psychological reasons for leaders not wanting a vigorous and knuckle-dragging debate in their midst. Who needs a free-for-all in a management meeting that might require a skillful leader to set the rules, exemplify good behavior and keep the dissension constructive, as Barra says? And, equally as important, who wants to have to break the tie when an impasse is reached? The answer to these questions is a leader who wants to have a healthy, productive and focused management and supervision team.

Look no further than Abraham Lincoln's cabinet, and the deft way in which he managed the decision-making process. As you'll read elsewhere in this book, Lincoln picked cabinet members based on their skills and abilities, even though many of them had been his personal or political rivals. He purposely sought differing views and encouraged broad and vigorous discussions, even if the views of his cabinet members were opposed to his. In the end though, Lincoln knew when to cut off the debate and make the tough decisions. Although early in his life he had a propensity to use his considerable oratory skills to demean and diminish rivals, he later became a master at overcoming resistance without destroying anyone's self-respect. Lincoln became widely respected for being a great listener, admitting mistakes and valuing constructive advice and opinions. He cared about people and showed concern for the wellbeing of his team members. In short, he won them over with a depth of character, keen leadership and an authenticity that disarmed even his most ardent critics.

The case of Donna Dubinsky illustrates my point of constructive dissension rather well (Leswing, Business Insider, 2-7-2016). Dubinsky was a middle manager at Apple in 1985 when Steve Jobs, who was Chairman of the Board at the time, proposed that the company's entire distribution model, which relied on warehouses to store and distribute product, be scrapped and replaced with a just-in-time system. Apple would assemble products as they were ordered by the customer and shipped overnight via FedEx. According to an anecdote told by Dubinsky in a book called Originals: How Non-Conformists Move the World, she thought the proposed change was a huge mistake and one that could cost Apple its future. She felt that Apple's success largely depended on its distribution model and argued vehemently with Jobs. She even threatened to resign unless she was given thirty days to come up with an alternate proposal. Jobs gave her the time to produce an alternative recommendation, which he ultimately rejected. Although Dubinsky failed to convince Jobs, and another executive would have bristled at her intensity, Apple promoted her to a senior position.

According to Dubinsky, she tells the anecdote to illustrate how Jobs was open to new ideas that didn't mesh with his thinking, even coming from those who were willing to argue with him. Jobs left Apple that same year after a clash with John Sculley, who was CEO and had formerly headed Pepsi. In an interesting postscript, Dubinsky claims that when she met with Jobs years later he told her: "There is no way I'm ever building a phone." You know the rest of the story! I believe that Steve Jobs, like any great leader and visionary, desperately wanted to hear contrarian views and ideas. While he may have had a talent for divining what products people would love before they knew it, he also understood that he needed to hear differing opinions. Even though he had intensely held beliefs regarding Apple products, he wanted people to challenge him and the direction of the company.

Regardless of your disposition for a particular course of action, allowing others to present their ideas and perhaps influence your thought process isn't merely an academic exercise. It is an intentional, purposeful way to ferret out ideas that could put any agency on the path to outperforming and achieving the goals of the department. Kaarlgard (the Soft Edge, 2014) believes that: "As a leader or manager, you have two choices. You can consciously build organizational trust, or you can allow petty issues and misperceptions, both signifiers of a fear-based culture, to erode trust." I don't underestimate how difficult it can be for any leader to put aside his long-held beliefs, ego and tradition, and welcome constructive dissension by giving up power to unleash a spirit of innovation and good works. It takes introspection as you've never experienced before, and a strong desire to do what's right for the organization. You, as the boss, are not omnipotent. Nor are you infallible. You are, in fact, human and subject to the biases and foibles that plague the rest of us. Thus, listen to what others have to say before making consequential decisions. As F. Scott Fitzgerald once said: "The test of a first-rate intelligence is the ability to hold two opposed ideas in mind at the same time and still retain the ability to function."

Consider Colin Powell, arguably one of the most effective generals in modern military history, when he says: "Don't be afraid to

Challenge the pros, even in their own backyard." In Leadership Secrets of Colin Powell (McGraw-Hill), Oren Harari explains that the "pros" are those in positions of authority and status in and out of the organization. They could be your boss or the executive team, or outside consultants or so-called "experts." It could even be your direct boss. Powell was known for constructively challenging authority, as when he openly questioned the invasion of Iraq and applied the pottery barn rule: "You break it you buy it," when he warned President Bush in 2002 on his plans to invade Iraq. How would the United States and its allies control a population of 25 million people, he asked? How would you govern or meet their needs and, more importantly, how would you maintain a relative peace in a country dominated by religion, tribalism, and status?

Or perhaps Kennedy's Bay of Pigs example illustrates why you should forcefully challenge so-called "experts," such as the CIA and military generals in his case, especially when the consequences of an ill-timed or poorly planned action are significant. History is replete with examples of leaders who thought they knew better, who considered themselves "Superhumans," as Friedrich Nietzsche called them, and who felt infallible. No historical figure has ever proven to be superhuman, and the best of them consciously sought the help and opinions of others to govern for the public good. Lincoln and his cabinet is a perfect example.

Police leaders have much to learn from the lessons taught us by relatively recent historical events. Especially those offered by Abraham Lincoln, who was arguably the most astute politician of our time. He understood the need to surround oneself with smart, capable people and, most importantly, listen to their point of view before charting the direction of the country. Too often, the internal political maneuverings of public and private organizations create a zero-sum game: For one person to win, someone else must lose. In some places, the art of negotiations for the sake of the enterprise isn't practiced well, if at all. Compromise is seen as a sign of weakness, fearing being taken advantage of by those with more strident positions. That sort of atmosphere most often emanates from the culture of an agency and, as we've discussed, that culture is a direct result of leadership and management failure. So all roads lead to Rome!

The bottom line is that police leaders must spend significant effort in developing a workplace environment that is conducive to seeking and vetting ideas and positions across the organizational spectrum without fear that one will be ridiculed or marginalized. There are sound ways to do that, including using outside professional help to educate the leadership team on the key elements of a constructive debate of ideas. But there are simple truths that will help anyone become a constructive dissenter:

Accept the fact you are not omnipotent and don't know it all. Regardless of how you see yourself in the scheme of things, there are others who are smarter and may have better ideas, or others yet who because of their life experiences can see things more clearly or creatively than you do. It doesn't mean they are better than you, only that they have a different perspective that could be valuable to the organization.

Make it clear to those in positions of leadership that you want the "rocks to tumble," as Steve Jobs believed. When you encourage that synergy created by different backgrounds, points of view and perspectives, the results of any effort will likely be more innovative, better positioned to succeed and more grounded in reality.

Check your ego at the door. You may find that frequently someone under your command will come up with better or more comprehensive approaches to problems. Rather than making you feel inadequate, that outcome should allow you to feel proud that under your leadership, folks are being creative or engaging in constructive dissension for the benefit of the organization. Give them credit and celebrate their contributions. More importantly, never take sole credit for your team's success.

Reward organizational courage. If you've created an environment in which folks aren't afraid to fail and are taking calculated chances on innovations and programs, you'll see a healthy culture that prizes pushing the envelope, and one that doesn't penalize well-intended failures. The caveat here is don't expect miracles if you haven't given folks the tools, training, and authority to try new things.

As the chief executive, make it clear you want—no, you must have— constructive dissension at all levels of the department. Don't just give it lip service, but follow up with concrete actions, so the message becomes loud and clear. Above all, as we discuss elsewhere in this book, don't ignore perceptions and don't lose your cool in meetings. That alone can destroy any potential for a collegial atmosphere where people feel free to espouse differing or dissenting points of view without being belittled or marginalized.

Lastly, you must model the behavior you expect from others. After all, that is the essence of leadership by example. There isn't a more powerful image I can paint for you than a leader who sets the example even in the most difficult times. Nothing is as powerful for influencing behavior as one's ability to walk the talk.

USING THE PROBATIONARY PERIOD
TO SUPPORT A HEALTHY CULTURE

*"To have an effective hiring process, the Department must conduct
meaningful evaluations of its probationary employees or run the risk
of repeating the mistakes of previous large-scale recruiting drives." —
Max Huntsman, Inspector General, Los Angeles County Sheriff's
Department.*

On a beautiful day in the 1980s after I had promoted to lieutenant, I
was sitting at my desk reviewing performance evaluations, when an
entry in the evaluation of a police officer trainee caught my eye. The
Field Training Officer (FTO) essentially wrote that the trainee was
unsure of himself, lacked command presence and was reluctant to
initiate field activity, usually waiting for the dispatcher or the FTO to
tell him what to do. I continued reading the document expecting the
conclusion to be a recommendation to terminate the recruit's probation. The FTO described how the officer wrote good reports,
conducted complete investigations and got along well with
teammates.

This document was the final probationary evaluation after a full
year of field training, so I scanned the report down to the end,
expecting to concur with a termination recommendation to the chief
of police. I was stunned to see that the FTO and his sergeant had
signed off on the recruit passing probation with two days left in that

period, after which termination would be subject to all civil service rules, thus making it much more difficult to terminate the employee. I looked again for anything I may have missed but found nothing. I looked at the recruit's file and saw repeated attempts to rectify his deficient performance to no avail. I summoned the team sergeant to my office.

When the sergeant sat down, I placed the performance evaluation in front of him and asked him if he'd read it, and if he concurred with the recommendation that the recruit pass probation. He viewed it for a minute and told me he did. I asked him about the persistent deficiencies, and he paused for a time, looking up at the ceiling. Keep in mind this was a good, experienced sergeant whom I respected. He finally looked at me and said: "Boss, this kid is a good person who has potential. I know he's got some problems, and the FTO wanted to terminate him, but I think we can work with him. "Besides," he said, "look at staffing. We can't even keep up with the pending calls on the board, and crime's out of control. It takes Human Resources a year to bring a new officer onboard, and he's not able to go out on his own for another six months after that. If we keep this kid he can answer calls and take reports. We can work with him."

It took me a minute to fully comprehend what the sergeant was telling me. I understood the personnel shortage and the conditions under which we were working; I had just left the field where I was a sergeant working swing shift. It was all fresh in my mind. The running from call to call; multiple shootings and other felony assaults occurring simultaneously; the shortage of officers and nights when we only had two sergeants in the field for a city of 400,000 residents or more during peak times. It was at times overwhelming, but thanks to our committed staff, officers and supervisors we always seemed to handle it. I understood what the sergeant was telling me, and it was tempting to agree and take the path of least resistance. We could let the recruit pass probation and then work with him to remediate behavior and build his confidence. We'd at least have a "call taker." But we could also end up with an injured or dead cop who couldn't control situations in a busy city like Santa Ana. I looked at the sergeant and asked him if he'd want the trainee on his team if all he could do was take reports and handle simple calls. He paused for a while and then said: "No, I guess not."

The trouble with that line of thinking was obvious. We'd spent a year trying to work with the recruit to no avail. In police work you either have the inclination and the skills, or you don't. You are either suited for the job or you're not. The probationary period is meant to help you determine whether recruits have the aptitude and determination to become a good officer. In most cases, if during that year a person does not show the capacity to learn and perform according to the agency's expectations, it isn't going to happen in subsequent years. Past performance is nearly always indicative of future performance. Some recruits recognize that principle and resign before being terminated. Others need the job and think they will make good cops but lack the competence to follow through. In all cases, it is important that those in command do everything they can to work with the recruit, but in the end make the right decision to terminate probation if the recruit lacks the necessary skills to do the job.

While tempting because of a lack of adequate staffing, or the difficulty in terminating a nice person from employment, supervisors and managers must always err on the side of the department. There are too many examples of how inadequate background investigations or failure to terminate during the probationary period have haunted an agency for decades afterward, or God forbid resulted in the injury or death of an officer. Look at Miami, New Orleans and others. In fact, look no further than Santa Ana in the mid-1970s, for examples that vividly illustrate the costs to organizations that don't do the right thing in terms of personnel decisions.

In a recent report by the Inspector General of the Los Angeles County Sheriff's Department (see link below), Max Huntsman said:

"For more than two years, the Los Angeles County Sheriff's Department has expended significant resources overhauling the Deputy Sheriff hiring process in an effort to alleviate a significant staffing shortage and quickly identify qualified candidates. However, it appears that the Department is missing a crucial opportunity to weed out low-performing and potentially problematic deputies during the one-year probationary period – the final stage of that process. Because civil service protections do not attach, the LASD has a heightened incentive to rigorously assess probationary employees over the course of that year and discharge those who do not meet department standards.

The statistics indicate that a rigorous assessment is not taking place. Of the 334 Deputy Sheriff Trainees who graduated from the Academy in 2014, not one was released for performance-related reasons. Moreover, an investigation by the Office of Inspector General revealed significant deficiencies in the probationary evaluation process, including incomplete personnel files and untimely and unsubstantial assessments. For example, 90% of one-year probationary assessments were untimely; occurring after the one-year probationary period had expired and leaving no time to remove a problematic trainee. Many of the written evaluations were form documents or included cut-and-pasted comments that lacked specificity and were not tailored to the individual trainee. In order to have a fully effective hiring process, the Department must conduct meaningful evaluations of its probationary employees or run the risk of repeating the mistakes of previous large-scale recruiting drives."

https://oig.lacounty.gov/Portals/OIG/Reports/OPT_Analysis%20 of%20the%20Deputy%20Sheriff%20Trainee%20Probationary%20Per iod.pdf?ver=2016-06-27-171131-467

These are often agonizing decisions. Don't ever let anyone tell you that it is simple to terminate someone's employment, no matter the reason. Over many years I had to end careers more often than I wanted, and it was always difficult regardless of the evidence of misconduct or the amount of documentation that someone wasn't up to the job. I'd always made it a point to talk to others I respected and get their input. I looked at the agency's history to search for similar situations. In the end I always tried to do the right thing for the department. On occasion I gave employees the benefit of the doubt when in my mind the redeeming values outweighed the factors supporting harsh discipline. On a few occasions those decisions came back to bite me in the proverbial behind.

On that day in my office, I asked the sergeant a series of questions to see if there was anything I'd missed in the file. I hadn't. All of the FTOs the recruit had been assigned to agreed he should not pass probation. They had all done their best to work with him and provided ample opportunities for improvement. He'd been remediated a number of times and, although there was slight improvement in some areas, he remained reluctant to initiate field activity, waited to be sent on calls, and when confronted with stressful field situations he lacked that command presence that you must have as a police officer to control and diffuse incidents—that amorphous but essential quality that often saves officers from injury or worse. One can see it in action when, without resorting to force, a crowd or suspect is controlled without force and chaos turns to order. It is the bread and butter in field policing; an ability without which cops get hurt or get their teammates hurt.

I told the sergeant that while I empathized with his concerns about staffing, I would recommend to the chief of police that we terminate the recruit. We brought him into my office, and I explained why his probation was going to end. To his credit, he understood and was seemingly relieved that this was all over. I could see it in his eyes. Afterward, I spent a significant amount of time with the team and discussed why the probationary period is critical for the agency and them. I also worked with our personnel department to beef up our recruitment efforts. Later in my career that day's experience, while not unique, helped me as the Human Resources Commander frame an aggressive but solid recruitment, hiring, and training strategy. As an agency, we also looked at our FTO program to ensure it was as solid as could be and gave recruits the training, support and time to prove themselves. That's all you can do. In the end, you must do the right thing to ensure your agency's best interests and those of existing employees and the community outweigh everything else.

THE WORKERS' COMPENSATION
SYSTEM

I know, you're wondering why I'm even dealing with this topic in a book about leadership—what could a system established to deal with injured workers have to do with leading men and women in policing? I'm doing it for three reasons: One, the use or abuse of the workers' compensation program in your department will likely be an indicator of the health of the organizational culture. Two, workers' compensation expenditures in California—and other states I'm sure—have exploded over the last couple of decades, representing a significant portion of an agency's budget. Three, there is substantial abuse of the system in some organizations, including at the top ranks, which sets the tone for the entire organization. Look no further than the Los Angeles Police Department's DROP program for an incontrovertible example of how the workers' compensation system can be abused to include criminal violations that result in felony charges against officers. Read the article at the following link for a concrete example:

http://www.latimes.com/local/lanow/la-me-ln-lapd-beck-drop-20180502-story.html

In a recent article, the Los Angeles Times highlighted how in Los Angeles the system is racked with fraud and abuse, and how expensive it's become to maintain it (Dolan, 11-18-15). The City's own audit criticized the police and fire departments for "a culture of filing 'excessive' injury claims at the two departments." According to the Times: "A disproportionate amount of the injury pay went to employees who filed consecutive claims, reporting a new injury just as a previous yearlong injury was about to expire...one fire captain took at least 18 separate leaves, including absences related to injuries sustained while playing handball, basketball and racquetball at the fire station at Los Angeles International Airport. From 2009 to 2013 he collected $242,500 tax-free while out recovering from claimed injuries."

http://www.latimes.com/local/crime/la-me-lapd-audit-20151117-story.html

In Orange County, California, a sheriff's deputy was indicted and charged with multiple counts of perjury and insurance fraud. According to the Orange County Register (Puente, 10-21-16), the deputy was accused of "engaging in CrossFit, a high-impact exercising [sic]. Prosecutors said he lifted more than 200 pounds in weights, and did box jumps, burpees, squats and other activities in contradiction to the limits imposed by his doctors. Prosecutors said he "didn't tell his doctors about his CrossFit workouts and then lied under oath during a deposition, denying that he lifted more than 20 pounds since his injuries." According to the Register, on February 21, 2017, the deputy pleaded guilty to six misdemeanor counts of insurance fraud, the Orange County District Attorney's Office said. In addition to jail and probation, he must pay $34,838 in restitution to the county and also $1,000 to the Worker's Compensation Fraud Assessment Fund, prosecutors said."

On the heels of that case, another Orange County municipal police officer was convicted of felony workers' compensation fraud, exposing him to years in prison. There are many examples of similar alleged abuse throughout the country, and while prosecutions for workers compensation insurance fraud may be relatively rare—although becoming more common—taking advantage of the system at all levels is more frequent, which damages the budget, morale, and culture of police organizations. Make no mistake, good cops resent those who file bogus workers' compensation claims and leave them to handle the full load of work in often understaffed agencies. They want and expect that their management teams will handle the fraudsters effectively. When that doesn't happen, they begin to lose confidence in the system, which erodes the agency's effectiveness and efficiency at all levels.

http://www.ocregister.com/articles/prosecutors-732973-zappas-injuries.html

http://www.ocregister.com/2017/02/21/orange-county-sheriffs-deputy-pleads-guilty-to-insurance-fraud-after-faking-injury/

I'll explain further why I think this is an important topic and what leadership has to do with it. But first, let me unequivocally state that any injured law enforcement officer is entitled to full and substantial care and compensation. I make no argument to do otherwise. When you risk life and limb in the performance of your duties and are injured, or when the job takes its cumulative toll over decades, the organization must take care of you and your family, making you whole to the fullest extent possible. This should be a non-negotiable policy of all law enforcement agencies to ensure confidence in the rank and file that should they incur an on-duty injury they will be properly compensated and provided competent medical care. What I will deal with is the waste, fraud, and abuse that can occur, and how that affects the morale and effectiveness of the workplace, eroding its shared sense of purpose. When cops see their leaders abusing the system, they see a department that lacks integrity, and which encourages some members of the organization to feel entitled to do the same. While it may be an unlikely topic for a book on leadership, it has everything to do with setting the example, being accountable and leading with integrity.

The workers' compensation system for law enforcement in California, and in some other states, is generous almost to a fault. It is meant to compensate injured workers when they get hurt at work or in their off time because of work. Justifiably so, it provides significantly better benefits than those given to civilians. I told you earlier that I spent six years as the Human Resources Lieutenant and got to know the organization's personnel system well. I also talked with professionals in other agencies and the issues are usually the same. First, the system was set up by the legislature to favor the claimant in a way that makes it easy to scam by those who are predisposed to take advantage of such systems. It is, by law, supposed to favor the injured worker whenever there is a dispute as to the injury or its origin.

While that is a laudable goal and works most of the time, it encourages abuse and leaves those who are hard, honest workers to carry the load—and employers and the retirement system stuck with the cost. I've seen a good number of officers that became disillusioned with their chosen career path and, in my opinion, used the workers' compensation system to retire and look for another line of work. I've also seen how management, wanting to get rid of problematic individuals, used the workers' compensation system as a means to do so, saddling taxpayers with the cost in the process.

CalPERS, the public agency that is charged with managing the retirement system in California, issued a circular in 2017 directing public agencies to more aggressively scrutinize IDRs (Industrial Disability Retirements) and toughening their stance on such retirements, which cost taxpayers millions of dollars each year. In the circular, CalPERS specifically addresses the practice prevalent in some agencies to use the IDR as a way to get rid of problem employees. The enhanced scrutiny includes looking closely at an employee's disciplinary record to determine if the IDR is being filed as a hedge against disciplinary action or termination; and looking at employees who are retired on disability more closely to see if their injuries have changed or resolved. In addition, the circular gives CalPERS a larger role in determining whether an employee is in fact disabled according to the law, something that was previously left largely to the public agencies. Keep in mind that these changes in policy are the result of what I believe is significant fraud and abuse in the system. Whether the new policies will become permanent remains to be seen, but it's a start. I suspect the system will be tightened to the point of perhaps hurting those who are legitimately injured—all because of the ongoing fraud and abuse. If you'd like to read Circular Letter #200-018-17 you can do at the CalPERS website.

The cost of fraud in the system isn't theoretical; it quickly adds up to millions of dollars in pension costs and in taxes that aren't collected by states and the federal government. For example, according to actuarial tables, a twenty-five-year-old officer who retires early on disability may be expected to live at least until the age of seventy-five. During those fifty years, he or she could collect several million dollars from the pension system, further straining resources for those that go the distance—or those who have legitimate disabilities related to their work. I remember a case where an individual had filed a workers' compensation claim and eventually a disability retirement application. I suspected the claim was fraudulent for a number of reasons, one of which was that this person also had another business on the side. Our agency took a hard line on the claim and the retirement application, fighting it in court and in front of an administrative law judge.

The individual in question called me one day and told me how unfair it was that we were fighting his claim when the money did not come from the department, and it would cost us "nothing." I spent the next twenty minutes explaining to him that the cost would indeed be borne by the agency and the city in the form of higher pension costs and workers' compensation contribution rates, to no avail. He felt he was entitled to the retirement and it wouldn't cost the City anything. I suspect there are others who think along the same lines and feel entitled to these benefits, whether they've suffered a legitimate injury or not.

The problems start at the top, with some agencies having many of their key executives retiring on disability pensions after having filed multiple workers' compensation claims as they neared retirement. I'm sure you've seen the headlines about the chief, sheriff or manager that got in trouble and soon after that became disabled and retired. How do you think the troops view that pattern? They can easily figure out that a significant number of these disability retirements are questionable and meant to reduce taxes and obtain financial settlements. Again, I'm not talking about the legitimate injuries suffered by many law enforcement officers that merit care and compensation to the full extent of the law. I'm not even referring to the cases where an on-duty incident exacerbates existing non-work injuries or conditions, which may also be covered. I'm talking about the actions of those who consciously and deliberately use the system to avoid discipline or to enrich themselves, and how their actions are perceived by the troops.

In a recent case in Los Angeles County, an article in the Los Angeles Times described a judge's reaction after a chief negotiated an employment agreement with another agency that would have given him a disability retirement at a later date: "The chief, the judge wrote, also wanted to keep confidential an agreement that would have eventually granted him a disability retirement, meaning that half his pension would have been tax-free." Keep in mind that this is a chief negotiating an agreement for employment that would have granted him a disability retirement prospectively.

While I'm not questioning the extent of any legitimate injuries this individual may have suffered, the perceptions created by his alleged actions hurt all of law enforcement. To be sure, many executives have legitimate injuries and are properly compensated for them, especially if they are forced to cut careers short or are unable to perform the full range of their responsibilities. But we should be concerned at the level of fraud and abuse associated with the workers' compensation system in a good number of public safety agencies. The road to fixing it starts with those in leadership positions acting ethically and responsibly.

The level of workers compensation system abuse alleged against the CHP, and especially its management team in the past, is breathtaking. For a more recent example of workers' compensation system woes and abuse in Los Angeles take a look at the link below. Without a doubt, this issue is significant and complex given the effect on an agency's budget and services to the public. The effects are not theoretical but practical and measurable. Managing workers' compensation costs, financial and cultural, should be a key leadership objective.

http://www.latimes.com/local/cityhall/la-me-sworn-injury-leave-20140928-story.html#page=1

So how do agencies minimize the potential for fraud or abuse? Here are some thoughts:

First, they establish effective claims reporting and investigation systems that ensure legitimately injured officers get all the benefits, medical care and compensation they deserve, and that their claims are processed promptly. This includes a sound investigative system that helps determine as quickly as possible whether a claim is legitimate. As I told you above, police management must work hard to process claims promptly so that the system works for everyone. Nothing engenders confidence in your injured officers like a competent claim system that ensures prompt delivery of services, which largely depends on establishing effective organizational systems.

Second, any claim deemed suspicious or for which there is credible evidence of fraud must be thoroughly and aggressively investigated. This includes conducting unbiased, timely and professional investigations that give you the best shot at making sound determinations on a given incident. Looking at the background of the claimant, including any misconduct history, pending disciplinary action or significant performance problems should be one of the follow-up steps. Of course, looking at a claimant's internal investigation file or other documents protected by statute must be done within the confines of the law. Consult with your legal advisor before allowing anyone, even if they work for the workers' compensation unit of your city or county, to delve into a claimant's personnel file. Often interviews with co-workers and others who know the person and may have knowledge of the incident in question will be enough.

Third, establish a program whereby injured officers are returned to temporary light duty as soon as practical. This is a good way to help ensure they don't lose the connection to the agency, prompting them to consider leaving all together. I can tell you from experience that the longer an injured employee remains off work the greater the chance he'll eventually retire or separate from employment. Conversely, when the organization is in frequent, meaningful contact with the employee to maintain a connection, the employee may return to work sooner.

Fourth, work with your leadership team to create an organizational culture that values hard work and shared responsibility for the agency's resources. That means rewarding those that lead by example and promoting ethical behavior in themselves and others.

I readily admit that making determinations of whether an injury is legitimate is no easy task, but the better and more competent the system is, the quicker you'll be able to resolve the claims. Work closely with your workers' compensation unit or administrator to the extent allowed by the law. They will be vital to the prompt resolution of these issues, and they'll play a big role in providing those who are legitimately injured with all the care and resources they need and deserve. If you, as the CEO or another manager of the agency, believe one of your employees is legitimately injured, fight for them to get all the benefits they have coming. On the other hand, if you reasonably suspect that the employee is abusing the system, insist on an aggressive investigation and defense to ferret out the truth. Whatever you do, don't use the system to get rid of bad apples or those that may be a thorn in your side. You'll be tempted to do it, as I've seen done on occasion because it's the path of least resistance. But if you succumb to the temptation to take that easy path, you'll create an environment of distrust and cynicism; a road that leads to mediocrity or worse. Most importantly, insist that your management team set the example and abide by the same rules you apply to supervisors and the rank and file.

7

THE EMOTIONAL INTELLIGENCE
IMPERATIVE

"To handle yourself, use your head; to handle others, use your heart." Eleanor
Roosevelt

I ntelligence Quotient tests, generally known as IQ tests, have been used for many years in both the private and public sector for a myriad of purposes, including employment, scientific and social research, and the military. The Civil Rights Act of 1964 and subsequent decisions have limited sole reliance on IQ tests to make employment decisions. In essence, any test that is used to determine suitability for employment must be job-related and non-discriminatory. The emphasis on job testing has always been to assess the skills, abilities and intellectual capabilities of applicants. Public safety agencies need to thoroughly test candidates for physical strength, common sense and capacity to think on one's feet, all of which are important indicators of potential success. What is much harder to determine, however, is the emotional intelligence—or EI—of those who seek line-level or leadership positions.

Some tests have been developed to determine an applicant's emotional intelligence, but they aren't widely used in selecting law enforcement applicants or those seeking promotion, even though EI is a much more accurate predictor of a person's ability to deal successfully with people. Albert Einstein once said: "We should take care not to make the intellect our God; it has, of course, powerful muscles, but no personality." It is evident to anyone that supervises or manages people, that personality, being able to deal with people, and empathy all combine to create good leaders who can get things done through others in ways that add value to the organization, the leader and the individuals in the team. While personality may not equate to a good emotional quotient, it nonetheless provides a base from which to build. Many believe you're born with your personality—like it or not—and you can't change it. Your emotional intelligence, however, can be developed to a certain extent with steady work and dedication. Putting the two together can equate to a powerful synergy that makes one practically invaluable to any organization. It is that combination that enables ordinary people to produce extraordinary results at all levels in a business or a police department. And if it can realistically be learned or developed, then focusing our efforts in this area on officers early in their careers is not only worthwhile, it is imperative.

What is emotional intelligence, exactly? According to Peter Salovey and John D. Mayer, influential researchers on the topic, Emotional Intelligence refers to one's ability to perceive, control and evaluate emotions in oneself and others, and using that information to guide one's thinking and actions (Salovy, Mayer, 1990). There are many articles that discuss EI in detail, so I won't spend much time on it. However, EI is a critical ability that, perhaps unlike IQ, many believe can be learned. Salovey and Mayer described a model for emotional intelligence that had four parts. I paraphrase it here for the sake of brevity: The accurate perception of emotion, including body language and other non-verbal indicators; the ability to reason using emotions to promote thinking and cognitive activity; the ability to understand emotion and determine the meaning of those emotions; and capacity to manage emotions, including controlling one's own, and responding appropriately to those of others. These are what many call the soft skills, as opposed to hard skills like technical expertise, budget planning or writing abilities. "Soft" may not be an apt descriptor given their critical importance to your agency, so championing them and including them in your organizational values should be a departmental priority.

We've all dealt with people who appeared to be emotionally tone deaf. They failed to perceive when someone else was going through a difficult time and exhibited little or no empathy given the circumstances. We've also seen those who say or do things without regard for how their actions will be perceived or interpreted. I worked for some good leaders, and one unique characteristic I remember most about them was their ability to build that emotional connection with others. Conversely, I also worked for a few who couldn't perceive or evaluate another's emotions if you tattooed them on their forehead. I worked much harder and with more enthusiasm for the former while resenting and lamenting the latter. These are the folks that tend to lower morale and productivity in organizations, yet we spend precious little time on testing for EI before promotions. Worse yet, we spend almost no time in attempting to improve the emotional intelligence quotient in those who need it most. I agree with those who believe EI can be learned, which is one of the reasons I wrote this book.

EMOTIONAL INTELLIGENCE IN PRACTICE

The ability to try and understand—indeed imagine—how another person feels or thinks in relation to stimuli around them or actions from you or others in the organization should be a non-negotiable skill for anyone intent on leading men and women in policing. This concept isn't merely theoretical, as some claim, but exceedingly practical when you consider than interpersonal interactions in your agency are the bread and butter of getting things done. No other skill or trait can help you be more successful than possessing and nurturing Emotional Intelligence.

Recognizing the emotional needs of employees and projecting the department's concern during a crisis is one way to forge the bonds that are necessary for any organization to become an effective team. Let me give you an example which left such an impression on me that I remember it vividly. I had heard from a supervisor that the husband of one of her employees was gravely ill. I always felt it was important to provide support to members of our department when a family member had a serious illness. I made it a point to seek out the employee and sat down with her to talk. I could tell her husband's illness was weighing on her. I told her I'd heard about her husband and wanted to make sure she was doing OK. I offered our assistance in any way possible and chatted with her for about 15 minutes. I also knew that her supervisor was staying close to her and working with her to lighten her load.

The next day she stopped by my office and told me how much she appreciated the previous day's overture and said she could see from the actions of her supervisor and the department in general that we cared about her. She felt as though everyone cared, and she could "see it in everyone's eyes" that we were a family. Her eyes welled up, and we had an awkward pause for a minute. She smiled and left without another word. I could tell she was in pain, but the reassurance from the agency and her colleagues meant she wasn't alone. I later heard from the supervisor, who also commented on how the employee felt overwhelmed that the Department was so supportive during her time of need. That employee remained highly productive and loyal to the agency until retirement and beyond.

During my tenure, there was never any question that when one of our officers was hurt, I wanted someone from our management team to be among the first to arrive at the hospital or wherever they were, regardless of the time. Given my assignments to Homicide, Internal Affairs, and Human Resources, I was used to getting called out in the middle of the night. I can't tell you how many hours we spent at hospitals with officers and their families. I remember one Thanksgiving night one of our patrol officers was involved in a severe crash during a pursuit. I got the call in the middle of our dinner with family and friends. Without giving it a second thought, I drove to the hospital. The officer was doing OK but was surprised to see a captain show up in the middle of the night during a holiday.

The great leaders I respected also felt the need to be there during difficult times, and I learned from them. The power of a simple yet meaningful act can't be overstated. It becomes part of the culture of the department and reinforces the need to think as a team which transcends any one person. When an organization feels as though the whole is greater than its parts, and that management understands and cares about employees, the results can be breathtaking. The opposite is also true: If individual members don't feel as though they are part of a larger purpose that transcends individuals and are not reminded of that purpose through leadership by example, they withdraw from the effort and tend to be ineffective. The organization gradually becomes mediocre, with members who are uncommitted and disinterested.

I happen to believe Abraham Lincoln was the best President we ever had. I admire him for his leadership and political astuteness, but also because of his compassion and love for the field troops. Keep in mind that when Lincoln was elected, he had little administrative or management experience other than running his law office and dealing with his clients' business. But, he had great insight into human nature and what motivated people. Lincoln was a student of behavior and the human experience. That helped him immensely when it came to leading men into battle, something he took exceedingly seriously. While he didn't get along well with some of his generals, when it came to the troops he was a master. He cared deeply about their plight and that of their families and often acted in contradiction to what some of his generals advocated. Lincoln went into the battlefield many times to see and feel the extent of the devastation and learn what he could about the war and its casualties. It's an undisputed historical fact that Lincoln spent much more time in the field with the troops than he did at the White House. He offers us all lessons in leadership hard to find elsewhere today. Think about the burden placed on his shoulders and what he was able to accomplish. Nothing short of miraculous!

Here's an excerpt from The National Archives Experience series of interviews with James L. Swanson, author of "Manhunt: The 12-Day Chase for Lincoln's Killer," referring to Lincoln:

"That one particular day he went to a hospital and refused to leave until he shook the hands of several thousand soldiers. It crushed him to know that he was sending them to their deaths. Lincoln was not like the generals in World War I of France and England and Germany who almost with impudent glee or vigor would send their men to the slaughter. Lincoln hated to lose those men. He loved them, and he loved the army. He was comfortable with military affairs. He was comfortable with the generals he liked. Sometimes we've had presidents who don't like the military or are afraid of the military or don't respect the military. Lincoln respected it, he loved it, and the soldiers knew it..."

Phillips, in Lincoln on Leadership, aptly captures the essence of why emotional intelligence is a critical ability in leaders who want to do the right thing: "If modern leaders don't intuitively understand human nature as well as Lincoln did, they should at least make an attempt to learn more on the subject. After all, the most important asset a business organization has is its employees."

I use these anecdotes to illustrate how critical it is for leaders to demonstrate genuine empathy and to care deeply and genuinely about those with whom they work. I was lucky. Empathy came seemingly naturally to me. Wiring, mostly I guess, but also a factor of my upbringing and life experiences, which included working at all levels in the Department. I knew what those who worked for me went through. I had done their jobs, including those of civilian employees. Don't ever underestimate the benefit of experience and having walked in the shoes of others you seek to influence and comfort. It is invaluable. Absent some character flaw, when you have a well-rounded background and have done most jobs in an agency, you possess legitimacy and credibility, which will help you sell tough or unpopular decisions. It is important to strive to build a solid skill and experience set—but more on that later.

My beliefs regarding the importance of emotional connections led me in the early 1990s to start our Peer Support Team. I understood early on how important it was to help employees deal with critical events, whether personal or professional. Post-Traumatic Stress Disorder (PTSD) was a relatively new concept in law enforcement at in the 1990s. The larger departments were starting to adopt practices to deal with it, but we were beginning to see the benefits of having a trained team with professional support to minimize the damage that is often done to individuals who are involved in critical incidents. There were critics to be sure, who claimed that it was "feel good crap," but there were also key supporters, like the late Lieutenant Greg Cooper, who as the SWAT Commander understood and encouraged the concept early on. And Chief Paul Walters, who took a chance on the idea and let me run with it.

The team has done exceedingly well and continues today thanks to the unselfish commitments from team members and leaders at all levels. While I try not to name individuals in this book to respect their privacy, I have to thank Dr. Eric Gruver, one of our departmental psychologists at the time, for his assistance and support while we worked to get the team selected, trained and operational. His insight was invaluable.

To be a trusted and respected leader, you must care about others in ways that may not come naturally to you. Not easy to do for some people, especially when you work in a large organization with many employees and competing demands for your time. But you must do it or risk losing the moral authority to accomplish organizational goals and help others be productive members of the team. The leaders I learned to respect during my career were those that set the example, were competent and demonstrated that they cared about the organization and me. Many of them were charismatic individuals, but others were quiet, introspective men and women who worked hard to show they valued your work and cared about you. They often put their cards on the table and were more introspective than considered safe in a paramilitary organization. What I mean is they trusted those around them by being honest and self-critical, revealing their fears and concerns to get good advice from others, including how to capitalize on strengths and reduce weaknesses. They opened up and, as I said earlier, gave up formal power to gain legitimate organizational power.

In their book Primal Leadership—Realizing the Power of Emotional Intelligence, the authors (Goleman, Boyatzis and McKee 2002) argue that it is the fundamental task of leaders to prime good feeling in those they lead. They further argue for the proposition that those good feelings are developed when a leader "creates resonance — a reservoir of positivity that frees the best in people." At its root, they argue, "the primal job of leadership is emotional." Primal to the authors means primary, first. Their book links the job of a leader and emotional intelligence to neurology and how our brains work. I read this book because I believed, and tried to practice, its tenets.

Before you dismiss EQ and resonance as "feel good" gobbledygook, I encourage you to think back and find moments when you felt inspired or encouraged by one of your bosses. Invariably in most instances, you'll find he or she was creating good will and relying on emotional intelligence to influence others. Emotional leadership doesn't mean you lose control, or regularly wear your heart or emotions on your sleeve. It doesn't mean sacrificing the hard management skills and the technical competence we all expect from our leaders.

The bottom line is that effective leaders should be reasonably intelligent, competent and lead by example. But, they needn't sacrifice emotional intelligence for intellectual capabilities, or cold and calculated competence. Sure, some problems or situations will require primarily hard skills, while others will largely depend on the soft skills that emotional intelligence brings with it. Great leaders blend the two in ways that achieve that synergy which makes it clear to those around you that you care; care for them, their families and the organization's well-being. If you care about those with whom you work, the rest follows. You can make a huge difference in how an employee sees the Department and themselves in it, by doing little but significant things. Learn the names of your employees and get to know them as much as practical. Write an employee a personal note for a job well done. Call them at home when they are ill or provide support when they suffer a personal crisis. Praise an employee in public. Critique someone by making it a learning and productive experience, rather than a demeaning one. These are easy things to do, and they pay handsome dividends in addition to being the right thing to do.

Conversely, there are things you say and do that can kill productivity, morale, and commitment to the organization. In the 1990s I was a lieutenant with responsibility for a number of divisions in the organization, some of which were technical in nature. In one of those units, we'd experienced errors that started affecting the systems our officers relied upon to do their jobs. Because of the problems, officers were being forced to jury-rig solutions that were either inadequate or downright improper. I sat down with the supervisor in the unit and one of the senior employees to discuss the issues and see if we could come up with a solution. The employee had already analyzed the problems and had come up with a potential solution, and he was eager to tell me about it. The employee hadn't said more than ten words when the supervisor jumped in and gruffly told him he had looked at his ideas and they were wrong. He dismissed the employee's possible solutions out of hand and, I could tell, made him feel so inadequate that he looked at the floor and hardly said a word throughout the meeting. I knew the employee, and he was a dedicated and knowledgeable person that worked hard to provide excellent service to the officers in the field, with whom he was popular and appreciated.

Even though I tried to salvage the conversation by trying to re-engage him in the problem-solving process, it was obvious the supervisor had killed any chance that the employee was going to feel like a valued team member and work hard to solve the problem. I later had a heart-to-heart conversation with the supervisor and explained how his demeanor had done nothing to resolve the problems our officers were encountering. I also spoke to the employee in private and tried to reassure him he was a valued member of the team. The employee had already experienced encounters with his supervisor that were similar to this one, but this particular one broke the proverbial camel's back: it was done in front of the boss. The employee was angered and remained so until the supervisor retired. The work remained adequate, but the employee's faith in the organization and his place in it were shaken.

When I retired over a decade later, that employee told me he'd never forgotten how the supervisor made him feel in that meeting and thanked me for trying to reassure him he was valued by the department. In Emotional Intelligence, Goleman concludes that: "Indeed, how criticisms are given and received goes a long way in determining how satisfied people are with their work, with those they work with, and with those to whom they are responsible." I find that when employees are critiqued constructively, with clear examples of work that can improve—and specifically how it can improve—given in a private setting, they tend to understand. The key, as most good managers and supervisors will tell you, is to show empathy and make constructive arguments that show the employee you care.

There are multiple definitions for the technical competence and the emotional intelligence that are needed to be a good leader. Job competence is generally manifested in the hard skills, such as writing and speaking well, knowing the budget or having a tactical background. On the other hand, the soft skills include emotional intelligence, empathy and the ability to act fairly and ethically. There are many other examples of both but suffice it to say an effective leader must have both. It is similar to the current debate regarding math and science versus the humanities in a liberal education. Many schools and universities throughout the world are rushing to eliminate classes on critical thinking, history or art, in favor of technology, math, and science. If we focus solely on the hard sciences, we'll end up with folks that can compute, but arguably can't deal with people or appreciate a good book or painting.

The key for anyone wishing to lead is to develop both realms and seek to understand how someone feels and thinks, as well as how they perform the hard tasks in their day-to-day work. In The Soft Edge (Jossey-Bass 2014), Rich Karlgaard plainly stated:

- Great, enduring organizations are masters at both the hard and the soft edges.
- Top performance depends on finding the right balance of hard and soft skills for any given situation.
- On balance, the soft edge is gaining currency. In this tough, global Great Reset economy, mastery of the soft edge will become as critical (or even more critical than) mastery of the hard edge.

Angela Ahrendts, the Senior Vice-President for Apple Retail, recently shared her hiring secrets on her LinkedIn page (https://www.linkedin.com/pulse/how-i-hire-my-guiding-principles-angela-ahrendts):

"By the time they have reached my office, I think it is pretty safe to say they are incredibly smart in their field. I want to make sure they are culturally compatible. Are they empathetic, compassionate, caring and giving of their mind and heart? My most overused quote, which is now often played back to me, is from Maya Angelou: "I've learned that people will forget what you said, people will forget what you did, but people will never forget how you made them feel." I want to sense if they truly care about the impact they make on people."

RECRUITING FOR EMOTIONALLY INTELLIGENCE IN THE CIVIL SERVICE

Organizations must develop job-related and non-discriminatory tests for EI for all applicants, especially for promotional candidates. It can be done, and it means a great deal for the success of your agency. The following link at monster.com highlights some strategies for including emotional intelligence aspects to applicant testing:

http://hiring.monster.com/hr/hr-best-practices/recruiting-hiring-advice/job-screening-techniques/emotional-intelligence.aspx.

I asked Orange County Sheriff Sandra Hutchens how her department handles recruitment in the face of dwindling competent applicant pools. She told me at the time that her agency was in the middle of reviewing all recruitment standards and processes to see where they can be adjusted to look for those who exhibit strong emotional intelligence and to help them complete the physical agility testing through training and skills development. She said: "Are we looking for folks that can handle people or those who can climb walls, even though the latter isn't done all that often?" While all requirements are important, Sheriff Hutchens believes diversity, strong people skills and the ability to do the right thing are fundamental requirements for law enforcement applicants. I wholeheartedly agree with her.

Kendra Cherry (see link below) lists several tests that have been developed to test for emotional intelligence. While your agency and its human resources professionals may balk at using these tests, they could, if properly validated for specific positions, provide valuable insight into supervisory and management candidates in particular. They are:

Reuven Bar-On's EQ-i — A self-report test designed to measure competencies including awareness, stress tolerance, problem-solving, and happiness. According to Bar-On, "Emotional intelligence is an array of non-cognitive capabilities, competencies, and skills that influence one's ability to succeed in coping with environmental demands and pressures."

Multifactor Emotional Intelligence Scale (MEIS) — An ability-based test in which test-takers perform tasks designed to assess their ability to perceive, identify, understand, and utilize emotions.

Seligman Attributional Style Questionnaire (SASQ) — Originally designed as a screening test for the life insurance company Metropolitan Life, the SASQ measures optimism and pessimism.

Emotional Competence Inventory (ECI) — Based on an older instrument known as the Self-Assessment Questionnaire, the ECI involves having people who know the individual offer ratings of that person's abilities in several different emotional competencies.

(http://psychology.about.com/od/personalitydevelopment/a/emotionalintell.htm)

EMOTIONAL INTELLIGENCE AND THE GOLDEN RULE

"I've learned that people will forget what you said, people will forget what you did, but people will never forget how you made them feel."
Maya Angelou.

Great leaders have empathy for others. They learn to walk in someone else's shoes to understand their perspective. As Atticus Finch said in To Kill a Mockingbird: "You never really understand a person until you consider things from his point of view...until you climb into his skin and walk around in it." Everyone will watch how you treat others in the workplace, including those who need time off to care for young children or need to support an ailing parent. They'll listen to the way you speak to others, give orders and make requests. Being flexible and finding workarounds for these issues engenders loyalty and pays big dividends. Single parents, for example, may need an accommodation to drop or pick up their kids from school or daycare. To the extent that you can, without jeopardizing the department's operations, try and accommodate folks. If you can't, take the time to explain why.

The only thing I hated more than being told "no" is being told "no" without an explanation. Think of it this way: how would you want your mother, sister or wife treated at their respective workplaces?

Simply put, treat others the way you'd want to be treated, and they'll hopefully model that behavior as well. It's the great contagion that pays dividends in perpetuity and makes your organization and its people better. It also translates into a more humane treatment of community members and broader engagement with community problems. It's really about a culture of respect that seeks to build a great workplace where employees are committed because they feel valued and appreciated.

The supervisors and managers with whom I worked that were flexible and cared about their subordinates were able to get more productivity and loyalty from those who worked for them. The leaders I respected most during my career were those that treated others and me with respect, often showing an interest in my career as well as my family. I could count on these individuals to look out for my best interest without shirking their responsibility to the organization. Often, they were charismatic, but there were some who were reserved and quiet by nature, yet still made me feel as though they cared about me. The adage that implores you to treat people they way you'd want to be treated works! As a leader, don't be afraid to demand it from those with whom you work. If you model the behavior and ask others to do the same, I can guarantee you people in your community will be treated better, and employees will likely treat each other better as well.

Lest you accuse me of being Pollyannaish, I'll readily admit they'll be those in your agency that for pathological reasons find it hard to treat others with dignity and respect. That's what the counseling and disciplinary processes are meant to address. If you can't do it any other way, you must use whatever lawful means are available to you to remove these folks from your agency. And you must be aggressive about it. I know how hard that can be as I've experienced it many times. If you take the path of least resistance and ignore the problem employees, be prepared to disappoint and diminish the good employees who will lose faith in you and think that you are unwilling or unable to do the right thing. In other words, be prepared for your organization to become mediocre! If you decide you want an enlightened workplace, you'll inevitably have to start at the top with your management and supervisory ranks. I found that in police departments that weren't a good place to work, it inevitably started at the top. Thus, finding staff members who are emotionally attuned to others and can hone their hard skills is of primary importance for the people in your community and your agency.

THE GRIT FACTOR

Lastly, don't forget about the Grit factor. In The Soft Edge, Rich Karlgaard (Jossey-Bass, 2014, 110) argues that: "In the real world, smarts isn't about looking for the next star student with a 4.0 or having an IQ that can boil water. Instead, it's about the importance of hard work, of perseverance and resilience. Call it grit. Call it courage. Call it tenacity. Call it a can-do attitude. These are such old-fashioned concepts, they're sometimes easy to miss." In police work the grit factor is critical because often the circumstances we face defy the most intelligent approach, forcing us instead to dig deep and find ways to solve problems with steadfast doggedness. I equate grit with emotional intelligence. The smartest person in the roll call room may not be the one with fire in her belly; the one who works hard and looks under rocks for crooks; or the steady and consistent problem-solver who learns to use the resources around him.

I sat on hundreds of background interviews designed to see if the applicant had what it took to succeed at Santa Ana PD. Invariably the ones that impressed me the most were the scrappers, the ones that overcame a difficult childhood or poverty, or the ones that, despite the odds stacked against them, were able to overcome adversity to make something of themselves. I looked for that grit factor, and all things being equal, I would hire a scrapper versus the polished intellectual any time. That philosophy served me well. When I first started in police work, I knew there would always be someone smarter and better educated than me, so I worked harder than anyone else and vowed to treat people as I would want to be treated. It always worked for me. So don't forget the scrapper!

Before I leave this topic, it's important that I address two common criticisms of this philosophy: There are those who think that the emotional quotient is all fluff, or "superficial crap," as someone once told me, which has no place in a police organization. Those of you who might agree with that sentiment are at this point getting ready to put this book on the shelf or toss the eBook into the virtual trash bin. And there are others who believe emotional depth and attachment to employees leads to a failure to maintain standards or impose discipline upon those who deserve it. You are wrong! Great leaders care, and they care deeply. They show it. They live it. They mean it. But, they intuitively understand the importance of imposing fair and timely discipline on those who deserve it.

More about this later, but effective leaders have the distinct ability to make decisions based on evidence and with the best interests of the organization at heart. Using your head and your heart are not mutually exclusive! The key is to learn to master both the hard and the soft skills. You ignore emotional intelligence and the ability to feel empathy at your professional peril. Sure, you'll have those who tell you what you want to hear: that you are wonderful and never let emotion get in the way of making "great decisions." Stick with those folks, and you may be on a train to nowhere, leaving behind a trail of disappointment and unfulfilled promise.

8

HUMILITY AND APPROACHABILITY

"True humility is not thinking less of yourself; it is thinking of yourself less."
— *Rick Warren*

I n 2011, Admiral William McRaven was the commander of the Joint Special Operations Command, home of Seal Team Six. As we all know, that was the team that carried out the operation that killed Osama Bin-laden in Abbottabad, Pakistan. In Operation Neptune Spear, McRaven was the architect of the plan and was involved in its execution from beginning to end. As a junior officer, McRaven himself was assigned to Seal Team Six and has a storied career in the military. If you ever want to hear a speech that not only moves you but provides life and leadership lessons like no other, watch Admiral McRaven's commencement address at the University of Texas at Austin in 2014 here: https://www.youtube.com/watch?v=pxBQLFLei70.

But back to the reason I write about him. In a recent CNN special about the operation that killed Bin-laden, President Obama described McRaven as "right out of central casting" when it comes to leaders that are competent and have the trust of their troops and the President of the United States. He described McRaven in terms like "accomplished, confident, cool," and trusted him to develop a plan that was designed to succeed even in the face of overwhelming odds. What struck me most about the admiral was his demeanor during the interview with CNN's Peter Bergen (who by the way was the first to interview Bin-laden before 9-11). He steadfastly credited the troops with the success of the mission and said the Obama team focused on doing the right thing without politics ever rearing its ugly head. He was complimentary of the President and the national security team for having engaged in robust discussion, and the President for having made a tough decision that could have easily backfired and made him a one-term president like Jimmy Carter after the failed hostage rescue attempt in Iran in the 1970s.

But what struck me most occurred when Bergen asked him about the effort that went into the Bin-laden operation. McRaven painstakingly credited the efforts of all those involved over many years and became emotional when thanking his troops. He teared up and asked that the cameraman cut the filming. McRaven is one of the toughest and experienced military men in the world, and he cried when thinking of the doggedness and bravery his troops exhibited before and during the operation. He didn't take credit for the operation, even though his leadership was instrumental in its success. He credited his team.

His humility was evident throughout the entire speech, and I couldn't help but wonder what it would have been like to serve under such an accomplished, competent and humble leader. These folks not only inspire their troops, but they also create an environment where everyone gives their blood and sweat to accomplish the mission, looking after each other in the process. Humility is, then, an indispensable quality in a leader that fuels the team to reach beyond their benchmark and accomplish the mission under the most adverse conditions. The leader who exhibits it honestly, genuinely is by far the most influential in the effort to make teams successful.

Humility isn't simply a great trait in successful leaders, but it is clearly better for the bottom line regardless of the business you're in. In an article in the Washington Post (December 8, 2016), Ashley Merryman makes a convincing case that when leaders are humble, their businesses not only prosper, but the workforce is better aligned with the organization's goals and priorities. According to Merryman, "True humility, scientists have learned, is when someone has an accurate assessment of both his strengths and weaknesses, and he sees all this in the context of the larger whole. He's a part of something far greater than he. He knows he isn't the center of the universe. And he's both grounded and liberated by this knowledge. Recognizing his abilities, he asks how he can contribute. Recognizing his flaws, he asks how he can grow."

Being humble then isn't about being humiliated or weak, it is about strength: Being secure in one's true self and allowing for one's weaknesses—opening up and being vulnerable to gain respect and more than willing compliance from subordinates. Some of the keys to humility, in my view, are admitting mistakes, being willing to listen to others, and openly celebrating the accomplishments of the team and its members.

In an Academy of Management Journal Article (June 1, 2016, Volume 59), Owens and Heckman wrote: "Our findings suggest that humility appears to embolden individuals to aspire to their highest potential and enables them to make the incremental improvements necessary to progress toward that potential." Their research found that the humble leader's followers are more motivated and work harder. They know their leader is counting on them—and their input matters—so they rise to the occasion. Non-humble leaders get their strength from a position of certainty. The non-humble leader promises that he does have all the answers, and he knows exactly what to do. He ignores information that might cause him to re-think his strategy. The inescapable conclusion to the research is that humility is an indispensable trait in those wishing to successfully lead men and women in policing. Humility, thus, is not a weakness but a powerful trait that allows you to understand that you are not infallible, leaving you open to better ideas and more information with which to make better decisions.

To read the article go here:
https://www.washingtonpost.com/news/inspired-life/wp/2016/12/08/leaders-are-more-powerful-when-theyre-humble-new-research-shows/?utm_term=.7477f9f0706b

ON HANDLING AUTHORITY

"The measure of a man is what he does with power"—Plato

It was 1985, and the badge on the lieutenant's chest must have weighed a ton. We'd been working the crime scene for a couple of hours, and our civilian CSI team was busy collecting evidence in what I can only describe as a bloody mess. A man in his twenties had been found dead, shot in the chest and face in an abandoned building in the central core of the city. He'd been dead for at least a couple of days, and the interior of the building heaped with trash, remnants of drug paraphernalia and assorted biological waste. As part of the homicide team, I'd been called at home and asked to handle the case. The officer acting as the scribe was young and had been employed for less than eighteen months. Doing his job, he approached the lieutenant to get his information for the log.

I could see the lieutenant was annoyed as he quickly gave short-riff to the request, continuing to walk to the crime scene tape delineating the border of the inner perimeter without giving the officer what he needed. As the watch commander, he had the absolute right to be there, but not without providing his credentials so the officer could properly log him in and out of the scene. Homicide scene management 101! I approached the officer and gave him the lieutenant's particulars. I also apologized to him for the lieutenant's attitude and told him that his reaction was not an indication of his (the officer) doing anything wrong. Without me saying it, the officer knew the lieutenant was wrong.

Over the years I worked with folks at all levels that got into law enforcement for the wrong reasons. I know Santa Ana is not unique in this regard, and such people are the ones that give us all a bad name. You can usually tell who they are. Just look for the supervisor or manager that abhors having his authority questioned, or who lets you know how he knows best in just about any situation. It isn't always the facts; it is how the circumstances are perceived and how the incident is told to others throughout the agency. The damage can be significant. I'll repeat one of my favorite quotes from Maya Angelou: "People will forget what you said, they'll forget what you did, but they'll never forget how you made them feel."

To be sure, I'm not talking about no-nonsense supervisors and managers who do their jobs well and demand you earn your pay. I respect direct and concise supervision and management. When I was the captain in charge of our Field Operations Bureau I was blessed to have experienced, respected and trustworthy watch commanders working for me. They included Jose Garcia, Ken Hall and Felix Osuna (who was one of the preeminent tactical experts in the nation). They probably had well over 100 years of experience between them. I could sleep well at night knowing they were in charge of the city. They had a reputation for not suffering fools easily, and for having high expectations for their subordinates. Keep in mind the watch commander's position is one that ensures the community is well served and that cops are doing their job. They make critical decisions all the time and are responsible for the operations of the department during their shift.

Even though these guys were not always popular, they were respected. They treated you with dignity and respect but wouldn't allow you to sit in the station and milk a report for hours while calls stacked up in the CAD system. Some were even feared a little bit, which is not necessarily bad when you have to maintain control and ensure the safety of a community of nearly half a million and dozens of cops in the field at any one time.

These watch commanders didn't isolate themselves behind a desk, but kept an open door and walked around the building often. They grabbed a patrol unit and went in the field, helping out when possible and keeping an eye on the conditions under which their officers and supervisors worked. When it was all said and done, we met frequently, and they weren't afraid to give me their unvarnished opinion and perspective, which I took to heart given their credibility and experience. I certainly appreciated their service, and so did the agency. The challenge for police executives is to train and mentor new lieutenants or commanders, so they develop the skills displayed by the veterans I described above. With the management ranks in many agencies getting younger and younger, it isn't easy. Some of these skills will come only with time and seasoning, but you can provide the foundation for growth and development by acutely training and mentoring your managers and supervisors.

Simply because you have stripes, bars or stars on your sleeve or collar doesn't mean you are better than anyone else in the organization. You have been entrusted with what I call a sacrosanct duty in leading men and women in policing. That means you have a heavy burden and must earn the respect of others to function properly. Humility gets you half-way there, and hard work, setting the example, competence, and integrity get you across the finish line. Think often about how your actions are perceived and internalized by others. If you can't, or won't be, that introspective, learn how. Ask others around you to honestly tell you how you are perceived and how your demeanor and interactions affect productivity and effectiveness in the department. Be wary of anyone that tells you how perfect you are and dig a little deeper to get honest feedback. When you do, don't kill the messenger. Take constructive criticism to heart and consider talking to those you respect about how you overcome deficiencies. Be humble and lose the attitude, and you'll see how people react. Give others credit even if you were instrumental in the accomplishment. Lend a hand to others without expecting anything in return. You'll feel better and those around you will as well, increasing productivity and loyalty to the department.

The other critical component of being a humble leader is not isolating yourself. Don't get so attached to the trappings of your office and position in the department that the troops begin to see you as arrogant and unapproachable. Given a choice, always elect to remain in the bullpen, close to the action and close to the sounds, sights, and rumbles of the work getting done. You'll be surprised how much more aware you become of the little things: the subtle but important aspects of the life and work of those around you. When your employees see you up close, unimpeded by walls or artificial barriers, they know you care and are interested in the quantity and quality of their work. They see you as part of the team, as someone who shares their goals and aspirations. If your office is enclosed, keep the door open as much as possible. Don't close the curtains unless necessary. Walk around and sit at someone's desk to talk and get to know that person a little better. I realize these are basic supervision and management principles, but they aren't always obvious to new and experienced leaders alike.

I remember one manager in particular that came to work and closed the door to his office, rolled down the shades, and finally emerging at lunch time. The speculation about what he was doing in there was worthy of a prime-time soap opera! Needless to say, he was neither respected nor liked, and he didn't care. There are times when your physical office may be some distance away from where the work gets done. If you absolutely can't avoid such a situation, then spend lots of time in the bullpen. I recommend you spend the majority of your time out of the office and amongst the troops. May not be easy to do, but it's vital to your success.

Donald T. Phillips, in his book Lincoln on Leadership (Warner Books, 1992), describes how Lincoln, On October 24, 1861, relieved General John Fremont from command of the Department of the West. In a letter to his successor, General David Hunter, Lincoln wrote: "He [General Fremont] is losing the confidence of men near him, whose support any man in his position must have to be successful. His cardinal mistake is that he isolates himself and allows nobody to see him; and by which he does not know what is going on in the very matter he is dealing with." Lincoln, the master communicator, made his point to General Hunter and unambiguously but subtly told him what he expected of him. Follow Lincoln's example and spend most of your time with folks in the agency and the community. No one ever won a battle, solved a community problem or led men and women in policing effectively from behind a desk.

Learn not to take credit for your team's efforts. If you do the job right, you'll ultimately get credit for having a great team and your collective achievements. Over the years I witnessed some instances where the supervisor or manager received an award for a particular project or action that was a team effort. Few things undermine morale more effectively than the boss taking credit for the team's hard work. It saps enthusiasm and gives folks little incentive to go the extra mile or show initiative.

Again, we talked earlier about the importance of being keenly aware of perceptions, and this is a fault that will fuel resentment among the troops. You may have been an essential part of the effort, and in the end, your leadership was instrumental in the accomplishment, but as Lao Tzu said: "...with the best leaders, when the work is done, the task accomplished, the people will say: 'We have done this ourselves.'" Your ultimate goal as a leader is to get things done through others and, more importantly, getting others to do it willingly, through legitimate persuasion and motivation. If they think you'll take credit for their work you'll be marginalized, and the results of any team effort will be lackluster, or worse yet, will be so deficient that it will reflect a lack of leadership.

LOOK TO THE POPE FOR INSPIRATION

I guess the best example of humility in modern times is Pope Francis. A little more than two years ago the white smoke wafting out of the chimney of the Vatican's Sistine Chapel announced that Rome, and the world, had a new Pope: Francis. Born in Argentina to Italian immigrants, Jorge Mario Bergoglio took a path to the papacy unlike no other, bringing with him the life experience, humility, and dedication that allowed him to turn the Vatican machine upside down. In a scant two years, Francis has managed to clean up and modernize the Vatican Bank—no small feat given the bank's notorious history. He streamlined Vatican communications, set a new direction for the clergy and instilled a sense of humility and purpose into an institution that was widely believed to be dysfunctional and focused inward rather than toward the Catholic faithful.

Whatever your religious beliefs or your feelings about the Catholic church, Pope Francis represents the best in leadership, team building and determination to do the right thing. He isn't just a symbol, but also a practical, clear example of humility that inspires others to follow him and, by extension, the teachings of the church. I'm not asking you to be a saint or that you compare yourself to Pope Francis; I'm asking that you look at what makes this simple man so consequential in our time so you can apply the principles of humility to your leadership style.

Francis was born in Argentina to Italian immigrant parents.

According to National Geographic Magazine (August 2015), he worked as a lab technician and was a bouncer at a night club for a period. Eventually, he entered a Jesuit seminary at 20 and almost immediately began to show the extraordinary qualities that allowed him to become Cardinal. Even then, Francis rode the subway and eschewed the many benefits that came with the office, staying close to the people and performing deeds such as washing the feet of prisoners in Italian jails. Showing an early talent for ministering and counseling, he became a spiritual advisor to other students. When Francis became pope, instead of moving into the ornate and luxurious papal residence, he elected to live in a simple apartment on the grounds nearby. He often avoids riding in limousines in favor of simple, small cars. The night he was elected, rather than wear the customary elaborate outfit, Francis wore a simple one and asked the gathered throngs to pray for him.

One particular story stands out in my mind as the perfect example of humility: The day he was introduced as Pope, Francis went back to the boarding house where he was staying to pay his bill. As the Archbishop of Buenos Aires in Argentina, he used to ride public buses, cook his own meals and lived in a modest apartment rather than in the official archbishop's residence. There are many examples of how Francis commands the respect of his flock, world leaders, and others by being a humble man who understands how flawed people are, including himself. Leaders in law enforcement can learn practical and employable lessons from Pope Francis. Some of them include staying humble; understanding that you are but a small part of the organization; not flouting the trappings of the office; seeking to understand the people with whom you work; and staying in close, regular contact with the line-level folks that do the work.

KNOW THYSELF

Getting people to give you unvarnished feedback about your skills, performance, and trustworthiness isn't easy. Many people that work for and with you probably feel encumbered by the organization's culture and the fear that if they are honest, you won't look kindly on them or their career potential. If on the other hand, you work for an agency where honest feedback and introspection is welcomed, you're golden! The essential task of getting feedback from others is more art than science, relying on the emotional connection and trust that is inevitably necessary to pave the way for a free-flowing exchange of thoughts and opinions. So how do you purposely use humility to open up the lines of communication? You have to actively seek negative feedback from those around you.

There is a tendency in some organizations to keep the boss happy even if that means withholding critical feedback or information. There is no quicker way to lead organizations astray than to inhibit constructive criticism of the leadership or management team. I spoke with individuals of all ranks in different agencies, and some of them told me that they dreaded giving the boss bad news or feedback they knew he or she wouldn't like or take kindly. When I probed further, I found that this attitude was more frequently a byproduct of the organization's culture rather than a single individual's idiosyncrasies. Great leaders use their empathy and self-awareness to monitor their own actions and see how others react to them (Goleman, 133). They consciously seek feedback regarding their leadership style and their ideas about work in general and specific projects. When the military and other government agencies use Red Teams to poke holes in their plans or initiatives, they recognize that there is always room for improvement. According to Goleman, there is a clear link between a leader's embrace of negative feedback and his or her performance.

Think about all the bosses you've had and their willingness or reluctance to be introspective and seek all manner of feedback about their performance. Then think specifically about those that consciously wanted to know the good, bad or ugly and welcomed your input. Then honestly assess their performance and look at the difference in outcome and the trust and respect they engendered. I learned from great leaders early on in my career that to be effective, one needed to open up, seek the opinions of others and be willing to look critically at one's performance. I worked for some bosses with whom giving them my unvarnished thoughts on all types of issues was easy. As long as I did it in a constructive, respectful manner, they welcomed my input.

These folks were without question the ones people aspired to emulate, and upon whom the employees bestowed trust. Although emulating them wasn't easy to do at times, I found that not only did it make me a better supervisor and manager, but it allowed me to get things done in ways that didn't require coercion or use of formal authority. The more I encouraged honest feedback and sought differing opinions, the more liberating it became. I found myself in an environment where people weren't afraid to come into my office to tell me I was wrong about a particular course of action. When I reacted poorly to negative feedback or bad news, folks were quick to push back because they knew I wouldn't take their heads off. Without any doubt, it made me a better person and allowed me to contribute much more to the success of the organization and, by extension, my team members.

It isn't one size fits all, however. People are wired differently, and it is hard to change their personalities, especially when they are accustomed to positions of power and influence. But there are ways to find a modus vivendi, or way of living with them, that makes it easier and more productive. I worked with some who had an authoritative leadership style that made some subordinates feel as though they could not approach them. One, in particular, had a gruff demeanor and was seen as someone you didn't want to cross or upset, lest you find yourself in his crosshairs. When I began dealing with him, I saw some validation of the rumors I'd heard, but I also found an individual who, if approached correctly, was not only willing to listen but was open to suggestions and negative feedback. From the start, I approached our relationship by making it clear I would be honest with him, but I also approached with respect and understanding for his positions and, more importantly, his way of making decisions.

Over time he learned that I had the best intentions and was looking out for the organization as well as his interests. If I had a difficult subject to discuss, I'd lay the groundwork by preparing him in advance and providing as much information as possible. I'd also come to him mindful not only with the nature of the problem but possible solutions as well. Those who modeled my approach were able to work with him productively. He never became a soft and cuddly manager, but we were able to accomplish objectives for the department, and I grew to respect and like him. I'd like to think those of us who learned to deal with him encouraged him to change as well. Although he never became an overtly humble individual, he nonetheless often showed a caring and empathetic side. So often it isn't about hard lines, but about learning to bend the borders to get things done.

9

BUILDING AND RETAINING TRUST

"If you once forfeit the confidence of your fellow citizens, you can never regain their respect and esteem. It is true that you may fool all of the people some of the time; you can even fool some of the people all of the time; but you can't fool all of the people all of the time." — *Speech at Clinton, Illinois, September 8, 1854.*— *Abraham Lincoln*

According to the U.S. Army's Field Manual 6-22, Leader Development (see bibliography), "Leaders shape the ethical climate of their organization while developing the trust and relationships that enable proper leadership." There is no single most important attribute that a leader must have than trust. It forms the cornerstone of any binding commitment from members of any organization. Without it, little is accomplished, and the agency becomes a rudderless, conflict-ridden workplace that is unable to create value for the community and its employees. In other words, trust in the executive and management team is absolutely essential to the well-being and effectiveness of any police organization. Trust is emotional as much as intellectual. People will look at what you say and what you do and form an opinion as to whether you can be trusted. That assessment happens over time and is greatly influenced by the emotional connection one can make with others.

That connection begins with how your actions are perceived, so the leadership by example discussions we had earlier become the key to engendering trust in relationships. Think back to how you viewed your supervisors and managers and what factors influenced your decision on whether to trust them. I'm willing to bet that those who walked the talk were able to earn your respect and trust. That assessment involved a gut reaction as well as a longer process of observing their performance and judging their competence. Your gut told you they were personable, warm or caring, while your brain looked at the person more critically over time to validate your initial observations and feelings. Over many years I learned to respect others by judging whether they cared about folks and whether their actions matched their words. Remember what Maya Angelou once said: "When someone shows you who they are, believe them the first time." So strive to build trust from the start of any relationship because most people will form those important first impressions right away.

These are Lincoln's words, and I couldn't agree more:

"When the conduct of men is designed to be influenced, persuasion, kind, unassuming persuasion, should ever be adopted. It is an old and a true maxim, that a 'drop of honey catches more flies than a gallon of gall.' So with men, if you would win a man to your cause, first convince him that you are his sincere friend. Therein is a drop of honey that catches his heart, which, say what he will, is the great high road to his reason, and which, when once gained, you will find by little trouble in convincing his judgment of the justice of your cause, if indeed that cause really be a just one."

Trust, then, becomes that glue that binds the organization together in good times and bad. It is the essential element in any workplace relationship, and it is paramount in a relationship with a supervisor or a manager. Rich Karlgaard (see below) defines trust as "confidence in a person, group or system when there's risk and uncertainty." Thus, trust is of particular importance during turbulent, difficult and trying times. Individuals that build that trust from the start are more productive and able to accomplish much more for the agency and its employees. While it should be entirely clear to all that trust is essential, it isn't always so obvious. I've seen a good number of folks in leadership positions violate that trust—or not develop it from the start—and lose their legitimacy in the organization, thus becoming a liability rather than an asset. Trust is a perishable asset and has to be nurtured. Once lost, it's nearly impossible to get back. Behavior that leads to that loss of, or inability to build, trustworthy relationships includes:

Engaging in misconduct. Violating organizational policies or committing crimes is one sure way to lose trust and your job as well. How can you expect to earn and maintain the trust of others if you can't be responsible for your actions? Likewise, failing to hold employees accountable when they commit acts of misconduct leads to cynicism and apathy among the good folks that make up the bulk of your department. They will conclude that you are unwilling or unable to do the right thing, making you ineffective or, worst, damaging to your employees. Strive to mete out disciplinary action fairly and promptly on sustained acts of misconduct. That may be difficult, but it's worthy of maximum effort on your part.

Failing to Share Information. Based on my conversations with successful executives and managers, and researching the qualities of thriving organizations, I firmly believe that sharing information often with employees and other stakeholders contributes to a trusting and productive relationship. Furthermore, disseminating information critical to those who do the work often leads to innovation and positive outcomes for the agency. Conversely, hoarding useful information, especially in difficult times, often leads to resentment, poor performance and insecurity among employees and externally in the community.

Mediocrity. Your performance is mediocre or worse, and you make little or no effort to excel in your position. How many times have you seen mediocre managers coast along in organizations that allow it to happen? Mediocrity, I propose, is perhaps the quickest way to kill the spirit of a workforce. Any chief executive or senior management team that allows it, especially in management ranks, is ineffective and worthy of dismissal. Mediocrity takes many forms, but it starts by those in positions of authority lowering the expectations and standards for employees and the organization as a whole.

Favoritism. Managers or supervisors favoring one person or another for the wrong reasons is another way to destroy the kinship spirit in police agencies quickly. There is a reason why the civil service process was created in public entities. The principle behind a meritocracy works well when those in power positions strive to make personnel decisions based on the experience, skills, and abilities of others. When you hand out assignments or projects, doing so in an impartial and legitimate manner goes a long way in establishing your credibility.

Going back on your word. Unless legitimate and unavoidable circumstances force you to change a course of action or commitment, sticking to what you've promised is one of those non-negotiable principles. If you must change course, make sure you sit down with those affected and lay out the reasons for the change and why it is, in fact, unavoidable. The key is to avoid setting expectations you know can't be fulfilled. You'd be surprised how often that happens. If you don't believe it's realistic to deliver on a promise or a course of action, don't set that course. Be honest with people and they'll understand if you try and fail.

Not admitting mistakes. Self-assessment and admitting when you're wrong is one of the easiest ways to maintain or regain the trust of your subordinates. It's a difficult thing to do, but it pays off in the end and sets the stage for building a better relationship with others. One key to that principle is learning from mistakes, so they don't repeat. Rigorously study the reasons for them and take steps to avoid them in the future. Also, do not forget to keep your thumb on the pulse of your organization, monitoring the morale index and addressing perceptions as quickly as possible, whether you think them accurate or not.

Letting your position go to your head. I can't tell you how many times I've heard folks complain about those in leadership positions becoming intoxicated with power and treating people like minions. The power granted to you by the respect and trust of subordinates easily trumps whatever formal power you have because of your position. I've seen supervisors and managers become largely ineffective because of the way they treat others in a condescending, autocratic manner. Sadly, many fail to see it and become the butt of jokes and scorn. As a legitimate leader, you must be humble and considerate of others. Ask, rather than order. Seek the opinions of others when possible and use them if appropriate. Treat people with dignity and respect and remember they hold the key to your success. Don't become so full of yourself that you start to take advantage of your position by engaging in internal and outside activities that are designed to make yourself look good or promote your private business, rather than the collective wellbeing of the organization and its members.

I've known managers who spend almost as much time pursuing outside interests or education as they did doing the business of the department in the name of "broadening one's perspective," with few if any results to show for it. I don't argue that education, training and improving your capabilities are a not a good thing. I simply feel that If you're going to pursue personal interests, they must mesh with and support the agency's goals and mission, as well as make you a better person. Ask yourself if what you're doing is primarily for the betterment of the organization or aimed at enhancing your chances for promotion or outside interests.

Appearing unable or unwilling to step forward during difficult times or while in the midst of an extraordinary incident. Building trust begins as soon as leaders assume positions of responsibility. That trust is fortified with time and under rigorous testing by members of the organization. But it is never tested as it will be during turbulent periods or when a major incident requires up-front leadership and visibility. I've seen police chiefs remain behind the scenes and allow their public information officers to address the press and the community at critical times. People and the media want to hear from their police executives in tough times. They want you to step up and provide as much information as possible, and they want you to tell them it will be OK, that you have the situation in hand. They want to see a dynamic, forthcoming individual at the helm that makes them feel better, and who gives them a sense of confidence in the management team. I've seen police leaders do just that. The difference in style is palpable.

I remember one day as I watched a sergeant in a medium-size agency step up to the podium in front of a throng of reporters and community members, to address an incident that had garnered international attention. I waited in vain for the chief to speak or at least make an appearance, to no avail. I was appalled. Conversely, I've seen police executives lead press conferences and meetings with aplomb and confidence, making me and everyone else feel good about that department.

Think of trust as a bank account that builds over time and is there when you need it. Let me give you an example. During the 1970s and 1980s, Santa Ana worked extremely hard to build and sustain its community policing program, reaching out to the community in many ways to educate and train residents and business owners. The outreach was all-encompassing and involved every single member of the department, from civilian employees to sworn officers of all ranks. The relationships we built and the policies we implemented were responsible for a precipitous decline in property crime and, more importantly, a marked increase in calls for service. We asked the community to call us anytime they had a problem they thought we could help with. So they called us. Many times, the calls had little to do with a crime or a suspicious situation, but a lot to do with community wellness and the fear of crime. Not unlike all police agencies, we were the only ones they could reach all hours of the day or night, and we were the primary link to other city services which weren't readily available in times of need. Rather than refuse to respond, we doubled-down and asked them to keep calling. Our managers often gave neighborhood leaders their cellphone numbers to maintain that critical link in times of emergencies or critical incidents. (Believe it or not, that privilege was hardly ever abused.)

We developed protocols for handling all sorts of problems that had little or nothing to do with the police, but everything to do with the trust the community had in their police agency and its ability to help no matter the reason. We printed informational materials and had officers and others carry pamphlets for public services and followed up on community requests for those services. A small army of non-sworn crime prevention officers (of whom I was one for two years early in my career) became the community's lifeline to many services and assistance it needed but didn't know how or where to find. That strategic approach eventually led to the department's modern community policing and problem-oriented policing philosophies that remain today.

The trust we built over decades was akin to a bank account, and there were many withdrawals over the years. When we needed information on a particular crime or crime series, they provided it, often leading to arrests. In difficult times, like an officer-involved shooting, we quickly and repeatedly met with the affected neighborhood and provided as much information as possible. As a result, I can only remember a few incidents that prompted demonstrations or disruptions. When we needed to build a new administration building and jail that cost over $100 million dollars and had to raise the utility user's tax to pay for it, Chief Paul Walters and City Manager David Ream reached out to the community with nightly meetings to answer questions and explain the project. They responded overwhelmingly. They taxed themselves because they trusted us. The strategy of socking away assets in that trust bank worked!

Employees develop a sense of trust in their department when they see supervisors and managers act competently and lead by example. That amorphous feeling of trust translates into loyalty and commitment to the organization and its principles, values, and goals. I remember talking to a young officer one day in our cafeteria. He had been with us for about seven years. We talked about how Santa Ana was a destination for lateral transfers from departments across the state, even the nation, and how we hardly ever had officers leave our agency unless it was to move closer to family or out of state. We had always had a stellar reputation and a salary schedule to match. I asked him why he stayed in our agency, and he told me he felt as though we all cared, collectively, for the community and the employees. He said there was a common sense of purpose and everyone pitched in to do their part. Sure, he said, there are some, as in every organization, who don't pull their weight or embarrass the department, but they are in the minority.

I asked him how much the money influenced him, and he told me he'd be lying if he said it didn't. But, he said, "that's not at the top of my list. I stay because I feel this is my family and the department cares about me and listens to my concerns." That's the kind of trust agencies must build. They can do it only over time, and it begins with a management and executive team that leads by example, is competent and trustworthy. In The Soft Edge, Karlgaard crystallizes the concept of trust in management when he says, "The very first step is understanding that trust isn't based on what the company is doing; it's based on what its leaders are doing." After all, the adage that leadership begins at the top is entirely correct.

BUILDING TRUST SIR ROBERT PEEL'S WAY

According to Wikipedia, on June 30, 1800, the authorities of Glasgow, Scotland successfully petitioned the Government to pass the Glasgow Police Act establishing the City of Glasgow Police, which was then the first professional police service in the country that differed from previous law enforcement in that it was a preventive force. The model was then implemented in other Scottish towns, which set up their police forces by individual Acts of Parliament. On September 29, 1829, the Metropolitan Police Act was passed by Parliament, allowing Sir Robert Peel, the then Home Secretary, to found the London Metropolitan Police, which was the first full-time, professional police force. The Metropolitan Police officers were often referred to as ´Bobbies´ after Sir Robert (Bobby) Peel. "They were regarded as the most efficient forerunners of a modern police force and became a model for the police forces in most countries, such as the United States, and most of the then British Empire." Wikipedia explains that Bobbies can be found in British Overseas Territories or ex-colonies such as Bermuda, Gibraltar or St Helena.

Sir Robert Peel is widely considered the Father of modern policing. He developed a set of principles—attributed by historians largely to Peel but may have been a collaboration with senior staff when the Metropolitan Police was founded—that was distributed to every new police officer in the Metropolitan Police in England starting in 1829.

The Principles, widely considered innovative at the time, retain a striking relevance to current times that should resonate with law enforcement executives everywhere and, if followed, could comprise the way forward in these turbulent times. I include them here (as listed originally, including original spelling) to illustrate why building community trust is essential to the survival of your agency, and why establishing clear community-based expectations should be the foundation of any police organization. It is uncanny how these principles are more relevant today than ever before. They seemingly show the path to improving police-community relations and elucidating the actual role of police in any community.

Sir Robert Peel's principles (as written then):

ONE: To prevent crime and disorder, as an alternative to their repression by military force and severity of legal punishment.

TWO: To recognise always that the power of the police to fulfil their functions and duties is dependent on public approval of their existence, actions and behaviour, and on their ability to secure and maintain public respect.

THREE: To recognise always that to secure and maintain the respect and approval of the public means also the securing of the willing co-operation of the public in the task of securing observance of laws.

FOUR: To recognise always that the extent to which the co-operation of the public can be secured diminishes proportionately the necessity of the use of physical force and compulsion for achieving police objectives.

FIVE: To seek and preserve public favour, not by pandering to public opinion, but by constantly demonstrating absolutely impartial service to law, in complete independence of policy, and without regard to the justice or injustice of the substance of individual laws, by ready offering of individual service and friendship to all members of the public without regard to their wealth or social standing, by ready exercise of courtesy and friendly good humour, and by ready offering of individual sacrifice in protecting and preserving life.

SIX: To use physical force only when the exercise of persuasion, advice and warning is found to be insufficient to obtain public co-operation to an extent necessary to secure observance of law or to restore order, and to use only the minimum degree of physical force which is necessary on any particular occasion for achieving a police objective.

SEVEN: To maintain at all times a relationship with the public that gives reality to the historic tradition that the police are the public and that the public are the police, the police being only members of the public who are paid to give full-time attention to duties which are incumbent on every citizen in the interests of community welfare and existence.

EIGHT: To recognise always the need for strict adherence to police-executive functions, and to refrain from even seeming to usurp the powers of the judiciary of avenging individuals or the State, and of authoritatively judging guilt and punishing the guilty.

NINE: To recognise always that the test of police efficiency is the absence of crime and disorder, and not the visible evidence of police action in dealing with them.

The point is clear: Building trust pays handsome dividends regarding effectiveness, innovation, productivity and a strategic advantage for the agency. The good will that accumulates over the years is especially critical during challenging times for an organiza- tion. Just read the papers or watch the news and you'll see many police and sheriffs' agencies struggling to maintain calm and order after an officer-involved shooting, a serious use of force, or another unfortunate incident that inflames tensions. Successful police chiefs get ahead of these events not only by using the good will banked over the years, but also by providing timely information and reaching out to stakeholders in the community.

Later in the book, I have a link to a YouTube video of a recent press conference in which the Omaha Police chief explains what occurred during a police response to an armed robbery that resulted in the deaths of the suspect as well as a sound technician from the show COPS who was riding with the officers. It's worth the time to watch. It's perhaps one of the best examples I can offer on how to handle such a press conference. (https://www.youtube.com/watch? v=pun2K52TO1s) Great police chiefs also ensure that the agency's supervisors and command staff practice these principles not only concerning the community but also in their dealings with employees in the organization. They insist on the leadership traits that build trust and ultimately produce the goodwill that allows for shared sacrifice, today more than ever before. They seemingly show the path to improving police-community relations and elucidating the role of police in any community.

DON'T IGNORE YOUR AGENCY'S MORALE

"The best morale exists when you never hear the word mentioned. When you hear a lot of talk about it, it's usually lousy." Dwight D. Eisenhower

I recently had a conversation with a seasoned officer from a relatively large agency in which he lamented the poor morale among the rank and file in his department. "It's crazy," he told me, "I have been a cop for over twenty years, and I've never seen it like this." I probed a little more, and he continued: "Sure, we've had problems before, but we've always gotten through the tough times because we knew that everyone, including management, felt we were in it together. It doesn't seem that way right now," he said. We talked for a while, and I asked more questions about the department's situation, and he gave me a litany of woes that were familiar to me, ranging from a lack of adequate staffing, experienced officers leaving for other agencies, to illogical disciplinary practices. But what caught my attention most was the officer's description of the attitude toward morale on the part of some in top management, which implied to him that it wasn't recognized as a problem. Perhaps management saw the problem but didn't actively acknowledge it, creating potentially damaging perceptions.

I had felt similarly some years back regarding an issue that some thought was hurting morale, which I failed to acknowledge. I simply felt it would go away on it's own. It didn't, and it took much more work to resolve than if I had tackled it head on much earlier. It had to do with a technology policy that I helped create and vigorously advocated, so I obviously had skin in the game. I started to hear rumblings that the rank and file weren't taking to the new policy and that it was creating bottlenecks in the flow of reports through the automated report writing system. We had been testing a new software system and had mandated it be used on certain reports. The problem was the program hadn't been thoroughly tested and a few critical bugs remained, causing delays in writing and processing of the reports. It took a couple of trusted friends in the agency to get me to see the damage the new procedures could cause the agency. When I listened to their arguments closely they made eminent sense and I scrapped the policy and started fresh—with more robust input from those who would have to carry it out. That debacle taught me an important lesson; one I remember to this day.

While it may be difficult to acknowledge a morale problem in any organization, it is essential that the management team quickly focus on the underlying issues which are ailing the agency. Then, promptly letting the employees know that management is aware of the perceptions and will work to fix the problems. More importantly, it is paramount that the chief executive displays a sense of shared sacrifice that exhorts all hands on deck, calling for the entire team to focus on the issues and begin the process of healing the damage caused by ignoring the obvious and persistent signs of a morale problem.

Sociologist Alexander Leighton defines morale as "the capacity of a group of people to pull together persistently and consistently in pursuit of a common purpose." Further, according to the widely-used corporate website mindtools.com, "Almost by definition, organizations with high morale experience higher productivity and staff engagement, they show lower employee turnover and absenteeism, and they have a happier workforce. What's more, they find it easier to attract and retain the best talent…while 'raising morale' can seem to be a nebulous goal, many of these other effects are measurable, and directly affect the bottom line." This definition accurately describes what many believe is an amorphous concept. The mindful well-being of the employees of any organization is definable not by hard-to-understand psychological terms, but by the concrete results that can be observed, measured and quantified by a competent management team.

A pernicious morale problem manifests itself in many ways, not the least of which is decreased productivity, lack of commitment to organizational goals, rumor mongering and, in some cases, covert guerrilla warfare by some who may be dubbed organizational terrorists. The latter take advantage of poor morale in the workplace to foment disorder and distrust of management, forcing you to focus your attention on them and not the entire department. I've seen them in action and have spent more than my share of energy trying to stop them.

So how do you deal with morale issues? First, keep your eyes and ears open and measure morale regularly. Take a look at the clothing company Patagonia. According to a Fortune Magazine article (Fisher, June 9, 2016), this highly profitable organization decided to improve employee retention and productivity by relentlessly measuring employee satisfaction. Dean Carter, Patagonia's head of Human Resources, "called on employee-engagement software provider High-Ground to set up a system similar to what he'd been using at Sears," where he previously worked and designed a simple system for measuring morale involving the selection of emojis as employees left work. Holding on to key talent means "companies need to capture the voice of the employee" in real time, observes Vip Sandhir, High-Ground's CEO. "A drop in morale almost always leads to a spike in turnover. But if you can spot it while it's happening, you have a chance to intervene."

That seems to be working at Patagonia, where Carter describes turnover as 'freakishly low.' The number of employees who have quit so far this month: One." I'm obviously not advocating that you ask your employees to pick a happy or sad emoticon to determine their satisfaction at work, but I am suggesting that you find ways (surveys, focus groups, etc.) to determine how satisfied your employees are with you, the management team and other organizational factors. A slow-burn of dissatisfaction can ultimately cripple your department and even cost you your job. Get ahead of it and do something about it before it becomes a more serious issue.

Second, do not ignore morale issues by assuming they are only perceptions that have no basis in fact. Whether your assumption is true is irrelevant; the perceptions become a reality for many—if not most—in the department and allowing them to fester will cause you headaches and a diminished return on your efforts to improve the situation. As I said above, tackle morale issues head on, promptly and by admitting there is a problem. Take a look at Winston Churchill's Call to Arms earlier in this book and ask for everyone's assistance and commitment to fix the problem as soon as possible. Be honest to the extent you can but remain optimistic and positive. Demand shared sacrifice from your managers and insist on leadership by example. Nothing less will work. Break down the problems into manageable parts and assign groups of employees to tackle each component under the leadership of individuals who are respected. Lastly, develop clear goals and a reasonable timeline for attaining them, keeping employees apprised of progress as well as obstacles. Above all don't ever lie or shade the truth.

There is no magic formula for dealing with low morale in any organization, but the key is dealing with it early and forcefully. Look at Bill Bratton, New York's now retired police chief who is credited as one of the most effective and enlightened police executives in the country. In every agency where he worked one of the first steps he took was to measure officer morale with an eye to increasing it. From his time as chief of the New York Transit Police to his role at the NYPD, Bratton has always sought to address morale. A caring leader readily acknowledges that he or she must deal with morale issues deftly and promptly to avoid the insidious problems that often follow inaction.

http://www.nytimes.com/1991/03/01/nyregion/for-subway-police-a-new-pride-over-duty-in-the-hole.html

10

CHALLENGE THE ESTABLISHMENT

JOHN F. KENNEDY - THE BAY OF PIGS VERSUS THE CUBAN MISSILE CRISIS

"Experts often possess more data than judgment." Colin Powell

L ike many of us, I have long admired John F. Kennedy. At the time of his death, I was barely nine-years-old growing up in Central America, so I have a sketchy recollection of that event. I remember a big to-do on television and my parents being very upset at the news, so I knew it was someone meaningful to them. Even though he never traveled much to Latin America, Kennedy was nonetheless beloved there for his charisma and his policies. When we emigrated to the United States six years later, I began to read about him and what he meant to the country. He was whip-smart and politically attuned to what was important to the common person on the street. Early on in his adult life and while his father, Joe Kennedy, was Ambassador to the United Kingdom, he made it a point to travel the world and learn about the strategic importance of many countries, meeting with political figures and laboring to understand their economic and political systems. He dove into their culture, engaging with the common man as well as the aristocracy of the time, all in an attempt to fully understand international issues and concerns.

By all accounts, Kennedy was a thoughtful, yet flawed, man.

According to the Washington Post (Sabato, November 20, 2013), "JFK had a dark side. The same internal fire that fueled his political success could also burn out of control. At 10, he noted in a letter to his father (requesting an allowance increase) that he had 'put away childish things.' He achieved that goal in many areas of life, but not in his irresponsible relationships with young, beautiful women—and even, on some occasions as president, with prostitutes. Kennedy's affairs included a White House intern, the mistress of a Chicago Mafia boss, Jackie's personal secretary and Mary Meyer, a prominent Georgetown artist. He risked his White House tenure, the welfare of his party, his policy goals and everyone he supposedly held dear." Despite his weaknesses, he was one of the most consequential presidents of the 20th century.

The international education he received during his travels would serve him well as a Senator and later as President. His untimely death cut short his full potential, so we'll never know what he was capable of accomplishing. Nevertheless, there are some lessons one can learn from historical events that undoubtedly resonate with public safety leadership everywhere. Before I talk about those lessons, I'll come clean and fully admit Jack Kennedy was a complicated individual with moral weaknesses, and frailties—multiple illnesses, including Addison's disease and severe and debilitating back problems—that threatened his effectiveness. He was in near-constant pain, including during some crises that threatened the nation. He labored through the Cuban Missile Crisis in excruciating pain yet mustered the physical and mental stamina to deal with all the issues that seemingly sprung up on a weekly basis during his presidency. While Kennedy's leadership lessons are many, I believe none are more instructive than the contrasting and diametrically different results of two incidents: The Bay of Pigs in 1961, and the Cuban Missile Crisis in 1962.

On April 17, 1961, a ragtag army of over one thousand Cuban exiles, trained and funded by the Central Intelligence Agency, landed on the Bahia de Cochinos (Bay of Pigs) on the southern coast of Cuba, with the intention of dislodging Fidel Castro and his revolutionary government from power. In three days the Cuban military defeated the exiles, killing a good number and capturing most, some of whom were later tried and executed. While the CIA-led invasion was conceived and planned by the Eisenhower administration before

Kennedy took office, he ultimately approved it after consultation with his advisors and military leadership. The Bay of Pigs proved to be a major embarrassment to the United States and President Kennedy. Some reports (http://www.faqs.org/espionage/Ba-Bl/Bay-of-Pigs.html) claim that U.S. B-26 bombers based in Nicaragua were supposed to provide support to the Cuban exiles, but missed their rendezvous because they misunderstood the different time zones.

According to historians, the intelligence was lacking, and the planning had been flawed at best. Plans for the invasion had been leaked in Miami and Castro had advance knowledge, allowing him to defeat the assault overwhelmingly. It was a devastating defeat for the CIA, the military and President Kennedy. More significantly, the military had arranged for certain contingencies, such as a U.S. Military invasion of the Island if the Cuban exiles failed in their mission, without telling the President, because they saw him as weak and indecisive.

So how does a mission so significant go so badly so quickly, and how does the President of the United States allow himself to be manipulated? Kennedy was a confident individual. He believed in his ability to make decisions, but he was a young president and had yet to develop his foreign policy chops that early in his administration. In my view, he was deferential to the military and had few if any trusted advisors. Many of those around him had been appointed by Eisenhower, his predecessor. He also relied on CIA assurances that the probability of success for the invasion plans was good and trusted them and others for information. Little did he know that the planning was faulty, the equipment mediocre and the intelligence assumptions false.

Complicating matters, Kennedy approved the plan but sought to hide the involvement of the United States in the invasion, contrary to assurances he'd made during the campaign that he'd forge an open administration that would take a centrist path. He was in the process of building a team he could trust in the midst of heavy lobbying by the CIA and others to act. Rather than delay the invasion until the plan could be vetted by those he trusted, or at minimum get fresh intelligence from the exile community in Miami, he gave approval. The results were disastrous, and he took it hard. In the aftermath, he was reluctant to commit American troops to theaters which probably required it. In turn, he developed a distrust of the CIA and the military leadership.

Contrast the Bay of Pigs with the Cuban Missile Crisis, where Kennedy was forceful, committed and well informed. Don't get me wrong, that was perhaps the most complicated and dangerous moment facing any American president in decades. In my view, even today there is no more consequential moment in history that had the life and death implications for millions of people throughout the world as did the Cuban missile crisis. It was an existential threat like no other and required thoughtful, strategic and timely action by Kennedy and America. Think of that moment, when decisions Kennedy made could spell unprecedented nuclear war and the destruction of the nation as we knew it. Kennedy had to use just the right mix of toughness yet remain engaged in the diplomatic process to diffuse the situation.

Remember that Kennedy had appeared belligerent to the USSR because of the ill-conceived and failed Bay of Pigs invasion, so the Soviets may have seen him as reckless. In fact, declassified papers show that the United States military presented Kennedy with plans for a nuclear first-strike against the Soviet Union, which he dismissed out of hand. Recovering from the perception that he was a war monger was critical. Janet Thomson from CBC News wrote a story in 2012 that quotes David Welch, co-author of The Cuban Missile Crisis: A Concise History: "It's hard for Americans, even Canadians, to understand this. We don't think of our own governments as aggressive and offensive, but other countries sometimes do...and it's a big part of the reason why the Soviets did something as dangerous and as risky as try to sneak strategic missiles into Cuba. They felt very threatened."

In the midst of the missile crisis, Kennedy surrounded himself with enough people he trusted, listened carefully and did not forestall political and diplomatic options. He knew he didn't know it all, and trusted advisors to fill the gaps, relying on still others—Bobby Kennedy for example—to vet the advice. According to some historians, he gathered those around him not to forge consensus, but to get all the information he could so he could make a decision. He knew he was the one who had to come up with the right course of action, as opposed to the Cuban missile crisis when he deferred to the CIA and the military. While he readied an aggressive military response, he arduously worked the diplomatic angle and sought to give Nikita Khrushchev a face-saving way out. Ultimately, the crisis resolved when the United States quietly promised to remove its own missiles from Turkey and never invade Cuba again. The Soviet Union removed its missiles from Cuba. No one knows how far Khrushchev was prepared to go, but what is clear is that the multi-faceted approach by Kennedy showed a determined and reasonable President that could be trusted to keep his word. More importantly, Kennedy eschewed the demand from military leaders to invade Cuba and use all military means to thwart the Russians. He knew instinctively that military force was not the answer, even though he was fully prepared to use it.

This approach presents clear lessons for law enforcement leaders. It goes to the heart of competence and the ability to analyze problems, develop alternatives and prudently implement solutions. It also goes to strategic thinking and the ability to surround oneself with a competent, honest and well-intentioned team—a team that is well rounded and chosen to complement the leader's weaknesses. A team, as Doris Goodwin would say, of Rivals. As I say elsewhere in this book, delegation is not abdication, so an effective leader learns to trust others, but retains a healthy level of skepticism, relying on one's instincts and having a go-to sounding board that one trusts implicitly to determine the best course of action. Don't get boxed in by artificial borders imposed upon you by those who profess to know more than you do, or those who claim to understand—better than you do—how police work should be done. While remaining receptive to new ideas and differing points of view, remain loyal to your own instincts and those whom you respect.

In consequential decisions, one would be wise to employ Red Teams (see section on Risk Management) to ferret out unforeseen weaknesses or contradictions in strategic or tactical plans. In the end, if you've done your homework and your team is a competent one, learn to trust your instincts and do the right thing. As Kennedy showed during his short presidency, one good man can make a tremendous difference in the lives of people. That includes presidents as well as police chiefs, sheriffs, command staff and line-level supervisors. There have been few leaders in history that soon after they assumed power were confronted with multiple major crises as did Kennedy. It is those moments that test your mettle and give you the opportunity to rise to the occasion. Someone once told me that it may be difficult to lead in good times, but much harder to do so in tough ones. If you elect to assume command in a law enforcement agency, be prepared to do both.

LINCOLN AND MCCLELLAN

The prosecution of the civil war for the Union by General George McClellan is another notable example of how leaders often defer to someone they perceive as a more experienced or able subordinate with less than ideal results. McClellan was a young commander who scored a number of victories early in the war. Lincoln, impressed with McClellan's achievements, had him take command of the Army of the Potomac in 1861. According to History.com, over the next nine months, he built a strong and dedicated army which under most accounts had an efficient command structure. "Young Napoleon" McClellan, as some called him, developed an antipathy toward Lincoln and ignored the President's suggestions and ideas on how to prosecute the war and pursue General Lee on several fronts. Lincoln deferred to McClellan for a period of time and saw the general hold back on several initiatives that could have gained ground and advanced the war efforts for the union. While McClellan remained contemptuous of Lincoln, he was unable to make the progress that would have proved him right. Phillips, in Lincoln on Leadership, writes that "McClellan began to dislike what he viewed as Lincoln's meddling...his attitude turned abrasive and disrespectful."

Again, according to History.com: "McClellan led the army down Chesapeake Bay to the James Peninsula, southeast of the Confederate capital at Richmond, Virginia. During this campaign, he exhibited the timidity and sluggishness that later doomed him. During the Seven

Days Battles, McClellan was poised near Richmond but retreated when faced with a series of attacks by Lee. McClellan always believed that he was vastly outnumbered, though he actually had the numerical advantage. He spent the rest of the summer camped on the peninsula while Lincoln began moving much of his command to General John Pope's Army of Virginia." Lincoln reluctantly once again turned to McClellan in late 1862 at Antietam, where he failed to pursue a retreating Lee, ignoring the President's messages and openly defying him. McClellan continued to snub Lincoln and others in the cabinet, further alienating himself from the President. Lincoln, convinced McClellan could not be trusted to pursue Lee as he wanted, finally removed him on November 5, 1862. McClellan would later run against Lincoln as the Democratic nominee but lost the election.

The McClellan lesson is important and arguably analogous to Kennedy and the Bay of Pigs. Doris Goodwin in Team of Rivals delves further into Lincoln's reluctance to question McClellan more forcefully when cracks in his strategy started showing up. Goodwin writes that at least one member of a congressional joint committee—created to investigate the pursuit of the war—believed that: "Lincoln did not think he had any right to know" McClellan's plans for the war as "he (Lincoln) was not a military man, and it was his duty to defer to McClellan." You get the similarities: a chief executive that was deferential to his top staff based on their experience even though he felt, or knew, the strategy wasn't working or could not work. In Lincoln's defense, he acted shortly after that and became much more involved in planning strategy for the war. The question is how many lives could have been spared had he acted sooner to question McClellan's strategy.

For a contemporary example of how challenging the establishment, including the "experts," look no further than Flint, Michigan. As you probably know, the city of Flint, operating under the leadership of an emergency manager appointed by the governor, switched its water supply from Lake Huron to the Flint River temporarily to save money. The "experts" failed to add corrosion inhibitors to prevent the old lead pipes from leaching lead into the water, leading to massive contamination of Flint's water supply. Thousands of families have been affected, including children. A number of officials have resigned after civil and criminal investigations were launched. In congressional hearings, the Governor of Michigan claimed he trusted "experts" and career bureaucrats when dealing with the crisis. The EPA administrator claimed her agency received inaccurate information from Michigan officials.

According to the New York Times (Abby Goodnough, March 18, 2016), "I kick myself every day," Mr. Snyder said repeatedly as he testified before the House Oversight and Government Reform Committee, saying his mistake was trusting employees—"career bureaucrats, " he dryly called them, and "so-called experts"—who consistently misinformed him that the city's water was safe. I wonder how difficult it would have been for the governor to dig a little deeper and ask the right questions about an issue that seemed relatively straightforward to figure out: you channel water with higher chloride concentrations through lead pipes, even though it is well known that the increased chemical concentrations will corrode the pipes and lead to contamination of the water supply.

I wanted to see how difficult it would be for a layperson to research the issue, so I did a quick Google search and within seconds came up with the answer from a document at the Centers for Disease Control published in 2013, two years before the crisis hit its stride. It's clear that higher levels of chemicals typically added to the water supply can lead to leaching from led pipes unless corrosion inhibitors chemicals are added as well. Either Governor Snyder had no one he trusted with whom to consult, or he blindly trusted the bureaucrats around him. Either way, it was a failure of leadership.

http://www.cdc.gov/fluoridation/factsheets/engineering/corrosi on.htm

My purpose in pursuing these historical and contemporary accounts—which seemingly abound—is to illustrate how deferential leaders can be with someone who may, on paper, have more experience or knowledge than them, even though their actions or proposals appear deficient or questionable. As I said earlier, delegation is not abdication, and it is imperative for leaders to look critically at the direction of projects or initiatives regardless of how experienced their advocates are. Again, this is not a question of trust, but one of vetting and troubleshooting ideas and plans that should be the norm for management teams. As long as the questioning is constructive and purposeful, no one should feel rejected or hurt if you've done your job in institutionalizing an approach of constructive dissension, as Mary Barra, the GM CEO would say. Look again at red teams for critical initiatives and even tactical operations.

Most importantly, as the leader who must make tough decisions, learn to trust your instincts. If you've done your homework and managed the process properly, you have to feel comfortable with your decision, and no one knows better where that comfort level lies than you do. Trust your instincts and work hard to determine what factors make you reasonably confident that the direction you've chosen is likely to be the right one. Just as important as the leader's critical thinking is establishing an organization-wide culture that encourages contrarian or critical views. People should be rewarded for questioning the direction of the department or any critical projects. Only when folks feel free to express concerns to management will agencies develop a culture of trust that often helps prevent failures and endless crises.

11

THINKING STRATEGICALLY

"Generally, he who occupies the field of battle first and awaits his enemy is at ease; he who comes later to the scene and rushes into the fight is weary." Sun Tzu in The Art of War.

U nderstandably so, much has been made lately about the decades-long loss of manufacturing and mining jobs in our country; jobs that used to provide middle-class livings for thousands of Americans. Politicians are quick to blame outsourcing as the only culprit, but it is undeniable that our political leadership and industry have been painfully slow to think strategically to overcome partisan divisions and create a plan that trains workers to qualify for advanced manufacturing jobs and other technology positions that often go unfilled. According to IBM's CEO, Ginni Rometty and the Department of Labor, there are over 500,000 technology jobs open in our nation today, but they go largely unfilled because companies can't find qualified workers to fill them. Think about that, hundreds of thousands of jobs that could go to American workers if they had the skills.

Why have we failed to look around the corner to see this crisis coming? Why didn't we start retraining workers that lost manufacturing jobs? In my view there is little doubt we often fail to think strategically, instead relying on government to provide unemployment and welfare to workers who lost jobs in the rust belt and elsewhere—all temporary and costly approaches that yield little and are unsustainable.

Looking at the macro level in law enforcement, are we approaching recruitment, hiring, training and community problem solving strategically, or are we simply providing short-term fixes to entrenched problems that demand a new approach? I say the latter. We are failing to work with educational institutions to develop critical thinkers and problem solvers to become police officers that have the skills to deal with the mentally ill, for example, or to look creatively at neighborhood problems that require long-term solutions. Likewise, our internal training programs pay little attention to building strategic thinking skills in our men and women in policing. The current policing crisis demands leaders who will unequivocally focus on all these issues and who will work with all private and public partners to build systems that can withstand the test of time, moving beyond tactics to strategies that build capacity to solve problems.

When you think about successful organizations, you nearly always come up with Apple, Google, Toyota and others who dominate entire sectors of the economy. What also comes to mind is their ability to think and act strategically. That is, having the foresight to have a vision, set goals to achieve it and employ effective initiatives to accomplish it. Yogi Berra once said: "If you don't know where you are going, you will wind up somewhere else." These companies chart their path by analyzing their strengths and weaknesses—as well as their competitor's—and look for opportunities to expand their business, ultimately controlling more of their respective markets. They are relentless in research and development, continually improving their services and striving for strident innovation. They are not afraid to fail while trying. They look for talented employees whose skills and abilities complement their strategic direction. They hire "A" players, vigorously shunning those who don't fit the culture of the organization or who wouldn't add strategic or tactical value to the company. The leaders in these entities—private or public—learn to see around corners, to anticipate, to figure out what they don't know, and to think strategically even when everyone around them is focusing on tactics.

Lastly, strategic organizations make the customer experience simply outstanding if not magical—read Enchantment by Guy Kawasaki; you won't regret it.

These companies pay attention to detail and relentlessly evaluate their actions to ensure support of their strategy and mission. They also create strategic plans that continuously evaluate the competition and build on the company's strengths, while at the same time admitting weaknesses and working to reduce or eliminate them. Given that public safety agencies don't generally have competitors, it is even more important to think strategically to create value for the community and the employees of the agency.

While public safety organizations don't have a profit motive, they do have the safety of their respective communities as their primary goal, and also the well-being and growth of their employees. Thus, for public safety managers and supervisors, the ability to think strategically is essential. I know what you're thinking: "as a manager or a chief of police, I don't have the luxury of picking the best and most talented, nor do I have the luxury of moving as quickly as private industry does. I am limited by the civil service process, the unions and a myriad of bureaucratic obstacles that tie my hands and make my life miserable." Look, I understand your frustration and empathize, but it's your responsibility as a leader to use the system and stretch it to its limits to accomplish the goals of your Department. The first step is to understand the process and identify its limitations thoroughly, then craft a plan to overcome them as much as possible. To do that you must be persistent and work harder than anyone else, focusing on results and staying true to the agency's vision and goals. It isn't easy, but it's the only way to be the best steward of the public's trust.

I'll give you a personal example. During the early 1990s and until the mid-2000s, law enforcement budgets were relatively stable, and the crime rate continued to fall below historical levels. Police agencies throughout the country were enjoying the rare benefit of being able to devote resources to experimental programs to further reduce crime and, more importantly, the fear of crime. Community Oriented Policing (COP) began to take hold, and lots of agencies began a paradigm shift to embrace Problem-Oriented Policing (POP) as a philosophy—looking for and treating the root causes of crime rather than its symptoms—with varying degrees of success.

I was intimately involved in my department's pivot to problem-solving and the effort to institutionalize it. We developed a comprehensive strategic plan, including redrawing district boundaries to include common neighborhood issues and natural geographic boundaries. We carefully looked at what was happening throughout the country and identified threats and opportunities. We used neighborhood and citywide data of all types, including calls for service and the opinions of residents and businesses, to qualitatively and quantitatively develop our strategic approach. We trained all our personnel using national experts and emphasized COP and POP as critical departmental initiatives.

While we had significant success in solving problems, reducing crime and making neighborhoods more livable, we didn't fully institutionalize COP and POP. By that I mean a full, unambiguous and consistent adoption of these philosophies as a way of doing business in every single nook and cranny of our agency. There were pockets where resistance was fierce, and we were only partly able to overcome it in the end. Don't get me wrong; I'm proud of what we were able to accomplish. We had done more and done it faster than the vast majority of agencies throughout the country were able to do. We had a rich history of community policing but institutionalizing these philosophies in a relatively large organization is difficult at best. Some folks simply did not believe in community policing, and others were inextricably wedded to enforcement and arrests as the sole remedy for their problems. That was the manly, sexy way to go in policing for decades, and no matter what we did a portion of the agency wouldn't play. Given civil service rules, achieving 70-80 percent compliance was a resounding success. Regardless, crime continued to decline, and we were able to capitalize on that phenomenon to strengthen services of all types.

The department's strategic thinking when crime was decreasing, and resources were more plentiful, resulted in what I call the "peace dividend in policing." I believe in the concept of regression to the mean," which, in brief, proposes that in time, statistics have a way of returning to their historical norms, or to put it simply, things tend to even out in the end. As you'll read below, Santa Ana made a strategic decision to adopt essential philosophies and devote precious resources when the peace dividend made it possible and likely to succeed and gave us the breathing room to develop strategies for when the crime rate regressed to the mean. I believe that cops can do a lot to reduce crime and fear of crime, but there are societal and economic factors about which we can do little. So crime trends happen despite the best efforts of the police. It took a while, but even though crime is still relatively low, we're seeing an increase in most major cities. Whether this evolves into a trend only time will tell.

At the same time the police department rolled out COP and POP, the City embraced the Quality movement spearheaded by W. Edwards Deming (https://www.deming.org), who had trained the Japanese to develop quality products using Statistical Process Control after World War II. His philosophy is widely credited with helping the Japanese go from making low-quality products that often broke and didn't last, to making high-quality products that catapulted them to the top in quality and efficiency. Deming's philosophy was simple: "Increasing quality would reduce expenses and increase productivity and market share".

https://en.wikipedia.org/wiki/W._Edwards_Deming

He was obviously right, and the United States would later embrace the quality movement in various forms. The City's adoption of Deming's principles was a natural and supportive step given that POP was established in the police department. The philosophies were similar in that they sought to address the root causes of problems and not merely the symptoms. They were synergistic concepts that would lead to better use of resources and higher customer (community) satisfaction. The concept was simple, yet it required a systematic change in culture and process. Rather than simply responding to calls for service and arrest violators, cops would now have to use a holistic approach, such as the SARA model, to take a deep dive into the factors and relationships that contributed to incidents, which created a problem. Similarly, the quality movement required using statistical process control methods to reduce defects at the front end of the manufacturing pipeline, rather than at the end when products were tossed or broke in the hands of the customer.

The timing was perfect. Critical community services such as code enforcement, neighborhood improvement, and building planning became tightly integrated with COP and POP, with community meetings and other efforts undertaken by representatives from all of these agencies. The holistic approach worked, and Santa Ana's neighborhoods saw not only neighborhood beautification efforts, but real gains regarding crime reduction, less fear of crime and a marked decrease in disorder. Employees began to use parallel development techniques in designing and implementing initiatives of all types, which created additional savings and efficiencies.

While in the past most departments may have acted independently to tackle a community problem, now the research and mitigation happened in close consultation with all stakeholders, inside and outside the organization. That meant that to a large extent, variables, resources, and disparate data would likely be identified and considered in tandem by all departments in the organization, reducing the need to go back and fix things when they broke. It worked, and it was possible because of strategic thinking throughout the entire organization.

STRATEGIES VERSUS TACTICS

Over the years I noticed that many leaders, including myself, at times confused tactics with strategies, blurring the focus of critical efforts in the agency. Liz Ryan (Fortune Magazine, May 2015) wrote: "One old boss of mine defined strategy as 'How to get out of the woods.' When someone asks you 'What's your company's strategy?' they are asking 'How are you going to win, to achieve your goals and do whatever you created the business to do?'" Jeremiah Owyang, the Founder of Crowd Companies Council (www.web-strategies.com, 2013), published a chart that showcases the critical differences between the two, which you can find here:

http://www.web-strategist.com/blog/2013/01/14/the-difference-between-strategy-and-tactics/

With regard to strategies and tactics, he believes that: "These two must work in tandem, without it your organization cannot efficiently achieve goals. If you have strategy without tactics you have big thinkers and no action. If you have tactics without strategy, you have disorder. To quote my former business partner, Lora Cecere, she reminds me that organizations need big wings (strategic thinking) and feet (capability to achieve)." The key for police executives is to ensure that all supervisors and managers understand the difference and broaden their thinking regarding how it all applies to their responsibilities. Too often we think tactically and fail to look for the "big wings" to guide and focus our approach. As is nearly always the case in law enforcement, the front-line troops know how to do the job, what they sometimes don't know is how their day-to-day work relates to the company's vision, strategies, and goals. It is management's job to make sure the troops can make that connection and vividly understand where the organization is headed.

Shortly after taking over the Field Operations Bureau of the Santa Ana Police Department in 2002, I reviewed available data to see where we were regarding community policing, field activity and in general anything that would tell me how well our troops and supervisors understood and embraced the department's mission and goals. I spoke with officers to get feedback as to how they viewed their jobs as they related to the bigger goals of community and traffic safety, crime and disorder, and productivity in general. I found that while many officers were engaged in problem-solving and the statistics showed a busy department, there were pockets where there was a disconnect between these activities and the overall goals of the agency. This disconnect included a mindset among some that because they were senior officers they didn't need to go the extra mile, take that extra step to become fully engaged with the community. A few even felt that seniority gave them a license to coast and not worry about productivity.

I also noted that more than a few of our younger officers didn't know the relationship between a good field interview (FI) and the subsequent identification of a suspect in a burglary or robbery. Given the uneven understanding of our mission, values, strategies, and tactics, I set out to attend roll calls, team meetings and work with officers in the field to reinforce our core beliefs in community policing and the direct relationship of good police work to less crime, reduced fear of crime and community wellness. I wrote a memorandum to everyone in the bureau that sought to tie it together in a practical manner, setting expectations early, communicating clearly frequently, and following up to ensure the strategies of the agency had a chance to succeed.

Strategic planning doesn't have to be difficult. Start by assessing your Department's (or your division, section, etc.) strengths and weaknesses, and using internal talent to help you build a strong strategic plan. Don't hesitate to bring in outside help if necessary to begin the strategic planning process. Depending on the size of your agency, the complexity of its problems and the resources available to you, you can develop a rudimentary strategic plan as described below. The key is not to be afraid to try despite obstacles and challenges. If you don't think strategically you will forever react to issues and problems rather than face them proactively, armed with a plan and data that will make your chances for success that much better.

The primary goal of any such effort is to develop a vision for the agency or division, along with the values that will guide you along the way. You'll then identify the broad strategic initiatives that will help you bring the vision to reality, along with the goals that will make up your plan, the objectives necessary to achieve those goals, and then the specific tasks that must be carried out to achieve each objective. Finally, you'll need to assign individuals to lead and manage each initiative, as well as those that will perform the tasks to accomplish the objectives for each goal.

There is one commonly used tool I will urge you to use in the strategic planning process: the SWOT analysis. This tool allows you to methodically analyze the Strengths, Weaknesses, Opportunities, and Threats that pertain to your organization. It is an essential component of the strategic planning process and is not complicated at all. While the model is often used in the private sector, it has application to public safety agencies and other government entities. SWOT means:

STRENGTHS - Assets and positive characteristics of the organization (or initiative if using it on a project) that will play a favorable role in the outcome. This part of the analysis will help you identify your agency's strengths so they can be enhanced and used appropriately in accomplishing objectives.

WEAKNESSES - The components of your agency that can be classified as weak or as liabilities in terms of the role they would play in accomplishing objectives and may place the agency at a disadvantage as it relates to opposing forces or conditions.

OPPORTUNITIES - The conditions that exist, mostly externally but can be internal as well, that the agency can leverage to its advantage, again relative to the objectives. Identifying opportunities is a critical part of the strategic planning process and must be repeated as the goals and objectives change.

THREATS - The present or emerging threats in the public safety environment that could create problems or work against the achievement of goals and objectives. These threats can be regulatory, financial, political, etc.

Whether conducting a SWOT analysis as a major part of a comprehensive strategic plan or in the process of planning a major project or initiative, it is an effective way to make sure you are indeed looking at all factors that can have an impact on that plan or initiative. When working on significant initiatives, don't skimp on any part of it as it will help you achieve desired outcomes. Remember that SWOT helps you collect the information and depict it graphically if you wish, but you still have to do the analysis. According to leader-shipthoughts.com, the following tips can help:

- Use a SWOT analysis to distinguish between where you are now and where you wish to be
- Be realistic about your strengths and weaknesses
- Be specific — only include key points and issues
- Relate strengths and weaknesses to critical success factors
- Always aim to state strengths and weaknesses in competitive terms
- Rank points in order of importance
- Finally, keep it brief — never more than a page

This and other strategic planning tools can be scaled up or down to fit your needs, so don't hesitate to use them for smaller projects or initiatives. On projects of lesser complexity keep the principles in mind to help you look at the issues more creatively. The bottom line is that thinking strategically at any level is the only way to remain relevant and well-positioned to help your organization transcend limitations and achieve meaningful results.

Finally, consider the Pareto Principle. Thinking strategically entails looking for ways to use your resources most effectively and efficiently, reducing the chances that you'll focus on the wrong objective or initiative. Pareto's Principle, also known as the 80/20 rule, basically states that you should focus your efforts on the 20% of activities that will get you 80% of the results that are likely to truly make a difference in your organization. For example, according to Paula

Rooney (October 3, 2002), Microsoft noted that by fixing the top 20% of the most-reported [software] bugs, 80% of the related errors and crashes in a given system would be eliminated.

The Pareto Principle is useful in many ways, and those of you in law enforcement will agree that a small fraction of the population will cause you most of the problems. According to Wikipedia, "several criminology studies have found that 80% of crimes are committed by 20% of criminals. This statistic is used to support both stop-and-frisk policies and broken windows policing, as catching those criminals committing minor crimes will likely net many criminals wanted for (or who would normally commit) larger ones." By focusing your efforts strategically on the subset of any issue that creates most of the problems you'll free your creative thinkers to gather the data, perform the analysis and determine what or whom that subset truly is. You can learn more about the Pareto Principle and how it's used in variety of industries go here:

https://en.wikipedia.org/wiki/Pareto_principle.

The point I'm trying to make is that in these times of lean budgets and dwindling support from the public, law enforcement professionals do not have the luxury of scattering resources in the hopes that some of the problems will get fixed. You've got to focus every officer, civilian employee, and technology like a laser beam on the areas or methods that are likely to have the biggest payoff. That also means that you must relentlessly employ analytical techniques that sift through noise and meaningless data to determine what's useful. More and more agencies are using crime analysis software to help them focus their resources. If you lack the resources to purchase or develop such systems, consider reaching out to a college or university to collaborate on a project that can result in a regional approach to shared crime analysis tools.

Many universities will provide interns or volunteers to help you with data analysis or software development. It doesn't have to be an expensive undertaking if you look around and reach out to community partners or businesses that have a stake in the outcome. There are some government and private organizations that award grants to recipients to develop analytical tools that can then be used by many agencies. Looking for these tools in places like The National Institute of Justice or the National Criminal Justice Reference Center is relatively simple and often yields results.

http://www.nij.gov/Pages/welcome.aspx

https://www.ncjrs.gov

The last point I'll make about strategic thinking relates to the chapter on management. Regardless of how brilliant your strategy, or how innovative your approach, none of it will see the finish line if you don't have excellent management skills and a good management team to back you up. Having a competent team that knows how to manage projects and initiatives is essential. I've seen good-intentioned and viable projects fail before they had a chance to make a difference because of poor management. While deriding good managers as inferior to "thought leaders" might be a popular sport, I never saw a project fully implemented by those who thought of it. It takes a cohesive team that includes technocrats and skilled managers to achieve success, so focus a lot of your efforts on making sure your department has one that can shepherd strategic initiatives through the administrative and implementation processes of your agency. Without one your great ideas will be left on the cutting floor languishing because having great managers was not at the top of the list for your agency.

SYSTEMS AND CONCURRENT
DEVELOPMENT

I can see your eyes glazing over...but follow me on this for a moment...I promise it will all make sense! If you look at great organizations, whether in public safety or the private sector, one of the key factors that contribute to their success is having systems in place to handle their day-to-day work and related activities. You'd be surprised at the number of police agencies that run their operations without a systematic approach. What I mean by "systems" is a set of programs or processes that interact with each other to produce a product or achieve results. In this case, the product is the delivery of your agency's internal and external services.

I like to describe these systems as the programmatic infrastructure that holds your agency together, akin to the human body's skeletal system. It's important to think of your interrelated programs as a system because they depend on each other and any ongoing or new initiatives must take into account the needs and capabilities of the other. Don't forget that this concept also includes the overarching organization, such as city or county government. Getting them all to work together, in sync and providing mutual support is arguably the most important management objective in your agency.

In all my years managing different divisions and programs in our agency I saw us do well in many areas, but we also made mistakes by not taking the systems view when developing new programs or initiatives. In other words, we failed to concurrently develop these initiatives, which then had to go back to the drawing board, often with additional costs or problems attached. Concurrent development is a term usually associated with engineering or software development but has application to public safety management. It simply means that when crafting any significant initiative or program, one needs to look at all of the interrelated system parts that may be affected to make sure the finished product reflects the needs and capabilities of the whole. This process is critical if you want to save time and money, as well as come up with the best solutions to problems or needs.

For example, if you are developing a new deployment schedule for your patrol officers, you need to meet with your fiscal unit (both your agency's unit as well as the that of the overarching organization, such as the city or county finance department), to work through how the new schedule will affect payroll and any computer programs. That includes programs that use algorithms to apply union contract provisions. If you are working on a crime problem and developing a solution, working with your jail, city or county attorney and other affected units is a must to avoid potential pitfalls and delays. When drafting or modifying policies or procedures, making sure you work with all stakeholders is critical.

I'm spending some time on what may seem like the obvious to you because I have worked with a good number of police professionals throughout the nation that failed to use the concurrent development process and wasted valuable time, effort and money. Concurrent development helps ensure that those involved can provide input and feel as though they are part of a team where everyone works together. To make sure you don't omit important players, make a simple swim lane chart to illustrate project activities and responsibilities and where each intersects into the realm of another department or organizational unit. You can use a software program such as Visio to make the charting process easy, or you can draw your own. Remember that form follows function, so don't make it too difficult. Google the term Swim Lane diagram, and you'll see many good resources.

Individual supervisors and managers can easily use a concurrent development process for everything they do that involves working with others on significant projects. Even if the agency does not have a general order dealing with the process, by looking independently at how others are affected, and working with them on the issues from the start, individuals improve the chances for success and a product that works. If your agency does not have one, I encourage you to institute a concurrent development process that will be used by all when working on significant projects, programs or policies. If possible, document that process in a general order or training bulletin and require your staff to at least do an initial assessment to see if it should be used. Define the process as clearly as possible and don't make it cumbersome. It can be as simple as a list of steps, including a scanning process to determine who the stakeholders are and a matrix to determine what impact, if any, the project will have on each of them.

BEST PRACTICES

"Good poets borrow, great poets steal!" Unknown, but often attributed to T.S. Eliot or Picasso

Great managers don't steal ideas, but they use benchmarks! Benchmarking is simply the task of identifying similar or like agencies (successful ones preferably!) and looking at their practices and results to see how they compare to the standard practices in the industry, and your own department's in particular. Benchmarking and the pursuit of best practices is of critical importance to public safety agencies looking to achieve extraordinary results. This quest often leads to saved time and effort by learning from other projects and initiatives without having to all of the research and development work. The public sector, unlike private industry, often shares strategies, tactics, and processes freely, but look for the data that tells you how successful those strategies have been. For example, the United States Conference of Mayors publishes an annual Best Practices guide that can be searched online. You can search by keyword or select a Best Practice Collection. Nothing beats a site visit though, or a thorough review of published results.

http://www.usmayors.org/bestpractices/

Another useful resource is the National Criminal Justice Reference Service (NCJRS), which can be found here:

https://www.ncjrs.gov/. This website is useful because it includes information on grants, training and other criminal justice areas all in one search engine. If you're looking for evidence-based ratings and reviews of crime reduction and prevention programs, the Office of Justice Programs Crime Solutions website may be your answer (It can be found at link below). I like their approach, which gives you some reliability in looking for proven solutions. For the program to be listed, Crime Solutions reviews all available literature and research and thoroughly vets the program. While not perfect, it's a good resource.

http://www.crimesolutions.gov/default.aspx.

Get used to benchmarking in terms of strategic initiatives, community policing, problem-solving and any other task of importance. Don't forget to look at the results that other entities produce and compare them to the standard, including statistics and metrics that tend to show capabilities and effectiveness beyond your own. Investigative units often do benchmarking analysis to see how their case clearance rates compare to other agencies, and how those rates are accomplished. It's nice to find out you're doing things well, but it's much more useful to find another organization doing better than you are and learning from them.

DISRUPTORS

"You have to seed internal disruptors. You need sources of internal disruption. They don't guarantee your survival, but you have got to try." Anand Mahindra

Above I've told you how important it is to relentlessly pursue best practices whenever possible to make use of previous research and strategies that have proven successful or hold promise. Now let's talk about the "disruptors." According to Josh Linkner from Forbes Magazine (http://www.forbes.com/sites/joshlinkner/2012/03/26/your-new-job-disruptor/), "Disruptors challenge assumptions. They shake the status quo. They are curious and creative. They adapt and improvise. Disruptors push the boundaries and love shattering conventional wisdom. They'd rather forge new ground than blindly salute the flag of the past. Disruptors squirm at phrases such as 'we've always done it that way,' 'that's just the way things are done here,' and 'if it ain't broke, don't fix it.' They know that speed and innovation now trump rigidity and conformity. They know that discovering fresh solutions and unleashing new ideas are top priority for both success and sustainability."

Every organization has disruptors, but not many public safety agencies look for and nurture these folks in a systematic way. More than likely the model that permeates many police departments is from the familiar and somewhat outdated paramilitary environment, where following orders and adhering to departmental policies is sometimes valued more than the innovative spirit that is required to reach beyond the fringes and fundamentally change the way you do business. The problems and challenges in modern policing require not only adherence to policy and constitutional requirements, but also the relentless pursuit of new methods, strategies, tactics and, most important, philosophies that are rooted in community policing.

In other words, many paramilitary organizations reward conformity, but that's changing. Enlightened police leaders everywhere have quietly but doggedly started to change the cultures of their respective organizations, so that "outside the envelope" thinking is encouraged, nurtured and rewarded. Many of them have built into their performance evaluation systems the ability to partially rate their officers on their ability to analyze community or organizational problems and come up with strategies to address them. The test, in many cases, is not whether the strategy worked—although it helps— but whether the officer used critical thinking and attempted to impact the problem with innovative and resourceful methods. Some agencies are even building problem-solving performance standards into their performance evaluation systems, clearly setting the tone for institutionalizing such thinking throughout the agency.

The trends are on the right trajectory, but there are headwinds. The economic downturn created a severe shortage of personnel for many departments, and in some cases, problem-solving took a back seat to the primary task of answering calls for service. While researching this book I spoke to police managers from several agencies, and they universally lamented the lack of resources for community policing strategies. Nonetheless, many, if not most, remain committed to giving their employees the time and the tools to look at policing differently, and hopefully developing worthy strategies to reduce fear of crime or solve long-standing community problems.

So how do you encourage innovation in your agency? I make the following recommendations based on my experience and the examples I saw while traveling the country and meeting police and sheriff personnel from small and large agencies.

Hire the best and brightest if you can but look for that spark that questions the status quo. Not easy to do, I admit, and dwindling candidate pools make it even harder. But it can be done if you design, and market, police jobs to challenge the intellect and intuition of applicants. It isn't enough anymore to offer good pay and benefits, as those you most want for your department will likely go where they are challenged to make a difference. Design your recruitment outreach to look in non-traditional candidate pools, including folks that may have liberal art aptitudes. Studies have found that those who possess the soft skills can make great problem solvers that look at issues from different perspectives. Many businesses—especially the ones that serve or deal with the public as a primary function—are finding out that the liberal arts often provide the critical thinking skills and the ability to deal with people. In a recent article on Fast Company, Elizabeth Segran wrote:

"While the tech boom is partly responsible for the spike in students majoring in science, technology, engineering, and math, many tech CEOs still believe employees trained in the liberal arts add value to their companies. In 2010, Steve Jobs famously mused that for technology to be truly brilliant, it must be coupled with artistry. 'It's in Apple's DNA that technology alone is not enough,' he said. 'It's technology married with liberal arts, married with the humanities, that yields the results that make our hearts sing." Other tech CEOs across the country agree that liberal arts training—with its emphasis on creativity and critical thinking—is vital to the success of their business.

Challenge your employees to solve persistent and entrenched community problems and give them the time and tools to do it. Train them to look beyond appearances and the obvious, and to look deep into circumstances that can and often are related, and insist that they test their assumptions. Looking at the SARA model or its hybrids as a starting point can encourage folks to think differently about community and organizational issues.

Design and implement training programs that exercise the critical thinking skills of your employees by not only providing theoretical models but practical application as well. Don't forget that educational institutions and private industry will often allow your employees to tag along or attend their own seminars and participate in their own initiatives.

Keep in mind that while finding and nurturing these outliers is difficult enough, creating a workplace that challenges them and provides the right incentives can be as, or more, difficult. Paramilitary organizations have long encouraged conformity with rules and regulations; in other words, staying within the box. The challenge for police agencies is to find ways to entice employees to, as the wildly successful 1984 marketing campaign for the Apple Macintosh urged: "Think Different." Look for ways to loosen the reigns and create opportunities for breakout performance and innovation. I know, it's hard to do when we all have reams of policy manuals and directives, but the fundamental need to retool our strategies and tactics to solve critical problems and regain community trust should prompt you to find a path forward. Start out slow and test ideas and methods; create small teams to find new ways of doing business; develop a set of incentives that transcends money but appeals to self-actualization; and reward those who dare try, even if they fail.

The bottom line is that contemporary public safety agencies must look at issues and problems differently than they have in the past. In order to solve complex community problems with limited budgets and personnel, cops need to think creatively and more deeply about all manner of challenges and obstacles. We all know that society has largely abdicated its responsibility for many ailments that cops have to deal with every day, such as mental illness, poverty, the lack of parental models and drug addiction. So rather than lament that state of affairs, police agencies must lead to set the tone and provide the impetus for new and more practical approaches.

IMPLEMENT AND MANAGE CHANGE
THOUGHTFULLY

Let me tell you about another period in my early tenure as the Captain of the Field Operations Bureau that I remember vividly. I remember it so well because in that particular instance I failed to manage change effectively. In fact, I wasted valuable time and community goodwill by forging ahead with half-baked ideas that I should have vetted much more thoroughly. I learned from that failure and vowed not to repeat it.

In the early 1970s, the Santa Ana Police Department had implemented an innovative and widespread community-organizing program partly through the use of federal and state grants. It was Called Community Oriented Policing (COP). I was part of that effort, which was aimed at training community members to properly secure their homes, implement Neighborhood Watch and learn to protect themselves from criminals while partnering with the police. Let's call it an early and seminal version of its modern cousin, Community Policing. It was widely successful, and property crime rates decreased steadily during the next few years. Santa Ana became the talk of the nation, won a slew of awards and a feature in the 60 Minutes program on CBS. This was a tremendous effort that brought all resources to bear on the fight against crime and disorder in the city. COP was first and foremost the quintessential strategy summoning all hands on deck, inspiring the community to achieve the level of wellness it sought by working with cops and others who believed that it could be done. It started with a police chief, Raymond C. Davis, who had a vision and was willing to think big to accomplish it.

Fast-forward to 2002 when I took over the Field Operations Bureau and began to look at how we were doing business and what needed to change. I had noticed for years that the COP program appeared tired and suffered from a lack of participation from the Latino community, which grew steadily to make up nearly seventy-five percent of all residents. Many of these folks worked two or three jobs to put food on the table and found little time to get involved in civic activities. As a result, the old guard dominated COP meetings and activities, which had been entrenched in the program for decades.

Don't get me wrong; these were great people who loved the city and devoted countless hours to make it better. But, there was only so much they could do without the active participation of all neighborhoods. The changes in the community over the previous twenty years were many and fundamentally altered the ability of community organizations to mobilize the residents and businesses. The city went from a predominantly white and middle-class population to a mostly Latino and labor-driven one. The dynamics changed, and we had to change with them or risk losing what we worked so hard to build over decades.

I began talking to community members and others internally to get a feel for what could be done to reinvigorate and modernize the program, which was vital to our policing efforts. I used the services of a consultant to assist us in reaching out to external and internal stakeholders, held several meetings and then drafted a strategic plan. Part of that plan included, based largely on my perceptions and ideas, a recommendation that to encourage fresh thinking the COP board's role and name needed to change. Rather than the COP Board, I wanted to call it the Police Advisory Board. Rather than bore you with all the details and dynamics, suffice it to say that I forged ahead with the changes. I was not prepared for the backlash that ensued. Keep in mind that politically the COP Board's members were deeply invested in the program and cherished the COP brand. After all, the program had been in existence for over thirty years, and the executive board members enjoyed their leadership role.

My ideas were not to be, and although I fought valiantly, I eventually recognized defeat, but not before I wasted six months and set back my efforts to improve how we did business by a year or more. I had good intentions, but I failed to heed the concerns of some community members who were entrenched in the program as it had been for decades, and who had enough political influence to scuttle any change they thought inappropriate. I also let my own biases and perceptions override what others advocated. I didn't listen well enough.

I tell you that story because it illustrates a glaring mistake by a new police captain. When you're going to change an established program that is politically and operationally vital to the organization, make sure you do your homework. Make sure you engage all stakeholders and listen to them. If necessary, use Red Teams (more about them later) to broaden your perspective and test your assumptions. That was a critical lesson early on in my role as captain, and one that stayed with me until I retired. It was, as I liked to say, that scar on my rear end that I'd feel and remember when I was about to make decisions on important matters.

The experience taught me to think through the implications of change and how to properly evaluate dissent and other ideas. Our strategic plan was partly successful, but my failure with the COP program changes remains a powerful lesson. Don't ever shy away from effecting change in your organization. Just do it smartly. Strive to understand human behavior, resistance to change and the value of intrinsic incentives for those to whom change may seem scary or uncomfortable. Consult with all stakeholders early in the process and have trusted advisors try and poke holes in your plan—see Red Teams below. Lastly, develop reasonable and obtainable objectives and a realistic timeline for critical checkpoints and milestone review. Don't make the same mistake I made: Listen well and take a retrospective look at what you're trying to accomplish and how you plan to do it.

EAT YOUR OWN DOG FOOD

In technology, the term "eating your own dog food" is used to denote companies that use their own products or software internally, which theoretically signifies that their products are good enough even for themselves, or they want to test their products to make sure they work as well as expected. Ultimately, any public safety agency executive must ask this question: Would I like to live in a community where the police or sheriff's department operated as we do; used the tactics and strategies that we do; and treated its residents and employees as we do? Personally, managers must also ask whether their leadership and behavior would be acceptable to their families or friends.

This self-examination often takes place in great organizations and leads to innovative, effective strategies to serve your customers externally and internally. I know, the use of the word "customers" to describe those whom police agencies serve is frowned upon by many because some of them are the crooks. Get over it! The truth is that those you arrest or investigate are indeed your customers, and if you want to keep your community safe and your agency out of trouble, learn to look at them that way. You don't need to coddle them, but you do need to treat them with dignity and respect while providing professional services.

Eating your own dog food, so to speak, is of paramount importance to any organization that serves the public. It's like IBM, for example, using the database and server management programs they create to manage their own data. What would it say about the quality and utility of their products if they did otherwise, say using Oracle products? Same goes for Microsoft, which according to Cult of Mac, once banned employees from using Macs as work machines, and wouldn't allow employees to purchase Macs with company funds. What does that say about the company when you have to ban your employees from using a competitor's products?

Whenever you institute a new program, community initiative or internal process, ask yourself whether you would employ similar measures in the town in which you live or expect your family to be similarly treated. It's always good to personalize whatever you plan to do in your community or department. Would you want your family or friends to experience those services or tactics? Eat your own dog food, and you'll act in the best interests of your workplace.

USING DATA, METRICS AND TECHNOLOGY

"In God we trust, all others must bring data." W. Edwards Deming

I recently saw an interesting debate on television regarding the relevance of the Gross Domestic Product (GDP) to a nation like the United States, which is long passed its industrialization period and is now primarily a service and technology economy. The argument against laying all your eggs in the GDP basket is that it measures production of goods and services, but not how those metrics relate to improving the lives, wellness, and happiness of the population. While GDP might be a good measure for developing countries, the argument goes, it's not wholly relevant to the American economy. Humor me on my economic policy detour so I can make a point: Law enforcement organizations, and their respective cities and counties, tend to measure variables such as arrests, traffic collisions, the crime rate and officer/deputy productivity to determine how well the agency is doing.

I call these "hard" metrics, which are valuable and useful in many respects. In this book I strongly advocate for audits and data collection, but many agencies fail to capture the data that may mean the most in reconciling the output—the organization's work—and the result, which includes the opinions, thoughts, and perceptions of the community. I call these the "soft" metrics. One needs to focus on both to understand what's going on in the field and the organization. Look at companies like General Electric, IBM, Apple and others, and you'll see the systematic collection of hard and soft data to help shape strategic decisions about customers, products, employee wellness and market opportunities. They don't sacrifice one set of data for another, nor do they underestimate the critical nature of the less edgy information that's harder to obtain, such as opinions, views, and feelings of customers and employees.

A report (Porter, Stern, Social Progress Index for 2014) recently concluded that the United States has fallen behind a slew of countries regarding social progress, including some from the third world. The report's authors define social progress as: "The Capacity of a society to meet the basic human needs of its citizens, establish the building blocks that allow citizens and communities to enhance and sustain the quality of their lives, and create the conditions for all individuals to reach their full potential." From that definition, they articulate the three dimensions of the social progress index framework: basic human needs, foundations of wellbeing and, finally, opportunity.

The report can easily be found on the Internet and will open your eyes, which I can see glazing over wondering why I'm even citing the findings of this report to a bunch of cops and public safety professionals. But many progressive law enforcement leaders believe that one essential responsibility of their agencies is advocating for and supporting social progress in the community. My point is that a public safety agency doesn't exist in a vacuum, and it must complement and support the mission of the overarching organization, whether that's a state, county or city. Agencies that see themselves as islands, rather than parts of the whole, are destined to underperform in many categories.

I witnessed firsthand how some police supervisors and managers scoffed at the idea that police departments should concern themselves with issues other than responding to calls for service, making arrests, or issuing traffic citations. That attitude can easily permeate throughout the agency, setting up an "us versus them" culture that has repeatedly proven harmful to the community as well as the organization. Working within your capabilities—and leveraging the capacity of others—in innovative and traditional ways, can be a force multiplier. Make it your mission to look for ways in which your agency can support the efforts of your city or county to increase the social progress and well-being of your community. This integration with, and support of, the overarching organization's purpose and goals needs to be part of your strategic plan to gain the trust and respect of the community. For law enforcement agencies community policing principles define the way forward.

So what metrics help you determine the state of your community beyond arrests, citations, and reports? They include: Do your residents feel safe? Is the fear of crime—whether you believe it justified or not—so pervasive as to blunt the hard work of your department? How does your community feel about their municipal services and, in particular, their police or sheriff's department? To what extent does the public have access to your jurisdiction's strategic planning process, and what input are they afforded to help shape policy? Do residents have easy access, online or through the local library, to educational materials, referral networks or counseling services? Do neighborhoods in your city or county appear neglected and, at times, lawless? These questions and others are seldom asked by agencies, although they have the potential to reveal the most useful insight into the state of their population. A community can have a relatively low crime rate without having a feeling of security or normalcy due to visible signs of disorder, rampant petty crime or a discourteous and uncaring police force. Furthermore, residents may feel isolated and powerless to change their living conditions when they lack access to services and information, and a police department is ideally situated to provide critical information about resources and opportunities since it is often the first to interact with community members.

Look for signs that your community isn't thriving or even minimally surviving based on the three dimensions in the social progress index. There are relatively inexpensive things your agency can do to help, but it takes commitment and looking beyond the obvious.

In a recent blog, the Rand Corporation described how its researchers are attempting to redefine what it means for cities to thrive and measure success. They call it the Wellbeing Index. Similar in nature to the social progress index, Rand's project involves the City of Santa Monica, which is seeking to "improve not just the safety and comfort of their residents, but also their happiness, their satisfaction with life—their wellbeing." In a community, the law enforcement agency is a fundamental component in that effort given that its employees are in constant contact with residents and businesses. The partnership requires a commitment not only to community policing, but also to reaching beyond traditional goals and objectives focused on arrests, the crime rate, and other numerical indicators, by trying to influence change in the soft metrics as well.

http://www.rand.org/blog/rand-review/2016/03/a-chance-to-thrive.html

As the Rand blog explains: "That word, wellbeing, is meant to go beyond just moment-to-moment happiness. Project leaders use it to describe the health of a community, its sense of connectedness and ability to reach full potential—happiness as a state of being, not just an emotion." Lofty ideals and foreign to most police planning and strategic tools, until now. More agencies are trying to redefine their purpose. They know that reaching beyond traditional metrics to gauge the result of their efforts is not only a good thing, but it is also a necessary thing.

This new and broad way of looking at your purpose and role in the community provides better job satisfaction, and it's good for business. The more contented the community becomes, the more it is apt to cooperate with the cops in traditional enforcement and problem-solving. The more they know their neighbors because of your efforts, the less likely they are to look the other way when they see something suspicious, and the more likely they are to become real partners in community policing. None of this is easy or a panacea, but it is the future. To read more about RAND's Wellbeing Index and find resources go here:

http://www.rand.org/search.html?query=wellbeing%20index

Knowing how the community feels and thinks should be an ongoing, systematic and top-driven effort. The chief executive and senior staff should lead the push to understand the community's priorities, fears, and desires, using that information as well as hard crime data to shape policy and programs. I always tell folks to personalize theory and think of their own circumstances to get an idea of how police initiatives affect others, so ask yourself when the last time was that your police department or municipal government asked for your opinion; on anything? I bet the answer is never or so infrequently as to render your input useless or dated. Why is that? I can tell you from experience that law enforcement in general has a tendency to think it knows best how to determine priorities and strategies.

I started out my career as a crime prevention officer, interacting with the community daily and building bridges to reduce crime, so initially, I felt it was critical to know our residents' perceptions and priorities. As time went on and I rose in rank, I began to think I knew better because I'd known their thinking early on. I started to neglect the strategic importance of community surveys, focus groups and other ways to take its pulse. I began to think that occasional neighborhood meetings and even less frequent town halls were enough. They aren't! To be sure, you'll know how the "regulars" feel; those that attend every meeting and often give you an earful. But you'll assume you know how the other ninety-nine percent feel. You won't! You'd be well served to consciously seek to understand the needs of the community, refreshing the data as frequently as possible.

Keep in mind that to varying extents, Santa Ana PD was a community-oriented department from the early 1970s. We were recognized nationally for being on the cutting edge of crime fighting as well as community outreach. We devoted tremendous resources to education, target hardening and block-by-block neighborhood organization to improve the lives of our residents. All of the chiefs I worked for in thirty years had that commitment to understanding and acting on the community's priorities and concerns. However, the execution of those strategies, as informed as they were, largely depended on personalities and competencies at the management level. Some managers made community policing a priority, while others felt that enforcement and directed crime suppression should take precedence. Some were able to skillfully blend the two to get results; both in numbers and in community satisfaction.

We often achieved satisfying results, but there were times when we struggled and didn't seize opportunities to take policing to a whole new level. To be fair, budgetary constraints played a significant role when our performance was underwhelming, but politics and the diversity in the execution of our vision and strategies also affected how we all approached our work. In any agency, the chief executive has the unique responsibility to focus all strategies and tactics to support the goals of the organization, even in the face of management resistance. Only the chief or the sheriff can apply the pressure or dangle the carrots to keep managers and supervisors on the same page.

The agencies that excel at understanding the underpinnings of the community's priorities get their input in a variety of ways, some of which can include formal surveys crafted by academics; focus groups that include a realistic sample of the community's economic, social, racial and geographic makeup. And don't forget the population on which you spend untold resources: arrestees and inmates. Whether you like it or not, they are your customers, so to speak. Learning to mine their thoughts and information through one-on-one or group methods can yield invaluable information as to how your department is doing.

If you run a jail, develop a program to periodically and randomly interview inmates to determine their perception of how they were treated or the opportunities they were given. Look, I know how difficult this can be, and I'll grant you that most managers and supervisors are loath to ask a crook for his opinion of the treatment he's received while in your custody. But if you're truly committed to improving how your organization does business, you'll need to be aware of how your systems are working or how your employees do their job when you aren't looking. Depending upon your agency's strategic planning cycle, you should conduct these activities as often as once a year or more frequently if appropriate. The formal research may then be supplemented by the agency's regularly scheduled community meetings and interactions with groups of all types. The picture your management team can paint when you combine these methods is often much clearer and useful to the development of strategies and programs.

The other side of this coin is the tactical data collection that populates your regular statistical reports and helps you shape your strategies. I won't spend a lot of time on this, but it is important to remember that, as Drucker wrote, "what's measured improves." As a young lieutenant, I had an interesting experience one day in the early 1990s. I was seated at my desk looking at a panoply of charts and graphs I'd pinned to the wall. They depicted activity in my district that included robberies, burglaries, assaults and officer-initiated activity such as field interviews, arrests, and citations. As I always did,

I had been trying to identify hotspots to encourage competition among officers to seek out these areas and increase our activity and presence there. I'd often meet with district sergeants and officers to talk about the stats.

As I studied them, a more senior manager walked in, looked at me and shook his head and said: "One day you'll figure out that these stats don't matter, it's community policing and problem-solving that matter. I wouldn't even have them up there." We discussed it for a bit and I understood what he was trying to say, but he walked out of my office before I'd had a chance to engage him further. He was right in that you can't look at this data in isolation, but the way he said it left me wanting a more thorough discussion. He wasn't alone in his thinking and even some academics agreed that arrest statistics aren't always meaningful. I disagreed. I felt it was essential to look at all indicators to get a complete picture to design good policing strategies. I wouldn't dismiss one set of statistics for another, but rather use them all in crafting our strategy. That's what the problem-solving SARA model (Scanning, Analysis, Response, and Assessment) advocated by Herman Goldstein called for. Besides, not every crime pattern or activity calls for a full-blown SARA model approach. Many times, focusing attention on patterns through crime analysis and spurring competition among the troops to lock up serial criminals is all you need in a particular situation. It's called good police work.

THE ALLURE OF BIG DATA

A more recent approach enabled by technology is the mining of big data—that is the exploitation of massive amounts of data from many sources to help solve crimes and pinpoint the most frequent offenders or the probability that a particular crime will occur in a geographic location during a specific time window. Doug Wyllie, Chief Editor at policeone.com, defines Big Data as the "ability to mine huge amounts of data from diverse sources, understand the accuracy and reliability of that data, and then make critical analyses—and sometimes difficult decisions—based on what you've learned." In Kansa City, the police department is using a computer model to analyze large amounts of data to identify those most likely to commit violent crimes or to be the likely victim of one. According to a New York Times article (Eligon, Williams, September 24, 2015), "the strategy, known as predictive policing, combines elements of traditional policing, like increased attention to crime 'hot spots' and close monitoring of recent parolees. But it often also uses other data, including information about friendships, social media activity, and drug use, to identify 'hot people' and aid the authorities in forecasting crime."

In essence, this is link analysis on steroids. While controversial because of its use of large data sets, the model shows promise and makes eminent sense. In cities like Chicago, the police department there has identified some offenders who are disproportionately responsible for a good chunk of violent crime in the city. Other jurisdictions have validated the approach, although much needs to be done to develop algorithms that are relatively accurate, and which give the police actionable and lawful intelligence. The point is over the last decade we've had a technology leap that could allow us to be more efficient in using precious resources. The more a supervisor or manager knows about technology and its relationship to policing, the more likely he or she is to support the agency's efforts.

Take Predpol, a software program that collects three data points per incident from a department's Records Management System—crime type, crime location and crime date/time—and applies algorithms and creates predictions for where and when crimes are most likely to occur. According to Predpol, it pinpoints small areas of 500x500 feet that are generated each day at the beginning of each shift. Officers can then act on the information by concentrating patrols in those locations to ostensibly prevent crime or make arrests for crimes in progress. This type of technology has been adopted by at least twenty large agencies, including the Los Angeles Police Department. The chiefs of police argue that they aren't going to get more money or more officers, so using predictive technology is essential as a force multiplier to help them focus scarce resources in the right areas and against the right suspects.

While the value and efficacy of big data predictive policing has yet to be fully settled, the American Statistical Association (ASA) concluded that predictive policing technology, especially ETAS (epidemic-type aftershock sequence) models, "predict 1.4–2.2 times as much crime compared to a dedicated crime analyst using existing criminal intelligence and hotspot mapping practice. Police patrols using ETAS forecasts led to an average 7.4% reduction in crime volume as a function of patrol time, whereas patrols based upon analyst predictions showed no significant effect. Dynamic police patrol in response to ETAS crime forecasts can disrupt opportunities for crime and lead to real crime reductions." In a recent Washington Post article (Jouvenal, November 17, 2016), UCLA Professor Jeff Brantingham defined ETAS: "Just as earthquakes happen along fault lines, Brantingham explained research has shown crime is often generated by structures in the environment, like a high school, mall parking lot or bar. Additional crimes tend to follow the initial event near in time and space, like an aftershock." There is no question that the technology has promise despite concerns by civil libertarians, some of whom argue that focusing police patrols on high-crime areas based on predictive policing technology may predispose officers to think that everyone in those areas could be a criminal, thus coloring their approach.

https://www.washingtonpost.com/local/public-safety/police-are-using-software-to-predict-crime-is-it-a-holy-grail-or-biased-against-minorities/2016/11/17/525a6649-0472-440a-aae1-b283aa8e5de8_story.html?wpisrc=nl_rainbow-nonsub

http://amstat.tandfonline.com/doi/abs/10.1080/01621459.2015.1077710?journalCode=uasa20

The utility of Big Data may also aid police agencies in building trust with the community by giving us the ability to gather and thoroughly analyze nationwide data on officer-involved shootings, uses of force and, potentially, racial profiling. There isn't a current standard for reporting, collecting and analyzing data from law enforcement agencies throughout the country. The old Uniform Crime Reporting (UCR) and the more-recent National Incident-Based Reporting System (NIBRS) do an adequate job of collecting basic incident data from departmental records management systems, but the quantity and quality of the information is not good enough to make judgments in terms of what factors contributed to specific police shootings or incidents involving excessive use of force. For example, factors such as the tactics that preceded an officer-involved shooting; the number of previous shootings in which the officer was involved; his level of experience; or the number of sustained complaints related to excessive force—all data that can be collected from hundreds of departments without identifying an individual, for the purpose of nationwide analysis. There is no question that mandated reporting of this type, coupled with cutting-edge analytical tools and Big Data solutions, can lead to better analysis of these incidents and much more informed policy making at all levels.

Take a look at a white paper on Big Data and law enforcement from ctolabs.com: https://core.ac.uk/download/pdf/30678906.pdf

Some top-tier software companies offer Big Data solutions for law enforcement, including the following:

SAS:

http://www.sas.com/en_us/insights/articles/risk-fraud/big-data-analytics-for-law-enforcement.html

Microsoft:

https://enterprise.microsoft.com/en-us/industries/government/fighting-crime-with-big-data-analytics/

IBM:

https://www-01.ibm.com/software/ebusiness/jstart/downloads/bd_LawEnforcement.pdf

While predictive policing computer models are excellent tools, don't forget about the good old human intelligence sources departments have in their field officers and detectives. Their knowledge has traditionally remained in silos; but some departments have mastered the art of drawing on these resources, melding them and coming up with timely information that can be applied in conjunction with computerized models. The key is harnessing human knowledge in your agency and marrying it to whatever technology you have, so nothing is missed, and the data has a chance to be validated.

Mining the data is one thing, but your cops and detectives can tell you why, for example, a particular gang is feuding with another and what's likely to happen next. Based on their experience they can refine the analysis, making it more timely and relevant. For example, a patrol cop who knows the players may be able to tell you about recent assaults or graffiti in his area that makes retaliation likely. The computer models can analyze spatial and geographic crime data that might predict the time and place of the retaliation, thus giving you a better chance of acting in time to prevent the crime. Don't forget: it is people and machines that work together, and don't exclude either for the other.

There is another aspect to relevant metrics that you'd be wise to consider: the administrative data that can help you diagnose and treat organizational symptoms of dysfunction and waste. Law enforcement agencies tend to focus analysis on data related to crime but often neglect data related to metrics such as sick leave use, workers compensation claims, and grievances filed. I believe that the latter are much more indicative of organizational wellness, including morale, than surveys or anecdotal observations can ever be. Smart departments make it a point to track these metrics on a regular basis and monitor any fluctuations in real time via management dashboards or monthly tripwire reports. The data, devoid of names or other identifying information, is a critical indicator worthy of regular review.

Let me give you an example that illustrates my point. A police department developed a software program that provides managers with a desktop dashboard which allows for real-time reports to be generated at the push of a button, as well as queries over time. The data not only includes crime-based information and calls for service but also data related to all administrative functions. In aggregate terms, the system can tell you how much sick leave is used on a monthly basis and in which divisions it's being used. It can tell you how many workers' compensation claims are filed and for what reasons.

An increase in the number of events in these and other areas allows management to analyze trends to design corrective programs or actions when problems begin to crop up, or it can help you diagnose a morale problem department-wide or in specific divisions of your department. A sudden and significant increase in sick leave used in the patrol bureau, for example, can give you early warning to scheduling problems or systemic issues affecting your agency. Use of force reports is another metric that, taken as a whole, can be indicative of serious problems with training or morale. Don't neglect the collection and real-time analyses of administrative data, as it can be a great tool to help fix organizational problems early.

SENTIMENT ANALYSIS AND SOCIAL MEDIA TOOLS

In 2015 IBM, the technology behemoth, began an effort to revamp its performance review system to better reflect the company's workforce, values, and culture. To obtain employee feedback, according to an article in the Atlantic (Wadell, September 29, 2016 - link below), IBM's "HR department set up a forum to solicit feedback on proposals for a new system and received tens of thousands of responses. Instead of assigning a team of analysts to comb through the reams of feedback, IBM set Social Pulse loose on the data." Social Pulse is IBM's version of sentiment analysis software, which uses algorithms to analyze vast amounts of data to determine how employees and others feel about their organization or an initiative in the development process. During that process, IBM determined that employees were unhappy that their performances were being graded on a curve, and the company quickly scrapped that system.

According to the Atlantic, Sadat Shami, IBM's manager for Center for Engagement & Social Analytics, said: "Without our social listening capabilities, we wouldn't have been able to surface that in time to make that decision. What traditionally happens in a month or two, we did in real-time." Sentiment analysis is a relatively new tool, but it is being used by many corporations and government agencies to mine and interpret data quickly to determine how customers, employees and other stakeholders feel about a host of issues. It is also in the early stages of testing in anti-terrorism efforts. I believe the technology has untapped potential for law enforcement in many respects, but in particular to determine how the community and the workforce feel about the department and specific projects or initiatives.

To read the story in the Atlantic go here:

http://www.theatlantic.com/technology/archive/2016/09/the-algorithms-that-tell-bosses-how-employees-feel/502064/

Think about the potential of this technology to help manage the culture of the organization and improve strategic planning efforts. A number of companies are or have developed similar software for sale to others, and I can foresee attractively priced off-the-shelf packages that can be modified for police agencies to use in a variety of ways, including crime analysis. In particular, I believe there is direct application for employee and community surveys that have somewhat open-ended questions that can be mined for critical sentiment and data in near-real time. What is often unwieldy work because of the reams of data and answers can become manageable and useful.

Think about what that means for community policing and assessing how your employees feel about important issues, thus allowing you to develop policies and initiatives that have been assessed by stakeholders at all levels. According to an abstract from Sentiment Analysis and Opinion Mining (Bing Liu, the University of Illinois at Chicago), "Sentiment analysis systems are being applied in almost every business and social domain because opinions are central to almost all human activities and are key influencers of our behaviors. Our beliefs and perceptions of reality, and the choices we make, are largely conditioned on how others see and evaluate the world. For this reason, when we need to make a decision we often seek out the opinions of others. This is true not only for individuals but also for organizations."

While this technology is emerging, there is no doubt it has the potential to help police executives and managers make critical decisions about their own employees and especially their communities. IBM's example above is but one of many—Twitter and Intel use it as well—where algorithms have been used to relatively quickly determine the sentiments and opinions of large groups of people. For example, human resources managers who analyze emotions in employee surveys can use the information to determine how internal programs and working conditions are faring in the minds of their employees to improve retention and operations. The strategic value is undeniable. The more reliable data analysis becomes, the more your organization can act and react to internal and field conditions. For an excellent story by the Wall Street Journal on Sentiment analysis software, go here:

http://www.wsj.com/articles/how-do-employees-really-feel-about-their-companies-1444788408

The other promising area in which sentiment analysis can help is in social media analytics. In an article at policemag.com, (Social Media Analytics in Law Enforcement, September 2012) Lieutenant Dale Peet from the Michigan State Police aptly describes how these tools can be used: "Sentiment analysis technology now exists that can analyze thousands of posts around certain keywords, such as "anti-government" and return negative sentiment scores to identify individuals who pose real threats. Perhaps someone is blowing off steam in making a threat. By analyzing information over time, officials can narrow the 100,000 posts that may be classified as critical to the 5,000 that could pose real threats and need further analysis. They can assess whether sentiment is changing over a period of time, either reducing or increasing the concerns of law enforcement about a serious threat." Social media sites provide not only intelligence about gang recruitment and activities, but the data can be more extensively analyzed to determine the mood in certain communities or groups, allowing for proactive monitoring and intervention. At the very least, it provides law enforcement with leads and information that can be pursued through further analysis and investigation. For example, agencies that have a cruising problem can leverage social media analytics to look for patterns and keywords that will help identify potential cruising locations and even planned violence at these events.

TECHNOLOGY AND THE COMPETENT
MANAGER

Whether you like it or not, technology is a major engine that fuels efficiency and effectiveness in the 21st-century law enforcement organization. Today's supervisors and managers must be what I call techno-literate. That is, they must understand the technological tools that help make the agency successful but make them individually productive as well. Technology tools in law enforcement include those online that make research easy, such as Google and online databases, but software that allows for the spatial and temporal (time and space) analysis of crime and crime data is particularly helpful. Geographic Information Systems (GIS) are an excellent example of technologies with which managers and supervisors must be familiar. GIS depicts data based on layers that include locations, times and frequencies that can be manipulated and mined to produce management reports. It's the basis for "hot spot" analysis and predictive policing. These are critical tools that are used by police organizations and must be championed by leaders. An excellent primer on GIS for law enforcement can be found here:

http://www.esri.com/library/bestpractices/law-enforcement.pdf

The other tools that are indispensable for competent managers are productivity programs such as email, word processors, spreadsheets and organizational tools such as Microsoft Outlook and others. Add to that the current batch of tablets and smart cell phones, and you've got a set of devices that makes management and monitoring of systems, programs, and operations much easier and. Thus, ensuring that all supervisors and managers possess technological skills is no longer optional for police organizations. Many have incorporated technology requirements into the hiring and promotional process, and some now conduct all testing via computer. It seems as though nowadays there is an app for just about everything. Whether rooted in Apple's iOS or Google's Android operating systems for portable devices, apps now exist that makes the public safety job easier and often more productive.

Whether it's a community member sending you real-time video or information, or an officer taking a report on an iPad, many agencies are adopting this technology and working with tech companies to solve problems. There are always individuals in organizations that are tech savvy or have degrees in computer science. Find them and groom them to help your agency without having to pay thousands of dollars to consultants. By all means, make sure they are competent and give them clear goals, but use them and help them develop their talents. If you doubt that being techno-literate is essential for today's police leader, you don't need to look further than your own agency to see what the impact has been of failed or subpar technology projects.

In my thirty years on the job, I saw a good number of projects mismanaged to the point where they had to be scrapped, abandoned or implemented without key features. To be sure, technology projects are risky and difficult to manage even under the best of circumstances but having a manager and supervisor that has a basic understanding of enterprise technology in-charge of the project can improve the odds of success. That includes knowing what you don't know and getting outside expert help to complement internal talent.

When I served as a police lieutenant, I managed the agency's computer services division for several years. The chief of police asked me to take over the task because he knew I enjoyed technology and had managed critical projects in the past. At the same time, I was in charge of the human resources and fiscal divisions for an organization of seven hundred employees. This was around the time when we were building a new police facility and jail and needed to ensure the new buildings had the best technology infrastructure we could afford, including fiber optics and state-of-the-art networking platforms. When I began to get familiar with the task ahead, I quickly realized that my technology knowledge was woefully inadequate for the task. The stakes were tremendous, and I recognized I had to quickly expand my understanding of these issues.

I remember going to the bookstore and buying several texts on enterprise computing, client/server architecture and networking systems. I spent several days reviewing what was perhaps the driest material I'd ever read as my eyes glazed over terms and concepts boring enough to put a caffeine addict to sleep. I had done the same when I took over Human Resources, so I could at least be conversant in the areas of workers compensation, labor law, and equal employment issues. I always tried to recognize what I didn't know, so I immersed myself in reading materials and experiences that brought my knowledge in certain areas to a level that allowed me to manage the critical projects and initiatives in my area of responsibility. I didn't become an expert, but I knew the basics and understood the issues.

Thankfully, when I managed computer services I had a technically-adept sergeant and an experienced and knowledgeable systems administrator to help guide the IT staff during this period. I brought in an outside consulting firm, and we developed a technology strategic plan to shepherd the difficult projects ahead. I soon saw that nearly everyone with whom I spoke had a different idea as to what platforms, models, and consultants we should use. Internally, staff was divided, but when they threw out technical terms and other suggestions, I was able to ask relevant questions and make sound recommendations to our agency's senior management team. Eventually, Santa Ana brought the projects to completion and opened a 450-bed jail with a functioning jail management system that we developed in nine months.

Those were stressful times that required a close working relationship with the City IT staff and the vendors with whom we partnered. Police organizations need to train and encourage their employees to become technically savvy and to apply those skills in finding lasting solutions to community and departmental problems. That means looking for those employees that have a technical aptitude and encouraging them to expand it to help the agency solve problems. It also means ensuring that everyone has a minimum level of competency with computers, software, crime analysis and productivity tools. That includes training your personnel to understand trend data, hot spot analysis, geospatial tools, and the relationship between cause and effect so they can engage in problem-solving more effectively. The earlier you start building that skill set, the more productive and satisfied members of your organization will be.

13

DEVELOPING YOUR PERSONAL AND PROFESSIONAL SKILL SET

"The only source of knowledge is experience" — *Albert Einstein*

Without a doubt, experience in one's craft or chosen profession is the one quality that is indispensable in any supervisor or manager. Without it, you will falter more often than you should, have to work harder to get the respect of the troops, and will make your path to competent leadership more tortuous. Believe me, broad experience—along with integrity and humility —will make it easier for you to obtain willing compliance and hard work from those you seek to influence. The road to competence in your public safety career started with your life experiences and formal education. It continued when you attended the police academy (or whatever basic training program your organization uses) and continues until you retire. In the middle of that long journey, you'll have opportunities to attend more training, work different assignments and get involved in projects that will broaden your experience base.

Those that aspire to leadership positions seek out these opportunities early in their careers and make the most of them. If you look at the resumes of most successful candidates for promotion, you'll find that most didn't pigeonhole themselves by staying in one assignment for years and years. They obtained as much knowledge and experience as possible and, after they mastered that job, tried to move on to other and more challenging roles. I don't mean you must hop assignments frequently, but you should look for opportunities that build on the experience you already have. When you do, you become more versatile and valuable to the organization, allowing you to consider problems from different perspectives.

The U.S. Army Field Manual on Leader Development identifies six transition points that illustrate the growing need for development of skills and attributes as the assignments become more complex and demanding. The first level is at entry points into the service, which require the soldier to understand organizational frameworks and provide direct leadership to others. From there the continuum includes leading at the organizational level, leading functions within the Army, and commanding larger bodies such as battalions, where leaders establish and communicate a vision and work to accomplish it through others. The last two include leading large organizations such as a brigade and an entire enterprise that includes frequent and complex interactions with outside entities. The Army recognizes that regardless of emerging technologies and other force multipliers, there is nothing like a well-educated, trained and experienced individual to accomplish the mission, so they start that development process early.

I remember my thought process when I was a gang investigator in the early 1980s. I loved the job. There were only four of us back then, and in an agency of 400 cops, it was viewed as an elite assignment. I had been there several years when I decided that I needed to get some formal supervisory experience, so I applied for the field corporal position when it came up. In Santa Ana, the corporal designation is just below sergeant and is viewed as an entry-level, full-fledged supervisory position. When I interviewed for the job, one of the board members asked me why I wanted to leave one of the best details in the department. I explained my reasoning, and they seemed satisfied. In the end, I was ranked high on the list and went back to the field as a corporal. The members of the interview panel later told me that my wanting to leave a great job for shift work in the field weighed heavily in my favor.

Don't be afraid to leave a good assignment if the move will give you more varied experience and improve your chances for promotion. If a promotion isn't one of your objectives, that's OK, I've known plenty of great cops who wanted to do front-line work, whether in the field pushing a black and white around, an administrative post or in the detective bureau. There is nothing wrong with not wanting to promote as long as you find fulfillment in the work you do and give it all you have. Some, however, stay in these assignments because they want to coast or don't want a challenge. They are comfortable and find no incentive to stretch and look for other opportunities. Sometimes it is these folks that grow tired of the job and cease to find the fulfillment they once had in our profession. The problem is that some of them will stagnate and hold on to valuable positions that should go to those that need the experience and are willing to work hard. That's precisely why some departments have mandatory rotation—perhaps every five years—to keep folks fresh and motivated in their assignments. To mitigate the loss of experienced individuals, some favor having a few anchor positions in every division to maintain institutional knowledge and train new personnel.

I believe in well-rounded supervisors and managers. There is no substitute for hands-on experience, from which you can grow and make the best decisions. Think about problems or situations you've confronted that prompted you to harken back to lessons learned in the past. You probably made a better decision or solved the problem more readily than if you had no reference point to use. Remember that we often learn from our own mistakes or those of others. All things being equal, leaders who are well-rounded and have done the jobs they now supervise or manage tend to have more credibility, and their subordinates usually accord them more respect than those who've never done the job. It doesn't mean that you can't lead a crew of folks if you haven't done their job. You can, and many do. It simply makes a difference to have walked in their shoes.

I remember situation that arose when I was a captain in Patrol. The Crisis Negotiations Team (CNT) was operating with an antiquated throw-phone system that we had purchased in the 1980s, when I belonged to the team. Although the unit could still help us accomplish the task—albeit with significant difficulties—the equipment lacked modern technology, like a camera and a recording device. When the CNT supervisor asked that we purchase a new unit, he didn't have to do too much talking to convince me it was needed. I remembered the days we had to make use of it and wished we had a better system. I'd been there, done that, so it was an easy decision. I can give you multiple examples of how my experience helped me make better decisions more quickly.

On other occasions it was my investigative experience that helped me see through deficient or incomplete administrative or criminal investigations. I had done both many times, so when reading or supervising one, I was able to point out issues or concerns, or simply guide others to do a better job. The fact that I had those specific experiences gave me the gravitas to constructively provide feedback and get good results. My point is simple: Get as much experience as you can in as many fields as possible. I realize that in many public safety agencies promotional opportunities do not abound, so it's easy for me to tell you to get those experiences, but probably much more difficult for you to do it. Despite that reality, you can make the most of even the briefest of projects, temporary assignments, committees and other opportunities that contribute to your value to the department.

I suggest you volunteer to take on challenging problems, both in the community and administratively within your agency. Take college courses that emphasize your area of interest and the needs of the department or seek training opportunities in areas in which you have little or no experience; and, look for a mentor—someone who has been successful in the organization—who is willing to share experiences, pitfalls and the path to success. There are so many ways to broaden your base and show your agency your potential. Take advantage of them and document them carefully, as they'll come in handy come promotional time—but more about that later.

Police executives nowadays don't have the luxury of waiting many years to develop good supervisors and managers. Given the number of cops on the job when compared to previous decades, and the relatively young age of officers in the field, agencies must develop more compact, intense and effective training programs. One way to do that is to design boot camps for supervisors and managers in a continuum of time relative to their experience. For example, you could build in two weeks of training at the time of promotion that could be front loaded with basic leadership principles, as well as the technical and procedural elements of the job, including those specific to your agency and jurisdiction. Six months or a year later, when they've had an opportunity to experience the nuances of the job, you might build in another week of intense, practical application training that explores in detail the soft skills needed to lead people and develop trust. The training could include role-playing and tabletop exercises that help the participant understand the critical elements of leadership by example, competence, and integrity. You can design periodic refresher programs to reinforce and renew these principles, just like mandated continuing professional training is required in many states to maintain certification. The soft skills are, by implication, essential to the well-being of the organization. They can be perishable, so regular training and practice are just as important as the hard skills required for the job.

SPEAKING AND WRITING CLEARLY AND PERSUASIVELY

"Of all the talents bestowed upon men, none is so precious as the gift of oratory. He who enjoys it wields a power more durable than that of a great king. He is an independent force in the world." Sir Winston Churchill

There are few skills more important to public safety supervisors and managers than the ability to speak and write clearly, succinctly and persuasively. The reports, memoranda, and papers you will author throughout your career will be scrutinized by criminal and civil courts, juries, lawyers, and others. Your assessment of situations and conditions, as well as any recommendations or proposals you make, will depend largely on how much credibility your spoken and written work carries. So, how you speak, the words you use and your relative facility with the English language will present you in a certain light to others. Even e-mails can influence how others perceive you, perhaps even more than reports or memoranda.

How you express yourself in writing is often your first opportunity to make a strong first impression as a leader, an opportunity for which you rarely get a second chance. Frequently, the person or reader forms these perceptions subconsciously, but they are created nonetheless. Think about how you view colleagues and others when they speak haltingly, or when you read a document they've written that is riddled with grammatical or spelling errors. Unless you know the redeeming qualities in that person, you probably won't trust his/her assessment or conclusions. Sadly, your perceptions will likely extend to other areas in the individual's performance. As the Los Angeles Times recently pointed out, consistently bad grammar and other mistakes tend to show a lack of attention to detail, which engenders distrust of whatever you say or write.

The ability to speak clearly and persuasively is even more important for managers and executives, as it allows them to use language skills for a higher cause: to rally members of the organization behind a common, worthy cause. You must be able to orally paint vivid and worthy pictures that not only inform but also inspire others to want to follow you as a leader. In an article at Inc.com, Hitendra Wadhwa, founder of the Institute for Personal Leadership, writes about Abraham Lincoln's ample oratory skills and how, early on, he cultivated them and used them to tear down opponents and perceived enemies. Later, he came to realize how making a point through stories and anecdotes was immensely effective in getting things done. He used rhetoric so effectively that few think he could have achieved his legacy without it. Wadhwa writes:

"Lincoln was undoubtedly one of the greatest communicators among all American presidents. His words—as a public speaker, writer, debater, humorist, and conversationalist—continue to entertain, educate, and inspire us to this day. With only one year of formal schooling, Lincoln consciously cultivated this mastery of language and expression. As a young boy he would practice public speaking by gathering his friends together and stepping onto a stump to address them. During his days as a lawyer in Illinois, Lincoln would frequently meet up in the evening with friends at a tavern where they would engage in story-telling contests. And he gleaned valuable lessons in rhetoric by diligently studying Shakespeare."

To read the entire article go here:
http://www.inc.com/hitendra-wadhwa/lessons-in-leadership-how-abraham-lincoln-became-americas-greatest-president.html

Bennis and Nanus emphasize that for vision and purpose to be crystallized and fulfilled, they must be communicated in a way that inspires others to action and captures the imagination. "The management of meaning, mastery of communication, is inseparable from effective leadership." (Leaders, 1997, page 31.) Writing and speaking are twins in the leadership skills continuum. Many believe that the quality of our education system creates applicants for public safety positions who are often ill-prepared and lack basic speaking or writing skills. As I mentioned earlier in this book, I had the privilege of directing recruitment and testing efforts, as well as the supervision of police academy recruits. I saw first-hand how a deficit in these skills kept many from getting these jobs to start or affected their career advancement if they made it.

There are some police officers, sheriff deputies and firefighters (private industry isn't immune by the way) who can't write at the level required to perform the duties of their positions or to write in a way that accurately informs the reader. Sure, some get by with rudimentary abilities to communicate and write a simple report, but at what cost to their credibility in the justice system and their careers? I realize I may be painting a bleak picture, and to be sure there are many good writers in public safety, but I believe that these skills can be improved if agencies act soon after they hire recruits.

In fact, some agencies act even before someone has decided to apply for a job, by pointing them to remedial courses at the high school and college level that they have advocated for and helped create. Once the person is employed, the agency's management team must design and implement remedial measures, even to the point of contracting with local institutions to deliver remedial courses on site. Be careful in your implementation, however, as those who must take the courses may feel singled out and embarrassed. The earlier in an individual's career that they attend these classes the better, as they will feel as though the agency cares about them and the improvement efforts are a part of the organization's culture. Management may find it easier (remember that dreaded path of least resistance) and less controversial to simply look the other way, hoping the person will, on their own, improve with time and experience. It doesn't work that way. Unless these problems are identified and corrected early on, they only become more engrained and difficult to confront as someone's career progresses. The ideal time for this work is upon hiring and during someone's probationary period. Following these efforts, develop ongoing mentoring programs to foster the continued improvement of your employees' skills in these areas.

You get my point. If you want to be a respected supervisor or manager, you must hone your speaking and writing skills. Here are my recommendations for agency executives and for individuals who want to command credibility through their speaking and writing:

Assess your writing abilities early and honestly. I realize that one's ego and self-image may preclude an honest assessment of one's skills and abilities, but it is essential to look at oneself as others do and make the necessary improvements, incrementally or otherwise. Have several people you trust and respect give you feedback on your oral communications, as well as look at and criticize your written product. To get a fresh perspective, don't be afraid to include those not involved in police work.

Based on the feedback you receive, draft a remediation plan that may include formal courses, self-improvement books and practical exercises that can, once again, be reviewed by those you respect. Many short books can show you how to write clearly for work. There are also clubs and organizations (Toastmasters International at http://www.toastmasters.org is one example) that can be invaluable in giving you a platform to test and improve your public speaking.

Write to communicate, not impress. Over the years I've read many papers and memoranda that are replete with long and uncommon words that were meant to impress the reader, rather than communicate a clear point. Use simpler words when possible and write with the intention of being understood by your audience. Resist the urge to fill the page or e-mail with long words with which you hope to show how intelligent or gifted you are. Instead, write simply and clearly.

Master the art of outlining. You'd be surprised how many people fail to properly outline a document or paper and miss key points, or submit disjointed and confusing material. Simple outlining (includes mind-mapping for complex tasks) can help you organize your thoughts and explore areas you may otherwise overlook. Outlining and mind-mapping will help you be better prepared when speaking to groups and individuals as well.

Use all the tools available to you to make your writing stronger and clearer. Word processors not only provide contextual spelling and grammar checkers, but most have focus screens that allow you to view your document without distraction. Learn to use these tools effectively, but don't rely on them exclusively. Allowing a word processor to correct grammar or spelling won't give you the understanding of how persuasive documents should be drafted.

Look at the writings of others whom you believe are good communicators and pick out the style elements that make out his/her products a standout. Emulate what works and avoid what doesn't.

Push your organization to establish a mentoring program to help individuals overcome deficiencies and become better supervisors and managers, which may include mock interviews and presentations. This step is one of the most effective ways to assist the members of your organization to become better prepared to assume leadership positions, but executives often ignore it.

Finally, learn to tell stories. Abraham Lincoln was a master storyteller who learned early on that the wisdom imparted by a story well told was more likely to be understood and used. He once said: "They say I tell a great many stories. I reckon I do; but I have learned from long experience that plain people, take them as they run, are more easily influenced through the medium of a broad and humorous illustration than in any other way..." Lincoln was a man who understood human nature and enjoyed hashing out real life tales and examples of that humanity. Research has found that when leaders find a way to communicate with real examples and anecdotes they become more human and trusted in the eyes of their subordinates. Most importantly, learn to orally paint vivid pictures of your vision and exhort from others the support you need to accomplish organizational goals.

14

MENTORING AND SUCCESSION PLANNING - THE BUILDING BLOCKS OF COMPETENCE

"The single most exciting thing you encounter in government is competence, because it's so rare."

—*Daniel Patrick Moynihan*

I remember fondly the friends and colleagues that played a mentoring role for me during the early years of my law enforcement career. Back then mentoring was largely thought of as an informal role by seasoned veterans, and it carried with it little or no encouragement from the organization. Nonetheless, there were those who spent time with me and helped me develop principles of leadership, hard work and a penchant for doing the right thing. These folks were informal leaders of the agency and commanded respect, not because of their rank, but because they cared and could be trusted. I learned an awful lot from slicked-sleeved patrol officers who had the literal and figurative scars to prove their bonafides. These folks thrived on police work and had fun doing it, bringing you along with their zest for police work and the knowledge and experience needed to make it successful as well as fun. To a certain extent, this informal mentoring system worked well at the time, but think what it could have accomplished if it had been formalized and delivered systematically.

Take, for example, the senior officer who took me aside early in my career and gave me examples of those in the Department that had been fired, demoted or prosecuted for misconduct on and off duty. He took the time not only to tell me what they'd done, but what had led to it and how I needed to be aware of the pitfalls and temptations in the job. He also emphasized the necessity to work hard and earn your pay, not simply to let dispatchers tell you where to go and what to do. Some of the advice took the form of well-intentioned crude analogies and metaphors, but they worked and got my attention. His help continued even after I'd left the field for an investigative assignment, and up to the last few years before I retired. It used to be that law enforcement had hundreds of applicants for each vacancy, and many more tested for promotion in the first seven years of their careers.

That era is long gone, and now agencies all across the country struggle to fill positions with qualified applicants. After Ferguson, it is even harder to attract good candidates, and positions often go unfilled for months or even years. Making the position attractive again must be a high priority for police chiefs and sheriffs everywhere. And by extension, departments must work hard to use the precious human resources it has, taking care to mentor and groom good cops to become supervisors and managers. Informal, seat-of-the-pants efforts are no longer appropriate or effective. Enlightened agencies develop and institutionalize formal mentoring programs and give it the resources necessary to succeed.

Many of today's modern public safety agencies still largely rely on those informal mentoring systems that worked well in a different era and can still yield some results today, but which can't adequately deal with the complexities of modern law enforcement organizations and the demands placed upon them by the public and the courts. Mentoring programs must be recognized, formalized and deployed with mentors who exhibit the highest standards of the agency. These individuals must be trained and recognized with incentives to help form the behaviors and patterns that will drive organizational effectiveness for decades to come.

A police officer's career should be about growth and development; that slow, incremental exposure to new and more challenging situations that ultimately help forge a leader's mettle. Departments have to create these opportunities for their employees, in particular for those that show the potential to add value to the organization and the people in it. Great law enforcement agencies don't become that good by accident; they think strategically, plan relentlessly and seize opportunities with a vengeance.

In addition to sound succession planning and the gap analysis I described early in this chapter, a formal mentoring program can help executives respond to changing economic, societal and legal trends. Without these strategic initiatives, police agencies often find themselves in a position of weakness when experienced workers retire, or external pressures require the department to rely even more on personnel who lack the necessary skills. I saw it to some extent in my department and in many others with which I dealt. It doesn't have to be that way, but it does require a management team and chief executive that are willing to spend the time, effort and capital to design a sound system, even in times of short-staffing and economic pressures. It is precisely because of these conditions that mentoring is necessary. Look at it as a strategic investment in the future of your organization; one that has the potential to make it better and reduce the number of blind corners you must navigate.

Don't be afraid to include some of your senior executives as mentors not only for staff officers but also for new officers and supervisors. If you want to integrate your agency with the overarching organization (the City or County), reach out to them and get respected non-police supervisors and managers as mentors for your team members. I found that when police employees understand the structure, concerns, and objectives of the entire entity, including how police actions impact their operations, they tend to make better decisions and collaborate more for better results. This axiom applies in particular when it comes to problem-solving and community policing efforts. If your agency subscribes to these philosophies, and it should, then willing cooperation from other departments becomes essential.

So, what are the elements of a good mentoring program? Following are my recommendations for a baseline program that can you can implement without major expense or significant loss of work time by the participants. There are many examples of mentoring programs, especially in private industry, such as PepsiCo's "conn3ct" program. There are also police mentoring programs, and I include some links below. Look for them and take what you can use and adapt it to your needs.

Define the purpose, scope, and importance of a formal mentoring program. Take care in communicating how the program is aligned with the agency's strategic initiatives and the level to which the chief executive is behind the program.

Formalize the program, its goals, objectives and operational guidelines in a departmental policy document.

Develop peer leadership skills by fostering a culture where everyone in the organization is encouraged to take the initiative to do the right thing, solve problems and set an example.

Develop a set of metrics that can be tracked over the short, medium and long term to validate the design and implementation of the program. The metrics must be clear enough to measure elements of the agency's performance in a variety of areas. Be careful to set realistic goals for which data can be attained relatively easily.

Train your mentors. If necessary, reach out to a consultant or college professor to help you define the needed skills and abilities, as well as the areas of competence required to succeed.

As the chief executive, define your expectations of the program and what you are willing to do to make it successful.

Give your mentors the necessary time to reach out to those with whom you've matched them. If necessary, consult with your agency's psychologist to help match individuals, but take care not to stigmatize anyone by implying they need help.

Make participation voluntary for more seasoned individuals but consider making it mandatory for less experienced personnel. Remember that even those who seemingly have little potential for leadership can surprise you. So don't be constrained when you select participants, but develop a set of key indicators by which you can measure progress.

Keep in mind gender differences and enlist the help of your female staff as well. They can often give a more relevant perspective to your female recruits and officers, and it's entirely possible that barriers were erected in the past in many agencies that have diminished the potential that female officers have for promotion. Consult with any formal female officer group at your organization as well.

Meet with the union and enlist them in the development and structure of the mentoring program. It will be better received and more effective. While there may be some resistance, if you've got the majority of your organization onboard, the union will come around because it's in their best interest to retain members and help them be successful.

Don't be afraid to bring in a professional consultant that has developed mentoring programs for police. I recommend you have an outside party look at your systems and give you suggestions for improvements. Here's the link to a brief article on how the City of London Police went about crafting their program:

http://www.management-mentors.com/resources/september-2008.

Take a look at successful police mentoring programs in communities across the nation to see if you can adapt the best of them to your environment. Here are several articles, resources, and programs that merit review:

http://inpublicsafety.com/2015/02/putting-experience-to-work-the-value-of-a-formal-mentoring-program/

http://www.theiacp.org/Portals/0/pdfs/Publications/BP-Mentoring.pdf

https://www.fdle.state.fl.us/Content/getdoc/e4d2bc31-a0a3-443b-8667-052ff430a908/Aviles-Mark-Research-paper-pdf.aspx

http://www.management-mentors.com/resources/september-2008

Your results with succession planning will depend largely on how effective you've been in mentoring and preparing your employees to assume more challenging and varied responsibilities. If you start early and provide the necessary resources, your task will be much easier, and you won't have to scramble when that inevitable crisis strikes. Look, for example, at the wave of retirements that occurred in California after an enhanced retirement formula was introduced and passed by the legislature at the turn of the century. Many experienced supervisors and managers retired a few years early, leaving agencies with the unenviable task of replacing them quickly with individuals who, for the most part, had not had the time to gain the minimum skills to comfortably do the jobs for which they were promoted.

To be sure many of these folks did well despite their lack of experience, but too many struggled to perform at that level. And what has been the cost? Look at the newspaper headlines, your civil liability records and drill down to see how much inexperienced supervisors and managers cost your agency not only in treasure but in good will from the community. The moral of the story is not to procrastinate and to start early to plan for succession of command at all levels. Coupled with mentoring and training programs, early planning will certainly pay off.

The last point I want to make in the area of mentoring and succession planning, is that you should focus all of your efforts on ensuring that the skills and strengths of your people can carry the organization beyond any one leader; beyond any one person that through the intensity of his or her personality dominates the agency. The systems, teams, and individuals must be able to carry the agency beyond any setback or periods of distress. The only way to get to this state of readiness is by using a systematic and strategic employee development roadmap and sticking to it over the long haul. There is no option but to take mentoring seriously and invest in the human capital that drives the success of the department.

GAP ANALYSIS

Knowing where you are and where you want to be is arguably the most important element of any organization's strategy for success. By that, I mean that any agency must take an honest inventory of its assets, capabilities, and deficits on a relatively regular basis, say every year or two, but definitely in conjunction with any strategic planning effort. That snapshot in time can then be compared with the organization's goals and objectives to determine the gap between where you are and where you want to be. That gap analysis is crucial to the timely accomplishment of goals, objectives and strategic initiatives, and gives the management team the data it needs to prepare a clear roadmap. Without this analysis your organization will be adrift in a sea of uncertainty and mediocrity, leaving to chance the critical decisions and actions that are required to succeed.

Implicit in this concept is that for gap analysis to work it must consider the skills and abilities of all members of the organization, your most valuable asset. The management team of any public safety agency should regularly conduct gap analysis for itself and members of their teams. That is, determining where competence levels are, projecting where they need to be, and then developing a plan to close the resulting gap. The process must dovetail with the strategic plan for the agency and should begin with a list of skills and abilities that every individual should have within a set period. That desired level of competence can stretch out over a continuum of time fixed by the agency. Then you conduct an inventory of each individual's skills and abilities to determine a baseline from which you determine the gap. The organization then develops a plan to close or eliminate that gap through training, assignments, formal education, etc.

Once you establish a baseline and the roadmap, you should set fixed checkpoints to ensure your plan of action is working or if you need to make adjustments. This process is a critical task for supervisors and managers and holding them accountable should be non-negotiable. As a first step, I suggest approaching gap analysis as one rung in the strategic planning ladder that is implemented in phases. This step includes a clear and firm statement from the chief executive that explains the agency's need for this course of action and what's in it not only for the department and the community but individual employees as well. Rather than pushing your team members into participation, pull them along with sound and inclusive steps that get them involved in the planning and execution of the plan. It's well known that when employees are involved in, and contribute to, the planning process, the results are much better, and the employees are more satisfied with their role in the agency.

As you've read elsewhere in this book, competent managers are essential to achieving the organization's goals and objectives, let alone increasing employee morale. Consider establishing a formal rotation program for all managers to expose them to every area of the organization, which increases their readiness levels to assume command of any team or division at a moment's notice. The U.S. military does this rather well, and their commanders are more competent because of it. Also, managers and supervisors who have broad sets of skills and abilities will make better decisions. They will help employees analyze their organizational gaps without having to defend their own shortcomings in experience. I firmly believe that a broad set of experience, skills and abilities, coupled with the principles discussed in this book, enables your leaders to command respect and drive the agency's strategies forward. Take a look at the U.S. Army's Army Leader Development Strategy (ALDS), which I believe is one of the best in existence. It is comprehensive and well thought out, and it has analogous implications and methods for law enforcement. The following paragraph succinctly describes the army's approach:

"Talent management complements leader development. Talent management takes into account the individual talents of an officer, non-commissioned officer, or Army Civilian—the unique distribution of his or her skills, knowledge and behaviors and the potential they represent. The Army looks to develop and put to best use well-rounded leaders based on the talents they possess—talents that derive not only from operational experience but also from broadening assignments, advanced civil schooling and professional military education, and demonstrated interests. We will restructure promotion timelines so that leaders have the opportunity for a broader set of experiences, which, taken together, improve an individual's leadership skill set. As we build teams comprising better-developed individuals, we improve the Army. At the same time, we are redesigning our rating system to include revamping the officer efficiency report to evaluate the talent of individuals more thoroughly. We are also implementing 360° assessments which include input not only from superiors but also peers and subordinates. Such a system will help individual leaders identify strengths to sustain and weaknesses to eliminate."

http://usacac.army.mil/cac2/CAL/repository/ALDS5June%20201 3Record.pdf

15

MANAGING RISK IN POLICING

"If it's predictable it's preventable." —Gordon Graham

According to the Los Angeles Times (Winton, April 9, 2017), the Los Angeles County Sheriff's Department pay-outs for lawsuits rose tenfold over five years, costing the taxpayers nearly $100 million. The City of Los Angeles is now considering issuing judgment bonds to pay for liability claims and jury verdicts against the Los Angeles Police Department. The legal cost of doing business for law enforcement agencies throughout the nation has risen steadily over the last decade primarily because of officer-involved shootings, uses of force and traffic collisions involving officers and deputies. While there are serious misconduct cases, such as LASD Deputy Jose Rigoberto Sanchez, who pleaded no contest to a charge of rape under color of authority and cost the county $6.15 million, these three areas account for the bulk of the payouts.

According to the article, Jurors are now less likely to give law enforcement the benefit of the doubt and more likely to award larger sums to plaintiffs, driving up the cost of judgments and emboldening attorneys to seek larger settlements during negotiations, experts said. "The social climate of today has had an important impact on trials and outcomes," said Steven H. Estabrook, litigation cost manager for the Los Angeles County counsel's office. "Higher awards and higher costs are getting more common." The costs are siphoning funds from other areas such as hiring, training and community policing, stretching resources and knocking agencies on their heels at a time when crime appears to be rising after decades of decline. Now, more than ever, police leaders must embrace risk management as a primary, essential function that has to become institutionalized to reduce liability. In other words, police leaders have to be more anxious and less complacent.

Tom Fox, Vice President at the nonprofit Partnership for Public Service and a guest contributor to the Washington Post's On Leadership section, recently interviewed Cass Sunstein, who wrote Wiser: Getting Beyond Group Think to Make Groups Smarter (Harvard Business Review Press). In an article summarizing the interview in the Los Angeles Times, Sunstein told Fox:

> "A complacent leader is someone who is upbeat, optimistic, who has a clear sense of direction, who is quite confident that things will be fine and who has a degree of sunniness. An anxious leader is someone who may be easy to get along with but also is thinking about all the things that could go wrong and always seeing the worst-case scenario. There is no question that the anxious leader is much better than the complacent leader. The anxious leader is able to redirect energies, listen to information from employees and won't continue the course of action if it's failing. The anxious leader also will be flexible and inventive and will foresee things that could go wrong. There's a saying that goes, 'If you make a plan, God laughs. If you make two plans, God smiles.' The anxious leaders are making two plans."

The U.S. Army Leader Development Manual puts it in clear terms: A leader who thinks critically "seeks to obtain the most thorough and accurate understanding possible," and he "anticipates first, second and third consequences of multiple courses of action." So while I want you to be a confident leader, I also need you to be an anxious one. That means anticipating results, opportunities and consequences on multiple levels. For example, the risk management eye should look closely at personnel and other systems that tend to be responsible for the majority of the liability payouts in an agency. Consider that in Los Angeles three cases accounted for nearly half of the $81 million in payouts in fiscal year 2016, including a wrongful conviction judgment and two officer-involved shootings.

Risk management (RM) isn't sexy, but it must be one of your top priorities, period. It's the responsibility of everyone in the organization, but in this section, I'll focus primarily on how you can help reduce or control risk. The concept of looking around corners to anticipate and mitigate risk is not a foreign one in police work—vehicle maintenance, wearing body armor, tactical plans, qualifying at the firearms range and many other activities are aimed at reducing risk—but few agencies practice it with the devotion and timing that's required to manage the situations that bring liability knocking on your door.

Whether your organization is small, medium or large, the art of risk management should be a key topic in your training program for your leadership team, paying particular attention to the field incidents that patrol sergeants handle routinely, such as uses of force, vehicle pursuits, traffic collisions and complaints from the public. These incidents probably constitute the bulk of your recurring liability claims and ought to be routinely monitored and examined to identify common causation factors, the frequency with which they are occurring and how they can be mitigated to the fullest extent possible. You won't find the answers to these questions unless you develop a systematic approach that relies on reliable data that is available almost in real time and is pushed to the desks of those tasked with the analysis. And, as is the norm in most paramilitary organizations, the members of your agency won't look at and act on the data unless you, the chief executive, makes it a priority.

I'll talk about such a system in this section of the book. I'll cover the basics for a rudimentary system that will work and can be scaled up when your needs or the size of your agency require it. It's not rocket science, and it can be implemented in stages and with a relatively small budget. The data collection and analysis can be done with a relational database or a spreadsheet. Obviously, the more sophisticated and versatile the tools you're using the better, but remember that no matter how great your tools are you can't use them unless you are capturing, storing and distributing the data to those that need it.

That means investing in a process; one that is simple and well designed to focus narrowly on the metrics, data, and processes that are relevant to risk management and upon which you can have the most impact. In other words, don't try to build a Swiss Army Knife! Focus relentlessly and practically on the areas that give you the most headaches. Your agency should already be collecting data on liability claims, whether through the risk management office of your city or county or through an in-house section that performs that function. Get a hold of the data and drill down to find your "frequent flyers" so to speak, so you can prioritize the areas that need the most attention.

While newly assigned as my agency's Training Sergeant one day back in the 1980s, I was attending a council meeting and noticed in the agenda a number of claims against the City that were to be discussed in closed session, which is the practice for reviewing or settling claims before they turn into lawsuits. The agenda listed at least six claims against the police department, most of which related to traffic collisions involving patrol units. Some of them were for collisions that occurred while officers were backing up. I remember thinking, "Here I am as the Training Sergeant, and I had not seen any of these claims." I found out later that the cumulative total of the six claims was more than $90,000; not a pittance by anyone's measure, even for an agency of 400 officers. That was real money, and who knew what else was slipping through the liability cracks. While we had a competent risk management unit, I quickly saw the disconnect between it and the folks that could make a difference in reducing these claims. The Chief of Police and our Internal Affairs unit saw the claims, but there was no analysis that looked at the cause and effect in the claims.

The next day I made it a point to walk over to City Hall and meet with our risk manager, who was a tall, lanky man with an affable disposition and a head for numbers. I told him I was familiar with the serious collisions and the large claims, but I'd not seen regular data or reports on the minor accidents. He opened a drawer and pulled out a thick report that listed every claim against the City that involved the police department for that year and told me he could get the data going back a decade or more. He explained how the PD usually got a report every six month that listed the claims, but it wasn't widely distributed within the agency. The reports normally went to the Chief's Office, and someone from management reviewed them, but they contained little useful information other than the basics. No one took the time to pull the related documentation and analyze it for more details upon which we could act. While we did get the reports, it wasn't frequently enough or in a format that gave us the critical data we needed at a glance—once the microcomputer revolution took hold later in the decade, management reports of all sorts became commonplace on the virtual desktops of police supervisors and managers.

As I studied the report, I was shocked to see how much money the City was spending on settlements for relatively minor claims involving collisions and uses of force. When I added them up, they totaled in the hundreds of thousands of dollars every year. Again, not chump change by any means. I asked to be kept in the loop and be sent a report on a monthly basis. I started looking at each claim to determine the cause of these incidents and identify any common factors.

We found enough actionable information that we sent one of our sergeants to be certified as a driving instructor by California Peace Officers Standards and Training. He studied the liability claims and developed four and eight-hour courses with a curriculum aimed squarely at the causes of most of the accidents. Surprisingly quite a few of them involved backing up, so we designed a hands-on course to address that factor. The officers involved in the collisions attended first, but eventually, everyone went through the training. Over the next few years, we reduced at-fault collisions by more than forty percent. That made me a believer in risk management—and I reached out to Gordon Graham.

Almost everyone in public safety, fire or police, has heard of Gordon Graham. He is the foremost risk management guru in our field and has been evangelizing agencies on the virtues of "predictable is preventable" for decades. He spent over thirty years in the California Highway Patrol and retired as a Captain and a lawyer. If you have not heard of him don't worry, you will. Before we go on, full disclosure: After I had retired from the Santa Ana Police Department I worked for what was then Gordon's and Bruce Praet's company,

Lexipol, for several years and got to work with agencies throughout the country. It was an experience I would not trade for anything, and it exposed me not only to the premier risk management company that is Lexipol but the problems and issues all public safety agencies seemingly face. I'd met Gordon back in the 1980s when I attended one of his seminars. In an article at urgentcomm.com on June 9, 2009, Glenn Bischoff described one of Graham's lectures as follows: "His topic was risk management, and his message was remarkably simple: nearly every bad outcome is predictable and thus preventable.

He used several historical examples to illustrate the point. The one I found most interesting was the most recent. He showed a copy of yesterday's USA Today, which reported that nearly every "serious" regional airline accident over the past ten years involved at least one pilot who had previously failed a proficiency test. According to Graham, each of these incidents was predictable and preventable. "If your pilot can't pass the test, then maybe he shouldn't fly the plane," he said. In contrast, Graham then presented US Airways Capt. Chesley "Sully" Sullenberger, who landed his airplane in New York City's Hudson River in January after several birds flew into the craft's engines, rendering them inoperable. Sullenberger is a shining example of one of Graham's seven rules of risk management: training has to be constant and rigorous. "Every day needs to be a training day," Graham said. He spoke of something that Sullenberger said in an interview shortly after his heroic actions saved the lives of everyone aboard Flight 1549. Sullenberger said that he tried, throughout his flying career, to make small deposits each day into his memory bank, knowing that one day he would "have to make a massive withdrawal," Graham said. It was a sound strategy, Graham said, because doing so enabled him to make instantaneous, life-and-death decisions on that fateful day. It's a lesson especially adaptable to the public-safety sector, whose personnel make such decisions on a daily basis.

I found Gordon Graham so compelling because he delivered a relatively dry subject with humor, keeping you glued to his presentation. People listened to him, and his delivery allowed the relevant points to stick in your mind. At least they did with me, and everyone else with whom I've spoken feels the same way. In fact, I was so impressed that I hired him to do a four-hour class for all our supervisors and managers. I followed his career and kept up with his teachings, trying to apply his "Five Pillars of Organizational Risk Management" principles (see below) in all the assignments I held. They served me well.

If you haven't already, visit http://www.lexipol.com for a walk-through of Gordon's principles and the Tip of the Day. You can subscribe, and you'll be notified when the new tips are available. If you Google him or Lexipol, you'll find many papers online that will help you understand and implement risk management principles in practical ways. I no longer work for Lexipol or Gordon, but I remain a fan. Gordon defines the "five pillars" as People, Policy, Training, Supervision, and Discipline. He assigns risks to one of ten families, which you can easily find online. Sources of risk are as diverse and dynamic as any other policing problem can be. Please refer to Gordon's extensive writings for additional details. He can be reached at http://gordongraham.com.

So how do you develop a sound system for risk management? Here are a few suggestions that if implemented properly can help an organization use a systems approach to minimize liability or injury related to all manner of risk. Regardless of resources, there are relatively low-cost ways to impact the incidents that are prevalent in your agency or the major ones that don't happen often but have the potential to cost you millions.

First, make sure that the chief or sheriff makes the task mandatory at all levels, including the rank and file. Don't assume everyone in the organization accepts the premise that recognizing risky behaviors or conditions, and doing something about them, is a shared responsibility. The CEO of the organization should clearly and unambiguously make it a priority and codify it into a policy document. Second, explicitly define what the task entails and set a clear procedure for communicating with the appropriate units so that the situation is promptly remedied. If the risky condition is minor or can be easily mitigated, encourage your employees to do so immediately.

I remember one day walking through an interior courtyard in our brand-new police building when I noticed an officer moving an artificial shrub near the bottom of a stairwell. I asked him what he was doing, and he told me he'd nearly hit the bottom of the stairwell structure with his head as he walked close to it, and he figured others might get hurt. So he found the artificial shrub planter and placed it near the structure to block the path and force others to round it a bit further away. He said he'd notified our Property and Facilities section but wanted to do something in the interim. I thanked him for taking action. That's the sort of initiative that ought to be encouraged and expected from everyone in the organization. He couldn't do anything about the possible design flaw of the stairwell, but he could immediately mitigate it.

Second, develop a system for collecting and analyzing data to identify and prioritize risks in all of Gordon Graham's Families of Risk. Keep in mind that you don't need to be an executive to look within your sphere of influence to implement management systems, as long as they are consistent with your organization's structure and expectations. Whether the effort is department-wide or a section's database, the important thing is to collect the data. Obviously, one database for the entire organization will be much more efficient and will help you avoid duplication, as long as the data and actions are reconciled at the end. Some agencies have a single Records Management System (RMS), while others aggregate data from an RMS, a Jail Management System (JMS) and a Computer Aided Dispatching system (CAD). Whichever way your agency does it, assign someone the responsibility to look at each of Gordon's risk families and map them to activities and data captured by your databases. I'm talking about collecting data on pursuits, uses of force, traffic collisions, workers' compensation claims, grievances, shootings and complaints from the public, among others.

If your agency is small enough, you may be able to accomplish the task by using a simple relational database (FileMaker Pro©) or spreadsheet (Microsoft Excel©, Apple's Numbers©). I'd be willing to bet you have an officer or supervisor who's a computer aficionado that would gladly take the assignment of developing a simple yet workable data collection system. If you can, use an integrated RMS, as these advanced systems are usually user-friendly and have robust management reporting capabilities. There are several reputable vendors in the industry (see the Technology section of this book for additional information). A word of caution: some of the data your agency collects is protected by statute and probably agency policy, so take great care to work within the law and to safeguard not only the data but reports as well. Work with your legal advisor, city attorney or county counsel to ensure compliance with the law.

Third, once the data has been mapped as we discussed above, work with your risk manager or the person in-charge of the database, to create reports that can regularly be delivered to managers and supervisors. The reports should be scrubbed to eliminate any employee identifying information—unless the reports conform to law and policy and go to those who need and have the right to know. Typically, personnel and internal affairs data are not disseminated until they've been stripped of identifying information and contain only aggregate figures—we discuss early-warning systems elsewhere in this book. Any other data, especially that which identifies trends and potential problems, should be available to any supervisor or manager on a monthly or quarterly basis. You want many eyes on the activities of the agency, especially if you've made risk management a priority and involved all your employees in the process.

Lastly, consider developing query tools so that your folks can easily create ad-hoc reports at their desktops. Again, the reports should strip the data of identifying information when necessary but should provide enough specifics to make the analysis possible. For example, a supervisor or a manager ought to be able to produce a report for all uses of force that includes the mode (e.g. Baton, OC Spray or fists), the frequency and the trend over time for specific teams, shifts or individuals—following departmental policy. If you identify a trend, you can get additional information by reviewing the original reports, thus fleshing out a picture of what is or could be occurring. Without these tools, your data sits idle, occupying space but not providing any value.

Fourth, review the data and the original documentation if necessary, to look for any commonalities and determine the likely causation factors. These factors can include faulty or inappropriate equipment, lack of training or proficiency, lack of familiarity with departmental policy (or the lack of a sound policy), inattention and misconduct, among others. Look at events over different periods of time to see whether a trend is present, or the incidents merely represent anomalies. That means looking at the data over the short-term — weeks or months— or over the longer term measured in years.

Again, use the SARA model or similar process as a starting point. Above all, once you've done your homework, follow through and implement whatever changes or measures are necessary to correct the problem, and keep reviewing the data to make sure your corrective actions are working. If not, go back to the analysis and see if you missed anything or if you need to look for another fix. It's a constant process of improvement that should be engrained in all your practices.

Fifth, make sure that your policies and procedures are current, legally defensible and systematically enforced. This process is perhaps the risk management task that is not given the attention it needs for an agency to remain professional and effective. When I worked with departments throughout the country, I found some policies that had not been revised in more than a decade. Some were critical policies that should be looked at frequently, perhaps once or twice a year, or when laws or practices change. I realize that to keep policies and procedures current you've got to devote precious resources, but think about the liability you create when you don't keep them current and legally defensible. There are many resources out there that will help you develop and regularly update your policies—such as Lexipol and others—but you will have to devote personnel time to the process. It is, however, eminently worth it.

Sixth, develop a program for training, testing, and acknowledgment that directly addresses your policies. Regardless of how good your policies are, if you don't train your officers on each one and test them to ensure they understand them, they aren't worth the paper they are pinned on. Similarly, if you don't have a recorded acknowledgment by each officer that they received the policy, it will be difficult to prove in any court or a discipline hearing that the officer was aware of it. Lastly, periodic testing of all policies is the final component of a sound policy system. Testing can be done with technology in a relatively quick way and without expending too many resources. Again, there are many resources that help you accomplish this task.

Risk Management involves a plethora of activities that are focused on preventing adverse incidents, especially the high-risk/low-frequency events that Gordon Graham describes, and which cost your agency hundreds of thousands of dollars over time — or God forbid an injury to an officer. Many managers at smaller departments live under the illusion that they are exempt from these risky events. I'm here to tell you they aren't. Sound risk management practices that are systematically applied throughout an organization is the only way to keep risk and liability under relative control.

ORGANIZATIONAL RED TEAMS

Have you or someone in your department ever made a decision or developed an operational plan that turned out to be half-baked, lacked an understanding of the issues or failed to take into account relevant information from a variety of perspectives, both internal and external? I know I had and regretted it. I looked back to see what I could have done differently, and invariably reached the same conclusion: The decision-making process I used in some instances was flawed and lacked a broader perspective. I should have refined my approach, perhaps by employing a Red Team. By now you're probably ready to close the cover (or cyber cover if you're reading this on a tablet) on this book and brand me a madman. Hang in there, and I'll explain.

Wikipedia describes the U.S. Army's Red Teaming definition as: "structured, iterative process executed by trained, educated and practiced team members that provides commanders an independent capability to continuously challenge plans, operations, concepts, organizations and capabilities in the context of the operational environment and from our partners' and adversaries' perspectives." (TRADOC News Service, July 13, 2005). In short, a Red Team is a group of individuals commissioned by the agency (internally and from outside consultants) to review or study organizational issues, processes, plans, etc., and challenge assumptions, data, and operational concepts. I realize this approach has been used primarily in the military and federal government agencies—according to the Robb-Silberman report from 2005, the Intelligence Reform and Terrorism Prevention Act mandates the use of such teams to ensure that analysts conduct alternative analysis—and gained popularity after the Iraq WMD debacle. But, any organization, and those in law enforcement, in particular, stand to benefit from red teams as well.

Here's an example: Suppose your agency is studying the gang problem in a particular neighborhood and has formulated a plan to attack it. That plan was put together by the lieutenant in that particular district or area and includes input from her sergeants and officers. That plan has now been presented to the management team so it can be discussed, approved and implemented. If not rolled out smartly, critical operational plans such as this one can potentially lead to significant or catastrophic losses for the agency, including lawsuits and loss of community support. I've seen them go well but also end badly because the decision-makers failed to establish a comprehensive vetting process, similar to the SARA model (Scanning, Analysis, Response, and Assessment) used in problem-solving efforts across the country. It is precisely in situations such as this one that a Red Team would be worthwhile. According to the University of Foreign Military and Cultural Studies at Fort Leavenworth, Kansas, Red Teams "improve decision-making in planning and operations by broadening the understanding of the operational environment from alternative perspectives, and identifying gaps, vulnerabilities and opportunities." The Red Team Manual may be found here:

https://www.hsdl.org/?view&did=802233

This is not limited to tactical operations and can be used in developing strategic initiatives of all types.

If you don't like the term "Red Team," feel free to use whatever term you like. Just think about the practical application of such a concept, and it's potential use in your organization. You may want to establish a Risk Assessment collateral duty in your planning and research section; or assign and train a group of individuals from different units that can look at projects, initiatives or strategies in a systematic way to find the weak links or unintended consequences. Having the equivalent to a red team can work wonders.

As an exercise, take a significant project that has already been completed and assign a couple of uninvolved individuals to act as the

Red Team members. Train them and familiarize them with the environment in which the project took place and give them time to research the topic or issue. Then have them do a thorough analysis and a post-mortem on the project to see how their findings would have altered your approach. I bet it would be revealing. Don't get defensive but think about the heartache and expenses a thorough review will save you and your department. Most importantly, if you elect not to heed their criticism or recommendations, make sure you tell them why. Otherwise, you'll have a deflated team that doesn't believe you're sincere when you ask for their opinion. Look into red teams and see if they may be helpful to you and the management team. Click the link below to read an excellent article on red teams from The Police Chief, vol. 74, no. 2, February 2007, By Michael K. Meehan, Captain, Seattle Police Department:

http://www.policechiefmagazine.org/magazine/index.cfm?fuseaction=print_display&article_id=1111&issue_id=22007

EMERGENCY MANAGEMENT

The ability of a police supervisor or manager to handle emergencies of all types should not even be up for discussion. We all ought to be reasonably competent in this area, being able to step into just about any tactical situation and take command and control following emergency management principles and internal policies. Sadly, that's not always the case. As in most deficiencies in law enforcement, you'll find that the reasons for those failures are most often attributable to a lack of leadership. There are many systemic reasons for these deficiencies, but the lack of will to ensure tactical competencies in all supervisors and managers can be attributed to the agency's top leadership. Stick with me, and I'll tell you why.

In most agencies, there are a few individuals that are tasked with readying the organization to handle all sorts of emergencies. These folks then take on that responsibility and become experts in emergency management and invaluable in times of crisis. What we fail to do, however, is ensure that their knowledge and proficiency gets passed on, as much as practical, to all managers and supervisors. In many agencies, the emergency management experts are the SWAT commanders and supervisors. These folks take charge of virtually all major tactical incidents whether SWAT related or not. There are a few others who have that level of competency as well. As a result, they are used a lot and are, at times, overwhelmed by the work. While others are trained periodically, agencies may not develop an ongoing, robust emergency management training and exercise program to ensure that all supervisors and managers can step in at any time and with confidence to handle these situations. This lack of proficiency is perhaps most glaring in management ranks given that other responsibilities tend to take precedence. As my old boss Gordon Graham loves to say, it is the high-risk, low-frequency events that tend to go wrong, so it's critical that we're prepared to handle them at all levels of the organization.

While your agency may be different and can handle these issues superbly, my experience with some departments has been to the contrary. Thus, I advocate for a comprehensive, ongoing effort to train all supervisors and managers in emergency management, and regularly exercise those skills to prevent them from perishing. In these times of demonstrations, active shooters, threats of terrorism and other events, all supervisors and managers must be competent enough to step into a command and control position and handle an event. Those in administrative and investigative positions must focus on remaining proficient in emergency management, so regular training and exercise programs are critical to your agency's ability to handle emergencies and tactical situations. If you think about the incidents that tax law enforcement organizations and affect communities everywhere, active shooters are always at the top. Agencies prepare for these eventualities, but managers must do more to become proficient at handling these incidents, from the tactics to the media and the aftermath. Some agencies even send their managers to other departments during and after a crisis so they can bring home lessons learned. Emergency management and tactical skills are now more important than ever in a well-rounded police manager

REALLY...CHECKLISTS?

Just hang with me on this one! If you get nothing else from this segment, please read Doctor Atul Gawande's book The Checklist Manifesto (http://gawande.com/the-checklist-manifesto). It's less than 200 pages and an easy read. I read it in a few hours and found it applicable to government and public safety. The fundamental principle, which has been widely used in aviation and now in medicine, is that in a world where information and knowledge are so vast and complex, the only way to harness them in practical ways is by developing checklists. He argues persuasively that the development of a checklist process in surgery has saved many lives and has significantly reduced errors in the operating rooms that use them. I know it sounds simplistic, but I urge you to read the book. It is full of examples from many industries and includes not only anecdotes that will surprise you, but empirical evidence that checklists work. He advocates keeping the checklists short, perhaps ten or fewer items, for them to be used effectively.

If you consider that police operations have become more complex legally, socially and technically, it is easy to see the value in checklists that are simple and concise yet prompt you to ask critical questions that may be forgotten otherwise. I can think of several operations over the years that cost us hundreds of thousands of dollars in liability that could have benefited from a checklist before implementation. Especially suited are tactical initiatives, and projects with civil rights implications such as gang sweeps and other multi-faceted operations with liability potential. After reading Dr. Gawande's book, I came to the conclusion that general orders or other policy documents that govern operations should include a checklist that must be completed before implementation. It's not difficult to look at different scenarios and ask relevant questions in advance when you have the time and not under the stress of the moment.

For example, let's say your agency has a general order that applies to dealing with the homeless in a public space. Why not include a checklist before a tactical operation is implemented? It can include items such as contacting the city attorney or county counsel, having a suitable place to store belongings, working with social services and having alternative resources to incarceration, determining the proper booking procedures and handling the media. While your personnel are likely to do all these things, can you confidently say they will remember them all? Isn't it easier and more efficient to create these checklists during a brainstorming session and making them a component of all your critical policies and operations? You may not think so, but progressive agencies that understand liability and work hard to prevent it will embrace the checklist process. Can you afford not to?

16

DELEGATION IS NOT ABDICATION

"I stand here today humbled and filled with remorse for my mistakes as sheriff of Los Angeles County. I did not lead. Instead, I delegated the responsibility for this important duty, and I should not have." — *Retired Sheriff Lee Baca at his court hearing.*

When Ronald Reagan made the now-famous statement regarding the Soviet Union and the Strategic Arms Limitation Treaty, "Trust but verify," he was referring to having a clear process for verifying the principles and actions agreed upon were carried out. He was reinforcing what I believe is a similar and fundamental leadership principle. That is, one must trust those to whom projects, programs or tasks are delegated, but one never relinquishes the responsibility of making sure things get done. That means learning to delegate smartly, including giving subordinates the tools, authority, resources, and freedom to accomplish the goal, but also staying engaged and available, and having checkpoints to ensure progress and timely completion. It also means staying involved in the major projects and initiatives to imprint your vision and values in the outcome.

A leader must embrace delegation to empower subordinates at all levels successfully, and to accomplish organizational goals that would otherwise linger while waiting for the "indispensable" leader to take control. James R. Bailey, a professor of at the George Washington University School of Business, calls it (Los Angeles Times, July 3, 2016) the "Indispensability Syndrome, a fallacious, emotional urge rooted deep in our desire to be wanted and needed." The article goes on to describe how some managers feel compelled to remain tethered to the organization through email and other means under the belief that without them, despite capable subordinates and sound systems, the team will suffer and their dependence on the manager will be diminished. For the most part, I agree with Bailey's conclusions. But, getting to a point where you, as a leader, can feel confident that the workplace will endure without you for a few weeks takes an understanding of delegation: what it is and isn't; how you ready your department or section to thrive without you; and how you engage subordinates to embrace autonomy yet understand the responsibilities that come with delegation.

Another perspective in a recent British Broadcasting Company (BBC) article by Sydney Finkelstein that appeared in their Capital section titled "In Praise of Micromanagement," makes the point that people such as Steve Jobs and other successful leaders are micromanagers because they care deeply about their products and want their vision implemented faithfully. The story explains that for sure, these leaders micromanage selectively and have trusted seconds-in-command that take care of many of the associated details of projects or initiatives. They are also experts, or highly competent, in the field or project at hand. They have to be. Otherwise, they have little credibility with the teams they manage.

Finkelstein says it best: "The modern executive is taught—in business schools and in many jobs, that to manage people effectively is to delegate, and then get out of the way…delegating is only step one. It's not delegate and forget; it must be delegate and be intimately involved with what happens next. You don't want to, and can't, do everyone else's job for them. But why would you walk away, as so many managers do? When you have deep passion for your business, your job, you also have a responsibility to be involved with how your vision is executed. You will likely step on some toes along the way and you may go too far on occasion, but which is worse: occasionally butting in on a subordinate's work to make a point, or not providing real-time feedback to help that subordinate grow and excel?" If you'd like to read the entire piece click here:

http://www.bbc.com/capital/story/20131003-in-praise-of-micromanagement

I remember one day shortly after I was promoted to sergeant when I took over an administrative function for a veteran sergeant. He was showing me what his work entailed. He pointed to a pile of documents on the side of his desk and told me the papers represented the "less important" assignments from his lieutenant. He said he used the "sixty-day" method for handling them. If, after sixty days, the boss did not ask him about the papers, he'd file them in the "round file," and pointed to the trash can. After I had picked myself up off the floor, where I'd landed after I fell laughing, I asked him what he'd do if the lieutenant ever asked about the papers, and he said he'd been doing it for a couple of years and he had never asked.

Now, folks, I venture to bet people all over the world use the "sixty-day" method in some form or another when they can get away with it. It is delegation at its worse, leaving potentially valuable ideas or projects in the dustbin because the boss failed to follow up in any meaningful way. Remember, you are not a micromanager simply because you establish a sound delegation system, using periodic checkpoints to measure progress and gauge compliance with organizational values.

THE CASE OF LOS ANGELES COUNTY
SHERIFF LEE BACA

The curious case of Lee Baca is particularly instructive. The now-retired Sheriff of Los Angeles County—who held that job for many years—was recently convicted on a range of federal charges, including lying and obstructing federal agents about a probe the FBI was conducting in his jails. Although this case has lessons in many facets of leadership, it is a prime example of delegation gone wrong. Baca could face up to twenty years in prison. His now-retired Under-sheriff Paul Tanaka was convicted in April 2016 of conspiracy and obstructing a federal investigation into brutality and corruption by sheriff's deputies in the county jails. Baca and Tanaka were once at the pinnacle of law enforcement, with authority and responsibility for tens of thousands of employees. In my opinion, they had the opportunity to do the right thing, yet hubris got the best of them. Unfortunately, they are not alone.

I'd met Baca several times over the years, and he was always congenial, articulate and seemingly dedicated to providing the community with excellent service. He believed deeply in community policing, treating people as though they all had value. He was also a runner, and you could tell by his rail-thin physique. I'd heard him speak several times and knew he was quirky and a bit odd, but his thinking was progressive. He often talked about law enforcement not relying on arrests to solve problems and using focused community work and alternative problem solving and resolution instead. Those were policing concepts we now embrace. He was a visionary that at times sounded Pollyannaish, even unhinged, prompting some in his agency and beyond to call him "Sheriff Moon Beam." But, he was popular with the community and respected throughout the vast neighborhoods of Los Angeles County. He was a fixture at community events, where he often preached racial harmony.

I liked him. If you talked with him for any length of time, you couldn't help but like his personality and straight forward demeanor. He made you feel important and focused his attention on you and your issues, irrespective of your economic or social status. I remember the day when President George W. Bush visited Santa Ana on July 5, 2002. As the captain-in-charge of all uniformed services and the SWAT team, which provided VIP security, I had the ultimate responsibility for ensuring the event at the Bowers Museum went according to plan from a local perspective. I also had two SWAT lieutenants (Ken Hall and Felix Osuna) who were the best in the business and handled the heavy lifting in terms of the liaison with the Secret Service and other agencies, as well as all the planning for the event.

Sheriff Baca was flown in via helicopter and landed not far from the venue. Although we'd met before, I was sure he wouldn't remember me. I was surprised when he walked directly to me and extended his hand. He introduced himself and almost immediately asked me about my last name, which he could see on my name tag. I told him I was born and raised in Honduras, but my father was of Middle Eastern origins. He then began what turned out to be a ten-minute conversation about Middle Eastern culture and food and ended the conversation by asking all of us to take a picture with him. He was charismatic and quickly brought you into what felt like an inner circle of friends. When Baca was indicted, I was saddened to see such a warm and caring individual fall from grace when he had the world by the tail. My guess is that despite good intentions, arrogance and hubris got the best of him. Someone once told me that the longer you stay as the head of any organization you start to think you own it. To me, that sounds like Lee Baca.

The LASD, with nearly 10,000 sworn deputies and thousands of non-sworn employees, is one of the top three law enforcement agencies in the nation. Baca was a powerful elected sheriff, and he frequently tussled with Los Angeles County supervisors on budget issues—at times threatening to close jails and let inmates free if he didn't get the funding he deemed necessary. He frequently got his way. When things started going astray, no one can precisely say, but it appears that at some point Baca all but turned over the running of the sheriff's department to his undersheriff, while he focused on political issues and non-operational matters. During the last few years of Baca's administration, the department seemed to spiral out of control, with scandal after scandal erupting into public view, and some deputies arrested for felony crimes. The bad news about LASD kept mounting, and Baca seemed helpless in stemming the tide of misconduct, criminal behavior, and conflicts of interest in his department.

Finally, in late 2013, the United States Attorney unveiled indictments against 18 members of Baca's department, stating that the incidents "demonstrated behavior that had become institutionalized. The pattern of activity alleged…shows how some members of the sheriff's department considered themselves to be above the law" (Los Angeles Magazine, Fremon, May 14, 2015). Shortly after the scandals became public and U.S. Attorney announced the indictments, Baca began to lay all of the problems at Tanaka's feet, telling the media he (Baca) was not a "hands-on" manager and lamenting his trusting of Tanaka to run the department. According to Fremon's article, Baca was the mile-high thinker who came up with the lofty vision, and then delegated "broadly." Tanaka, who was seemingly aggressive and confrontational, willingly took the mantle of command and got things done—in his own way, based on his values and priorities, not Baca's.

It appears Tanaka was the one who actually ran the department, and Baca was the "Thought Leader," as I've heard him described. He apparently hated details and delegated many if not most of the critical tasks of running such a large organization to his undersheriff. In an interview with Inside OC (Rick Reiff, PBS), Orange County Sheriff Sandra Hutchens (a retired LASD official whom I interviewed for this book), gave Baca credit for doing good things at the department, but also faulted him for failing to contain Tanaka—in essence having a "blind spot" when it came to his Undersheriff. Hutchens said: "I left the department about three years sooner than I would have because of Mr. Tanaka and his influence, his negative influence," she said. "I saw the wrong people getting promoted, the right people not getting promoted and I talked to Lee, as many did, about that." As is the case when delegation becomes abdication, Baca's reliance on one individual, without consistent monitoring and a values-driven approach, led to the Sheriff's downfall and trauma that was and continues to be, painful to the department.

To read an engrossing account of the Baca/Tanaka debacle, go to: http://www.lamag.com/longform/downfall/

The Board of Supervisors in Los Angeles County appointed a blue-ribbon panel to look into the jail allegations. It was called the Citizens Commission on Jail Violence (http://www.lacounty.gov/files/CCJV-Report.pdf). The members included retired judges, the former head of the Drug Enforcement Administration and then Long Beach Police Chief (now L.A. County Sheriff) James McDonnell. The report was brutally critical of the Sheriff and Tanaka, describing cultural and systemic issues in the jails that went back decades. Speaking to the media, Robert Bonner, the former head of DEA under President George H.W. Bush, said: "The fact is that the sheriff does not seem to be someone, as a manager, who wanted to hear about problems...Like the proverbial ostrich, he seems to have had his head in the sand, happy to deal with other issues, ones that perhaps interested him more, but not minding the store when it came to running the jail in accordance with lawful and sound use of force policy" (See link below).

With regard to Tanaka, the CCJV report stated, in part: "Not only did he fail to identify and correct problems in the jails, he exacer-bated them...Over the course of several years, the Undersheriff encouraged deputies to push the legal boundaries of law enforcement activities and created an environment that discouraged account-ability for misconduct. His repeated statements that deputies should work in an undefined 'grey' area, contributed to a perception by some deputies that they could use excessive force in the jails and that their aggressive behavior would not result in discipline."

http://www.lamag.com/longform/downfall/4/#sthash.ujPLZCmi .dpuf

To an interested observer like me, it appears as though Baca was progressive early on regarding alternative policing and incarceration philosophies, especially those dealing with community relations, crime prevention, and race relations. All laudable areas of interest, but not at the expense of the administration of the department and the traditional policing efforts of the organization. Baca loved to travel and had meetings with policing leaders from throughout the world, often leaving Tanaka and others in charge of the department. He appears to have delegated nearly all day-to-day activities to his underlings without having the necessary checkpoints and controls that would have kept him informed and in touch with the real culture of the organization. According to the Los Angeles Times (Rubin, July 18, 2016), in 2010 the LASD hired nearly 300 officers from a little-known county police force that patrolled parks and government buildings, many of whom had serious misconduct on their records, including about 100 who had issues with dishonesty. When things started going south with some of the new hires, Baca blamed his undersheriff and said he had no idea people with such records were being hired.

The apparent history of Baca delegating critical functions without the necessary controls goes back decades and crystallizes the need for competent police executives and managers never to abdicate their responsibilities in the name of delegation. Was he a poor judge of character? A poor manager? Someone who had vision but not the leadership and competency skills needed to run such a large agency? Perhaps all of the above, but just think how differently things might have turned out for the LASD and Baca himself, had he exercised even a modicum of oversight on Tanaka and others. I have no doubt he would have been the sheriff for many years and his personal and professional lives wouldn't be a mess.

Ultimately, Baca and Tanaka retired under a cloud of allegations, leaving one of the largest police agencies in the nation rudderless and in turmoil. I suspect that when Baca left the department, he knew in his heart of hearts that an indictment was in the offing and that he would be the subject of it. If his own statement in court when he was going to plead guilty is accurate, he knew he'd lied to federal investigators and would ultimately be held to account. The tale of Lee Baca is a sad and cautionary one for law enforcement leaders everywhere, whether elected or appointed. Baca and Tanaka thought they owned the department and were kings at the LASD. The voters had handily reelected Baca several times, and Tanaka was his heir apparent, as well as his confidant and all around "get it done" guy.

Although we'll never know for sure the extent to which Baca abdicated his role and delegated his official duties, it is certain that whatever the case, it led to his retirement and the loss of trust by the rank and file of a huge public safety organization, and ultimately his convictions in court. People in his agency—rank and file, supervisors, and managers—went to prison. Credibility with the community suffered. Los Angeles County spent millions of dollars on civil judgments, lawyers and corrective measures to bring the jails up to a reasonable standard of compliance with generally accepted correctional and management principles. After serving on the CCJV, Jim McDonnell (the former Long Beach police chief), saw an opportunity and ran for Sheriff, winning the election. The hopes of the community and the thousands of workers in the LASD now rest with him.

Baca was due to be sentenced to six months in federal prison in accordance with a plea agreement, but the judge rejected the arrangement. He told Baca and his lawyers that the sentence was too light, especially given the five-year sentence he gave Tanaka, Baca's second-in-command. The judge, a George W. Bush appointee who is known as a no-nonsense jurist, said the nature of the crimes for which he had sentenced others to years in federal prison, called for a harsher sentence to regain the trust of the community in law enforcement and to deter others. Because of the rejection by the judge, Baca withdrew his guilty plea and decided to take his chances with a jury trial. According to the Los Angeles Times (Rubin, Chang August 2, 2016), Baca spoke to reporters after the plea deal fell apart and said he was going to trial to clear up inaccurate statements made by the judge and the U.S. Attorney's office. In his original trial, the jury hung 11 to 1 for acquittal.

The USA took an entirely different approach the second time, introducing evidence regarding Baca's alleged untruthful statements to the FBI. The judge also ruled for the prosecution on some key issues, barring the introduction of several witnesses favorable to the defense. The tactics worked, and Baca was convicted. This entire ordeal has stained Baca's legacy and has tainted whatever life he has left. As if that wasn't enough, the Los Angeles Board of Supervisors refused to indemnify the former sheriff in a 2013 lawsuit regarding a beating at the jail in which Baca was found personally liable. As of this writing, he'll have to pay $100,000 out of his own pocket. What is clear is that his delegation of command to Tanaka is something he regrets on personal and professional levels. The lessons learned in this case for law enforcement managers and executives are invaluable and should become a case study for all new police leaders. On May 12, 2017, the judge sentenced Baca to three years in federal prison, although he remains free awaiting appeal.

WHAT SMART DELEGATION
LOOKS LIKE

I spoke with a number of current and retired lieutenants, captains and chief executives about delegation. One individual in particular summed up his primary consideration: "Trust." He told me that tries to build a measure of trust with subordinates by developing relationships with them, so he can delegate without having to check on someone constantly. He looks for the skills and willingness to take ownership of a project. If he doesn't find them, rather than give up, he'll look further to see if training or more confidence will give the individual the ability to do well. He told me he gives folks enough of a "leash" so they can feel free to look for innovative ways to accomplish the task, but depending on the project he'll have regular contact with the person to assess progress and see if he can remove obstacles. On the big, critical projects, he told me, he looks for someone better than he is or has skills better suited to the task than his. He emphasized that police managers need to realize they don't know everything and using the knowledge and experience of others on critical matters ought to be the only way to do business.

One of his comments particularly caught my attention: "Find a Doubting Thomas," he told me. "You want someone to challenge your thinking" and tell you why and how you might be on the wrong track. The important point here is that smart delegation is indispensable in a leader. There are supervision and management books that cover delegation ad-nauseam, so I'm not going to bore you with theory. However, I've seen too many people fail to delegate properly —with disastrous results—so I'll offer some suggestions that may seem obvious, but which often are not practiced. They certainly helped me over the years. These principles apply whether you're a field supervisor or the chief. Keep in mind that without a sound delegation system, which allows your subordinates to do their jobs properly, you put at risk important projects and initiatives that can get you and the organization in trouble. Further, if you don't learn to delegate, you'll start doing everyone else's jobs for them, eventually making you sick or causing you to burn out. Delegate smartly and you'll accomplish more.

Here's a simple system that should help anyone delegate with confidence, and which I found helpful throughout my career:

The person(s) to whom you delegate must understand your vision and values, and the overarching framework within which they will assume the delegated responsibilities or tasks. Resist the temptation to tell people precisely how to get the job done. Give them the general outline of the mission, coupled with a precise definition of their authority and the tools and resources they'll have at their disposal.

Make sure when you delegate a task, the desired outcome, scope and deadline are stated and acknowledged. Make it clear you are there to help remove obstacles and help work through problems.

Decentralize decision-making as much as possible to facilitate innovation and problem-solving, perhaps by using small, autonomous teams that you task with specific projects that don't require frequent input from management. There is no better way to spur new thinking in the workplace than allowing small teams with the right leadership to tackle problems relatively free of the bureaucracy.

Ensure that the person to whom you delegate has the capacity to accomplish the task or project. If he or she doesn't, provide the necessary training or mentoring.

Don't rely exclusively on those whom you know can deliver and get a task done. Look for those who have potential and work with them to develop their skills. Sure, it will require a bit more attention and the project might take a little longer to get done, but you'll be developing a back bench of capable individuals that can take on progressively more challenging tasks in the organization.

Establish checkpoints at reasonable intervals depending on the complexity of the task—not too frequently so the project doesn't get bogged down—to ensure adequate progress and completion of milestones, and make it clear with your subordinates that they need to keep you informed as to the key issues and primary obstacles on the project. Don't fall into the trap of having too many updates or useless meetings just to satisfy what could be your insecurities. If you find yourself obsessing over whether those to whom you've delegated can do the job, something's not right, so review the fundamentals and go back to step one.

Communicate the relative importance of the task or project, as well as your concerns and expectations. Remember, you can delegate authority but you can't delegate risk and ultimate responsibility, so clear communication is essential.

If the project is substantial, use software or another method to track progress. It can be as simple as Microsoft Outlook or a simple task management program that allows for task or project assignment to others. Even if you do it with pen and paper, track and monitor progress. On the more complex projects, learn to use project management software that helps you meet deadlines and gives you warning of the potential for missed milestones. I used software to help me manage large technology projects that involved a multitude of tasks and crossed organizational lines, often using outside contractors. On everyday delegation, consider a simple tickler file that prompts you to follow up on important tasks.

Give the person to whom you delegate the authority and responsibility for the work and help remove obstacles within your sphere of influence.

Lastly, if you've got a sound system for tracking progress and have provided the authority, training, and flexibility, trust the folks to whom you delegate, but stay involved. As the Lee Baca debacle points out, delegation is not abdication.

17

THE POWER OF AUDITS: DEVELOPING A SYSTEM

"Auditing is a cornerstone of good public sector governance. By providing unbiased, objective assessments of whether public resources are managed responsibly and effectively to achieve intended results, auditors help public sector organizations achieve accountability and integrity, improve operations, and instill confidence among citizens and stakeholders." — The Institute of Internal Auditors.

I have always been a firm believer in audits, which are often mandated by laws or regulations. The adage that what gets measured or reviewed gets done right and repeated is true. Organizational audits are an essential component of any governance plan that seeks to empower local governments to become worthy stewards of the community's trust and resources. According to the Institute of Internal Auditors, "The public-sector auditor's role supports the governance responsibilities of oversight, insight, and foresight. Oversight addresses whether public sector entities are doing what they are supposed to do and serves to detect and deter public corruption. Insight assists decision-makers by providing an independent assessment of public sector programs, policies, operations, and results."

Police agencies that have robust and well-organized audit

programs not only have the best potential for effective financial controls but often have the data they need to create sound strategic initiatives. On the macro side of the equation, there are many employees whom you don't need to audit because they take on and complete more than their share of work and are intrinsically honest. However, there are others who will take advantage of a lack of systems and controls. Even if the laggards are few, they can get your organization in deep trouble politically, financially and even criminally. I formed that opinion after years of conducting audits and managing the audit function in Internal Affairs and Human Resources.

You're probably already calling me a control freak who doesn't trust the systems in any organization or his employees, but commonsense dictates that a good audit program is necessary to fulfill an agency's responsibilities concerning community expectations and applicable laws. I assure you that Reagan was right: trust but verify! How do you know if you're doing things right if you don't audit your systems? Look, for example, at a recent audit conducted by the State of California on its CalGangs system, which is the statewide shared criminal intelligence system on suspected gang members. The database has strict guidelines for entering individuals and spells out admit requirements to exclude and remove people entered in error or who no longer fit the criteria for inclusion in the system. The audit concluded, in part:

> "Although it asserts compliance with federal regulations and state guidelines—standards designed to protect privacy and other constitutional rights—little evidence exists that CalGang's governance has ensured these standards are met. As a result, user agencies are tracking some people in CalGang without adequate justification, potentially violating their privacy rights. Further, by not reviewing information as required, CalGang's governance and user agencies have diminished the system's crimefighting value. Although CalGang is not to be used for expert opinion or employment screenings, we found at least four appellate cases referencing expert opinions based on CalGang and three agencies we surveyed confirmed they use CalGang for employment screenings. Although these practices do not appear to be

commonplace, they emphasize the effect CalGang can have on a person's life."

There are three types of audits in police agencies: Financial, performance, and compliance. I'll briefly talk about each one and give you some resources that can help you establish a good audit system and learn more about industry standard practices.

Financial audits should be used more often in police agencies but are traditionally limited to areas where they are required by federal or state grants, or in response to a complaint or a crisis. But in my view, there should be regular audits of areas such as the property and evidence room, overtime and premium pay practices, vice and narcotics banks, and in general any function where financial transactions take place. I have personally supervised investigations of missing evidence money more than once that could have been avoided had proper safeguards and regular audits been in place. And, the amounts of money missing (likely stolen) were not insignificant.

No other area can benefit more from regular audits than the property and evidence room. It tends to be the bastard child of many police agencies and is frequently neglected by management because it's tedious work and "not what cops signed up to do." Out of sight, out of mind doesn't usually work in this case. You would do well to purchase or check out at the library the book titled Property and Evidence by the Book, by Joseph Latta and Gordon Bowers, both retired law enforcement managers. I consider it the best and most practical text on police property and evidence rooms. You can find it at http://www.iape.org/book_new.php or Amazon.com. Believe me; it's money well spent for any police manager or executive.

Another area ripe for regular financial audits is the premium pay structure of your organization. Most agencies have them built into union contracts, and they may include longevity pay; shift differentials; educational incentives, senior officer pay, etc. Unless you audit your premium pay ledgers on a regular basis you're probably wasting money. I'll give you an example. While managing the Human Resources division of my agency I also had responsibility for the Fiscal unit. One of the non-sworn lead persons in HR was a competent, energetic and dedicated person. She cared deeply about the agency and hated to see money wasted. She came to me one day and suggested we look at the premium pay structure to make sure those receiving the pay were contractually entitled to it. Given the complexity and number of monthly changes, she was right in worrying about errors.

I assigned her full-time for a month to do nothing but audit the books. I was shocked when she came back with the many mistakes she found, including some that had gone uncorrected for years, to the tune of thousands of dollars wasted or misspent. That audit alone saved the city a couple of hundred thousand dollars or more when you consider that mistakes would have gone on in perpetuity. I know, you think your agency is immune from these mistakes and you are God's gift to policing because you don't allow waste in your organization. Just call me when you get your head out of the sand, and we'll talk.

Compliance audits are those the agency usually conducts because they are mandated by grants, legislation or agency policy. They help ensure that the department is complying with specific requirements, such as those imposed on police agencies by federal and state laws on the gathering, use and maintenance of criminal intelligence files, such as the CalGangs example I cited above. Government and private grants of all types nearly always have both financial and compliance audit requirements that must be thoroughly performed and documented lest the agency lose certification or be forced to pay back grant funds. Any manager or executive who doesn't take compliance auditing seriously is flirting with disaster and risks not only loss of the grant funds in question, but future monies as well. We'll talk about the best system for the audit function in a minute.

Before we leave the compliance area, let's review an area seldom audited by law enforcement agencies: compliance with the Fair Labor Standards Act (FLSA) and state-specific labor laws. The FLSA, in particular, can cost you lots of money, particularly if a court finds that you violated the Act purposely and with little regard for the law. Depending on the circumstances the damages may be multiplied by a factor of three. And that doesn't include attorney's fees! I realize that most agencies don't set out to violate labor laws and any problems stem from either ignorance of the law or a lack of systems to ensure compliance. Also, labor laws and union contracts must be interpreted correctly to avoid liability in these areas.

If you want to avoid expensive problems for your agency, I suggest you contact your county counsel or city attorney and ask them to conduct an FLSA audit. If they don't have a template for the review, I'm sure the federal Department of Labor (DOL) will provide all the guidance they need. In any case, don't take no for an answer and seek outside help to ensure you're complying with relevant federal and state laws, including paying your employees correctly for their regular rate of pay and overtime, as well as handling compensatory time off according to law. The DOL website contains a wealth of information and can be found here: U.S. Department of Labor. For a quick fact sheet that briefly summarizes the main areas of interest for law enforcement vis-a-vis the FLSA go here:

http://www.dol.gov/whd/regs/compliance/whdfs8.pdf.

The other audit topic I consider critical is in the use of force arena. There aren't many agencies that collect and thoroughly analyze use of force data to determine whether agency policy is being followed and, just as importantly, whether the policy is good enough to withstand a Pattern and Practice investigation by the U.S. Department of Justice. I won't go into detail about these inquiries by DOJ, but I assure you that most police departments don't spend nearly enough time on them even though they can be devastating to your organization. Take a look at this Time Inc. article on Pattern and Practice cases for some insight into how they can affect your operations:

http://time.com/police-shootings-justice-department-civil-rights-investigations/?xid=newsletter-brief.

You can easily find additional resources in the Department of Justice's Civil Rights Division website at http://www.justice.gov/crt/about/spl/police.php. I recommend you spend some time looking at all the factors that DOJ reviews when conducting a preliminary review as well as a full investigation and then build those data points into your audit system.

Performance audits are perhaps the most neglected and under-performed in most police agencies, but they are the most influential in an organization's efficiency and effectiveness. A progressive police department wants to know how it's doing with respect to its strategic goals and tactical objectives. It must also understand how it stacks up against the industry standards (more about metrics later).

Having an effective performance audit system helps you make those determinations and gauge how well you are serving stakeholders, including the community and your employees. These audits can be either qualitative or quantitative, but both are necessary to get a clear picture. Whatever you do, make certain that you publicize the results of these audits to the extent possible and that you address the results. There is nothing that undermines an organization like building expectations that you care enough to audit, but you don't follow up on the results of your examination. That's worse than if you did nothing.

While the subjects of performance audits are many, here's a quick example of one that should be the norm in all agencies. When I became the commanding officer of an investigative division of the department in the early 1990s, I conducted a complete review of its operations and spoke with virtually all the employees and supervisors assigned to it, most of whom were seasoned and dedicated professionals. I soon discovered that there was no audit system to help determine whether cases and investigations were being followed up correctly and whether the division had the resources it needed to do the job with which it was entrusted. From talking with the members of each unit I also found out that a significant number of them felt that some of their co-workers were not carrying their share of the load. A system of checks and balances did not exist at all.

We then put in place an audit system that included a supervisory monthly random review of select cases assigned to each investigator. The review would look at whether and when the investigator followed up leads, contacted the victim, and wrote additional reports on each case. The supervisors also judged the quality of the investigation based on predetermined criteria. What we found astonished not only me but the supervisors. While we found that most investigations were completed on time and appropriately, we discovered a significant number of cases, including felonies, that had laid dormant for weeks or even months with no follow-up whatsoever. While the audit results led to disciplinary action in a few cases, it primarily helped us assess resources and establish a system for continuing review of operations. Again, what gets measured and reviewed generally gets done properly.

The elements of a baseline audit system include:

Create a comprehensive list of all areas in the organization that need to be audited and determine how often that will occur.

Assign the audit responsibility to specific individuals in a particular functional unit of the agency. Consider Internal Affairs or your planning and research unit. If your department is small, assign the audit duties to an individual whom you trust and respect, or do it yourself. But understand that agency size or lack of resources does not absolve you from the responsibility to have a sound audit system.

Train these individuals properly and give them the resources they need. A good starting point is the International Law Enforcement Auditors Association (ILEAA). Their website can be found here http://ileaa.org/

Coordinate efforts with the overarching organization's audit team to eliminate duplication of effort. Sharing data and results may also lighten their load and provide insights they wouldn't otherwise have.

Codify the audit function and responsibilities in a general order. Make sure you spell out what level of cooperation you expect from everyone regarding audits, and what data must be preserved beyond that required by internal systems.

Confer with your attorney or legal advisor to determine the most advantageous way to document your audits to minimize liability. I often found that we decreased liability by conducting audits and addressing weaknesses. Juries in civil court like organizational introspection and self-initiated corrections of deficiencies. They've told me so after ruling in our favor or minimizing damages.

Don't limit the audit process to non-financial areas. If necessary, bring in someone from the outside to help you design and implement an effective audit system for all your financial systems that reinforces good stewardship of the agency's resources.

Create an audit template for each area to be audited, modifying it when criteria or legislation changes. This attention to detail will avoid audits that miss critical areas or are done each time differently.

Work with your county counsel or city attorney to make sure you have all the legal support needed and have them review all audit templates for compliance with federal and state law. If you change them, have the lawyers review the changes and document it.

18

LABOR-MANAGEMENT RELATIONS: DEALING WITH POLICE UNIONS

"The cycle of conflict, confrontation, and discord between labor and management has become a comfortable way of doing business. The communication between police unions and police management is often nonexistent, which creates a potential for disruption of police operations and delivery of services to the public. " U.S. Department of Justice

I belonged to a police union (rank and file as well as management) for all of my decades in police work. Many unions in California started out as social entities to benefit widows and orphans and to conduct activities to promote the common good of members and their families. While a few still play a largely social role, most unions in small to large agencies are multifaceted and represent their members at the bargaining table and the misconduct investigative process. They have fiduciary as well as fair representation duties to their membership, meaning that they are bound contractually to act in the best interest of their members and represent them not only at the bargaining table but also when they are accused of misconduct.

Unless you hail from a right-to-work state, unions typically rely on legislation that defines the bargaining process to provide the necessary parameters and structure within which they operate. That law in California is codified in Government Code Section 3500, the Meyers-Milias-Brown Act. While I am not an attorney, nor do I plan on engaging in extensive legal discussions in this book for obvious reasons, it is instructional to note the stated purpose of the act:

"It is the purpose of this chapter to promote full communication between public employers and their employees by providing a reasonable method of resolving disputes regarding wages, hours, and other terms and conditions of employment between public employers and public employee organizations. It is also the purpose of this chapter to promote the improvement of personnel management and employer-employee relations within the various public agencies in the State of California by providing a uniform basis for recognizing the right of public employees to join organizations of their own choice and be represented by those organizations in their employment relationships with public agencies..."

I include that partial definition, and this topic in general, because during thirty years in the business I saw unions evolve and their power grow significantly for reasons I'll discuss in a minute. But, in some cases and for a variety of reasons, I did not see a consistent, concomitant increase in management's sophistication to deal with that increased power, especially in a political context. Thus, the strategies employed by unions placed management in a reactive and adversarial role from the start. In fact, some police managers I know characterize their relationship with the rank and file union as one of the most stressful in their careers. It is seemingly and endlessly adversarial—a state which some managers described to me as a drag on the effectiveness of an agency.

I also saw how police management made some terrible decisions, prompting more legislation such as California's Assembly Bill 301, which the legislature enacted in the 1970s as a result of perceived abuses by management in large agencies, such as the Los Angeles Police Department. It is much like criminal case law: if you look at the facts in many seminal case decisions that still affect us today, you'll see some flawed police work or tactics. The resulting legislation often goes beyond the need to fix whatever problem may have existed, placing more draconian controls on law enforcement. You can say the same for legislation that's enacted to facilitate labor-management relations, which tends to enact restrictions on management actions that aren't always in the best interest of the agency as a whole.

To be sure, the increased power of police unions based partly on their political action committees and their support—or non-support—of political candidates, places police management teams at a disadvantage. A rank and file union can employ resources that have an impact on elections, which management unions simply can't normally muster because of their size. Also, I've always believed that police managers ought to tread carefully in the political arena, as the public could easily see political meddling as an attempt to benefit themselves rather than the community.

My deeply held beliefs in this area were a subject of debate when I was part of the leadership in the police management union at my old agency. That's not to say police managers shouldn't work with elected officials to educate them as to the disciplinary process, working conditions and community problems—even how their support of the union in some instances might affect the agency. But to adopt a formal political action framework can be wrought with problems and harmful optics that can erode employee and public confidence in management. I admit that a good number of police managers disagree with me and favor aggressive lobbying of elected officials to advance the management union's objectives. Those efforts have achieved mixed results. I'm fundamentally uncomfortable with the prospect of management being beholden to politicians in any way. In my view, it just doesn't look good and tends to be counterproductive.

Many managers still view rank and file unions as obstacles to their authority, including the implementation of effective policies and strategies to combat crime, such as community policing. Little empirical research has been conducted to validate that view, so the evidence is mostly anecdotal. Some argue that unions, with their influence and intrusion into traditional management prerogatives—such as discipline, deployment and scheduling—help breed mediocrity in organizations by providing cover and protection to those who choose to commit misconduct or take advantage of the system in other ways. There is a group in every organization that relies on the union to simply get by without having to pull one's weight. I saw that dynamic most often when we, as managers, failed to think strategically and didn't anticipate the issues, or didn't deal with them competently, fairly and effectively.

I also saw flawed disciplinary policies and due process systems contribute to the problem. To be sure, there are instances where unions flatly and overtly oppose a management decision or practice simply because they don't like it, even when it may be the right thing to do and is beneficial to most of their members. On some occasions no doubt, a couple of members complaining loudly to the union leadership may sway them to take positions they would not ordinarily take.

In misconduct cases in particular, the interests of the accused individual may not line up squarely with those of the general membership, or the department. As we discuss in the misconduct and discipline section of this book, some of these errant employees damage the organization, and some see the union as complicit. But unions have the duty to represent members regardless of their popularity. It is that duty to represent individual members, some of whom may not be well liked, or whose actions the membership finds abhorrent, that often feels contradictory and inappropriate to police management and to some police supervisors who may be represented by the same union. This dichotomy has always created divisions in police unions and is often at the core of a cop's view of right and wrong when contrasted with the collective benefits unions provide their members.

If I had a dollar for every instance in my professional life when a supervisor or a manager came to me complaining about the power of the union—and how it had thwarted a good policy or management decision or got a bad cop off without consequence or with too little discipline—I could play a round of golf at Pebble Beach! Look, I'm not arguing that management is wrong, and the unions are right (although surprisingly they are more often than you think). I am saying that regardless of how we perceive the union's power, it's a reality with which we must deal constructively, intelligently and consistently.

That means educating managers and supervisors on employment law and honing the agency's disciplinary investigations and processes; conducting investigations as quickly as possible; ensuring that accused employees get the rights to which they are entitled; and developing policies that are clear, succinct and enforceable. It also means working with union leadership to understand their point of view and resolve issues before they become hopelessly adversarial. That entails understanding the union's point of view and admitting when we, as managers, make mistakes or handle an issue less than competently or fairly. Learning to deal with that reality is a core management duty, so the quicker one arrives at that realization and makes adjustments in strategies, the quicker the business of the department can move forward.

On the other hand, the unions also have a duty to their members not to do anything gratuitous or underhanded to help bad cops survive disciplinary action that is carried out promptly and equitably. In the PEW Research Center survey I cited earlier, fully 72% of those surveyed said that errant officers are not held accountable by their departments. Unions need to look at how they contribute to those feelings by going beyond their required role to represent and advocate. They need to develop policies that not only meet their fiduciary and representational requirements but also consider the well-being of the membership and the department as well.

When union leaders have a myopic view of their duties it can result in a dysfunctional, counterproductive relationship with management that in the end will cost members financially, as well as a loss of job satisfaction. Labor and management need to stop looking at their relationship as always adversarial, and instead should strive to play their roles honestly and with the best interests of the department, the union and the community—and not necessarily in that order—at heart. Cultivation a professional atmosphere that relies on problem-solving can help both sides achieve that goal.

One experienced police executive from a relatively large agency told me that when he was a police sergeant, he felt as though the union and the department had essentially the same concerns for the rank and file and the department as a whole. When he promoted to lieutenant, he began to change that view when he tried to discipline an officer he knew was a bad cop and trouble for the department. He was shocked to see the degree to which the union supported the officer even though, in his mind, they knew how damaging the officer was to the reputation and morale of the entire organization. He had trouble processing the union's allegiance to someone who should have never been hired or should have probably been fired long ago. Eventually, he grew to accept the union's role in opposing management grudgingly, so he slowly began to look at ways to improve his chances of having discipline upheld and management rights preserved. He demanded better and timelier internal investigations and looked for ways to work with the union to point out why bad cops don't belong in any police department.

He firmly believes, as do I, that a small percentage of the agency is disproportionately responsible for a significant amount of the misconduct, so learning to focus on those individuals legally and competently is the key to holding them accountable. In the end, he worked with the union as much as possible, but there were times—more often than not in his view—when the department's interests diverged from those of the union. In those instances, he tried to do the right thing and stand by his convictions. As we spoke over lunch, I noticed a certain melancholy in his voice. I could tell he'd had some bad experiences with the union that left him pessimistic about management's ability to conduct the business of the agency, especially when unions can reach out to politicians with political action committees and backchannels. In the end, he told me he did what he could and wasn't going to let it bother him. Despite his words, I could tell it did.

The bottom line is that unions often have significant power over the affairs of any public safety agency. Aside from their political power, it's designed that way by the law, which was probably enacted due to management overreach or downright poor treatment of cops under investigation for misconduct. That power is bolstered by the political process, which allows for political action committees (PACs) that can help elect council members, county supervisors or state and federal legislators. So that's the sandbox and seemingly unleveled field in which we must play, which tends to erode management rights. Learning the game and dealing honestly and productively with the opposing side is critical to further the needs of the organization.

Chief executives must ensure management is an active steward of the public's trust and money, while at the same time leveraging the union relationship when possible to help accomplish the goals of the agency. The interests of the organization and those of the union are not generally mutually exclusive unless you or the union leadership want them to be that way. While you usually can't change the political process or the law, you can work with the union with the best interests of the entire organization at heart. It just takes the will to move beyond the fringes!

Remember, police management's relationship with police unions isn't a zero-sum game. There doesn't necessarily have to be a loser in every instance. Sheriff Sandra Hutchens from the Orange County Sheriff's Office told me: "They may be the union's members, but they are my employees." She went on to explain that it is imperative for chief executives to find a way to work with unions by making progress on some issues where agreement is possible, making it a positive outcome for the organization even when significant areas of disagreement remain. During our conversation, the Sheriff readily admitted that there are times when she can't move off a particular position because she firmly believes it is the right thing to do. After all, she is responsible for the ultimate performance of the sheriff's department. Nevertheless, she actively seeks ways to find common ground and achieve agreements that are both good for the union's membership—her employees—and the organization, which by extension includes the community. While there may be obstinate parties on both sides of these issues, I find that often there are ways to bridge these gaps by acting honestly and fairly.

But, there will be times when politics and the influence of the union will trump your resolve to achieve an agreement. I was part of negotiating teams throughout my career (on both sides), and there were times when I stood my ground, only to be overruled by the chief of police, who had himself been overridden by the city council. That's just the way it is sometimes and cursing a union negotiator for doing his job within the law and gaining the upper hand on an issue is counterproductive. Instead, look at your strategies, tactics, and creativity to see if there could have been another way to handle the issues.

There are times when police management needs to be relentless in its zeal to rid the organization of truly toxic employees—at all ranks and levels (see the section on Internal Affairs). Allowing bad cops, or others, to remain employed in your department, hurts not only the community and other employees but also creates the liability and loss of community trust being experienced by some agencies throughout the country. I have outlined the best way to accomplish this critical objective elsewhere in this book, but it comes down to the three core principles of which I've spoken extensively: Leadership, Competence and Integrity. Learning to lead by example and doing the right thing even if it's difficult and unpopular; having the competence in your organization to thoroughly and effectively investigate misconduct; and having the integrity to treat those accused fairly, providing all rights and due process required.

That means resisting pressure to cut corners and adhering to all laws and regulations in your jurisdiction when investigating and prosecuting misconduct. Being right some of the time isn't enough anymore; police managers must strive to deal with misconduct effectively, working with the union and others to set up robust systems that leave little to chance. Only then will you restore the public's trust in your department.

I argue that it is also in the best interest of police unions to look more critically at the conduct of some of their members. Gone are the days when police officers could use excessive force with a degree of impunity knowing that union contracts and political influence could provide the cover necessary to survive. Arbitration agreements, in particular, have at times had the unintended effect of protecting bad cops to the detriment of the agency and the union. In 2014 The Atlantic Monthly did a piece on the disciplinary process for cops (Friedersdorf, December 2, 2014) in which they list a litany of examples which, in their view, illustrates why the system is broken. While I disagree with their premise and their call for cops to become at-will employees—politics and bad managers would make a mockery of that system—the examples they cite leave you begging for a better system to weed out bad cops.

Friedersdorf's article states that: "There are, of course, police officers who are fired for egregious misbehavior by commanding officers who decide that a given abuse makes them unfit for a badge and gun. Yet all over the U.S., police unions help many of those cops to get their jobs back, often via secretive appeals geared to protect labor rights rather than public safety. Cops deemed unqualified by their own bosses are put back on the streets. Their colleagues get the message that police all but impervious to termination."

There is some truth to the argument that when bad cops win reinstatement or a markedly reduced punishment, it has a tendency to diminish other employees' trust of the system. You may not hear it said publicly, but I heard it privately many times. Regardless of who was at fault—a flawed presentation of the case or gullible triers of fact—seeing toxic employees return to work creates a sense of injustice and a disincentive to work hard and abide by the rules. In some cases where our personnel board overturned terminations, I had good employees in my office wondering why the system favored those who had no right to be employed by our department. Everyone knew they did wrong, and irrespective of the reasons for the results, they sometimes blamed it on management. But on a significant number of cases, rightly or not, they put the blame squarely on the union. My guess is that these cases slowly erode the support workers have for unions until the workers themselves need representation. So you see, it can be a vicious circle. But unions would do well to rethink a policy of relentless defense of truly toxic employees, lest they not only lose support from their members but the community as well.

There are common sense ways to strengthen your position and that of the organization when dealing with union issues. Below are my recommendations. As with any critical change, please run these recommendations by your legal advisor to make sure their implementation is consistent with your memorandum of understanding as well as applicable state, city or county ordinances or laws.

Ensure that you train all managers and supervisors (especially new ones) in all applicable laws with respect to the role of the union. That includes any legislation which governs the bargaining process and any procedural bill of rights in your state that regulates how you'll conduct misconduct investigations. As I mentioned earlier, in California AB 301, codified in Government Code sections 3300-3313, is the relevant law that you must follow in this regard. Having thorough, documented and ongoing training in these laws will likely yield fair, impartial and efficient investigations that are upheld on appeal. I know what you're thinking: knowing the law and being able to conduct competent investigations is a different thing. I agree. We'll talk more about the misconduct investigation process in the Internal Affairs section of the book. But for now, understanding these laws is a great start. And by the way, don't overlook your field supervisors out there pushing a black and white around. They are critical to making the system work. Look at the section on Checklists for a relatively simple way to ensure that your investigators follow all pertinent laws and regulations on every internal investigation your agency conducts.

Work with the union leadership to plan and implement a series of periodic roundtables with management with the aim of identifying issues that you can resolve early. Be careful not to create a process by which the union simply complains about management or managers without a framework for solving problems. Likewise, work in close cooperation with your legal advisor to ensure that the process is allowed under the Memorandum of Understanding with the union. Document all the issues and make sure someone tracks them and provides feedback to participants if the matters are not confidential under law or policy. Lastly, if you set up expectations that the meetings may lead to resolution of problems or improved relations, be sure to follow through and keep everyone informed. A note of caution: be sure to keep this process separate from bargaining sessions, which have their own rules and procedures and are subject to state and federal law.

Identify a staff officer at the rank of lieutenant/commander or above that will become your agency's management liaison with the union leadership. During the years I spent as the Human Resources Lieutenant or the Executive Officer, I frequently worked with the union leadership to identify problems early and attempt to resolve them. We developed ground rules for confidentiality and regular communication and stuck to them. I got many calls about potential liability issues, and I called them about emerging problems. We couldn't always avoid a showdown, but together we resolved many problems before they escalated or wound up in court. Above all, work hard to establish trust and do what you say you'll do. Nothing destroys a working relationship faster than going back on your word, not following through on a promise or ignoring a potential problem.

Likewise, demand that those on the union side adhere to the same standards. Sheriff Hutchens told me that was one of her key moves after taking over the Orange County Sheriff's office. She selected a trusted and respected lieutenant to work closely with the union to nip problems in the bud early and provide a line of communication between the union and management. Smart CEOs understand that working with unions to accomplish mutual goals and solve problems is not only shrewd but vital to the well-being of an organization. While you won't be able to address all problems, you'll likely exhaust any reasonable means of coming to an agreement before having to go to court or the labor relations board. Develop a set of principles by which you and your management team operate when it comes to contract negotiations. That includes:

- Being as honest as practical during the process
- Doing what you promise to do
- Looking for common ground even when you believe your position is the correct one
- Being prepared by having solid knowledge of the issues up for discussion
- Applying critical thinking skills to the most sensitive elements under consideration
- Understanding that in the end, you are responsible for the performance of the agency, so get the best deal you can.

Most importantly, learn not to take it personally. Lots of things are said at the table—on both sides—that tend to upset one person or the other. Most often, the offending statement or language is posturing and meant to have an effect on the parties' psyche. Roll with the punches and set the example by being civil, honest and pragmatic. If you take the high road, you give the process a chance to work.

Learn to understand that management-labor relations will often become adversarial and that for unions to justify their existence there has to be some conflict or issue with which they can rally the troops. Seldom do you find a workplace where there is perpetual labor peace. Some are calmer than others, and in some, the unions are constantly at odds with management. It's the nature of the beast, and the actions of some managers fuel that discord. So understanding the dynamics and knowing that the union isn't generally aiming its path at you, will go a long way to help you deal with it productively.

These are essential elements of a healthy and relatively respectful relationship between management and rank and file unions in law enforcement organizations. There are many things you can do to strengthen that relationship. There are several worthy publications that will give you a comprehensive look at these issues and I've listed them below. My parting shot on this topic is simply to remind you that you're not in this alone, and you're not the only one with ambivalent and at times distrustful view of police unions. Learn to deal with them and you'll be more successful and less stressed.

Publications:

Police Labor-Management Relations:

Perspectives and Practical Solutions for Implementing Change, Making Reforms, and Handling Crises for Managers and Union Leaders

U.S. Department of Justice

Office of Community Oriented Policing Services

Volume One: https://ric-zai-inc.com/Publications/cops-p110-pub.pdf

Volume Two: https://ric-zai-inc.com/Publications/cops-p110b-pub.pdf

Michael Polzin and Ronald DeLord

19

MANAGING THE MEDIA
RELATIONSHIP

"It takes 20 years to build a reputation and five minutes to ruin it. If you think about that, you'll do things differently." – Warren Buffet

M edia relations is a topic that has caused and will continue to cause, countless sleepless hours for police executives and managers. It's the nature of the beast, but also a medium that holds great promise for agencies that handle it correctly. There are simple principles that can make the relationship easier to manage and more productive. I'm not a media relations expert by any means, but over the years I've dealt with enough thorny issues in policing that required media contact, including providing information to news organizations on all officer-involved shootings and major incidents. For a chief executive and the community, there is no more stressful or impactful incident than a police shooting, especially when the outreach and dissemination of information are handled poorly.

The essence of what I'm about to tell you comes mostly from personal experience and my observations of how agencies throughout the country have handled these incidents. In this segment, I'll outline the seven principles I consider key to having a healthy relationship with the media and, by extension, a community that is informed and trustful of what you do and tell them. These principles are interrelated and dependent on one another, so I consider them a system for handling media-related issues of all types.

Principle #1: Get it all out as quickly, accurately and prudently as you can. I have seen so many examples of how to violate this tenet it's almost comical. Some folks believe that if you give the media the barebones minimum and hide the rest, they'll go away. It doesn't work that way. Reporters aren't stupid, and they readily recognize attempts to deceive them or hold back on critical information. They'll not only make your life miserable, but you'll lose their trust and prompt them to print adverse stories that don't contain the agency's point of view. Make it a practice to give them whatever relevant information you have as soon as you can. If for some reason you can't be forthcoming or have to hold something back, tell them why to the extent that you can. If it's a significant or potentially controversial event, conduct a triage as quickly as possible so that you're reasonably confident that whatever information you put out is accurate. It can be done, and it should be done.

Be straight with the media, and they'll respect you for it. I know some current and past law enforcement public information officers (PIOs) who are respected and trusted because they do just that. Remember, if you don't get your version of events out there, the media is likely to use whatever information they can dig up, from any source who's willing to talk to them, including anti-police radicals or anarchists who'd love to sully the reputation of your agency.

Principle #2: Consider the short and long-term impact of your decisions. Suzy Welch, the author, and wife of the legendary General Electric CEO Jack Welch wrote a book called 10-10-10: 10 Minutes, 10 Months, 10 Years; A Life Transforming Idea (Simon and Schuster/Scribner). The author advocates a system for making decisions that considers the consequences of those decisions in ten minutes, ten months and ten years. While the analysis may be a little more complicated, 10-10-10 certainly simplifies the process. I'd like you to apply that concept to media relations in public safety agencies and consider the implications of your decisions regarding the media. If you are the media relations officer, give your boss the best possible assessment of any media-worthy topic keeping in mind that your actions could impact the agency and the community not only in the short term but for years to come.

Principle #3: Be as honest as you can and follow-up on your promises. There is nothing that will get you cross with the media like lying to them or not giving them all the facts, even though they may well be entitled to them. I've seen police managers and executives shade the truth, only to find out later the media learned it from other sources. It's almost impossible to re-establish that relationship once it has been compromised. If you make a promise, keep it, or don't make it in the first place. You'll be surprised how understanding and cooperative the media can be if you are honest and level with them about why you can't reveal certain information. Don't impose unreasonable deadlines or artificial limitations on information that the media is entitled to have. While you may reasonably regulate the timing of the release, the best policy is to provide as much honest, vetted information as quickly as possible.

Principle #4: Assign the best you have to the PIO function. We've all seen or heard PIO's on television or radio that should have never been assigned to those duties. If your PIO isn't articulate, reasonably intelligent and honest, your agency will pay the price at some point in time. Don't set someone up for failure in what is arguably the most visible position in your organization. Consider creating a simulation as part of the selection process and include a member of the media and the community in the panel. Get a medium-term commitment from the selected candidate, as the learning curve is steep and it takes a couple of years for someone to feel comfortable in the job and build the necessary relationships with the media. As the chief executive, make it crystal clear to everyone in the organization that the PIO has your support and authority to obtain information and disseminate it in compliance with policy and consultation with section heads. I was a homicide detective for years and was reluctant to release information to the press. I understand the reluctance to give up details, but I also knew we had an obligation to the community to get them as much information as possible without jeopardizing the investigation.

A NOTE OF CAUTION: having a PIO doesn't mean the chief executive relinquishes the responsibility to be visible in high-profile cases. When you've got a particularly sensitive situation, such as a controversial officer-involved shooting or the homicide of a child, the community wants to see their police chief or sheriff up front, reassuring them that the agency will act appropriately and aggressively to ferret out the truth and ensure that justice is done. When a chief executive is reluctant to lead from the front in such situations, the agency begins to lose trust from the media, the community and the department's employees. Give your PIO the authority to release information as he or she sees fit based on departmental policy. Unnecessarily delaying the release of information creates problems for the media, which has tight deadlines. Trust your PIO but make sure you have input in critical situations. Once again, delegate doesn't mean to abdicate. In times of crisis, the chief executive must be up-front and reassuring to members of the community and the employees of the organization.

Principle #5: Don't play favorites. It is perhaps the most natural thing for a new PIO like one reporter more than another. When he or she starts dealing with different personalities, there will inevitably be some who endear themselves to the PIO more than others, a dynamic that may cause the PIO to play favorites with breaking stories or sensitive information. All things being equal, you must treat members of the media the same across the board. Doing otherwise will cause them to treat your agency less than fairly or slant articles or stories in a different direction than you might have liked. I realize that there will be times when certain media representatives will behave badly or publish inaccurate quotes or information out of context. If that's the case, approach them, then their news director or editor, and work out the issues if you can. If not, put them on notice that you will not deal with them if the problem continues. Tell them precisely what the problems are and give them an opportunity to correct them. Remember, treat them fairly and let them do their jobs. If you do and they don't reciprocate, then document it and treat them accordingly.

Principle #6: Use social media as much as you can but control the message and assign responsibility for all outgoing messages to the PIO and a trustworthy manager or supervisor as back up. I don't have to tell you how critical social media outlets like Facebook, Twitter, Google Plus and others are to an agency's mission. However, many departments use the medium haphazardly and fail to create sound, defensible policies that govern how it will be used. I've seen agencies all over the country get in trouble for disseminating information through social media when it was wrong, disjointed or didn't ask for specific information, leading to frustration and wasted time. Look at national model social media policies that have been tested, such as those from Lexipol (http://www.lexipol.com), my preferred source, or the International Association of Chiefs of Police (http://www.theiacp.org), then modify them to suit your agency, but always in close consultation with your legal advisor. You might even consider having a respected media member look at it. After all, your policies in general will and should be a public record.

Principle #7: Create an overarching media relations policy that spells out exactly what everyone's role should be in the organization, and what information each person can release. Even though I prefer that the PIO deal with most media requests, in many agencies that will be nearly impossible. I also know that the PIO will not always be available to speak with the media, so it is critical that you give your supervisors and managers the appropriate authority and training to handle these duties when necessary. Once again, each state has laws and regulations that govern how police agencies will deal with media requests. Whether it's disclosure of public information, such as the Public Records Act in California, or when to provide media access to disaster scenes. They are all different, so make sure the policy is well researched, lawful, clear and widely disseminated.

In the end, smart police chiefs and other executives understand how important it is to have a sound media relations policy and a competent PIO. They also realize that in the current environment, which is chockfull of social media apps and outlets, police agencies must use this technology smartly and to their benefit, as well as the community. You should view an honest, productive and sustainable relationship with media outlets as one of the cornerstones of any chief's community outreach efforts. Embrace it smartly and reap the benefits. Ignore it or do it badly and it'll become a drag on the agency and your organization, chipping away at the trust you have with your residents and businesses.

As I worked on this book, a friend, who is a public information officer for a large agency, sent me a link to a video of the Omaha Police Chief's press conference regarding the accidental shooting of a COPS show employee during the response to an armed robbery. The sound man, Bryce Dion, was riding with Omaha Police officers as is customary during filming and entered the building with the officers as the suspect started shooting at the officers with what appeared to be a large handgun. As the suspect made his way to the exit of Wendy's restaurant, he exchanged gunfire with the officers, and Dion was struck by an officer's bullet in the vestibule, where he'd entered the building. The suspect and Dion were killed, and his handgun was later determined to be a pellet gun, but looked, sounded and worked just like a real firearm.

A tragic incident for sure, and one which could have easily deteriorated given that it occurred shortly after the Ferguson, Missouri officer-involved shooting and subsequent riots. If you're interested in seeing a good example of what a police press conference should look like, click on the following link to see Omaha Chief Todd Schmaderer as he deftly handles the media. The video clip ought to become mandatory viewing for police chiefs and PIOs everywhere.

https://www.youtube.com/watch?v=pun2K52TO1s

HANDLING MISCONDUCT AND DISCIPLINE

"Only 27% [of cops surveyed] agree that officers who consistently do a poor job are held accountable." — PEW Research Center Survey

There are millions of police car stops and encounters with the public in the United States every year and relatively few of those result in a shooting or violent confrontation. But there can be no coddling of those few who commit flagrant and wanton misconduct, so police management and police unions must work together to purge police agencies from toxic cops. If we don't do it together, it will be done for us by the courts or civilian oversight, with disastrous consequences for our credibility even within our own ranks. The handling of internal investigations becomes a key imperative for departments everywhere, and the competence, timeliness and fairness of these investigations will be tested multiple times during the process. If you believe, as I do, that a small number of bad cops is responsible for most of the problems departments face in terms of excessive use of force, inappropriate shootings and other misconduct, then you'll likely agree that dealing effectively with the bad cops is necessary to protect the good ones—many of whom are losing faith that management is up to the task.

Consider that some cops are starting to recoil from proactive policing because they don't want to risk politically motivated termination, incarceration, or worse. In my view and that of many others, like ex-FBI Director James Comey, the so-called "Ferguson Effect" is probably real and—despite denials by politicians—is contributing to a serious increase in violent crime in America. Rather than pronounce police shootings as racially motivated, as the Minnesota governor did a few hours after one shooting in his state, each incident ought to be carefully examined, dissected and analyzed to see what factors contributed to the outcome. Having spent decades in the business, a good number of those years investigating officer-involved shootings, my guess is only a tiny fraction of these incidents would be found to be racial in nature. Instead, most would be seen as justified and in compliance with U.S. Supreme Court Decisions; some as accidental (admitted or not); and yet others as training or tactical failures.

But the media is replete with dramatic, high-profile incidents that appeal to those whose view of policing is cynical and pessimistic. Even the folks who are open-minded, when incessantly barraged with less than honest information, begin to react in ways that make them feel more distant from their police forces. There is no question that some police shootings appear to be clearly out of policy and could qualify as criminal, such as the shooting of Walter Scott in 2015 in Charleston, South Carolina, which resulted in a twenty-year sentence for the officer. Some incidents can be legitimately blamed on police departments and may involve predictable actions by officers that should not have been hired, were retained despite overwhelming evidence of their incompetence, or who were not supervised appropriately or held accountable for their actions.

It is these incidents that damage police agencies and lead to the loss of trust from the community. These are self-inflicted wounds sustained by the good cops and other employees when management fails to act to deal with the bad ones. In the last few years, the issue has become an existential one for many agencies, primarily due to these high-profile incidents. Adding to the problem is misconduct and underwhelming performance by more than a few managers on critical events, important projects, and initiatives. Look no further than the evening news for heart-wrenching examples of how cops are under attack seemingly everywhere. In some instances, the criticism is due to failed public safety leadership, and in others, it is clearly due to the hype created by the media and special interests. In all cases, the community and the good cops suffer.

A Wall Street Journal article (December 30, 2016, Rednofsky/Elison) explained why confidence in police leaders to control errant cops is now in question more than ever. The Journal examined over 3400 criminal and disciplinary records in public documents from every state and found that many police officers who committed serious misconduct that resulted in criminal charges either retained their jobs or resigned and obtained employment with other agencies. According to the Journal, its analysis "gives credence to the notion put forth by some law-enforcement officials that police misconduct—which has become a point of national debate after a series of high-profile shooting deaths, some on video—might in part stem from the presence of a small but persistent minority of 'bad apple' officers who are allowed to stay on the job."

Some of the chiefs or sheriffs interviewed admitted that disciplining errant officers is difficult, particularly given the extensive due process rights and substantial union support many officers enjoy. Also, the research found that states vary on decertifying officers from eligibility to do police work because there is no national licensing authority or database that controls who may be licensed as a law enforcement officer. As a result, some cops who were arrested and fired were able to find work in another state or even another jurisdiction. Another impediment to the vetting of cops who were fired and sought employment elsewhere is the practice of "file sealing." I've personally seen officers resign in lieu of termination provided the department seal their files—usually subject to review with a proper waiver—so they could apply for employment elsewhere. The tactic may appeal to a police chief who wants to get rid of a bad apple but doesn't want to deal with the due process and appeals afforded cops virtually everywhere. I don't argue we should reduce the due process rights cops have earned over decades, but I do believe there should be a balance vis-a-vis the community's right to have accountable and professional police forces.

A more recent study conducted by the Washington Post and American University (Kelly, Lowery, Rich - August 3, 2017) found that since 2006 the nation's largest police departments have fired 1881 officers, and that 451 have been reinstated by arbitrators or citizen panels. Some officers have been fired and reinstated twice. According to the article, "Most of the officers regained their jobs when police chiefs were overruled by arbitrators, typically lawyers hired to review the process. In many cases, the underlying misconduct was undisputed, but arbitrators often concluded that the firings were unjustified because departments had been too harsh, missed deadlines, lacked sufficient evidence or failed to interview witnesses." Some of the reversals may have been done by arbitrators who could have an ideological position to support the union and officers in general, but the data show that the majority of the reversals were probably due to procedural or due process errors or lack of timeliness in the internal investigations. Some of the reversals appear to be self-inflicted wounds by agencies that lacked the competence, resources or systems to conduct thorough, fair and timely investigations. Whatever the cause, putting bad or toxic cops back in the field damages not only the reputation of the department, but the morale and loyalty of the good officers and other employees.

These results undermine the premise that cops serve the community and become subservient to its needs based upon a common set of norms, one of which is that management will competently deal with misconduct to protect the public and other employees. That social construct has never been more at risk of collapse than it is today. For evidence that the good cops want the bad ones out—and expect management to do it effectively and fairly—look at the research conducted by the Pew Research Center I cited earlier, which found that most cops are losing faith in their management team's ability to weed out the bad apples. The issue of bad cops who are disproportionally responsible for acts of misconduct and bad shootings that seriously harm law enforcement's mission is not going away, so establishing sound systems to deal with the problem ought to be at the top of the list of any municipality's goals. Think of it in terms of return on investment: Dealing with the bad apples effectively and in compliance with due process requirements will not only add value to your agency, but will slowly help you build a culture of trust and willing adherence to departmental policies.

To read the extensive Washington Post article go here: https://www.washingtonpost.com/graphics/2017/investigations/

police-fired-rehired/?
utm_term=.21bf1e62055f&wpisrc=nl_evening&wpmm=1

Given the staggering investment police agencies make in new officers, there is no question police chiefs everywhere have a difficult job of recruiting the best candidates and keeping them. Hiring qualified cops has been a difficult proposition for decades, but it is particularly onerous today when departments are under crushing scrutiny, and individual officers are vilified publicly by the media. Some departments—especially smaller ones—are taking calculated risks on hiring officers who may have been terminated from other agencies, or who may have serious misconduct on their records. Some of the gambits pay off, and the officers do well, while others end up in disaster for the agency, with the officer committing additional misconduct, getting arrested or costing the department precious dollars in liability. I remember several officers whose probation was terminated by the Santa Ana Police Department who went to work for smaller agencies. Some did well, while others failed again because of their pathological failure to learn from mistakes.

The bottom line is that if we in the industry don't fix this mess, it will be fixed for us—and we may not like the results. It's about time we developed a national licensing authority and a database that tracks not only criminal behavior by officers but serious misconduct as well. According to the Journal article, "Advocates for stronger reporting say records should follow officers systematically. Some urge focusing on misconduct, not just convictions. A commission President Barack Obama created after the 2014 Michael Brown shooting in Ferguson, Mo., calls for the national decertification database to be expanded to all police agencies. St. Louis University law-school professor emeritus Roger Goldman, among America's pre-eminent experts on police, points out Congress has made such reporting mandatory in medicine, requiring data on practitioner's malpractice payouts and disciplinary actions be sent to a central repository. 'With all the concern about bad cops,' he said, "you would figure the feds would have something similar for law enforcement."

In my 30 years in the business, I saw first-hand how a handful of bad cops can knock an agency on its heels. There should be little debate that a few individuals can make life difficult for good employees and members of the community. Thus, enlightened and forceful leaders must learn to deal with toxic employees skillfully, lawfully and efficiently. If all else fails, good managers must get them out of the organization. Having leaders that aren't afraid to take action is particularly important in these turbulent times, when cops are under scrutiny for real or perceived grievances, and when dedicated peace officers are being murdered simply for wearing the uniform. These problems require leadership that withstands political pressure to malign good cops for the sake of expediency but is unrelenting in weeding out the bad ones. Only steadfast commitment to doing the right thing will allow agencies to earn back the respect of the community.

The hiring process for law enforcement employees, and in particularly sworn officers, is a system of interrelated parts that requires massive amounts of resources and time. It takes months to bring an employee on board, and a year or more for these employees to be productive. While we spend much time and effort on this task, we don't spend nearly enough time in putting systems in place—including training for supervisors and managers—to deal with disciplinary issues and toxic employees in particular. According to Michael Housman and Dylan Minor (Toxic Workers, November 2015), who have studied the extent and effects of toxic workers across the country, the effects of bad employees can be debilitating and at times devastating to the organization. "at their most harmless," they assert, "these workers could simply be a bad fit, leading to premature termination and a costly search for and training of a new worker. However, more damaging to the firm is a worker who engages in behavior that adversely affects fellow workers or other company assets; we label this type of worker "toxic."

I'm not revealing any secrets here. We've all known too many toxic employees in our respective organizations who wreaked havoc on the workplace, with management at times unable or unwilling to deal with them. Even if these employees constitute a small—even tiny—minority in the workplace, they can damage morale to the point where the good people in your department come to believe those in positions of leadership are unwilling or unable to do their jobs. If you doubt the importance of dealing with toxic employees, just open the newspaper or turn on the television, and you'll see the loss of community trust, the cost of liability and the demoralization of police workplaces everywhere. Aside from having the courage and political will to take on those who may be ruining your agency, you'll need a sound and credible system to investigate misconduct, take appropriate disciplinary action and provide robust due process. Nothing less will do. For a wealth of information and data regarding toxic employees, look here: http://michaelhousman.com.

Take a look at Los Angeles County for an example where flawed or incompetent individuals not only get to keep their jobs but get promoted as well. The Los Angeles Times (Sewell/Theroly, September 25, 2016) describes how under a new policy, L.A. County workers "can be promoted despite past arrests or disciplinary action." According to the Times, there are over 50 employees working in the county's juvenile lockups who received promotions despite serious disciplinary problems or criminal arrests ranging from mistreatment of children in custody and arrests for drunk driving. Apparently, the controversy dates back years when the county refused to promote certain individuals due to sustained misconduct or arrests for off-duty behavior. The union sued, lost and then appealed. The county, wanting to "improve relations with employees," settled the case and created a new policy that allowed more employees with disciplinary records to be promoted. The interim probation chief went further, telling the Times that even though the county won the lawsuit, "we still had a big mess in terms of employee relations."

I was incredulous as I read the article. One of the beneficiaries of the new policy, according to the Times, was an officer who was disciplined for excessive force after slamming a boy's head into a bed frame. He was given a fifteen-day suspension and was later promoted. When asked about this case, the probation chief replied, "Excessive force. Slamming a kid's head. Yeah, I don't like that," he said. "I didn't look at any of the specific cases. You just had to meet the new policy, and he must have." Give me a break! To be sure, I've taken a chance on an employee that had made a mistake in the past, but it depends on the severity of the incident and whether there were previous ones that constitute a pattern or an unwillingness to change. We all make mistakes, and we deserve an opportunity to redeem ourselves. However, serious, willful misconduct or criminal charges ought to be a red flag for retention, let alone promotion.

Adding to the problem is the lack of national uniform standards and a clearinghouse for police misconduct, Take a look at the case of Sean Sullivan. According to the New York Times (Timothy Williams, September 10, 2016), Sullivan was a police officer in a small Oregon town in 2004, when he got caught kissing a ten-year-old girl in the mouth. He was apparently convicted, and his sentence barred him from taking another job as a police officer. But in 2005—only a few months after his conviction—Sullivan was hired by the Cedar Vale, Kansas, police department, not as a police officer, but as its chief of police. According to the Times, while at his new department Sullivan was again investigated for an inappropriate sexual relationship with a girl and convicted of burglary and criminal conspiracy.

According to the Bend Bulletin quoting the New York Times, "Sullivan, 44, is now in prison in Washington state on other charges, including identity theft and possession of methamphetamine. It is unclear how far-reaching such problems may be, but some experts say thousands of law enforcement officers may have drifted from police department to police department even after having been fired, forced to resign or convicted of a crime." Yet there is no comprehensive, national system for weeding out problem officers. If there were, such hires would not happen, criminologists and law enforcement officials say. Either Cedar Vale didn't do a thorough background investigation, or they gave Sullivan the benefit of the doubt.

Regardless, there is no national, comprehensive system to check on the status of law enforcement officers as they apply for jobs in law enforcement agencies. Likewise, there is no national licensing authority that controls the professional status of cops and provides the necessary data to potential employers. As a result, errant and criminal cops may end up hopping from one agency to the other, especially when some departments do not conduct adequate background checks. As the Sullivan case illustrates, the consequences on the community and individual agencies can be devastating. This case and many others show the lack of accountability in our current system, which feeds the activist narrative of cops out of control. Without the political will to set up national systems that both management and labor can support, cops who are fired or resign in lieu of termination will continue to have employment options, further damaging police-community relations.

INTERNAL AFFAIRS AND THE
DISCIPLINARY PROCESS

In 1997 our chief of police appointed me his Executive Officer—a lieutenant's post that had responsibility for the internal affairs (IA) unit, the Chief's office operations and as liaison on all legislative and legal issues for the agency. A few years before I had ended a six-year stint as the Police Human Resources Lieutenant, which, as I told you before, was without question a revealing and formative period in my career. I was going from one high-pressure assignment to another, yet I knew that IA was a function vital to the credibility and effectiveness of our department.

Some years before, the management team had sought to emphasize the importance of internal investigations, so the Chief doubled the number of sergeants in the unit to four. That allowed him to assign most investigations to IA, freeing field and detective sergeants for other duties, including use of force investigations. At the same time, the move ensured that the investigations and reports were standardized, improving quality and consistency. In theory, the move also spurred him to pick the best individuals for the job. Ideally, they would be experienced investigators who were respected throughout the agency for their fairness, investigative skills, and writing abilities.

We also assigned a corporal to the unit to investigate civil claims and handle all Pitches motions—named after Los Angeles County Sheriff Peter Pitches; these legal motions are filed by defense attorneys seeking information from an officer's personnel or IA file for review by a judge in-camera to determine relevancy in a criminal case. While there are non-criminal uses for a Pitches motion, it usually deals with criminal offenses. The corporal would then search for any files on incidents responsive to the motion and bring them to court for the judge's review, who would then make a determination as to whether any materials—such as the names and addresses of previous complainants—would be released to the defense. The handling of these motions was an important function which required a corporal with impeccable credentials and reputation, as the judge relied on his or her word when seeking and reviewing confidential personnel records. The process had wide-ranging implications for the agency, and getting them done right was imperative.

Having a sound system for investigating complaints of misconduct and assigning the best individuals to the job is paramount in any police organization. Not only does the public expect it, but so do the members of the agency. Whether they tell you that or not, trust me when I say that the overwhelming majority expects a fair, competent and timely resolution to misconduct and disciplinary issues. They also expect that disciplinary action will be imposed when appropriate. When an agency fails to provide swift resolution to these matters, or when it metes out discipline that is unfair or disproportionate to the violation, it invites a lack of trust from everyone, and you start to lose even the most committed employees. Our agency made a commitment to assign the necessary resources and establish the needed practices to manage internal investigations properly.

The process mostly worked, but there were some instances where we made mistakes, resulting in lawsuits or inappropriate discipline being meted out. After having been involved in the IA process for many years and with the benefit of hindsight, I recommend the steps below so your agency can enhance its IA process and minimize mistakes and lawsuits. For a comprehensive discussion of the internal affairs process and an excellent guide for any organization, take a look at the Department of Justice's Community Oriented Policing Services publication called "Standards and Guidelines for Internal Affairs: Recommendations from a Community of Practices." It can be found here:
http://ric-zai-inc.com/Publications/cops-p164-pub.pdf.

The International Association of Chiefs of Police has an excellent

publication called Internal Affairs, Strategies for Smaller Departments, that gives you a brief overview of the issues and provides recommendations for small departments.
http://www.theiacp.org/portals/0/pdfs/BP-InternalAffairs.pdf

Recommendations:

Develop a comprehensive internal investigation policy that complies with state and federal laws and regulations. I like to use the "concurrent" development process, which means that from the start you identify the stakeholders, including the legal advisor, the union, and others, and begin to develop each policy with their input. It doesn't mean the union has veto power or calls the shots, but getting early input on concerns and critical issues will help you craft a document that will be practical and withstand scrutiny. In time, even if you live in a right-to-work state, you may need to meet and confer with the union on this and other policies that change employment terms or working conditions, so consult with your legal advisor. There are many model policies available but be careful with generic templates that may not include legal statutes and generally accepted principles from your state. When you design the process and document it in a policy document, write it so that even an eighth-grader can understand the workflow and each step involved in the continuum, including due process and appeal rights.

Develop an internal investigation manual and provide training. The manual should be a how-to document that you can distribute to all your supervisors and managers. This document must be well tested and reviewed by stakeholders to ensure compliance with statutes and generally accepted practices in your jurisdiction. Remember that the courts or legislature will likely deem your policy and manual a public record, subject to disclosure even without a subpoena, so make it a living, changing document that quickly adapts to changing conditions, laws and legal precedent.

Establish a time limit for investigations, so they are concluded in a timely fashion, and in compliance with any statute of limitations imposed by the legislature. In California, any internal investigation must be completed within a year of the discovery of the misconduct by someone empowered to take action, and the employee must be notified of any proposed punitive action within that same year. The law provides for some exceptions, including when criminal charges are involved. Many agencies have policies that generally require misconduct investigations to be completed within 90 or 120 days, which in most cases should be more than enough time. Not only is timeliness good for the agency and the accused employee, but also helps establish your credibility with the community. And don't forget to notify the complainant in plain language of the outcome of the complaint and any action taken by the department. Again, make sure you comply with privacy laws or other statutes when releasing any personnel information.

Decide whether the investigator or a manager will come up with the conclusions and findings of the investigation. Some agencies allow the principal investigator to articulate the summary and conclusions from the evidence and statements, and to list which, if any, policies were violated. Others ask the investigator to lay out all the evidence and then task a manager with the responsibility of pulling it all together and recommending whatever action is appropriate. I prefer the former, as the administrative investigator is closest to the facts and can best articulate a sound conclusion. However, I believe a manager must always review any internal investigation and should feel free to dispute any findings she believes are inaccurate or not supported by the facts. She should also be given the latitude to ask for additional investigation or clarification of any material contained in the investigation.

Either way, it is the manager who should determine the conclusion of the case and make any recommendations for discipline. The option you choose should be consistent with the laws of your state, your own policy and any memorandum of understanding with the union. Moreover, the chief of police should always retain the responsibility of thoroughly reviewing and concurring with the recommendations of others.

Develop a sound complaint intake process that doesn't discourage anyone from making a legitimate complaint and makes it clear your agency will investigate it and get back to the complainant with whatever information can be revealed under the law. Deciding up front whether a complaint is legitimate is a difficult thing to do most of the time. I caution you not to allow supervisors or others to dismiss accusations as illegitimate or questionable without careful review by a manager. It's a slippery slope that can create problems for your department. Instead, train your supervisors to carefully analyze the situation and determine if the complaint relates to some service issue or a grievance with the department's call response policy that had nothing to do with the employee in question. If that's the case, the supervisor should attempt to resolve the issue at that time and fully explain the facts to the complainant. If they are entirely satisfied, that should conclude the process.

The supervisor's actions should then be documented—including any training or policy issues—and kept for a reasonable period for easy retrieval should new information surface later. Pay close attention to your state's laws on negative comments regarding employees that may be placed in a personnel file. When in doubt err on the side of safety and get the employee's signature. This practice, when implemented appropriately, tends to help the department become more efficient, identifies policy issues and prevents the employee from having to go through the formal investigative process.

Establish some method for determining whether the punitive action you are considering is generally consistent with discipline previously imposed under similar circumstances. Some agencies develop so-called "bail schedules" that list ranges of punishment for specific offenses depending on whether it's the first, second or even third offense. These guidelines can be helpful in guiding the chief's actions but be careful in relying on them without looking at all the variables, including the employee's record, his experience, the underlying facts of the violation and any other relevant issues. I've often found that an open and productive discussion among the employee's supervisor, manager, and the chief will yield the right course of action.

Remember though, that you will have to justify any punishment, or the lack of, to the organization—and don't think others won't find about it, because they do, and quicker than you think. The informal pipeline in the department will have analyzed and passed judgment on your decision within days, so do it right. The most important element in discipline is that it should be fair, swift and predictable. Imposing discipline devoid of clarity and uniformity destroys trust and encourages systemic chaos. Swift, fair and certain should be your agency's motto on discipline. Nothing else will work.

Establish an early-warning (EWS), data-driven system to identify employees who may be in need of counseling, training or additional measures to correct behavior. More has been written about these systems than perhaps many other topics in managing misconduct. I won't go into detail about how they work or what they can accomplish but will comment on their methodology and effectiveness. There are software programs that cost thousands of dollars that capture just about every action an officer takes in her career, her job assignments, her training, etc. If your agency can afford one of these integrated solutions, they are great when used appropriately. They can give you a snapshot of your employees that can help you determine how best to help them succeed, or when to intervene if it looks like she's going down the wrong path. However, most agencies in the United States are small, many with 25 officers or less, so spending large amounts on software is generally prohibitive. Remember that data conversion, or capturing the data, to begin with, can be onerous, and that there are cost-effective ways to accomplish the task.

It doesn't need to be that elaborate. Using a relational database or a spreadsheet can be just as effective, and the agency often has an employee who can use both. The key is determining the data fields you'll need to capture from an existing system, or the data you'll need to input into the program after an event—use of force, shooting, complaint, etc.—and how often you'll query the system to determine if anything needs attention. For example, you can set up a monthly check of the database that includes a tripwire that notifies you when an employee has had more than two complaints in a six-month period, or three or more uses of force in a year. Then the critical imperative is to determine what, if any, action is required.

The EWS is not a punitive system, but one designed to provide managers and supervisors with early prompts to meet with the employee and see if the department can help in any way via training, counseling or another positive step. The EWS is a tool that if used appropriately can help you identify and correct problematic trends before they turn into disasters for the employee and the agency.

I don't mean to simplify the implementation of an EWS because it can be complex and demanding and, if implemented casually, can hurt a department. I recommend reading available literature and talking to other agencies, and shamelessly copying whichever programs work. They may even share their software with you if they developed it in-house. It isn't so much the EWS, as the folks implementing it, running it and acting on its alerts. Some departments are diligent, while others simply give it lip service because of a consent decree or pressure from the community. Take a look at:

http://www.dailynews.com/government-and-politics/20140907/early-warning-systems-aim-to-id-troubled-police-officers).

Look for models at www.ncjrs.gov or the Police Executive Research Forum. Most importantly, ensure that the EWS is consistent with your policies, the MOU with the union and all applicable laws regarding employee privacy and personnel file confidentiality. If you've done your homework, an EWS can help you save the careers of some of your employees and reduce your litigation and liability expenditures.

Provide for robust due process for your employees. The United States Constitution requires due process before a government employee can be deprived of property rights, and many federal and state cases have expanded those rights over the years. Some police agencies have personnel boards, boards of rights, administrative hearing officers or other mechanisms for hearing employee grievances and appeals to punitive actions. Some states are even required to grant due process hearings even before the chief executive renders decisions on discipline. You'd be surprised how many departments don't have a systematic, reliable and tested method in place to satisfy these requirements. One way to look at it is how would you, if accused or charged with misconduct, want to be treated. What kind of investigation would you want? What forum would you think is fair to plead your case or appeal it if you were charged? What would you expect in terms of discipline? Figure out your expectations, and then ask someone you trust and respect to give you her thoughts.

Once you begin to think in terms of fairness, coupled with doing the right thing, you can develop a sound disciplinary and due process system that meets legal standards but also passes the fairness test with your employees. The process also requires that you, as the chief executive, support your managers when they try to do the right thing by disciplining employees who deserve it. It is sometimes easy for good folks to become discouraged when their efforts to discipline or rid the agency of toxic employees are thwarted by a personnel board or arbitrator. As long as the manager was trying to do the right thing using established protocols and in a fair manner, you must support that effort. If the disciplinary process failed, look for lessons-learned and improve it continuously.

Recommendations on the use of paid administrative leave:

Use paid administrative leave sparingly and judiciously, but don't be afraid to take action. The primary reasons to place someone on administrative leave pending an investigation include:

- The alleged offense could result in termination or criminal charges, and early review indicates the allegations may likely be sustained
- Removing the accused employee from the organization because sabotage or serious damage to—or misuse of—departmental records or equipment is possible
- Removal of the accused employee from the department is necessary because the allegations involve serious sexual harassment or other discrimination charges, and the employee cannot be isolated to prevent recurrences.
- Removal of the accused employee is warranted to facilitate an investigation, or the employee is being disruptive or threatening to other employees
- The employee has been arrested. Although misdemeanors may not cause you to place an employee on administrative leave, consider moral turpitude or theft charges as more serious than a simple misdemeanor.

Needless to say, placing any employee on administrative leave should be done in close consultation with the agency's attorneys and the Human Resources department. When you place someone on such a status, it creates a public perception that the employee is at least suspected of having committed some serious misconduct. Whether your intention is pure, your actions will likely create a perception of guilt, so doing your homework up front is essential. That means initially evaluating the charges carefully and taking great care not to embarrass the accused employee by walking him out of the building in front of others or doing anything that assigns premature fault. Once these perceptions take hold, fueled by inappropriate management actions, it's difficult for an employee to come back to work unscathed.

Furthermore, if your initial assessment was rushed or not sufficient to convince a reasonable person that administrative leave was necessary, you may be subjecting your agency to a lawsuit. Lastly, once the employee is placed on administrative leave, proceed quickly to investigate the charges in a professional, thorough manner. If the investigative process reveals serious doubts about the charges, consider bringing back the employee to full or limited duty, taking care to protect the agency and the other members from further harm. Most importantly, finish your investigation promptly and take the necessary action to conclude the matter without unnecessary delay.

As I've told you before, I spent six years as the Human Resources Commander and five as the Executive Officer in charge of internal affairs. During that time, we placed a good number of employees on administrative leave and we terminated most of them at the conclusion of due process. Making that initial decision wasn't always easy and required careful consultation with our attorneys, but by and large we were thoughtful regarding the accused employee and the organization. If possible, we made it a point to meet the employee outside the department to place them on leave, or we did it in the middle of the night when few people would witness it, taking care not to parade the employee out the door. Once we had enough information regarding the credibility of witnesses or the charges, we reassessed the employee's status.

If you were to ask me what can be done to reduce the stigma to the accused employee, and still protect the department and its employees, I would say do your homework, act reasonably and conclude the investigation as quickly as possible. Your leaving folks on paid administrative leave longer than necessary is a waste of resources and the department's money. It creates a deserved perception with the public that paid administrative leave is like a "vacation" for many—and many times it is. How can anyone justify keeping someone on leave for a year or longer? If you can't finish an investigation in a reasonable amount of time, something's wrong with your system.

Lastly, if you bring the accused back to work and he was exonerated, the Chief of Police should make a clear statement as to the employee's innocence, unless the investigation was inconclusive. Leaving doubt in the minds of his coworkers and supervisors will likely stigmatize the person and sour their attitude and loyalty to the department. Hopefully, when you put the employee on administrative leave you had a reasonable—or even strong—basis for doing it, so in the overwhelming number of cases the employee won't return. I realize there will be situations when a statement isn't possible, or the confidentiality of the investigation or employee's personnel file precludes it, but work with your attorney, the employee and his attorney on the best course of action. Above all, act reasonably and don't single out anyone for disparate treatment. Based on the circumstances, similar cases should be treated similarly.

Develop a policy that states when an administrative investigation should be referred for a criminal investigation, and to whom it should be referred. Some agencies refer them to their own criminal investigators, while others use another governmental agency. In my opinion, it is nearly always better to have an external body conduct criminal investigations of employees. I won't get into a detailed discussion on this topic because it would take many pages, but there are several important considerations. In most cases, results from administrative investigations can't be shared with criminal investigators lest you risk Garrity violations (Garrity v. New Jersey) or specific state laws, such as the Peace Officers Bill of Rights in California. In addition, there is an implied conflict of interest when an agency conducts a criminal investigation of its own employees. While some do, it's a tall order to construct a "Chinese Wall" to keep the administrative and criminal investigations separate.

Take a look at Garrity and look for model internal affairs policies that withstand legal scrutiny when drafting your own. Police departments often get into trouble not because of a particular event, but because they failed to adequately investigate all aspects of policy violations and neglected to consider the criminal aspects of a case. For a thorough discussion of Garrity issues, as well as how non-sworn employees fit into the picture and what rights they have, visit the following links:

http://www.garrityrights.org/faq.html.

https://supreme.justia.com/cases/federal/us/385/493/case.html

Deal with truthfulness issues promptly and decisively. I reserved the issue of lying during an internal investigation for last as it is a critical topic. In general, if an employee lies when asked a reasonably clear question by a supervisor, then he or she should be terminated. There is no place for liars in any public safety organization, and chief executives must make that a condition of employment. I shouldn't have to list all the ramifications to the agency, the community and the criminal justice system caused by dishonest police officers because there are too many. The loss of trust from the community and the courts in and of itself is catastrophic to an agency, let alone the liability that is sure to follow.

A recent article by Robert Lewis and Noah Veltman in WNYC News highlights the problem in several examples from the New York Police Department. Cops who lie not only damage themselves and the agency but create a cloud over every officer and employee of the organization. Trust me when I tell you that folks in police departments don't want liars in their midst and want them uprooted as quickly as possible. And that is exactly why you must have a sound investigative and due process system similar to the one I've outlined above. Despite the size of your department, you must spend the time and resources to get it right.

http://www.wnyc.org/story/hard-truth-about-cops-who-lie/

I once heard a discussion between police chiefs at a conference regarding the issue of termination for those found culpable for lying to a supervisor. One advocated swift and sure termination with no room for equivocation. The other felt the issue was more nuanced, citing concerns such as the employee's understanding of the question, and whether the question was about a material issue in the investigation. The discussion was spirited and both sides made good points. There will be times when the discipline could be less than termination if enough doubt exists as to the employee's intention to lie, or as to whether the employee understood what was asked. I've always felt that given the implications, to find an employee guilty of lying you should have more than the preponderance of the evidence to justify a conclusion that the individual lied. To put it another way, if you're going to fire an employee for lying make sure you truly believe the charges and there is little doubt in your mind as to the employee's guilt.

The duty of a chief executive to the organization and the community demands careful but sure action in these cases. If you retain employees who have been shown to have lied, you risk keeping "Brady cops"—a nickname given to such officers after Brady v. Maryland, a 1960s case decision that, in part, mandates disclosure of exculpatory evidence to the defense. A sustained case of lying or dishonesty is one instance that is considered a disclosable event. "Brady cops" pose grave consequences for the prosecution and the agency, and likely won't be of much use to you in the field or any assignment where veracity is indispensable. There are many cases and discussions among police circles regarding Brady and its implications. It's a complicated issue, so consultation with your legal advisor is essential.

However, you need to look no farther than the current slate of news articles that describe how officers throughout the nation—who had known and troubling pasts—have been involved in questionable shootings and other incidents. If you look closely at these folks and their agencies, you'll see that in many cases the employers ignored glaring misconduct or hired officers after they had been fired or disciplined for serious matters in their previous agencies. In a significant number of cases, the incidents highlighted in the media were an indication of leadership failures and a reluctance to do the right thing. On top of the list of misconduct for which a police department should fire someone is lying. There is no redemption for a law enforcement officer who knowingly lies about any material issue while engaged in work-related matters. Period. Reluctance to deal with this and other misconduct will ultimately catch up with any agency that chooses to ignore it.

Take the case of the Los Angeles County Sheriff's Department in 2015. Since Chief Jim McDonnell took office in 2014, he made the issue of truthfulness a key component of his plan to restore the agency to a trusted, effective organization. He's fired some employees for lying—by some accounts many more than the previous sheriff, Lee Baca, fired in the last five years of his tenure. The county's civil service commission has reinstated a few of those terminations citing previous cases where some who lied were not terminated, forcing McDonnell to take them back and assign them to positions in which they have no investigative or enforcement contact with the public— essentially making them Brady cops. According to the Los Angeles Times (Chang, 2015), some of the reinstated deputies admitted to lying on police reports and to supervisors investigating claims of misconduct. In one case a deputy tried to take a photograph of a woman by kneeling down and sticking his cell phone under her dress. The deputy denied the allegations at first but later admitted them. The commission reinstated him and cited cases were admitted liars got training or education in lieu of termination under Baca. See the section on Delegation for a more thorough look at what may have gone wrong with Baca's tenure.

Even if McDonnell fires every employee who lies, he still needs to deal with a significant number of tainted employees from the Baca administration. Sad state of affairs for a proud and storied law enforcement agency. Don't get me wrong, whether to terminate an employee for lying is a difficult decision based on our discussion above, but more often than not termination is the right thing to do for the organization. Consider that public defenders and other attorneys maintain a list of Brady cops in their jurisdictions so they can use that information to impeach them on the stand. If you've been branded a Brady cop, how do you appeal to a jury or judge that you have honestly testified when you have a lying offense on your record? How would an agency feel if a rapist or murderer was acquitted because the officer in question was the only witness to a confession or to finding critical evidence? These are the thorny issues with which police executives must deal, and which if not handled correctly will cause lasting damage to the department.

21

YOU ARE WHO YOU HIRE: BACKGROUND INVESTIGATIONS MATTER

"The best predictor of future behavior is ... past behavior" - Unattributed

The old adage that past behavior is the best predictor of future behavior remains true today. In the early 1970s, Santa Ana saw an unprecedented increase in crime, especially property crimes like burglary, theft and auto theft. The strategy to combat that rise in crime was two-pronged: One, the City instituted a utility users' tax to hire approximately 100 bilingual experienced officers; and two, the police department adopted Community Oriented Policing (COP) as its policing philosophy. The strategy was enormously successful and helped bring down crime rates, garnering nationwide accolades in the process. The television show 60 Minutes featured Santa Ana as an innovative community. Unfortunately, with success came problems related to some of the officers SAPD hired in a span of about two years. As with other cities that rapidly hired large numbers of officers, often cutting corners in their background investigations, Santa Ana felt the personnel problems for years to come.

We hired some really good cops who truly helped make the community much safer and proved to be wise investments. But we also hired more than a handful of problem officers from other agencies that cost us dearly in workers' compensation, litigation, and internal complaints. In the early 1990s, I took a look at how the lateral transfers were hired to see if I could glean anything that would help us learn any lessons. Although not totally surprised, I was astounded at the number of problems I found. You have to go back to understand the Department's dilemma. We had to hire 100 lateral transfers that were bilingual, primarily in Spanish, in a short period. There was no way to conduct all those backgrounds that fast unless we assigned current members of the organization to do them, so we had many folks pitching in to complete them regardless of their qualifications or experience. So, when I looked into it, I found some glaring red flags that showed the quality of our process had suffered. The urgency to hire laterals had trumped caution and acceptable standards.

For a more current example of how less than thorough background investigations can affect an agency, look no further than the Cleveland Police Department (CPD). In 2014, Tamir Rice, a twelve-year-old boy, was shot and killed by officers from the CPD. According to the New York Times (Mele, January 13, 2017), "Tamir had been playing with a toy pellet gun near a recreation center when someone called 911 to report him. The caller said Tamir was 'probably a juvenile' and that the weapon was 'probably fake,' but those qualifications were not relayed to the responding officers, who were told only of a report of a male with a weapon. Needless to say, the shooting was highly controversial and filled media coverage for months.

While the shooting may have been justified according to CPD policy and case law—the grand jury declined to bring criminal charges—one of the officers involved remains mired in trouble with his department and will face administrative charges for failing to disclose in his job application that he resigned in lieu of termination from his previous employment at the Independence, Ohio Police Department. Again, according to the Times, "He also did not disclose that while he worked there, he failed to secure his weapon and was insubordinate and untruthful to a superior officer, records show. The Independence Police Department concluded that he had 'an inability to emotionally function,' that he could not follow simple directions and that he had had an emotional breakdown." I hasten to add that the officer deserves full due process and only after the adjudication of the administrative process will a complete picture emerge. But given what we know, it appears as though the CPD didn't uncover the alleged information, or if it did, it decided to hire the officer anyway.

I could cite other jurisdictions that had similar problems when they lowered their standards or conducted less than complete background investigations. Miami-Dade at one point had over 100 cops in jail in the 1970s. New Orleans at one point had more scandals and investigations of their cops going on than troops in the field at any one time. So it isn't an isolated issue, and it points to the critical and non-negotiable nature of background investigations. Today, with the financial pressures on government to cut costs, the trend is to hire private contractors, at the local and federal levels, to conduct background investigations. I urge you to be cautious of that approach and not lose control of a fundamental process in staffing your agency with competent, ethical individuals.

I realize that you may, at some point, have to contract out some services, including backgrounds. But before you do, look hard and deep within your agency for options to keep this function in your shop, where those that conduct them are properly trained and have a vested interest in hiring the best. Otherwise, if you're set on using contractors—and there are good ones—do your homework to make sure they are well established, reputable and hire experienced background investigators. Most importantly, assign an individual from your shop to review the quality of the investigations and audit the contractor's files for compliance with state law and generally accepted principles. I also suggest doing a top to bottom review of at least one background for every ten they do for you, including visiting some references and confirming statements from others. Having an engaged and attentive customer will keep contractors on their toes.

Given the current toxic state of police-community relations and the seemingly never-ending scandals in law enforcement, it is becoming much harder to hire cops that are well qualified. There are fewer applicants in the community, and a significant number of those that apply are either rejects from other agencies or poor candidates for employment. It's a known axiom that for every 100 applicants to a law enforcement job the hire yield is two, at most. Think about that. One or two of every 100 applicants get through the process! With the economy recovering qualified candidates are becoming harder to find, prompting some agencies to lower standards and look away from even the recent use of marijuana. I'm not going to argue the value in rejecting previous marijuana users because this book would be 500 pages, but I want to illustrate how standards have evolved over the years and how desperate some departments are getting. Some agencies are even poaching candidates from other departments, often attending job fairs and advertising in each other's media markets. The competition among police organizations to hire good cops would certainly astound you.

The same problems don't exist in hiring firefighters. They have hundreds or even thousands of applicants for every opening. Different business, different dynamics and different relationship with the community when you don't ever have to put handcuffs on someone or take their children away. If you think I'm exaggerating the state of law enforcement hiring practices or the applicant pool, just call your local chief or sheriff and ask her. It's depressing! And don't forget that because of mandated basic training and field training programs, from the time you hire a new police officer to the time they are in the field on their own and being productive is generally between 18 months and two years. That's right, as long as two years! One can shorten that period by as much as half by hiring lateral transfers from other agencies, but you saw above that, as a rule, I'm not an enthusiastic supporter of that approach. While departments can hire some good lateral officers, unless you have a stellar background investigation program there is a better than 50/50 chance you could end up with serious problems when hiring laterals. The only thing you can do is insist on thorough and competent background investigations and resist the urge to hire the B and C players. Easy to say, tough to do.

I wish I could give you a clear answer to the problem, but there isn't one. There are, however, short and long-term strategies that agencies can use to maximize their applicant pool and hire qualified individuals. In the long-term category, many departments are starting to cultivate young men and women in their communities through police explorer programs, frequent mentoring of young people in local schools and developing internship programs that target folks in high school and college. Some agencies rightly believe that having a healthy internal culture with opportunities for self-actualization and encouragement of innovation are also great long-term strategies. They advertise these assets when recruiting young men and women for these programs. In the short term, having a relatively competitive salary and benefits structure is important, but doesn't need to be at the very top of the list. Many applicants are looking for good places to work with, again, healthy organizational cultures and a variety of opportunities for advancement and problem-solving. I believe that police departments must become marketing wizards and use all tools available at their disposal, including social media and public service announcements.

Look at behindthebadgeoc.com for an example of how police departments can take the initiative and portray a more accurate and favorable image of cops. (Disclosure: I am not associated with them in any way, but I do know the editor and some of the writers.) It's not the only model. There are lots of ways to get the word out about your agency and its working environment. But you'll need to be aggressive and unrelenting in your approach. Look at the entire hiring process and shorten it as much as possible, perhaps combining the written test with the physical agility and the entry interview, but don't dilute the critical value in each. Some agencies offer financial incentives for employees who bring a qualified candidate into the process, and he or she is actually hired. Others frequently attend job fairs and advertise in relevant trade magazines and publications. There isn't magic formula, but it takes a well-designed system to help you hire the best.

Lastly, consider including a group of respected rank and file employees in the interview process to test whether the candidate is a good cultural fit with your department. Don't assume you or the management team knows best. Having that extra input will make your decision more relevant to your agency and your community. The "culture fit" interview is used extensively in private industry, and it's been validated to produce better hires than those whose sole review is by management. Further, having multiple eyes on a candidate can help you assess whether he/she is suited for police work and will likely put in the effort in the police academy. Most departments can give you examples of police recruits that were hired at great expense, only to fail the academy or resign after a few months on the job because this wasn't their "type of work."

Google has recently started a shift in its hiring practices and is making significant changes. For example, instead of asking abstract and odd questions during interviews—such as "how many golf balls could you fit in a school bus?"—to asking structured questions about what applicants will actually be doing in the position for which they are applying. According to an article in Fortune Magazine (Friedrich, November 2015), "Google has since become a fan of evidence-based management, utilizing internal data through its People Analytics department (its version of HR) and built close relationships with academics." The lessons Google has learned about hiring, management, diversity and analytics have been incorporated into their corporate culture, and assembled into a website (https://rework.withgoogle.com), that is a wealth of research and studies related to how work is done, decision making, the value of management and how people interface and produce their work.

According to Google, "Hiring is one of the most important things an organization does. Every new hire affects the team, culture, and company direction. It pays to invest time, resources, and research into the hiring process. Making the wrong hire can be far costlier than taking the time to make the right one." While this statement is nothing new to police executives and managers, we too often fail to make the necessary commitment up front in the recruitment and selection process to hire the very best candidates with critical thinking skills and the emotional intelligence required to deal effectively with people. It is far better to spend money and resources up front than to deal with lousy employees or, worst, organizational terrorists. Google offers excellent tools, templates and ideas that can stimulate your thinking regarding how you recruit and hire employees (https://rework.withgoogle.com/subjects/hiring/). Also, use these tools to review and change your promotional processes. I realize Google is a private employer with much more flexibility, but we can learn from private industry and apply what we can and what works.

LET THE ROCKS TUMBLE

In a 1996 interview by Robert Cringely for a PBS special titled Triumph of the Nerds," Apple's Steve Jobs describes an incident from his childhood when an old man who lived in his neighborhood showed him a rock tumbler. The old man and Jobs went out and got a handful of plain old rocks, then put them into the can with liquid and grit powder. They closed up the rock tumbler, turned it on, and then the man told Jobs to "come back tomorrow." The next day, Jobs returned, and the man opened the can. Inside were these "amazingly beautiful polished rocks. The same common stones that had gone in through rubbing against each other, creating a little bit of friction, creating a little bit of noise, had come out these beautiful polished rocks."

Jobs' description of the rock tumbler is a perfect "metaphor for a team that is working really hard on something they're passionate about. It's that through the team, through that group of incredibly talented people bumping up against each other, having arguments, having fights sometimes, making some noise, and working together they polish each other and they polish the ideas, and what comes out are these beautiful stones." This is one of my favorite Steve Jobs stories that illustrates why you should seek to surround yourself with skilled, hard-working people that complement each other and create the conditions for success, even if you have to seek them out throughout the organization.

I remember when I was first assigned to our homicide unit. The sergeant-in-charge at the time was a veteran of many years and a no-nonsense supervisor. He was one of the young cops that had investigated the murder of one of our officers by members of the Black Panther Party in the 1960s. He was intimidating until you got to know him, and then you'd get great insight into his thinking and philosophy. It was obvious from the beginning you had to earn his trust before he'd confide in you or share personal details, but once you did his observations and advice were invaluable. He had a knack for synthesizing complex theories or concepts into a simple form that instantly made sense.

Even though he was a quiet, reserved man, he could make you feel as though you were an indispensable part of his team. Many felt he was aloof and unapproachable, but those who worked for him learned to respect him. I had left the gang unit a couple of years before and had been working in the field as a corporal when I applied to the Vice and Narcotics unit. One morning after I turned in my application I got a call from the deputy chief who told me I was going to be transferred to Homicide. I asked about the Narcotics job and he only told me I'd be a better fit in Homicide. Not wanting to argue with the boss, I thanked him and did as I was told.

When I'd been in the Homicide unit for a few months, I asked the sergeant why he'd picked me for the job when I had never even applied for it. He gave me what I call an unsolicited "life lesson" that stuck with me forever, and which helped shape how I thought of mentoring and succession of command. He told me he had learned a long time ago that smart supervisors learn to understand not only the needs of their units but their professional and personal strengths and weaknesses as well. He went on to explain how he had an opening for an investigator and had heard I'd applied to Narcotics, which he thought would be a "waste of my experience and talents." So he called the Deputy Chief directly, whom he knew well, and had me transferred to the unit. He said he had never been reluctant to use personal friendships for the benefit of the department. More importantly, he said, you have to create the conditions for success by picking people that complement your skills and help make up for your deficits, personal and professional.

The lesson seems to suggest that to be successful you should surround yourself with folks who bring different talents to the table and upon whom you can rely, and the rest usually works out. Learn to look at yourself and your command honestly and make decisions that make both stronger. Don't surround yourself with clones or base hiring decisions on friendship. That will get you in trouble quickly. I don't mean to suggest you bypass the selection process for most positions, but when the system allows, don't be afraid to "create" conditions for success; especially in critical jobs.

As I said, I took that talk to heart and learned to surround myself with folks that had skills and abilities that made my team and me stronger. There were times when I picked or sought out individuals for assignments who hadn't even asked for the job, but whom I knew brought to the table exactly what I, and the organization, needed. In many cases, I knew the folks I picked were smarter than me or had the expertise I did not possess. In some cases, their personality played a major role in their selection based on my assessment of the tasks in question. While someone may be highly skilled, if he or she can't handle people, you'll forever regret hiring them.

In other words, I always tried to create the conditions that added value to the agency and made success possible by surrounding myself with the right people. I wasn't always right (and I paid dearly for those few mistakes!), but the majority of the time my selections proved correct, benefiting the Department and me. All the smart and successful leaders I know took the same approach. What's more, members of the team learned from each other and gained skills they wouldn't have otherwise acquired. So, as Steve Jobs said, let the "rocks tumble!"

HIRE THOSE WITH PASSION
AND GRIT

Don't underestimate the power of grit! In a recent book (Grit: The Power of Passion and perseverance, Scribner 2016), Angela Duckworth argues that success and the ability to overcome life's problems is more a function of "passion and long-term perseverance," rather than genius or intellect. In defining the importance of grit, Duckworth describes how when teaching math, she discovered that the most successful students weren't necessarily the ones with a natural aptitude for the subject. Often those who displayed what she came to believe was "grit" were also able to succeed by overcoming obstacles and displaying a keen ability to stick to goals despite limitations or problems. Duckworth tells the New York Times that grit is "a combination of passion and perseverance for a singularly important goal" and can be measured through what she calls the "grit scale," which predicted a broad range of outcomes based on a person's ability to face adversity, the courage to face difficult situations, having the resilience to endure struggles and being able to aim for excellence rather than perfection.

http://www.nytimes.com/2016/04/10/education/edlife/passion-grit-success.html

I came to the United States at the age of 15 as an immigrant from Honduras, Central America, one of the poorest countries of the world. While I spoke a little English, I wasn't fluid in the language by any means. It didn't take me long to figure out that I was at a disadvantage in so many ways, that I'd need to work twice as hard as anyone else if I wanted to make something of myself. When I began my work in law enforcement I put that belief into practice. I told myself that there would always be someone smarter and more experienced than me, but I would work harder, longer and more effectively than anyone else if I could help it. When they asked me to get one arrest, I got two or three. When they said we should get a couple of good field interviews (FIs) a day, I got ten. I wrote more reports and handled more calls than even more senior officers. I got to work two hours early to check the report boards for crimes that had occurred in my area so I'd be prepared during my shift. In other words, I worked my ass off, and it worked. It helped that I loved police work and took it quickly a scant six years after arriving in the U.S. as an immigrant.

Police work is a natural profession for those who exhibit grittiness. While intelligence and education are desirable for sure, it's easy to see why the grit factor can be an invaluable commodity in law enforcement. Cops who have lots of life experience and who have overcome adverse circumstances often make the best problem solvers. In my experience they are generally more resourceful, are empathetic and can work their way through crime problems a little easier than their counterparts. They can also readily display command presence and take control of volatile situations. I fully admit I'm generalizing here, but absent the perfect police candidate; I'd rather hire one with grit than a polished, well-educated one who lacks life experience. It's also been my experience that if you bring a determined officer into a team, those qualities tend to start rubbing off on the others over time because cops don't often want to be shown up. Cops that possess grit are invaluable to any organization, so look for them, nurture them and encourage others to model that behavior. And remember, the adage "hire for attitude and train for aptitude" is spot on for police agencies.

CONSIDER INCLUSIVE LEADERSHIP
TO DIVERSIFY THE WORKPLACE

Amidst a changing landscape in how policing is done in America, as well as the diversity of communities, cultures, demographics and ideology, police chiefs everywhere are realizing that diversifying their organizations is an absolute necessity. Some studies have shown that the organizations that hire with the specific intent to diversify the workplace outperform the others. According to Deloitte University Press (Bourke/Dillon, April 2016), "Diversity of markets, customers, ideas, and talent is driving the need for inclusion as a new leadership capability".

http://dupress.deloitte.com/dup-us-en/topics/talent/six-signature-traits-of-inclusive-leadership.html?id=us:2sm:3tw:4prmention,dup3072,dup3046:5eng:6Consulting:201 60915::deloittetalent&linkId=28067969.

Given the state of police-community relations and the challenges facing communities now and in the foreseeable future, the same can be said for public safety organizations. The more diverse police departments become in terms of gender, race, cultural background and experience, the more they can respond to emerging needs and problems. Police departments have traditionally been male-dominated organizations that tended to recruit from the military, especially Vietnam veterans returning from the war in the 1970s.

The aggressive outreach to minority communities started in the 1980s and many departments have significantly increased the number of Hispanic and Asian officers. In Santa Ana the city council, and especially City Manager David Ream, saw the trend early and made the necessary adjustments, resulting in a workforce that now closely reflects the racial makeup of the community. For example, in the 1990s as the city became largely Hispanic—with many speaking Spanish as their primary language—and a police department that was overwhelmingly white, he instituted bilingual requirements for hiring officers. In a decade, the department increased the number of bilingual officers by over forty percent.

Unfortunately, you can't say the same for women. Most agencies have failed to hire enough women by any appreciable amount. With exceptions, women constitute between ten and fifteen percent of officers in most agencies—in some the number is two to three percent. Studies show that women tend to look at problems more intuitively and creatively, and they tend to de-escalate situations more effectively than their male counterparts. They get fewer citizens' complaints, use less force and cost less in terms of liability.

For comprehensive data on this topic, go to this link for a landmark study conducted by the National Center for Women in Policing:

http://www.womenandpolicing.org/pdf/2002_status_report.pdf.

Some studies worldwide have shown that generally, women make excellent police officers and tend to improve an agency's effectiveness and risk management. However, law enforcement has seemingly been unable—or unwilling in some cases—to markedly improve the hiring and retention of women. In her comments to the Presidential Task Force on 21st Century Policing in 2015, Chief Barbara O'Connor, President of National Association of Women Law Enforcement Executives, said:

"NAWLEE agrees that our police agencies should mirror the diversity of the communities we serve. As an organization we are passionate about policing in a fair and impartial manner. But in order to achieve this we must increase the number of women in policing. As you may know, the national average of women serving as police officers has remained stagnant at 12%. However, we know women bring many valuable attributes to policing and a recent study done in 2005 titled:

"Women Police: The Use of Force by and Against Female Officers" by Schuck and Rabe-Hemp, found that female officers generally use less force in police-citizen encounters than do their male counterparts. Overall, the findings support assertions that women and men perform policing duties differently and that hiring more women as police officers may help to reduce excessive force."

To read the entirety of her comments go here:
http://www.nawlee.org/announcements/Oral%20Testimony%20
01%2030%2015-Culture%20and%20Diversity-FINAL.pdf

There is little doubt that, all else being equal, more diverse police agencies will outperform their counterparts in nearly all categories for which data is available. So what does it take to focus on diversity in the workplace, and what specific traits in police executives are needed to make this a reality in a turbulent, more complex world? According to Deloitte (see above), there are six traits that clearly identify an inclusive leader:

Cognizance: Highly inclusive leaders are mindful of personal and organizational blind spots and self-regulate to help ensure "fair play."

Curiosity: Because different ideas and experiences enable growth.

Cultural intelligence: Because not everyone sees the world through the same cultural frame.

Collaboration: Because a diverse-thinking team is greater than the sum of its parts.

Commitment, because staying the course is hard.

Courage: Because talking about imperfections involves personal risk-taking.

Recruiting women will require innovative, aggressive and focused outreach that not only expands beyond the traditional methods but also paints a more comprehensive, inviting and challenging picture of the police workplace. We will have to make a case that women can indeed find fulfillment as peace officers and that career tracks can lead to advancement—all the way to the chief or sheriff's corner office. We'll have to make community policing and its attendant principles a cornerstone of all policing efforts. That means moving beyond rhetoric to real, tangible changes in how we do business, and making institutionalization of these policing philosophies a top priority for the organization.

Attracting women also means providing services and benefits that are relatively uncommon in current workplaces, such as affordable child care—perhaps onsite—and maternity leave that rivals that which is provided in private industry. Inclusive leaders will have to work hard with their city managers, county executives and elected bodies to make policing an occupation with real potential for women who haven't imagined themselves strapping on a gun and armored vest to make a living. But it must be more than just a job—the work must be challenging and rewarding. The best way to do that is to make solving community problems an intellectual—as well as emotional—proposition. In his 1954 book Motivation and Personality, Abraham Maslow described his hierarchy of needs to underpin a human being's fundamental desires. He argued that rather than simply earning a paycheck, people in organizations look to reward their need for self-esteem and self-actualization. They want to be challenged and they aim to meet those challenges.

In addition, we will need to develop marketing plans that will show police agencies in a much better light than has the media, especially in the last few years. That will take creative methods to reach out to the media organizations and make a case that more women in policing is not only desirable and laudable strategy, but paramount to better community relations and reduced crime and community fear. I believe that the corporate world—with its deep pockets—and media executives, when confronted with data and a will to do the right thing, can become partners with law enforcement to help diversify our workplaces. Agencies will need to produce marketing products such as public service announcements and other professional materials to make their efforts more productive. Again, forming partnerships with universities and other public entities can yield significant in-kind contributions to any outreach plan.

Beyond marketing, police agencies need to look at their hiring practices to remove or modify obstacles to hiring a diverse workforce, especially women. I managed our hiring process for six years, and I can tell you that the biggest impediments to hiring qualified female officers were: one, our inability to attract women to apply for the job; and two, the low pass rate for women in our physical agility testing. As Orange County Sheriff Sandra Hutchens told me, "are we looking for people that can climb walls or those who can deal with people?" Her agency is actively reviewing all parts of the hiring process, especially the physical agility test, to see how the organization can help more qualified women applicants complete the process while retaining high hiring standards. Improving workforce diversity will require a focused, pragmatic approach that begins by honestly analyzing the modern job of the police, determining what skill sets are required to do the job, and then developing and attracting applicant pools that have or can obtain those skills. Not an easy task by any means, but one which must become a high priority for police executives.

AN INSPIRING EXAMPLE

Retired Police Sergeant Irma Vasquez-Mandell is what I consider an inspiring example to female officers everywhere. I knew her for decades and there is no one I respected more for her work ethic, skills and affection for the community. She grew up in the Delhi neighborhood of Santa Ana—a working-class area known for gang activity dating back to the turn of the century. Delhi was formed largely by Mexican immigrants, many of whom were fleeing the war in Mexico and had to abandon homes and businesses. The founders still have descendants that live and work in the area, which has remained tightly knit and mostly Hispanic.

The neighborhood often filled with sweet aromas wafting from the sugar beet factory nearby, and many worked in factories and machine shops located within a mile or two of Our Lady of Guadalupe, one of the oldest churches in the city where most neighborhood residents still worship. Mandell became an Orange County deputy sheriff in the early 1970s, working at the women's jail in Santa Ana. The jail undoubtedly gave her the experience she needed to feel confident handling inmates without always resorting to force. Two years later she was hired by the Santa Ana Police Department as a police officer.

Sadly, my good friend Irma Vasquez-Mandell passed away prematurely recently after a year-long battle with cancer. I knew her for over forty years, and before she fell ill I sat down with her to get her impressions of women in policing and the challenges departments face in hiring and retaining them. She remembered going to the Orange County Sheriff's Academy with few female officers. She had to wear a uniform skirt, making it an embarrassing proposition to do the necessary physical exercises in an overwhelmingly male class. To remain a viable candidate, she felt it was important to work hard and not let disadvantages slow her down. There was no question in her mind that back then being a woman in police work was tough because the physical requirements taxed women much more than they did men, who dominated the field. Completing a police academy anywhere is no small feat. But doing so as a woman in the 1970s was particularly daunting.

I also started as a deputy sheriff in Orange County in the 1970s, and although OCSD is a great agency, like many in the business, I admired the Santa Ana Police Department. I remember doing a roof check at the Men's Central jail and looking down on Fourth Street as Santa Ana units drove by and thinking that that's where I belonged. It wasn't just the allure and excitement of being a Santa Ana cop, but the feeling that to do "real police work" one had to work in a busy city known for doing outstanding police work. Mandell moved to SAPD for the same reasons.

During her career, Mandell developed a reputation for being a no-nonsense professional who worked hard and never gave up. She had assignments in Patrol, Narcotics, Juvenile and Homicide, where she distinguished herself as a thorough, effective and dedicated detective. She also worked as the supervising sergeant in the Human Resources unit, where she was responsible for hiring and training new recruits, as well as administering the polygraph examination for police applicants. If there was anyone who could give me useful insights regarding women in police work, it was her. She remembers feeling inadequate to do the job because the academy didn't train her to solve problems, she told me. Sure, it provided structure and taught her the law, tactics and how to subdue suspects, along with the other hard skills officers need to survive and put crooks in jail. However, the intensive training didn't teach her "how to think critically, make better decisions, solve problems," which were sorely needed skills for avoiding unnecessary fights and shootings, and to solve community problems.

Mandell told me she didn't think she had the physical prowess to do the job—especially in an active city like Santa Ana—so she had to rely on her "brain and ability to talk her way out of tough spots. "I had lots of siblings," Mandell said, "so I was lucky in that I knew how to navigate difficult situations and talk my way out of problems." She recounted how one day while patrolling the streets of Santa Ana she had to arrest a large man for being drunk in public. She was barely 5'4," and the suspect was tall and sturdy. As soon as she went to handcuff him, he began to fight. Mandell knew she would probably be on the losing end of the deal, so she asked him: "What's the matter with you? Don't you have a wife? Why would you want to fight me? You should be ashamed." Suddenly the suspect paused, then stopped and apologized, allowing her to cuff him. Mandell was able to control a dangerous situation by using her gender as a tool, and by reasoning with the suspect. I can tell you that in many instances, had the officer been male he would have used physical force to subdue the suspect, potentially resulting in injuries to one or both of the combatants. I know because I used force in similar situations because I knew it was justified, not because it was the only way to solve the problem.

Mandell told me she believes most women in police work feel as though they need to use their brains more than physical force to do their jobs. "We think differently," she told me. It has to be difficult for a female officer working in the field, surrounded by male cops, who may see a woman talking her way through a difficult situation as a weakness. "Women don't want to show weakness," she said, especially in front of their male counterparts.

I understood what she was saying because I'd witnessed similar situations. I remember an incident that occurred a year barely after I was hired as an officer. I was on a domestic violence call with two senior officers, one of whom was a woman. The couple was shouting at each other as we stood between them. The husband began to approach his wife when the female officer stopped him and began to reason with him, telling him he didn't want to spend the weekend in jail. The husband continued to argue, refusing to move back, but was settling down. I could see he began to listen and I felt we had the situation under control. Suddenly, the male officer—a seasoned veteran— walked up from behind us and pushed the husband back onto the couch. The fight was on.

We finally handcuffed him, but not before he suffered minor injuries and we had to call a supervisor for a citizen's complaint. As is common in domestic disputes, the wife took her husband's side, claiming that we brutalized him. I spoke to the female officer afterward, and she felt as though the use of force was premature. Even though she felt she was right, she still felt as though she'd shown weakness and worried if the incident would get around to the other officers. I felt for her and actually thought she'd done the right thing. I've also seen female officers use force needlessly because they didn't want to appear weak in front of their peers. That was the culture in many police organizations back then—and I suspect some are still mired in the same dynamics today.

Mandell was one of a handful of women in the department at the time and she didn't have a mentor—or anyone in whom she could confide to vent or simply ask questions. There were few women in policing and the formal peer support systems of today didn't exist. As paramilitary organizations that have long been dominated by men, police agencies have struggled to attract and retain women. It isn't just that the "macho" culture of the past that lingers, but the nature of the job often attracts males more readily than qualified females. As a result, the formal and informal systems that govern the behavior in organizations were largely created by men.

While we have more female officers and police chiefs than ever, changing the culture of any organization is often a tortuous task that even the best-equipped leaders find daunting. It isn't enough to rewrite an agency's policies and sit back to watch change happen. Lasting, meaningful change can only come from a deep commitment at the top to make police departments a welcoming and productive environment for anyone with good intentions and the desire to serve the community—especially in these turbulent times.

I asked Retired Sergeant Irma Mandell what she would do about this problem if she were queen for a day. If law enforcement agencies want to attract and keep women, she said, they have to focus on making the workplace more challenging and appealing to their sense of community and purpose. Their sense of belonging if you will. "Women want to feel as though they are part of a worthwhile effort to serve communities and solve problems." She added that by and large women are good problem solvers and want to feel as though their skills are being used for the betterment of the agency and the community. They want to use their interpersonal skills to deescalate tense situations before using force without concern that others will see them as weak. They need to feel fulfilled by doing worthwhile work, especially in challenging places like Santa Ana.

In short, they want to make a difference and aren't afraid to roll up their sleeves to do so. Most of all, she said, "The police chief has to have a vision for the organization that makes me want to be a part of it." I could see she grew more animated as she made the point, and she continued: "That vision has to take into account what's important to the cops on the street, so they feel as though there is a shared purpose."

But it isn't enough to hire women, she said. The department has to develop systems so that the officers are supported throughout their careers, but especially early on as they acclimate to the organization. Perhaps assigning personal mentors who open up lines of communication and with whom the officers can discuss thorny or weighty issues without fear of ridicule or reprisal. Women like a personal approach, she said, especially when they are new to the workplace and are getting used to the culture, which tends to be the most critical time in a new officer's career—male or female. Mandell emphasized the need for a robust support system for women in law enforcement. Otherwise, departments face a significant risk that their recruitment and training investment will come up short. Given the current political environment, the law enforcement community must look inward to retool our agencies and make them feel welcoming to all qualified people.

THE STRATEGIC IMPORTANCE OF CIVILIANS IN THE POLICE SERVICE

When I entered the police service in the 1970s, I did so as a civilian, a Community Service Officer (CSO). Becoming a sworn officer back then was extremely competitive, with hundreds of applicants lining up for a handful of positions. So I became a CSO in Santa Ana with the hope of eventually finding a job as a police officer. As you read elsewhere in the book, working as a crime prevention officer was an invaluable experience for me and gave me skills and insights I would use for the next three decades. Aside from practical experience, I saw first-hand how civilian employees could perform police functions traditionally associated with sworn officers at a much lower cost, and with greater zeal and effectiveness—and for which sworn powers were not needed or desired.

I remember conversations with officers who felt relieved that a CSO was doing the things they hated to do, or which took them away from field duties they considered their primary focus. Let's be honest, cops usually get into police work to conduct investigations, solve crimes and arrest criminals. Having them organize and do Lady Beware seminars and neighborhood watch fireside chats back then was not considered a good use of scarce resources. Officers did participate and interacted with the community in these settings during their shift, but the organizational and logistical heavy lifting fell to the CSOs and other non-sworn personnel.

At its peak, Santa Ana employed about thirty CSOs and PSOs

(Police Service Officers) whose sole task was to organize the community, lead seminars, conduct home and business security inspections and engage in community policing. Later, the department expanded the use of civilians to crime scene investigations, accident investigations and even assigned them to the detective bureau to work crimes such as domestic violence, fraud and other cases that didn't need a sworn officer until an arrest was imminent. The strategic decision to use civilians in this way wasn't an easy one, as the union bristled at the loss of sworn officers, and the politicians feared that community safety would suffer if gun-toting cops didn't attend to the community's every need. Eventually, the union recognized that they would get additional members in the civilians, and the city council grew to love having these friendly, attentive and resourceful workers to organize and help folks in the city.

This small non-sworn army was not only focused and useful; it was cost effective as well. An agency back then could hire about two civilians for the price of one police officer. While that ratio may be a little different today, it's still much cheaper to hire civilians than sworn officers—especially when most departments still suffer from the effects of the Great Recession. According to most sources that analyze police staffing, police officer ranks across the nation have steadily decreased over the last decade, and municipalities show little appetite for strengthening them. The costs, including retirement plans, are prohibitive, especially when measured against cuts in other services such as schools, libraries, streets, etc. Luckily, the crime rate is about the lowest it has been in decades, allowing police forces to cope with less personnel.

In Denver, Colorado, civilians are filling many jobs traditionally held by sworn officers. According to the Denver Post (McGhee, 2012), "Budget constraints have led to a drop in the number of Denver officers to about 1,386 today, from 1,450 before White was sworn in almost a year ago. Since his appointment by Mayor Michael Hancock last December, White has been working to get more police on the streets. The department employs about 240 civilians, including crime analysts and staff assistants. Police departments across the country have been cutting costs by replacing officers with civilians, said Richard Brady, president of the Matrix Consulting

Group, which provides analytical services to state and local governments."

The use of civilians in selected jobs in law enforcement is becoming a strategic necessity if agencies expect to overcome the fiscal problems they face. Consider, for example, how crime analysis has become an integral part of any department's response to crime, and how most of these crime analysts are civilians who are highly trained professionals. How about paraprofessionals that act as counselors, mediators and quick-response teams to domestic violence and other family-related events?

Don't forget civilian collision investigators that free officers for other duties that require their skills and equipment. In other words, thinking way outside the box to determine which duties and responsibilities can benefit by hiring civilians is not only effective, but necessary. Union attitudes are also softening given fiscal constraints throughout the country, and some now support these efforts because many of the civilians end up belonging to the police union. If you want to develop a successful civilianization program, it's critical that you meet early and often with your stakeholders, including the affected unions. I firmly believe this trend will continue, so the leadership teams of law enforcement agencies must think strategically to maximize results and reduce costs. Hiring non-sworn personnel for appropriate duties should be one element of your strategic plan.

According to SF Gate (July 25, 2010), the San Francisco Police Department "Under a $955,000 pilot project to begin in January, 15 civilian investigators trained to interview victims and witnesses, write reports, take crime scene photos and collect fingerprint and DNA evidence would respond to less-serious cases where the crime occurred some time ago and no perpetrator is believed to be nearby. The civilian investigators would work in one or two of the ten district stations." While this is not a new concept (Santa Ana pioneered it in the 1970s), more agencies are finding that using civilians to perform tasks traditionally carried out by officers, leads to more productive and satisfied employees, and work that is done well. That was also my experience.

In Mesa, Arizona the police department embarked on a civilianization campaign that increased morale, reduced response times and allowed sworn officers to focus their skills on calls and crimes that needed them (Cote, 2010). There is always institutional pushback for new programs or innovative initiatives. However, those that have merit and yield results tend to melt away opposition relatively early once the data is analyzed. The only caveat will always be officer safety. No agency can afford to reduce its sworn ranks to the point where officer safety suffers. There isn't a quicker way to end a potentially good program than to have it threaten the safety of the cops in the field. In my travels throughout the country I saw little or no evidence that civilianization reduced safety for cops.

Consider the Los Angeles Police Department, which employs about 10,000 sworn officers and a little less than 3,000 civilians. According to a Los Angeles Times article (Winton, April 16, 2016), the LAPD has 621 sworn officers filling civilian positions, jobs which could easily be done by non-sworn personnel and cost approximately $44k less per position than hiring cops. If you do the math, not only does it pay to hire civilians to do work they can perform—often better than cops--but it increases the number of officers that departments can put out in the field. Unfortunately, politicians often tout hiring cops as campaign promises, and everyone likes a big round number, like 10,000. Like elsewhere in the nation, hiring cops in Los Angeles is an activity muddled in political rhetoric, not strategic thinking. It makes for great theater to publicly pronounce how they'll hire lots of cops, but it doesn't always make sense in practical terms.

In Los Angeles, the Mayor ordered an audit that identified many positions that could easily be filled by civilians. In light of an increase in crime, he's called for a multi-year hiring plan that has received broad support, even from the police union, which in the past had opposed hiring civilians at the expense of sworn positions. Keep in mind this isn't a rigid formula for success, and while I support hiring non-sworn personnel for many functions, there are other considerations. For example, any hiring plan must improve officer safety and provide for the proper balance between responding to calls for service and giving officers the opportunity to initiate directed activity in the field. That means doing extensive analysis of all available data to determine the best deployment model. Civilians can give an agency more leeway in how they tackle crime and build a relationship with their communities.

The same goes for correctional facilities and jails at the municipal level. More and more county jails are embracing the direct supervision model (see USDOJ, National Institute of Corrections, http://nicic.gov/directsupervisionjails) and using civilians to fulfill their mission. It simply makes sense, assuming they are selected appropriately and trained well. The benefits can be measured financially and, often, in terms of effectiveness and career satisfaction, as most civilians who work as correctional officers or detention officers at the municipal level will likely report a greater degree of satisfaction with their career choice.

That was my observation during decades of hiring, dealing with and investigating civilian detention officers in Santa Ana. Most did not want to become sworn officers and made a conscious decision to work in corrections. Things change when you get to the state level and the prison systems. While I have no direct knowledge of that working environment for civilians in state prisons, the inmate populations are somewhat different and pose additional challenges to working conditions. In California, being a state correctional officer is about as hard as any job gets, so using civilians in front-line enforcement positions is probably not yet an option. Regardless, state officials are making use of civilians in nearly all non-enforcement functions.

According to a report by the Chief Justice Earl Warren Institute on Law and Social Policy, University of California-Berkeley School of Law (What Works in Community Policing? A Best Practices Context for Measure Y Efforts — November 2013), civilianization is a key strategic option to deal with reduced budgets and understaffed departments. The report states:

"In this era of limited budgets in which police departments are expected to do more with less, jurisdictions across the country are increasingly using civilian employees as a source for human resources, as they are generally relatively inexpensive compared to sworn officers. Indeed, civilians comprise as much as 30% to 50% of the staff of many departments. In this process, commonly referred to as 'civilianization,' non-sworn personnel are used to handle support roles such as administration, dispatch, crime scene forensics, record-keeping, and other administrative duties. The infusion of civilian workers to handle these tasks has enabled many departments to free up sworn personnel to focus on direct law enforcement duties and community policing efforts. Indeed, federal legislation, such as the Violent Crime Control and Law Enforcement Act and community policing grants through the COPS' program Making Officer Redeployment Effective, has specifically required agencies to hire and use civilian employees so that officers can be redeployed to community policing efforts. Although cost-savings are the most common motivation, a 2008 national review of civilianization in U.S. police departments found that among 76 surveyed agencies, 59% cited 'support of community policing efforts' as a motivation to hire more civilian workers."

https://www.law.berkeley.edu/files/What_Works_in_Communit y_Policing.pdf

As the report clearly shows, perhaps the most attractive area in which to use civilians is on jobs that don't require powers of arrest. I'll go one step further. Most cops get in the business primarily because they want to help people, but many also want to chase crooks and put them in jail. They want to do criminal investigations and bring them to a conclusion by putting handcuffs on the suspects. It's a natural inclination which the media and recruitment materials reinforce. How many recruitment brochures have you seen that show an officer meeting with residents to help them solve a community problem? Maybe a few, but I'd venture to say none. Most recruitment materials show the K-9 unit, airships, SWAT and other enforcement-related functions.

Unfortunately, we have yet to change the allure of adventure and action in police recruitment, and many get into the profession to do just that. So my recommendation is that you explore using civilians for dedicated community outreach, organizing and training, bringing in sworn officers as needed. That will sound like heresy to some community policing purists, who feel that everyone in an agency must be extensively used for community outreach, even to the exclusion of the traditional policing role. I worked with some folks that felt that way despite evidence that excluding or minimizing the traditional police role was a mistake. There is value in the significant strategic and tactical role that cops play in field contacts and arrests. Having cops in the field in their traditional enforcement role matters.

Most sworn law enforcement officers don't set out to do some of the community outreach—meetings, seminars, training—partly because they feel, rightly or wrongly, as though calls for service and putting crooks away suffers in the process. Most agencies nowadays are woefully understaffed and don't have the luxury of assigning squads of cops to focus exclusively on community policing and problem-solving. So why not hire non-sworn personnel to free up officers, but also to carry out some of the community outreach and organization that is key to successful community mobilization? The crime prevention model Santa Ana used in the 1970s is a perfect example. It worked! The officers and supervisors were substantially engaged in the effort, but the critical tasks I described above were largely carried out by civilians.

I don't see a disconnect between this approach and the most innovative community policing programs. Someone has to do the legwork, and in understaffed departments, non-sworn personnel can do it just as good or better than the cops—and at a much lower cost. No one has yet to declare that they have the best and only community policing or problem-solving model. Even the legendary guru of Problem-Oriented Policing (POP), Herman Goldstein, never claimed to have developed the only way to do it. In light of the financial and staffing problems facing law enforcement agencies, it's time to look civilianization as a useful strategic tool to do more with less.

22

FOR CITY MANAGERS AND COUNTY EXECUTIVES

"Public safety agencies consume more than half of a city's budget, so developing a good working relationship with police leaders is critical." - Experienced City Manager

The relationship between a city manager or county chief executive and a police chief or sheriff—and their management teams—is at times one of the most difficult ones to maintain, yet it is arguably one of the most important. The city manager is the chief's boss, although he or she must work with city council members as well. An elected sheriff is primarily responsible to the voters, but the board of supervisors holds the purse strings, so keeping them relatively content is no small task. Regardless of the political or employment arrangement, public safety chief executives have to work well with elected officials as well as top executives of the overarching organization. The key for the law enforcement executive—as I was told decades ago—is to be politically astute but apolitical. That means one must understand politics and the agency's political environment, navigating them astutely, but not acting with political motivations to benefit anyone in particular. It's at times a tricky balance to strike, but one which police managers must incorporate into their practices.

In addition to my own experience and relationships with chief executives over the years, I interviewed current and former city managers, executive assistants and department heads in preparation for this book. I found that their stories, complaints, and suggestions were remarkably similar, and they also dovetailed with my experience and observations over the years. I've incorporated them into the various sections of the book, but I also found some of their thoughts especially relevant to how different departments in a municipality find common ground to work together well and use each other's resources to fulfill the organization's strategy and goals. These are key points worth emphasizing, and they are critical to the success of the overarching organization.

Develop a comprehensive strategy that unifies the priorities of all departments. Without fail, one of the most common suggestions from seasoned municipal government veterans was to develop a long-term strategy that successfully blends and incorporates not only the vision and goals of the entity, but also incorporates each department's goals and objectives in ways that create synergy rather than competition for funding. One former manager told me it was akin to herding cats at times, especially when funds were scarce and public safety consumed the majority of the budget. The strategic objectives of a city, for example, include areas such as literacy, infrastructure improvements and community capacity to create a nurturing environment for children and families. While public safety is a critical component of any strategic plan, there are costly elements that aren't specifically related to the activities of a police department.

Developing a sound strategic plan, I was told, requires each department to see and understand the priorities of the other and, more importantly, how they interrelate to support community priorities. It involves having a city manager or county chief executive that can work well with department heads and elected officials, putting aside implicit or explicit biases and genuinely encouraging what Mary Barra, General Motors' CEO, calls "constructive dissension." That means being approachable and paying attention to the details embodied in every department's needs and aspirations, and the ability to encourage and listen to constructive criticism.

One executive manager told me about how the CEO of his municipality felt he knew better and often eschewed details for a "big picture" approach, which ultimately resulted in bad decisions or a failure to consider critical issues. According to the manager, the CEO felt he alone could handle the organization's strategies and had no one who was competent, knew the bureaucracy and paid attention to details. Another told me strategic thinking isn't easy in bureaucracies, but having a sound strategic plan with annual or biannual reviews is essential in times of scarce resources and competing community demands. Another said it's crucial to have a second-in-command for any CEO that is not only a competent manager but who knows the organization well and can focus on details and the implementation of initiatives.

There is an argument to be made for a CEO that focuses on high-level strategic thinking, the "care and feeding" of the elected officials, and the decision-making process that is necessary to break logjams and competing views from managers. But, that approach requires a second-in-command that complements the CEO's skills and makes up for those he/she lacks. It also requires someone who can listen and give up power and information to gain the respect and confidence from the organization. One manager told me that he stopped offering opinions on critical issues unless asked explicitly because the feedback was either ignored or glossed over. That's a recipe for failed initiatives and lackluster organizational performance at best and a miserable place to work at worst.

Develop a mix of internal training programs and events that purposely include members of all departments, especially supervisors and managers. Facing a changing municipal landscape and headwinds in solving entrenched community problems in the 1990s, the City of Santa Ana created the Public Business Academy (PBA) for all managers in the organization. It was designed to bring together managers from every department and provide them with training and interaction opportunities to emphasize the strategic approach the City had adopted. Private industry embraced the quality movement created by W. Edwards Deming, and police departments were refining their community policing philosophies to include Problem-Oriented Policing (POP).

These strategic shifts—which had lots in common—signaled an inflection point for municipal government: police agencies and their respective overarching organizations had to find new, more effective, ways to do business together to solve community problems and improve the quality of life in their jurisdictions. They had to leverage their respective capabilities into a synergistic force to focus on community problems. To do that, in the early 1990s the City of Santa Ana adopted Total Quality Management (TQM) as its guiding philosophy and used the PBA as one tool to bring supervisors and managers from throughout the organization to instill a common philosophy for problem-solving. The PBA sought to impart a set of processes and terminology that would become the City's philosophical and practical toolkit, which would be used to work within and across agencies.

As part of that process, the City created what I call an overarching strategic plan, which included a unified purpose and vision Statement, a set of values to guide the actions of all employees and the attendant goals and objectives for each department. The idea was to have departmental goals support the overarching goals of the City. Keep in mind that the City had dabbled in the quality movement in the 1980s with lackluster results, mostly attributed to lack of support from supervisors and managers. The TQM initiative meant to avoid the problems in previous attempts by getting these folks on board early and by providing training opportunities that highlighted the roles each of them played in achieving the goals of the City.

In my view, getting supervisors and managers together was perhaps the most significant move the city manager made to advance the quality movement. The idea was to create one team that was focused relentlessly on the community's problems and could draw on each other's strengths and capabilities to effectively and efficiently advance departmental and overarching initiatives. It worked.

I remember how through the program I got to know folks personally and professionally, allowing me to understand their perspective and priorities. It also emphasized for me how the police department could capitalize on the resources other departments had. I remember listening to a manager from the community development agency describe how she had to cut a position from the budget that was part of a team that conducted code enforcement inspections—a tool that the police department used extensively in problem-oriented policing. That tidbit of information allowed us to find ways to work together to create efficiencies and support our respective goals. We found resources and opportunities because we understood one another's priorities, needs, and concerns. If you've been a cop for a long time, you know that kind of cooperative relationship isn't always the norm in medium to large organizations.

I also got a deeper appreciation for their responsibilities and the synergy that we created when departments used each other's tools to further common goals and objectives. Interestingly, it also gave me a better understanding of budgetary constraints that cut into my long-held belief that the police department budget was the most important —yes, cops can be prima donnas! I began to understand why we had to develop a closer working relationship to use scarce resources more efficiently, and why I needed to walk in their shoes to truly get an understanding of their perspective.

The lessons I learned at the PBA stuck with me forever, and we were able to build relationships and accomplish objectives together much more frequently. We began to think in terms of "one team," rather than different units that had little in common. For example, do all police managers know what a city planner does, and how that may affect traffic enforcement or overcrowding in the future? Or does a community preservation officer know what crime prevention strategies and tactics cops used to reduce future calls for service? Knowing the relationship between different components of the organization can yield better informed, more productive managers that make better decisions. That is where exceptional organizations make their biggest gains: they ensure that everyone has the tools, knowledge, and commitment to be more effective together than apart.

The key is to create a culture of systematic cooperation among departments. Municipalities create artificial barriers between departments and foster unhealthy competition for funding and resources. Based on a common understanding of organizational-wide and departmental priorities, CEOs should strive to create a common set of terms and systems to analyze and address problems, issues, and community concerns. These systems need not be complicated and can be created using the parallel development process I described earlier in this book. Only when each organizational subdivision is acutely aware of the goals and concerns of the other will a culture of cooperation work. To create and sustain such a culture, the CEO must lead by example, asking for and welcoming honest feedback to help shape strategy, policy, and tactics.

One seasoned city manager told me that all managers—whether they have projects before the city council or not—should attend council meetings. I can tell you that initially that wouldn't be a popular thing to do, but eventually, it would help create one team, with one mission, that is acutely aware of the context in which they operate alongside other managers and departments. That same individual suggested it ought to be mandatory for all managers to spend some time—at least a couple of months—in the city manager or county CEO's office. An experienced police manager told me that his assignment to the city manager's office for several months changed his thinking and perspective on other departments in the City. He was able to see the needs and priorities of others and how they, too, were critical to the organization. Once individuals are exposed to all the aspects of work across the overarching organization, you begin to provide the awareness that people need to make emotional and intellectual connections with others, thus gaining a better understanding of the entire enterprise. This, in turn, can yield better strategies and a more cooperative approach to problem-solving.

To make sound decisions that add value to the organization and the community, seek diverse opinions, listen more than you talk, and then make up your own mind. This is perhaps the best and most critical task any city manager or chief executive has when dealing with police agencies. The CEO's objective should always be to select police chiefs that he/she can trust implicitly, but as Ronald Reagan once said about the Russians in the Strategic Arms Limitation Treaties, "Trust but Verify." That means developing mechanisms and metrics to determine how effective and efficient a police department truly is. It also means identifying good people in the department and in the community whose judgment and insight can be gleaned from time to time to assess how things are going. I'm not advocating spying on the police chief. What I'm saying is that when a municipal CEO has only one inflow of information, she risks having filtered information.

I'll give you a photography example. Semi-professional cameras have the ability to focus on a specific point in a scene or on multiple points—as many as 80 in some—to come up with a truer depiction of the overall scene. While focusing on a specific point will crystallize it, the rest of the picture may be blurred. Depending on your goal, you may not want to ignore the other focus points if you want to get the desired result. There is nothing wrong with looking at multiple data points and opinions to inform one's decision-making process. In fact, it is critical. The CEO may not want or have the capacity to conduct the outreach, so having a second-in-command or a trusted aid that can do that will help the organization have a better perspective on a range of issues. Don't let it deter you if there is pushback or resistance from the individual departments because there will be those who are insecure or feel threatened by your attention. Those who have the best interest of the agency at heart will welcome you wanting to look beyond the obvious when you have good intentions and do it constructively.

A final note for municipal CEOs: When you look at your own police agencies honestly, do you see leaders who have the trust of those they lead, or do you see supervisors or managers that rely on the bars on their collar or chevrons on their sleeves to command respect? The answer to that question will largely determine whether the agency is able to deliver results for the community and for its employees. Too often municipal governing bodies don't demand from their law enforcement CEO a strategic plan to ensure that people in command positions are superb leaders who possess the respect and trust of the troops.

I fully understand that a city manager will trust her police chief to do all these things, but a completely hands-off approach won't work when cities and counties have immense investments in their police and fire agencies. The CEOs who care about the future of their organizations should require written strategic plans for leadership mentoring, training and succession of command. These plans should also be modified periodically and when major changes occur in the organization. You should trust the police chief or the sheriff but understanding the organizational culture and capabilities will give you a better handle on how your cops are doing.

UNDERSTANDING AND MANAGING
THE BUDGET

Remember when Captain Barbossa (from the famed Black Pearl in Pirates of the Caribbean) tells Elizabeth after he had promised her freedom if she complied with his request, that Parley, part of the pirate's code of behavior, is more like "guidelines?" That's how cops often think of budgets. Cops don't sign up to look at spreadsheets all day long. Nor do they like having to adhere to rigid budgets. After all, police investigations and operations are unpredictable, and one never knows where they'll lead. Similarly, SWAT actions and other emergencies don't happen according to some schedule. "The bean counters ought to just leave good cops alone and focus on those that make widgets; those that can control their production rate and have more sedentary and predictable duties."

I can't tell you how many times I've heard similar laments (and even thought them myself) during thirty years of police work. After all, there are components of police work where adhering to budgets gets challenging (e.g. homicide investigations, emergency SWAT operations, riots, etc.). Should cops be expected to craft realistic and achievable budgets and adhere to them? The answer is yes, but with caveats.

Once you assume the role of a supervisor or a manager, budgeting becomes a necessity of paramount importance, especially in the lean times of the last decade and beyond. However, most in law enforcement are not familiar enough with, nor thoroughly trained in, budgeting principles as a matter of doing business. City and county managers must pay close attention to this deficit and hold the chief executives of their public safety agencies accountable for ensuring all managers are well versed in, and held to, the organization's budget materials. They must also keep in mind the fluidity with which police operations change and provide a timely process for modifying that budget based on unforeseen circumstances. Don't wait until the end of the year to acknowledge that the overtime budget has been depleted, then go into crisis mode to address the deficit. Public safety budgets comprise between fifty and seventy-five percent of the budget for most cities or counties—more in some jurisdictions.

These budgets must be proactively and aggressively managed through forecasting and frequent data analysis. If I were to give a new police chief or sheriff the best piece of advice I could about budgeting, it would be to find a highly competent, honest individual in the organization who has the aptitude to learn and manage the budget. Then cultivate that interest and trust him or her to proactively engage with the management and supervisory team to keep the numbers under control. This advice is even more important if you as the CEO are not detail oriented or inclined to work with financial data.

Here are some basic recommendations from someone who managed, and at times struggled with, budgets. Although simple, these thoughts will help any agency manage their budget a little better. These recommendations include the role of the overarching organization, such as city or county management.

Provide all managers and supervisors training on the topic of budgets. Including a general budget primer on the different types of budgets and the one used by the overarching organization. Don't simply gloss over the type of budget the organization uses and its major components. Take a deeper dive into the budgetary realities and sources of revenue, as well as limits on discretionary spending. There was a time when as a supervisor—or even as a young manager —when I knew little about the city's budget. I felt as though the world revolved around the police department and saw few instances when we needed to focus on the priorities of other departments. In other words, I was making decisions based on my assumptions, not those used to create the city's budget. That context would have given me a much better perspective on what it took to run a city and what the financial issues were.

I remember the first day I heard City Manager David Ream say that the business community generated two-thirds of the city's revenue and used one-third of the services, while the residential community generated one-third of the revenue but used two-thirds of the services. He was trying to point out the need to attract businesses and commerce so that the residents could get the services they needed. That explanation stuck with me as I rose through the ranks, prompting me to work with the business community to help them do well.

Ensure that managers understand the big picture concerning the city or county and how the safety budget affects all other expenditures. Emphasize how the police budget affects the ability of other departments to carry out their responsibilities. In many cities and counties, police and fire departments are viewed as prima donnas who consume most of the resources. Working with these folks cooperatively and honestly goes a long way toward building trust and teamwork, and it starts to chip away at misconceptions and suspicions about each other. You might consider assigning supervisors and managers to other agencies for a few days when they first promote, and to have their representatives participate in any orientation program you may have for them.

Develop an organization-wide budget team. The team should be one that works together to build the budget and ensure members of all departments understand each other's needs. Until the decision makers have a broader view of the budget needs across the organization, the allocation of resources will continue to be devoid of focus and accountability, failing to focus on the needs of the community. Having a unified budget team can help develop better budgets.

Create a financial triage system for each department. Insist on an exercise or assessment of each department's activities and develop a matrix to classify each in terms of which are mandated by law, which the agency must do as core responsibilities, and which are optional, or just nice to do. The optional activities must then be prioritized and justified. Then build your core duties around all of these activities with the first two categories taking budgetary precedence.

Develop performance metrics to determine organizational effectiveness for each activity and tie it to actual outcomes. This is critical to establish the return on investment for each budget dollar. Make the metrics realistic and the goals achievable. They must be realistic and tied to performance standards that are well articulated. Don't make this just another exercise. Build it as an important component of your budget process. More importantly, follow up!

Create a budget early-warning system and budgetary milestones across departments. Design monthly checkpoints and a mid-year budget review for each division or bureau to ensure there are no budgetary surprises at the end of the fiscal year. Also, devise an early-warning system based on financial metrics that will alert departments about impending budgetary shortfalls that can be tracked on a monthly basis, such as departmental spending down to the account level. Build that system as an enduring financial instrument that endures over time and turnover in management ranks.

This is perhaps one of the most critical actions any municipality can take to avoid financial problems. Look no further than San Bernardino, California for a prime example. Forced to declare bankruptcy in 2012 it is emerging from that process. While many factors contributed to their problems: confusing and inadequate charter giving the mayor and city manager dueling authority; frequent turnover of leadership positions; and spending more than their revenues.

One, however, stands out glaringly: their inability to detect and act upon signs of management and fiscal dysfunction. Andrew Belknap, regional Vice-President of Management Partners, was quoted in a Governing Magazine article by Liz Farmer (August 25, 2016): "Belknap said the city's overly complicated system of checks and balances in its 48-page charter and extreme turnover essentially created a stalled government: Between 2004 and 2014, the city cycled through five city managers, five police chiefs, four finance directors and five public works directors. The situation was so disorganized that by the time officials realized the full magnitude of the city's finances, it was too late to declare a financial emergency. Instead, San Bernardino officials had to declare insolvency, or they weren't going to make payroll. 'They didn't have the political and management systems in place to see this coming or act ahead of time,' Belknap said."

http://www.governing.com/topics/finance/gov-story-behind-san-bernardinos-long-bankruptcy.html

Give each budget account a realistic figure and then hold all managers accountable for living within their means, understanding that unforeseen circumstances will occur. Don't make the same mistake my agency made from time to time by providing budget numbers and then bailing out those who couldn't hold to them (including me at times). Make them conduct a thorough analysis as to why the deficits occurred and a plan to help prevent them in the future to the extent possible. More importantly, focus on the early-warning system described above.

For the civilian executive and management team in overarching organizations there is no more consequential objective than creating a unified and committed group of supervisors and managers in their public safety agencies. The sheer amount of resources these departments consume should make it a top priority for any city manager or county CEO to understand their business and provide clear-eyed oversight for their functions.

23

SKILLS AND STRATEGIES FOR PROMOTION

"I've missed more than 9000 shots in my career. I've lost almost 300 games. 26 times, I've been trusted to take the game winning shot and missed. I've failed over and over and over again in my life. And that is why I succeed." — Michael Jordan

I was blessed to have worked with some great street cops and investigators during my career. Some went on to promote up the chain of command, while others chose to remain in the field. Their reasons for not wanting to promote varied, with some citing the seniority that gave them good days off, (in most organizations as a new sergeant you start at the bottom in terms of seniority), to the increased responsibility, for which the increase in pay didn't necessarily compensate them appropriately.

One of the best street cops I ever worked with told me once that he remained a patrol officer because he loved it, and because he didn't think he had the skills and personality to be a good supervisor or manager. He didn't want to take responsibility for a team of officers or do the attendant administrative work. In short, he wanted to do what he loved without being encumbered by supervisory duties. I respected him not only because he was such a good cop, but because he knew what drove him and made him happy. He recognized he didn't have the personality to lead others in a formal role.

Some who seek promotion fail to take an introspective look at their motivations and skill set, thinking that the formal authority will compensate for their deficiencies. Some look at the money as the only motivator, but soon find out that it never makes up for a lack of interpersonal skills it takes to lead people effectively. In my view, the best cops in the agency won't necessarily make the best supervisors or managers. Don't get me wrong; these folks are key to the agency and you want to nurture them and value their work. And being an outstanding police officer gives you a leg up on the promotional process as long as you have the soft skills to go along with it.

My advice to anyone considering promotion is to do a comprehensive inventory of their skills and abilities to see if they are compatible with those needed in supervisory or management roles, and then to assess their motivation honestly. If money is one of those motivators, that's fine, but they ought to ask themselves if they are ready to assume more responsibility and be responsible for the lives and work of those who will become subordinates. If you've done that assessment and conclude that you want to promote, read on.

Most people start preparing for promotion too late. They squeeze all of their efforts into the last month before an interview—some wait until the week before and expect to do well, rather than think of it as a career-long endeavor, with an intense period of preparation in the weeks or months preceding the exams. They prepare tactically rather than strategically!

That's how I saw it in the early stages of my career, not even giving it a serious thought during the years when I was in the field having too much fun to think about it in any other way. I remember wondering during those early years why anyone would want to give up the job of a patrol officer. It was nirvana for crying out loud! When I was promoted to Detective and assigned to the Major Enforcement Team, then to Gangs, the thought of promotion was still remote, although I was starting to think I could contribute more to the agency in different capacities.

Years later, after I'd gone through a corporal's promotional process, I began to think about it all as a system—one which made sense for the organization and me. As my career progressed, I began to help younger officers prepare for promotion by encouraging them to think in broader terms, avoiding the last-minute cramming and studying to pass an exam. Although that was important, it was a shallow way to think about it, and it didn't make you a better supervisor. Thinking about it in tactical terms may have worked for some, but it didn't give them the tools they needed to lead men and women in a physically and emotionally dangerous profession.

Looking at one's career strategically as well as practically helps round out your experience and sharpens your intellect, making you better suited for promotion. You'll notice I said: "practically" when thinking about your career. What I mean is not everyone is suitable for promotion, and you should not even attempt it until you feel comfortable with your level of experience, maturity, and knowledge of the job. I know that may be controversial, but I am a firm believer that you must have substantial experience in the first few rungs of your career ladder before you even think about promotion.

For example, if you're a new police officer, you should strive to learn and do the job of a patrol officer for at least several years. I don't just mean showing up and answering calls—I mean doing the job well and becoming effective in the field, gaining experience in all its facets until you can almost do it blindfolded! Then, look for investigative and administrative assignments, in that order. If they aren't plentiful, volunteer for them for short periods of time. Then, and only then, should you look for a promotion.

I believe that my career progression was based in part on my experience in the field as a patrol officer and investigative assignments. I don't mean you can't be a good supervisor or manager if you have limited experience in some areas. I've seen a good number of folks who were very good at what they did without touching every base. But it certainly helps if you are well rounded and have done a variety of jobs in the agency. I've seen how some individuals were promoted because they were good test-takers, or they were charismatic and articulate, without the substance to back it up. Almost always these individuals had a tough time making decisions and relating to the troops in the field.

All things being equal, having a varied set of experience gives you a leg up, and gives you the basis to do the job right. You've been there, done that, so no matter what gets thrown at you there is a place or situation you can reference! Don't be eager to promote too soon. Enjoy your job, do it well and seek assignment opportunities. It will pay off in the end.

I like to think of the promotion system as a three-part plan of action. The first part begins as soon as you have a few years of experience under your belt and you've decided that you want to contribute more as a supervisor, manager or executive in an organization. I call this the FOUNDATION phase, when you gather as much and as varied an experience base as you possibly can. This part of the plan is as long as your career and should be evaluated on a yearly basis. (review Gap Analysis earlier in this book.) This phase starts to build your reputation and the record upon which you'll seek promotion. The best advice I can give you is to work hard, use your common sense and learn to do thorough and complete investigations. That means doing more than they ask you to do and never letting the police radio dictate how busy you are in the field. If you're not on a call or a report, keep engaged through observation activity or solving community problems.

You know what I'm talking about: the cops that do the minimum or shy away from challenges end up pushing a black and white around for the rest of their careers. As I've said elsewhere in this book, being a competent patrol officer or detective is an honorable and commendable way to spend one's career in law enforcement. I've known and greatly respected good cops that didn't want to get promoted. They enjoyed their work and did a superb job. There were others that merely wanted to coast, doing the minimum to keep their jobs and their sergeant off their backs. These are the folks that turn a police department into a mediocre organization and, as you've read in this book, police management hasn't done enough to deal with them effectively. Hopefully you will learn from their mistakes.

The second part is the EXPANSION phase when you use your experience, insight, and talent to make even more valuable contributions to your agency in a variety of areas beyond your performance in the field. This phase tends to begin after four or five years on the job when your experience and skills help you define problems and find better solutions, and you begin to see more clearly the cause and effect of the most entrenched problems with which you deal. By that, I mean that you've dealt with a host of issues in policing and experienced circumstances that gave you a better sense of the job, the community, and your organization. That exposure provides a base from which you can build a more resourceful and useful career. During the first few years as a police officer, I focused on the basics of police work, enjoying my job tremendously and building a good reputation as a field officer. It was, without a doubt, the springboard to other assignments and more knowledge-gaining opportunities. Don't waste those years by coasting by or letting the radio tell you what to do. It behooves you to be proactive and inquisitive and develop a solid reputation for being a hard worker, good report writer, and competent field investigator.

The last part is the ROUNDING OUT phase, when the importance of relationships, resources, policing philosophies and data-driven analysis becomes more obvious, offering you the potential to be truly influential in your organization. This phase becomes a continuum, an ebb and flow of discovery and ideas that gets more pronounced with your desire to help the troops and your department make a difference in the community. This phase is when you further hone your interview skills and become adept at articulating your point of view. We'll talk about this in more detail but notice that I didn't mention what I call the CRAMMING phase. I didn't mention it because it should be obvious: the three to six months before the official promotional exam begins when you review all departmental policies, procedures, and programs that are relevant to the process.

Also, this is the period when your research takes you to laws, rules, and regulations, as well as the case law that governs everything we do in police work. We'll talk about this phase a little more, but we won't dwell on it. Don't worry too much about rigidly following a path that you believe will get you promoted. Rather, do the best job you can, learn as much as you can and experience as many facets of policing as you can to make you well rounded. More importantly, learn how to deal with people at all levels, from crooks to community members, to co-workers and supervisors. The ability to exhibit emotional intelligence and handle human relations will become your greatest asset. Using those skills to forge relationships is without a doubt anyone's greatest tool in any organization.

HOW TO ACE THE PROMOTIONAL
TESTING PROCESS

Let's talk about what most departments are looking for in their promotional candidates. Keep in mind that this topic alone could be two-hundred pages long, so we'll cover what I consider to be the key ingredients for success in getting promoted. Over the years I was a promotional panel member dozens of times and for all types of processes, including oral boards, practical exercises and assessment centers. I also graded written essays for management positions, including lieutenant and captain. After the first few you begin to see the common threads that distinguish the truly successful candidates from the mediocre. You can generally tell who's well prepared and who isn't, and who has that fire in the belly for promotion for the right reasons.

What usually wrapped it all up for me was the person's ability to connect with me viscerally and emotionally. If you read this book from the beginning, you know what I mean by that. Not that these processes are infallible, because too many go on to get promoted that never should have been. But if you do enough of these panels you can usually see through the insincere or superficial. It all comes back to the critical skills modern leaders need, and the ability to project them credibly. Let's talk about what you'll need to convey in an interview or another process that will bring you to the top of the pack.

First, police managers and executives want to know how you think, how you handle matters that challenge your integrity, how you deal with the community and how you solve problems. Second, they want to know if you are reasonably intelligent and whether your emotional IQ has prepared you to deal with employees and challenging situations with empathy and genuine concern. Third, they want to test your ability to break down complex issues and problems into manageable chunks, ultimately arriving at a reasonable conclusion.

Lastly, they want to see if you possess the right communication skills—writing and speaking clearly and persuasively. Your job, in forty-five minutes or often less, is to convince them you not only possess these abilities, but you've used them successfully. After all, if you're applying for a supervisory or managerial position, you should have a meaningful record from which to draw. So here are some of my recommendations for successful interviews or other selection processes. These aren't exhaustive, but they are the critical ones without which you probably won't get to first base.

Do your homework. There is little redeeming value in an interview where the candidate failed to do his or her homework about the job for which one is applying, or about the department's current vision, values or policing philosophies. Doing the research is not only smart, but it should be a precursor to all other preparations you undertake. I have participated in interview boards where candidates assume that their charisma, experience, and tenure have prepared them to answer factual questions about key departmental philosophies and strategic positions. Don't make that mistake! Devote all the time necessary to talking to others who may have good insights into the organization, reviewing planning documents and developing a good understanding of your agency's key metrics and issues. Whether you're applying for a supervisory or management position doesn't matter; the more you know about these critical issues, the better you'll come across.

Lest I regret to mention it, unless you've been instructed not to, do research the members of the interview panel to get an idea of what's important to them. Don't structure your preparation or answers to the idiosyncrasies of individual board members, but keep in mind their perspective as it becomes particularly important with answers that could offend a panel member. While their personal opinions or feelings are supposed to be subservient to the instructions given by the chief of police or sheriff, they may subconsciously take offense, creating an unfavorable impression of you that will be hard to overcome.

I remember sitting on a panel for police sergeant when I was a lieutenant. One of the board members was the SWAT commander in another agency. The question at play had to do with a barricaded suspect. Our aim was to see if the candidates would elect to make an entry when faced with the potential shooting of the hostage. It didn't take long for one particular candidate to make the decision to go in without building his case to do so, even before we'd interjected the shooting threat into the scenario. His comment was: "These SWAT guys are often late, and by the time they get here we've wasted valuable time." I chuckled and looked over at the SWAT lieutenant, who despite a kernel of truth in the matter, grimaced and almost reached across the table to throttle the candidate. My point is that despite having a legitimate viewpoint if you aren't sensitive to another's position or philosophy, you may end up at the bottom of the list. Be honest, but not brutally honest. Make your case constructively!

Reach out to those you respect for advice. Don't be afraid to talk with people you respect and those who hold credibility in the department to get advice. Whether it's your peers or superiors, look for those who exhibit the qualities you believe are desired in leaders in your agency and get their input on you, the promotional process and what issues or initiatives the organization is dealing with or will in the future. Remember form and function are both important. How you come across is just as critical as how knowledgeable and practical you are. I found that as I studied for promotional exams, I became more confident, and that allowed me to be more articulate and personable. It's tough to come across well if you haven't done your homework, so focus on all aspects of the process.

Review and develop your personal story. It has always astounded me how many candidates for promotion fail to think about and develop their personal story when going before a promotional board or when making an opening statement. Your personal history, as it applies to not only the position for which you are testing but the community and values of your agency, is as critical as your professional contributions. By that I mean the personal experiences and history that shaped you and make up your worldview. The folks across the table from you will want to know who you really are and how that translates into a better, more focused and thoughtful human being. You need to make that case for them in a few minutes at the beginning of the interview or the appropriate moment in the conversation.

Police agencies don't want automatons who simply read the book and follow the rules. They want supervisors and managers who have life experience and project a reasonable, thoughtful point of view. You have to accomplish this objective relatively quickly, so think it through and relate it to your qualifications for the position as you prepare for the process. One of the now high-ranking officers I mentored while at the Santa Ana Police Department was born and grew up in the city. He was a product of the city's school system, and despite living in an area where gangs were ubiquitous, was able to stay out of trouble, later earning a master's degree. He had a compelling story to tell that spoke directly to his desire to improve and give back to the community.

Be Yourself. Not being authentic is often the downfall for some who feel obligated to change their personality or assume a new identity just for the interview. While you may be a good actor and may get away with it, the odds are against you. Who you truly are should be what the board gets, as sincerity trumps polish nearly every time. That doesn't mean you go in unprepared hoping your personality will carry you through. What it means is you prepare exhaustively and practice your delivery relentlessly, focusing on mannerisms and distractions upon which you can improve. You are not changing your persona; rather you are polishing your delivery and learning to control bad habits. Let me give you an example.

In a promotional interview for police sergeant, this particular candidate was someone known to me. I knew his personality and reputation, and I knew he was smart and capable. He sat down across a long table from the board on a rolling office chair. There were four of us. A few minutes into the interview, each time one of the two board members on the edges of the table asked a question, this individual would scoot up on the chair to that end to answer the question. When the board member on the other end asked a question, he'd roll back the other way. It got to be so comical that regardless of what the candidate did from that point on, the interview was effectively over. I couldn't figure out why an experienced individual would do such a thing in front of a promotional panel. Again, be yourself and control the impulse for theatrics or other measures that will turn people off. I do advocate you allow your personality to come through and let your passion for the job speak for itself. Don't be afraid to lean in a little bit when you're giving an important answer or use controlled mannerisms to make your point in a systematic but passionate manner. There is nothing wrong with allowing your positive personal traits to come through, including a smile when appropriate. Just be aware of any negative mannerisms and control them.

Assess at least one of your weaknesses and be ready to discuss it. You will likely be asked about your weaknesses, so the time to think about them is early in your preparation. Don't simply turn whatever it is into a strength immediately, as the Board will see right through that and may think you're insulting their intelligence. I recommend you consider whatever weaknesses you may have and pick one that—with work and initiative—can be improved and potentially turned into an advantage. You don't have to be brutally honest, but you need to tell them you are not only aware of the weakness, but you've worked on it, and you've gained insight into how anyone can become introspective to become a better person and police leader. That ability to look inwardly, identify faults and improve is one quality that makes a great leader—and the interview panel knows that.

Don't suppress your speaking DNA—just manage it. As I said above, interview panels expect to see and hear the real deal. Too often the candidate will go to great lengths to prepare by attempting to create an entirely different speech pattern or, worst, adopt a vocabulary filled with ten-syllable words that are meaningless unless that's your natural speech pattern. As someone told me long ago, speak to communicate, not impress, so speak plainly, naturally and directly. It's OK to pause momentarily—as long as it isn't too long—to consider the question and the appropriate answer. I always respect a candidate who appears thoughtful and considers her responses, as opposed to blurting out an answer that makes little sense or is devoid of the critical elements sought by the question. If you pause, don't do it for more than a few seconds and avoid looking up at the ceiling as if seeking divine guidance. It makes you look indecisive rather than thoughtful. Look in the space between panel members instead, or at a slightly downward angle toward the table.

I once had someone advise me to sit on my hands during the interview because I always used them when speaking. They were correct that I did use my hands when I spoke, particularly when I was animated. I thought about it and quickly dismissed the advice. Using my hands while talking was in my DNA, so I simply used it to my advantage. I used my hands only to make a point or used my fingers to depict the number of options. In other words, I didn't discard my speaking DNA, I merely controlled and channeled it. Don't try to be anyone you really aren't. It's the kiss of death in an interview.

Make eye contact—but don't stare. Think about how you feel when someone doesn't make eye contact when they interact with you. Does it inspire confidence in the person, or do they seem shy or unsure of themselves? Conversely, how do you feel when someone's eye contact is so intense and relentless that you feel compelled to look away? Those are the extremes, but you'd be surprised how often candidates for promotion make those mistakes in an interview. The key to making appropriate eye contact is to periodically and systematically make eye contact with all of the board members. When folks ask me for advice on this topic, I tell them to play it naturally, as if they were having a conversation with a friend with whom they want to exchange valuable information.

For example, when one board member asks you a question, you'll naturally be looking at him, but during your answer you will also briefly make eye contact with the others, not lingering too long on any individual in particular. Near the end of your response, you'll shift your focus to the board member who asked the initial question. You don't want to make anyone uncomfortable, but you want them to know you are acknowledging each of them throughout the interview.

Think out loud—thoughtfully. This is perhaps one of the most important areas for which you can prepare. Often, candidates will regurgitate a rehearsed response and fail to show the interview panel how they arrived at the answer. It is fine to give them a factual answer if the question calls for one, but practically anyone can read books and memorize data and information. Most interviewers will quickly determine if the candidate is merely spouting facts from memory or if she is thoughtful and analytic. One way to convey your thinking process is to identify the key elements of a question and tell the panel why the topic is important. Another method is to identify alternatives, eventually picking one and telling the panel why you picked it.

Remember, all of this happens very quickly, and some questions may only call for a short, factual answer. But many questions lend themselves to thoughtful, but brief, analysis. Any hypothetical question calls out for you to let the panel see how you think (see below). I don't mean babbling or unintelligibly thinking out loud. I mean telling the panel the elements you considered and then methodically crafting an answer that shows how you deduced the answer and why. This isn't always easy to do, so I recommend you enlist the help of friend or colleagues to sit on mock interview panels.

The more you practice the more at ease and comfortable you'll feel in the real process. Thomas Jefferson once said: "I'm a great believer in luck. I find the harder I work, the more I have of it." The more you prepare for these selection processes, the better you'll do. It's really that simple.

If possible, try and find common ground with panel members early in the interview. The panel may ascribe to Maya Angelou's adage that "when someone shows you who they are, believe them the first time." I've always believed that when trying to make a good impression, the first few minutes are critical. This is unquestionably the time to show your personality. If you can establish a rapport with the board right away by finding common ground or a shared interest —often in the form of small talk—it is likely that it will set the tone for the rest of the interview and you may score higher in the end.

According to the Wall Street Journal (How to Build Instant Rapport in an Interview, Shellenbarger, 11-29-2016), in a recent study of 163 mock interviews, the interviewers were asked to rate candidates' competence after two to three minutes of introductory small talk, then score candidates' performance on a series of 12 job-related questions. According to the article, "Candidates who managed to find common ground with interviewers and spark a sense of trust before the interview received higher overall scores from interviewers than those who performed equally well on the interview but failed to generate that early sense of connection, according to the study led by Brian W. Swider, an assistant professor of organizational behavior at the Georgia Institute of Technology, Atlanta. An applicant's ability to spark rapport seems to have a unique influence on whether he or she gets the job, Dr. Swider says."

While the following analogy may be imperfect, I can tell you that building rapport with crime suspects about to be interviewed works wonders. I was a homicide detective for years, and I explicitly tried to treat suspects with dignity and respect, often looking for small conversation topics before beginning the interview or offering a snack or drink. I pride myself in the fact that I obtained lawful confessions from the overwhelming majority of the murder suspects I interviewed. It isn't rocket science. Find common ground with anyone, and the results speak for themselves.

Make a visceral connection with the interview panel. There is nothing more powerful in an interview or in writing an essay than making a visceral connection with others. When I think back to all the selection processes in which I participated, I invariably remember the candidates who were able to make emotional connections with me or other panel members. By that I mean the candidates who showed they cared about people, their department, the community and their subordinates. For example, the young sergeant seeking to become a lieutenant who gave me a thoughtful answer that came from his heart. Or the commander who wanted to be a captain and gave me an example of an incident he handled that drained him emotionally but taught him humility and made him a better person. Or perhaps the officer who gave us an eloquent description of why as an FTO he took a chance on a young probationer because of his intrinsic qualities, and who later proved to be a good officer, father and husband.

Almost anyone can memorize facts and figures, but few can allow an interview panel or essay grader inside their heart, showing them not only their intellect but also displaying the emotional IQ that is key to relationships and trust. All things being equal, I'll go with someone that can build sound, healthy relationships with others, rather than the clinical, calculating thinker who presents the factual solutions easily. Remember another Maya Angelou's quote: "I've learned that people will forget what you said, people will forget what you did, but people will never forget how you made them feel."

When asked a hypothetical question, learn to identify the key

issues, define a couple of alternatives if appropriate, and then make a decision. When you're asked a factual question during an interview, it's OK to say you don't know the answer; trying to bluff your way will probably land you on the reject list. Hypotheticals are different. They are designed to elicit your response one way or the other, and in law enforcement the possible scenarios are endless. In other words, they want to know if you can identify the key issues presented in the question, look at the alternatives if appropriate, and then come up with a plausible answer that you can defend. You can't, ever, say you don't know what you would do, although I've seen many do just that. Regardless of how well you do on the other portions of the interview if you don't give them an answer on a hypothetical question you'll likely fail the process.

I define a hypothetical question as one in which the panel provides you with a set of facts or conditions, and you're asked to assess them and give an answer that may resolve the issue within the realm of possibility. There generally isn't one way to do that. I've given answers to the same question that all made sense, but what usually makes the difference is when one systematically identifies the key issues and then gives an answer that one can explain and support. They want to know if you can think critically on your feet and can communicate your thinking in an orderly and persuasive manner. The answer doesn't necessarily have to be the most correct, but how you articulate your support of the answer matters most. Don't get me wrong: a stupid, nonsensical answer will always be incorrect no matter how well you defend it. But if your answer is plausible, then how well you back it up with reason should carry the day.

Assess your soft skills and lead the interview with them in mind. Law enforcement has and will continue to adopt technology as a force multiplier. There is no question that being able to do more with less and leverage data sources to develop strategies and tactics is critical to the efficiency and effectiveness of any police agency. Departments will continue to value technical and hard skills in applicants, but it remains that the soft skills—emotional intelligence, being able to deal with people, showing empathy—will almost always trump other skills all other things being equal. Your ability to relate to the board and express yourself in ways that showcase your soft skills, as well as your technical abilities, gets you to the finish line.

You must come across as genuine and interested in the outcome not simply for yourself, but for the organization and the community as well.

Assessing your soft skills ahead of time and developing clear examples you can articulate to the panel will let them know you prepared and thought about the process. Remember, often it is the little, nuanced things that separate candidates on a list. In a recent survey (Titled "The Soft Skills Jobs Seekers Need Now,") of HR and recruiting professionals by iCIMS, a talent acquisition software company, those surveyed said that all things being equal, the candidates who possess soft skills such as enthusiasm, active listening, presentation skills and written communication skills, generally have an edge.

According to the research described by Forbes Magazine contributor Carmine Gallo, "A full 94 percent of recruiting professionals believe an employee with stronger soft skills has a better chance of being promoted to a leadership position than an employee with more years of experience, but weaker soft skills." As I said, I have participated in hundreds of promotional processes, and I can't emphasize enough the importance of developing and honing one's soft skills.

To read the article at Forbes Magazine go here:
https://www.forbes.com/sites/carminegallo/2017/08/17/the-interview-skill-guaranteed-to-give-you-an-edge/

Have a powerful closing statement. Irrespective of how you think the interview will go, you need to have a closing statement that seals the deal. The panel needs to know that you truly want the promotion, have worked hard to prepare for it, and you are ready to help make your organization and community better. Even if you feel good about the interview, don't assume they got that from your previous answers. Given that most promotional exams are highly competitive, you want the interview panel to remember you in a way that makes you stand out from the crowd— preferably in a positive way!

Thinking about and crafting a closing statement is critical. It may be that during the interview you failed to bring up an important point, or perhaps you didn't think you connected emotionally with the panel. The closing then could become a make or break proposition and the chance for you to redeem yourself. Keep it relatively short, but don't be afraid to take the opportunity to remind the panel why you are an excellent candidate, a good fit for the position, and why they won't be disappointed.

Participate in mock interviews. I highly recommend you get folks you respect to do mock interviews with you and have them video recorded. You'll be amazed how much you learn about yourself in front of a mock interview panel. It's revealing, and I guarantee you it will give you insights into your personality, mannerisms, and knowledge that you won't get anywhere else. It is time well spent.

In my view, these points form the nucleus of any effort to do well on a promotional exam. Aside from the practical, wrought portions you must prepare for, these are the most influential in any process. The more time you spend thinking about them and practicing your delivery, the better the chances are that you'll be successful. Remember, if you've decided you want to be a supervisor or a manager in law enforcement, preparation started when you decided you'd be a good, competent cop. That's the prerequisite for advancement, and if you aren't, I recommend you don't sit for interviews or seek to promote until you are. You'll do yourself and everyone in your department a disservice otherwise.

EPILOGUE

As I finished writing this book in 2018—three years after I began—I expected to see some improvement in police-community relations throughout the nation. I found that while some communities seem to have created a more trustful environment with their police agencies, most urban and minority neighborhoods still struggle to form productive relationships with their cops. I am cautiously optimistic however, that leaders at all levels in public safety understand the implications and are working hard to develop and mentor young officers to become outstanding and inclusive leaders. There really is no alternative. A number of police chiefs have told me they are working hard to hire and promote those candidates who possess the soft and hard skills needed to build trust in communities. Some are realigning priorities to include neighborhood-based objectives, and are instituting supervisory and management competence-based leadership development programs.

To that end I pray and hope that this book will help current and aspiring leaders do better, become more competent, and adopt the tenets I so firmly believe in, and which form the nucleus of this book.

I would also like to thank the many police leaders with whom I spoke in police agencies across the nation, as well as the civilian managers who oversee large organizations and who shared with me their critical thinking on cops and public safety in general. Their insight was invaluable.

Lastly, I want to thank the cops and detectives in my old agency and others in America who gave me their unvarnished opinions of their agencies and their leaders. It is for them that I wrote this book.

* * *

BIBLIOGRAPHY

Ahrendts, Angela. 2015. "How I Hire: My Guiding Principles." LinkedIn Pulse. August 21, 2015. https://www.linkedin.com/pulse/how-i-hire-my-guiding-principles-angela-ahrendts.

Ariely, Dan. 2016. Payoff: The Hidden Logic That Shapes Our Motivations. Simon & Schuster/ TED.

———. n.d. "Transcript of 'What Makes Us Feel Good about Our Work?'" Accessed January 12, 2017. http://www.ted.com/talks/dan_ariely_what_makes_us_feel_good_about_our_work/transcript.

Babwin, Don. n.d. "Personnel Records Show Years of Complaints against Officer." Yahoo News. Accessed November 10, 2015. http://news.yahoo.com/personnel-records-show-years-complaints-against-officer-072632494.html.

Bailey, James. 2016. "Managers, Take Your Vacations." Los Angeles Times, July 3, 2016, sec. Business.

Bennis, Warren G., and Burt Nanus. 2012. Leaders: The Strategies for Taking Charge. 2nd edition. HarperBusiness.

Biography.com Editors. n.d. "Alexander Hamilton - Political Scientist, Government Official, Journalist, Military Leader, Economist, Lawyer." The Biography.Com Website. Accessed November 11, 2015. http://www.biography.com/people/alexander-hamilton-9326481.

Bishoff, Glenn. 2009. "Risk Management Is a Laughing Matter." Urgentcomm. June 9, 2009. http://urgentcomm.com/policy-amp-law-commentary/risk-management-laughing-matter.

Black, Lauren Zumbach, Dan Hinkel, Lisa. n.d. "Gliniewicz's Personnel File Shows Troubled Tenure on Fox Lake Police Force." Lake County News-Sun. Accessed August 12, 2017. http://www.chicagotribune.com/suburbs/lake-county-news-sun/news/ct-fox-lake-cop-personnel-records-20151106-story.html.

Botelho, Elena, Kim Powell, Stephen Kincaid, and Dina Wang. 2017. "4 Things That Set Successful CEOs Apart." Harvard Business Review. May 1, 2017. https://hbr.org/2017/05/what-sets-successful-ceos-apart.

Bourke, Julliet, and Bernadette Dillon. 2016. "Six Signature Traits of Inclusive Leadership | Deloitte University Press." DU Press. April 14, 2016.

Bryant, Adam. 2011. "Google's 8-Point Plan to Help Managers Improve." The New York Times, March 12, 2011. http://www.nytimes.com/2011/03/13/business/13hire.html.

Chang, Cindy. n.d. "L.A. County Sheriff's Deputies Who Lied Continue to Draw Paychecks." Los Angeles Times. Accessed March 8, 2016. http://www.latimes.com/local/california/la-me-deputies-false-statements-20160308-snap-htmlstory.html.

Cherry, Kendra. n.d. "How Emotionally Intelligent Are You?" About.Com Education. Accessed November 10, 2015. http://psychology.about.com/od/personalitydevelopment/a/emotionalintell.htm.

Churchill, Winston. 1940. Their Finest Hour. Speeches. House of Commons, UK. http://www.winstonchurchill.org/resources/speeches/122-their-finest-hour.

"Citation for Staff Sergeant Clinton L. Romesha - Medal of Honor Recipient for the United States Army." n.d. Accessed May 2, 2016. https://www.army.mil/medalofhonor/romesha/citation.html.

Comey, James. 2018. A Higher Loyalty, Truth, Lies, and Leadership. Flatiron Books.

"Conceptual Thinking." n.d. Psychology Wiki. Accessed May 23, 2017. http://psychology.wikia.com/wiki/Conceptual_thinking.

Coté, John. n.d. "Civilians Take on Police Work in SFPD

Program." SFGate. Accessed April 12, 2016. http://www.sfgate.com/crime/article/Civilians-take-on-police-work-in-SFPD-program-3180624.php

"Crisis in Chicago." n.d. Accessed January 4, 2017. http://www.cbsnews.com/news/60-minutes-crisis-in-chicago-gun-violence/

Dana, Charles Anderson. 1902. Recollections of the Civil War; New York, D. Appleton and company. http://archive.org/details/recollectionsofc00danach.

Davey, Monica, and Mitch Smith. 2017. "3 Chicago Officers Charged With Conspiracy in Laquan McDonald Case." The New York Times, June 27, 2017, sec. U.S. https://www.nytimes.com/2017/06/27/us/chicago-officers-indicted-laquan-mcdonald-shooting.html.

Dolan, Jack. 2014. "L.A. Pays Millions as Police and Firefighter Injury Claims Rise." Latimes.Com. September 28, 2014. http://www.latimes.com/local/cityhall/la-me-sworn-injury-leave-20140928-story.html.

———. 2015. "No Reliable Way to Track L.A. Police on Tax-Free Full Salary Injury Leave, Audit Finds." Latimes.Com. November 18, 2015. http://www.latimes.com/local/crime/la-me-lapd-audit-20151117-story.html.

Duckworth, Angela. 2016. Grit: The Power of Passion and Perseverance. First Edition edition. New York: Scribner.

Eligon, John, and Timothy Williams. 2015. "Police Program Aims to Pinpoint Those Most Likely to Commit Crimes." The New York Times, September 24, 2015. http://www.nytimes.com/2015/09/25/us/police-program-aims-to-pinpoint-those-most-likely-to-commit-crimes.html.

Elmer-Dewitt, Elmer. 2011. "Steve Jobs: The Parable of the Stones." Fortune, November 11, 2011. http://fortune.com/2011/11/11/steve-jobs-the-parable-of-the-stones/.

Farmer, Liz. 2015. "The Story Behind San Bernardino's Long Bankruptcy." August 26, 2015. http://www.governing.com/topics/finance/gov-story-behind-san-bernardinos-long-bankruptcy.html.

"FBI Director Comey: 'Ferguson Effect' Causing Murder Spike."

2016. Newsmax. May 12, 2016. http://www.newsmax.com/Newsfront/FBI-james-comey-ferguson-effect-murder/2016/05/12/id/728510/.

"FBI Report: Media Narrative Inspires Violence Against Police." n.d. The Daily Caller. Accessed May 11, 2017. http://dailycaller.com/2017/05/05/fbi-report-media-narrative-inspires-violence-against-police/.

Fields, Gary, and Zusha Elinson. 2016. "The Hidden Hurt of Life on the Police Beat." Wall Street Journal, December 18, 2016, sec. US. http://www.wsj.com/articles/the-hidden-hurt-of-life-on-the-police-beat-1482090105.

Fisher, Anne. 2016a. "Why Performance Bonuses and Merit Raises Don't Work." Fortune Magazine, February 24, 2016. http://fortune.com/2016/02/24/salary-bonuses-merit-raises-effectiveness/.

———. 2016b. "Can Measuring Morale in Real Time Predict When Key Talent Is Planning to Quit?" Fortune Magazine Online, June 9, 2016. http://fortune.com/2016/06/09/patagonia-employee-turnover/.

Fremon, Celeste. 2015. "The Downfall of Sheriff Baca." Los Angeles Magazine, May 14, 2015.

Friedersdorf, Conor. 2014. "How Police Unions and Arbitrators Keep Abusive Cops on the Street." The Atlantic, December 2, 2014. http://www.theatlantic.com/politics/archive/2014/12/how-police-unions-keep-abusive-cops-on-the-street/383258/.

Friedrich, Tamara. 2015. "Here's What You'll Need to Know If You Wan to Work for Google." Fortune Magazine, November 15, 2015. http://fortune.com/2015/11/25/google-rework-secrets/?xid=soc_socialflow_twitter_FORTUNE.

Gallo, Carmine. n.d. "The Interview Skill Guaranteed To Give You An Edge." Forbes. Accessed August 20, 2017. https://www.forbes.com/sites/carminegallo/2017/08/17/the-interview-skill-guaranteed-to-give-you-an-edge/.

Garvin, David. 2013. "How Google Sold Its Engineers on Management." Harvard Business Review, no. December, 2013 (December). https://hbr.org/2013/12/how-google-sold-its-engineers-on-management.

Gawande, Atul. 2011. The Checklist Manifesto: How to Get Things Right. Reprint edition. New York: Picador.

Goleman, Daniel, Annie McKee, and Richard Boyatzis. 2002. Primal Leadership: Realizing the Power of Emotional Intelligence. 1 edition. Harvard Business Review Press.

Goodwin, Doris Kearns. 2006. Team of Rivals: The Political Genius of Abraham Lincoln. New York: Simon & Schuster.

"Google's Management Tools." n.d. Accessed August 23, 2017. https://rework.withgoogle.com/.

Greenleaf, Robert. 1970. "The Servant as Leader."

Harari, Oren. 2002. The Leadership Secrets of Colin Powell. McGrawHil,2002.

Hardy, Benjamin. 2010. "Servant Leadership and Sir Winston Churchill." http://digitalcommons.wku.edu/cgi/viewcontent.cgi?article=1291&context=stu_hon_theses.

Housman, Michael, and Dylan Minor. 2015. "Toxic Workers." Cornerstone on Demand and Harvard Business School. http://www.hbs.edu/faculty/Publication%20Files/16-057_d45c0b4f-fa19-49de-8f1b-4b12fe054fea.pdf.

"How Far Joe Will Go for Jobs." 2016. December 4, 2016. http://www.cbsnews.com/news/60-minutes-how-far-joe-max-higgins-will-go-for-jobs/.

Huntsman, Max. 2016. "ANALYSIS OF THE DEPUTY SHERIFF TRAINEE PROBATIONARY PERIOD: RECOMMENDATIONS FOR A MEANINGFUL ASSESSMENT OPPORTUNITY." Los Angeles County Inspector General.

Hutchens, Sandra. 2015—In Person Interview.

Irving, Doug. n.d. "A Chance to Thrive: What We Can Learn from One City's Effort to Transform Community | RAND." Accessed March 9, 2016. http://www.rand.org/blog/rand-review/2016/03/a-chance-to-thrive.html.

Jean-Paul, Ralph. n.d. "Napoleon Bonaparte's Guide to Leadership | Potential2Success." Accessed December 8, 2015. http://potential2success.com/napoleonbonaparteleadership.html.

Jouvenal, Justin. n.d. "Police Are Using Software to Predict Crime. Is It a 'Holy Grail' or Biased against Minorities?" Washington Post. Accessed November 18, 2016. Link.

Kamarck, Elaine C. 2016. Why Presidents Fail And How They Can Succeed Again. Washington, D.C: Brookings Institution Press.

Karlgaard, Rich. 2014. The Soft Edge: Where Great Companies Find Lasting Success. 1 edition. Jossey-Bass.

Karlsson, Gary L. Neilson, Ken Favaro, Per-Ola. n.d. "Report: 2014 Study of CEOs | Strategy&." Accessed April 18, 2017. https://www.strategyand.pwc.com/reports/2014-ceo-study.

Kelly, Kimbriel, Wesley Lowery, and Steven Rich. n.d. "Police Chiefs Are Often Forced to Put Officers Fired for Misconduct Back on the Streets." Washington Post. Accessed August 3, 2017. https://www.washingtonpost.com/graphics/2017/investigations/police-fired-rehired/.

Leswing, Kif, 2016 Feb. 7, and 2. n.d. "How an Apple Employee Once Stood up to Steve Jobs — and Got Promoted for It." Business Insider. Accessed February 14, 2016. http://www.businessinsider.com/donna-dubinsky-stood-up-to-steve-jobs-and-promoted-2016-2.

Liu, Bing. 2012. "Sentiment Analysis and Opinion Mining." Synthesis Lectures on Human Language Technologies 5 (1): 1–167. https://doi.org/10.2200/S00416ED1V01Y201204HLT016.

Maxwell, John C. 2011. The 5 Levels of Leadership: Proven Steps to Maximize Your Potential. 1 edition. New York: Center Street.

McGhee, Tom. 2012. "Denver Will Replace Some Police with Civilians." Denverpost.Com. November 12, 2012. http://www.denverpost.com/ci_21977602/denver-will-replace-some-police-civilians.

Mele, Christopher. 2017. "Officers Involved in Tamir Rice Killing Face Administrative Charges." The New York Times, January 13, 2017. https://www.nytimes.com/2017/01/13/us/officers-in-tamir-rice-killing.html.

Menezes, Gus Garcia-Roberts, Jack Dolan, Ryan. n.d. "LAPD Chief Calls for Change to Controversial Retirement Program." Latimes.Com. Accessed May 4, 2018. http://www.latimes.com/local/lanow/la-me-ln-lapd-beck-drop-20180502-story.html.

Merryman, Ashley. 2016. "Leaders Are More Powerful When They're Humble, New Research Shows." The Washington Post, December 8, 2016.

https://www.washingtonpost.com/news/inspired-life/wp/2016/12/08/leaders-are-more-powerful-when-theyre-humble-new-research-shows/?utm_term=.7477f9f0706b.

Mohler, G. O., M. B. Short, Sean Malinowski, Mark Johnson, G. E. Tita, Andrea L. Bertozzi, and P. J. Brantingham. 2015. "Randomized Controlled Field Trials of Predictive Policing." Journal of the American Statistical Association 110 (512): 1399–1411. https://doi.org/10.1080/01621459.2015.1077710.

Morin, Rich, Kim Parker, Renee Stepler, and rew Mercer. 2017. "Behind the Badge." Pew Research Center's Social & Demographic Trends Project (blog). January 11, 2017. http://www.pewsocialtrends.org/2017/01/11/behind-the-badge/.

O'Connor, Barbara. 2015. Oral Testimony Chief Barbara O'Connor, President of NAWLEE and Chief of Police, University of Connecticut Presidential Task Force on 21st Century Policing "Culture and Diversity." Washington, DC.

Oliver, Sam. 2015. "Angela Ahrendts Was Swayed to Apple Retail by Instant Personal Connection with Tim Cook." AppleInsider, March 26, 2015. Http://appleinsider.com/articles/15/03/26/angela-ahrendts-was-swayed-to-apple-retail-by-instant-personal-connection-with-tim-cook.

Owens, Bradley P., and David R. Hekman. 2016. "How Does Leader Humility Influence Team Performance? Exploring the Mechanisms of Contagion and Collective Promotion Focus." Academy of Management Journal 59 (3): 1088–1111. https://doi.org/10.5465/amj.2013.0660.

Owyang, Jeremiah. 2013. "The Difference between Strategy and Tactics." The Difference between Strategy and Tactics` (blog). January 14, 2013. http://www.web-strategist.com/blog/2013/01/14/the-difference-between-strategy-and-tactics/.

"P1 Poll Results: What Are the Most Crucial Skills a Cop Should Possess?" n.d. PoliceOne. Accessed November 11, 2015. http://www.policeone.com/chiefs-sheriffs/articles/8273599-P1-Poll-results-What-are-the-most-crucial-skills-a-cop-should-possess/.

Paul Ryan. n.d. "Paul Ryan Acceptance Speech." Paulryan.House-.Gov (blog). http://paulryan.house.gov/news/documentsingle.aspx?DocumentID=398412.

"Pay for Performance — Time to Challenge Conventional Thinking." n.d. Willis Towers Watson. Accessed March 9, 2016. https://www.willistowerswatson.com/en/insights/2016/02/pay-for-performance-time-to-challenge-conventional-thinking.

Peet, Dale. 2010. "Social Media Analytics in Law Enforcement." September 20, 2010. http://www.policemag.com/blog/technology/story/2012/09/social-media-analytics-in-law-enforcement.aspx.

Phillips, Donald T. 2013. Lincoln On Leadership: Executive Strategies for Tough Times. DTP/Companion Books.

"Police Labor-Management Relations (Vol. I): Perspectives and Practical Solutions for Implementing Change, Making Reforms, and Handling Crises for Managers and Union Leaders." 2006. Washington, DC: U.S. Department of Justice, Office of Community Oriented Policing Services. https://ric-zai-inc.com/Publications/cops-p110-pub.pdf.

Polzin, Michael, and Ronald DeLord. 2006. "Police Labor-Management Relations (Vol. II): Perspectives and Practical Solutions for Implementing Change, Making Reforms, and Handling Crises for Managers and Union Leaders." Washington, DC: U.S. Department of Justice, Office of Community Oriented Policing Services. https://ric-zai-inc.com/Publications/cops-p110-pub.pdf.

Porter, Michael, Michael Green, and Scott Stern. 2014. "Social Progress Index 2014." Social Progress Imperative. http://www.socialprogressimperative.org/system/resources/W1s iZiIsIjIwMTQvMDUvMjYvMTYvMzQvNTQvNzk5L1NvY2lhbF9Q cm9ncmVzc19JbmRleF8yMDE0X1JlcG9ydF9Xy5wZGYiXV0/Socia l%20Progress%20Index%202014%20Report%20e%20.pdf.

PUENTE, KELLY. n.d. "O.C. Deputy Accused of Collecting Workers' Comp for Injuries While Doing CrossFit." The Orange County Register. Accessed October 22, 2016. http://www.ocregister.com/articles/prosecutors-732973-zappas-injuries.html.

Queally, James, Kate Mather, and Cindy Chang. 2017a. "Police Arrests Are Plummeting across California, Fueling Alarm and Questions." Los Angeles Times, April 1, 2017. http://www.latimes.com/local/lanow/la-me-ln-police-slowdown-20170401-story.html.

"Police Arrests Are Plummeting across California, Fueling Alarm and Questions." Los Angeles Times, April 1, 2017. http://www.latimes.com/local/lanow/la-me-ln-police-slowdown-20170401-story.html.

Radnofsky, Louise, Zusha Elinson, John R. Emshwiller, and Gary Fields. 2016. "Why Some Problem Cops Don't Lose Their Badges." Wall Street Journal, December 30, 2016, sec. US. http://www.wsj.com/articles/why-some-problem-cops-dont-lose-their-badges-1483115066.

"Rebuilding Morale: Creating a Happy, Committed Workforce." n.d. Accessed June 14, 2016. http://www.mindtools.com/pages/article/morale.htm.

Reiff, Rick. 2016. "Inside OC: Sheriff Hutchens Says Likely to Run Again; Discusses Jail Break, Informant Scandal." Voice of OC. May 13, 2016. http://voiceofoc.org/2016/05/inside-oc-sheriff-hutchens-says-likely-to-run-again-discusses-jail-break-informant-scandal/.

———. n.d. "Reiff: Are Police Backing Off?" Voice of OC. Accessed May 3, 2017. http://voiceofoc.org/2017/05/reiff-are-police-backing-off-retired-cop-uci-prof-differ-over-rising-crime-rate/.

Report, Staff. 2017. "Board of Supervisors Votes Not to Indemnify Former Sheriff Baca." Westsidetoday.Com. May 3, 2017. http://westsidetoday.com/2017/05/03/board-of-supervisors-votes-not-to-indemnify-former-sheriff-baca/.

"Re:Work - Managers." n.d. Accessed January 14, 2016. https://rework.withgoogle.com/subjects/managers/.

Rooney, Paula. n.d. "Microsoft's CEO: 80-20 Rule Applies To Bugs, Not Just Features." CRN. Accessed April 12, 2016. http://www.crn.com/news/security/18821726/microsofts-ceo-80-20-rule-applies-to-bugs-not-just-features.htm.

Rubin, Joel. 2016. "For Baca, a Legacy Tainted by Misdeed." Los Angeles Times, July 18, 2016, sec. Front Page.

Ryan, Liz. n.d. "What's The Difference Between Strategy And Tactics?" Forbes. Accessed November 15, 2015. http://www.forbes.com/sites/lizryan/2015/05/17/whats-the-difference-between-strategy-and-tactics/.

Sabato, Larry. 2013. "Lead like John F. Kennedy." Washington Post. November 20, 2013.

https://www.washingtonpost.com/news/on-leadership/wp/2013/11/20/lead-like-john-f-kennedy/.

Salovey, Peter, and Mayer, John. 1990. "Emotional Intelligence." Imagination, Cognition, and Personality 9 (3): 185–211.

Scelfo, Julie. 2016. "Angela Duckworth on Passion, Grit and Success." The New York Times, April 8, 2016. http://www.nytimes.com/2016/04/10/education/edlife/passion-grit-success.html.

Scherer, Michael. n.d. "The Ashcroft-Gonzales Hospital Room Showdown." Salon. Accessed August 26, 2016. http://www.salon.com/2007/05/15/comey_testifies/.

Schou, Nick. 2016. "Santa Ana Police Department Fires Officers In Pot Video Case." OC Weekly. July 14, 2016. http://www.ocweekly.com/news/santa-ana-police-department-fires-officers-in-pot-video-case-7340514.

Seavey, Ho. n.d. "The Battle for COP Keating." Text. The American Legion. Accessed May 2, 2016. http://www.military.com/daily-news/2013/05/01/battle-for-cop-keating-afghanistan.html.

Segran, Elizabeth. n.d. "Why Top Tech CEOs Want Employees With Liberal Arts Degrees." Fast Company. Accessed November 11, 2015. http://www.fastcompany.com/3034947/the-future-of-work/why-top-tech-ceos-want-employees-with-liberal-arts-degrees.

Sewell, Abby, and Garrett Therole. 2016. "Youth Lock up Staff Benefit in Deal." Los Angeles Times, September 25, 2016, Morning edition, sec. California.

Shellenbarger, Sue. 2016. "How to Build Instant Rapport in an Interview." Wall Street Journal, November 29, 2016, sec. Life. http://www.wsj.com/articles/how-to-build-instant-rapport-in-an-interview-1480436936.

Spears, Larry. 2010. "Character and Servant Leadership: Ten Characteristics of Effective, Caring Leaders." The Journal of Virtues and Leadership One (One): 25--30.

Stelter, Leischen. 2015. "Putting Experience to Work: The Value of a Formal Mentoring Program." February 25, 2015. http://inpublicsafety.com/2015/02/putting-experience-to-work-the-value-of-a-formal-mentoring-program/.

Swanson, James. 2008. Symposium on Lincoln and American

ValuesPhysical. http://www.archives.gov/press/press-releases/2008/nr08-138.html.

"The Checklist Manifesto." n.d. Atul Gawande (blog). Accessed March 3, 2016. http://atulgawande.com/book/the-checklist-manifesto/.

The Dark Charisma of Adolf Hitler. 2012. Documentary, Biography, History. BBC.

"The Role of Auditing in Public Sector Governance." n.d. The Institute of Internal Auditors. https://na.theiia.org/standards-guidance/Public%20Documents/Public_Sector_Governance1_1_.pdf.

Times, TIMOTHY WILLIAMS New York. 2016. "Troubled Cops End up Back in Blue." The Bulletin. September 11, 2016. http://www.bendbulletin.com/nation/4649823-151/troubled-cops-end-up-back-in-blue.

Trueman, C N. 2015. "The Impact of the Blitz on London." History Learning Site. April 20, 2015. http://www.historylearningsite.co.uk/world-war-two/world-war-two-in-western-europe/britains-home-front-in-world-war-two/the-impact-of-the-blitz-on-london/.

Tzu, Sun. n.d. By Sun Tzu, by Samuel B. Griffith, by B. H. Liddell Hart The Art of War(Text Only)[Paperback]1971. Oxford University Press.

"U.S. Army Leadership Development Manual." n.d. University of California at Santa Barbara. Accessed June 19, 2017. http://www.milsci.ucsb.edu/sites/secure.lsit.ucsb.edu.mili.d7/files/sitefiles/fm6_22.pdf.

Vallano, Jonathan P., Jacqueline R. Evans, Jenna M. Kieckhaefer, and Schreiber Compo N. 2015. "Rapport-Building During Witness and Suspect Interviews: A Survey of Law Enforcement." ResearchGate 29 (3). https://doi.org/10.1002/acp.3115.

Waddell, Kaveh. 2016. "The Algorithms That Tell Bosses How Employees Are Feeling." The Atlantic, September 29, 2016. http://www.theatlantic.com/technology/archive/2016/09/the-algorithms-that-tell-bosses-how-employees-feel/502064/.

Weichselbaum. n.d. "Inside Chicago's Police Laboratory." TIME.-Com. Accessed April 24, 2016. http://time.com/chicago-police-3/.

Welch, Suzy. 2017. "Bill Belichick Reveals His 5 Rules of Exceptional Leadership." CNBC. April 13, 2017. http://www.cnbc.com/2017/04/13/bill-belichick-leadership-rules.html.

"What Works in Community Policing? A Best Practices Context for Measure Y Efforts." 2013. The Chief Justice Earl Warren Institute on Law and Social Policy University of California, Berkeley School of Law. https://www.law.berkeley.edu/files/What_Works_in_Community_Policing.pdf.

Winton, Richard. 2016. "L.A. City Controller Says Too Many LAPD Cops Are Cubicle Police; Civilians Can Do That Work." Los Angeles Times, April 19, 2016. http://www.latimes.com/local/lanow/la-me-ln-la-city-controller-cops-cubicle-police-20160419-story.html.

———. 2017. "Sheriff's Department Misconduct-Claim Payouts Have Soared, Topping $50 Million Last Year." Los Angeles Times, April 9, 2017. http://www.latimes.com/local/california/la-me-sheriff-lawsuits-misconduct-20170409-story.html.

Wyllie, Doug. 2013. "How 'Big Data' Is Helping Law Enforcement." PoliceOne. August 20, 2013. https://www.policeone.com/police-products/software/Data-Information-Sharing-Software/articles/6396543-How-Big-Data-is-helping-law-enforcement/.

ABOUT THE AUTHOR

George Saadeh came to the United States in 1970 at the age of fifteen as an immigrant from Honduras, Central America. Speaking little English and having only a rudimentary understanding of the culture, he became proficient in the language and eventually earned a bachelor of arts degree in management. In the years after his arrival, he became increasingly interested in police work and in 1975, a scant five years from his arrival in California, he went to work for the Santa Ana Police Department. George Saadeh worked as a non-sworn Community Service Officer for two years, spent six months working in the Orange County jail as a deputy sheriff, and the City of Santa Ana hired him as a police officer.

He spent over thirty years with the police department and rose through the ranks to retire as a Police Captain. He worked in every functional bureau and division of the department in front-line, investigative and administrative assignments, and was fortunate to be associated with some of the best and hardest working police professionals in the country. He received the honor of Investigator of the Year twice; once in the Gang Unit and then again in Homicide. During the last five years of his career, he was honored and humbled to lead the Field Operations Bureau, which included patrol, traffic, SWAT and generally all uniformed services. It was, without a doubt, the highlight of his professional life to be able to lead the men and women that risked their lives every day to keep the community safe. During that time he was also fortunate to play a leadership role in managing the homeland security efforts of Orange County with leaders from the City of Anaheim and the Orange County Sheriff. It was a team effort that the federal government recognized as a national model.

In the years preceding the writing of this book, Captain Saadeh owned and operated a consulting firm, and worked for a company that provided risk management and policy advisory services to public safety agencies nationwide. During that time he saw the impact of good and bad leaders on law enforcement agencies throughout the country, which reinforced his strong belief in proven, practical leadership principles. This book is a personal account of his experiences and observations over thirty-five years, and a roadmap for becoming an excellent police supervisor or manager through leadership by example, competence and integrity.

37066899R00255

Printed in Great Britain
by Amazon